ICONS OF HIP HOP

**Recent Titles in
Greenwood Icons**

Icons of Horror and the Supernatural: An Encyclopedia of
Our Worst Nightmares
Edited by S.T. Joshi

Icons of Business: An Encyclopedia of Mavericks, Movers, and Shakers
Kateri Drexler

ICONS OF HIP HOP

An Encyclopedia of the Movement, Music, And Culture

VOLUME 2

Edited by Mickey Hess

Greenwood Icons

GREENWOOD PRESS
Westport, Connecticut • London

Library of Congress Cataloging-in-Publication Data

Icons of hip hop : an encyclopedia of the movement, music, and culture / edited by Mickey Hess.
    p. cm. — (Greenwood icons)
Includes bibliographical references, discographies, and index.
ISBN-13: 978-0-313-33902-8 (set : alk. paper)
ISBN-13: 978-0-313-33903-5 (vol 1 : alk. paper)
ISBN-13: 978-0-313-33904-2 (vol 2 : alk. paper)
 1. Rap musicians—Biography. 2. Turntablists—Biography. 3. Rap (Music)—History and criticism. 4. Hip-hop. I. Hess, Mickey, 1975—
 ML394. I26 2007
 782.421649'03—dc22   2007008194

British Library Cataloguing in Publication Data is available.

Library of Congress Catalog Card Number: 2007008194
ISBN-10: 0-313-33902-3 (set)   ISBN-13: 978-0-313-33902-8 (set)
         0-313-33903-1 (vol. 1)   978-0-313-33903-5 (vol. 1)
         0-313-33904-X (vol. 2)   978-0-313-33904-2 (vol. 2)

First published in 2007

Greenwood Press, 88 Post Road West, Westport, CT 06881
An imprint of Greenwood Publishing Group, Inc.
www.greenwood.com

Printed in the United States of America

The paper used in this book complies with the Permanent Paper Standard issued by the National Information Standards Organization (Z39.48-1984).

10 9 8 7 6 5 4 3 2 1

Contents

List of Photos   vii

Volume One

Foreword, *Jeru the Damaja*   ix

Preface   xiii

Introduction   xvii

A Timeline of Hip Hop History, *Nicole Hodges Persley*   xxi

Kool Herc, *Wayne Marshall*   1
Grandmaster Flash, *H.C. Williams*   27
Roxanne Shanté, *Thembisa S. Mshaka*   51
Run-DMC, *Jeb Aram Middlebrook*   69
Beastie Boys, *Mickey Hess*   91
MC Lyte, *Jennifer R. Young*   117
Eric B. & Rakim, *Shawn Bernardo*   141
Public Enemy, *George Ciccariello-Maher*   169
Salt-N-Pepa, *Athena Elafros*   193
Queen Latifah, *Faiza Hirji*   217
The Geto Boys, *Jason D. Haugen*   243
The Native Tongues, *Aine McGlynn*   265

Volume Two

Preface   ix

Ice Cube, *David J. Leonard*   293
Dr. Dre and Snoop Dogg, *David Diallo*   317

Nas, *Susan Weinstein*   341
Wu-Tang Clan, *Jessica Elliott and Mickey Hess*   365
Tupac Shakur, *Carlos D. Morrison and Celnisha L. Dangerfield*   391
Notorious B.I.G., *James Peterson*   417
Lil' Kim, *Aine McGlynn*   439
Outkast, *T. Hasan Johnson*   457
Eminem, *Katherine V. Tsiopos-Wills*   481
Missy Elliot, *Joi Carr*   503
Jay-Z, *T. Hasan Johnson*   529
Kanye West, *Todd Dills*   555

Interviews:

Let 'Em In: An Interview with DJ Premier, *Shamika Ann Mitchell*   579
Word Up: An Interview with DJ Scratch, *Shamika Ann Mitchell*   591

Afterword: The Twenty-Four Most Overlooked MCs in Hip Hop,
    Masta Ace   603

Selected Bibliography   609

Notes on Contributors   613

Index   621

List of Photos

DJ Kool Herc (page 1) speaking at a news conference to launch "Hip-Hop Won't Stop: The Beat, The Rhymes, The Life," the first ever hip-hop initiative at the Smithsonian's National Museum of American History in New York, 2006. © AP Photo/Henny Ray Abrams.

Grandmaster Flash (page 27) performing live at Wembley Arena in London, 1985. © S.I.N / Alamy.

Roxanne Shante (page 51). © David Corio.

Run DMC (page 69), ca. 1985. Courtesy of Photofest.

Beastie Boys (page 91), 1998. Courtesy of Photofest.

MC Lyte (page 117). Courtesy of Photofest.

Eric B and Rakim (page 141). © Waring Abbott / Alamy.

Public Enemy (page 169). Courtesy of Photofest.

Salt n Pepa (page 193), ca. 1994. Courtesy of Photofest.

Queen Latifah (page 217). Courtesy of Photofest.

The Geto Boys (page 243) arrive at the 2004 Source Hip-Hop Music Awards at the James L. Knight Center, October 10, 2004 in Miami, Florida. © Orlando Garcia / Getty Image.

De La Soul (page 265), one of the founding members of the Native Tongues posse, along with A Tribe Called Quest, the Jungle Brothers, Afrika Bambaataa, and others. © David Corio.

Ice Cube (page 293). Courtesy of Photofest.

Dr. Dre and Snoop Dogg (page 317), 1993. Courtesy of Photofest.

Nas (page 341), 1994. Courtesy of Photofest.

Wu Tang Clan (page 365), 2000. © Kevin Winter / Getty Images.

Tupac Shakur (page 391), 1996. Courtesy of Photofest.

Notorious B.I.G. (page 417), ca. 1997. Courtesy of Photofest.

Lil' Kim (page 439) in the pressroom at the 2006 MTV Video Music Awards in New York. © AP Photo / Tammie Arroyo.

Big Boi and Andre 3000 (page 457) pose in front of the three awards they won at the 46th Annual Grammy Awards, 2004. © AP Photo / Reed Saxon.

Eminem (page 481), 2000. Courtesy of Photofest.

Missy Elliot (page 503) performs during the 2003 MTV Europe Music Awards in Edinburgh, Scotland. Courtesy of Photofest.

Jay-Z (page 529) rapper and CEO of Def Jam Records, 2001. Courtesy of Photofest.

Kanye West (page 555) performs "Jesus Walks" at the 47th Annual Grammy Awards in Los Angeles, 2005. © AP Photo / Kevork Djansezian.

Preface

Choosing the twenty-four most important hip hop artists of all time is no easy task. From Kool Herc to Kanye West, *Icons of Hip Hop* spans four decades of MCs and DJs, old-school pioneers and new-school innovators, to profile the figures who have made hip hop music what it is today. Hip hop music, once considered a passing fad, continues to thrive and evolve more than thirty years into its history. *Icons of Hip Hop* presents the stories of twenty-four important figures who have contributed to the music's development and success.

Our profiles begin with Kool Herc and Grandmaster Flash, two DJs who established hip hop's musical foundation with their invention of breakbeats and turntable scratching. These hip hop pioneers collected funk and soul records and transformed their record players into instruments that created new sounds through backspinning and scratching. These turntable techniques, along with digital samplers and drum machines, form the backbone of hip hop music. The sounds that DJs like Herc, Flash, Afrika Bambaataa, Pete DJ Jones, and Grandwizard Theodore invented have been built upon by three decades of DJs and producers, from Rick Rubin and Jam Master Jay to Eric B and the Bomb Squad to DJ Premier, DJ Scratch, Dr. Dre, and Kanye West.

At Kool Herc's block parties in the 1970s, the DJ was the focal point of the performance, and the MC, or rapper, served chiefly to call the crowd's attention to the DJ and to entice people onto the dance floor. As early MCs like Coke La Rock and Busy Bee began to develop more complex rhyming routines, the MC came into his own. Famous MC battles, such as the 1982 competition between Busy Bee and Kool Moe Dee, took rhyming to a new level as these MCs sought to win over the crowd with their rhyme structure, wordplay, and wit. Whether hyping up the DJ or boasting about his or her own skills on the mic, the MC was always a crowd pleaser. With the 1979 release of Sugarhill Gang's "Rapper's Delight," the first hip hop record to reach mainstream radio worldwide, the rapper became the face of commercial rap music.

"Rapper's Delight" also introduced mainstream listeners to the terms *rap* and *hip hop*. The song begins with the words, "I said a hip hop.... " From that early moment in hip hop history, when *rap* and *hip hop* were used in the title and first lines of the same song, the meanings of these two terms have been debated. When many fans and artists talk about hip hop, they explain that it is a culture that expands beyond music to include four central elements: graffiti art (aka tagging or writing), b-boying (aka break dancing, popping, and locking), DJing (aka turntablism, or mixing, cutting, and scratching records), and MCing (aka rapping or rhyming). On his song "9 Elements," KRS-One expanded this definition to include five more elements: beatboxing, fashion, language, street knowledge, and entrepreneurialism. In his lyrics to "9 Elements," KRS makes the distinction that to rap is merely an action that anyone can take, but "Hip hop is something you live." Both terms, hip hop and rap, however, are used to describe music. To distinguish between the two forms, the term *hip hop music* is often used to designate a song that holds true to hip hop's orginal aesthetic rather than appealing to a pop audience, and the term *MC*, as opposed to *rapper*, is often used to designate a hip hop vocalist who holds true to this same aesthetic. In an exclusive interview for *Icons of Hip Hop*, Roxanne Shanté explained the difference between MCs and rappers: "Rappers need videos, MCs don't."

Although Shanté eventually did make a video, she first made her name going head-to-head with other MCs in the street. Her record "Roxanne's Revenge," hailed as one of hip hop's first answer records, took rhyme battles into the recording studio as she responded to a single, "Roxanne, Roxanne," by the group UTFO. Roxanne initiated a series of answer records from several different MCs, and extended hip hop's competitive element to recordings and radio airplay. Video airplay would become even more important to Run-DMC, whose visual imagery of black fedoras, gold chains, and unlaced Adidas sneakers would introduce hip hop fashion to MTV audiences. As hip hop culture moved into mainstream outlets like MTV, listeners sought to preserve the original culture by making distinctions about which songs counted as "real hip hop" and which were created for crossover success on the pop charts. In the mid-1990s, MC Hammer dropped the "MC" from his name, claiming he was in the business of entertainment rather than hip hop, in response to criticisms that his pop hits like "U Can't Touch This" were selling out hip hop culture. Debates about what characteristics consitute rap or hip hop rage on today as artists like Defari claim to make "real hip hop" rather than pop rap.

Ideological distinctions aside, however, rap music is an inextricable part of hip hop culture. Artists and listeners will continue to argue about which MCs are making music to make money and which ones do it out of a pure love for hip hop, but even as these debates continue, we should remember that the shiny suits and diamond grills we see on MTV and BET in the twenty-first century are as much a part of hip hop as the Kangol hats and Fila jumpsuits worn by hip hoppers in New York City parks in the 1980s. Rather than debating which figures belong to rap and which to hip hop, *Icons of Hip Hop* showcases the inventions and innovations of twenty-four musical icons from 1973 to 2007. Even at two volumes, however, our icon profiles are not comprehensive. As with any collection, there are omissions. Throughout the book, however, we make connections to other MCs, DJs, and producers whose stories intersect with the twenty-four figures we have chosen. Each profile discusses and cross-references other artists connected with the icon at hand. A foreword from Jeru the Damaja, a rapper included in Kool Moe Dee's list of the top fifty MCs of all time, credits the artists who influenced his rhyme style. Nicole Hodges Persley's timeline of hip hop history highlights the innovations of artists like Kurtis Blow and Schoolly D, icons who are not included in our twenty-four in-depth profiles. An afterword by veteran rap artist Masta Ace lists the twenty-four most overlooked hip hop icons, who are worthy of further study. Exclusive interviews with Masta Ace, Roxanne Shanté, Mystic, and Kool DJ Red Alert, included in the Roxanne Shanté profile, provide a firsthand account of the development of the first female MC to spark a national trend. And finally, Shamika Ann Mitchell's exclusive interviews with DJ Premier and DJ Scratch give further attention to producers, the people behind the music, as icons.

The scope of *Icons of Hip Hop* is intentionally broad in that we seek to profile old-school orginators as well as new-school innovators, devote attention to the different regions that have contributed to what hip hop culture has become in the United States, and recover the stories of lesser-known artists. As the editor, I sought to pay homage to those artists, like Ice Cube and Eminem, who typically come to mind when hip hop is mentioned, but also to call attention to groups like the Native Tongues and Eric B. & Rakim, that haven't matched Ice Cube's sales but that rank high on many fans' lists of the best rappers of all time. In short, the twenty-four artists profiled in these two volumes were chosen based on their unique contributions to the development of hip hop music, style, and culture: Grandmaster Flash made the turntables an instrument, Eric B. & Rakim created more complex rhyme flows, MC Lyte proved that women could rap with aggression, Outkast shifted attention to Southern hip hop, and the Native Tongues provided a much-needed critique of hip hop culture itself. Each essay ends with a section on the legacy of the artists, which emphasizes their influence on hip-hop today and their importance to hip hop in the future. We include producers and DJs as well as MCs, fan favorites as well as platinum-selling artists, women as well as men, and Atlanta and Houston as well as New York and Los Angeles. With this approach to selecting its subjects, *Icons of Hip Hop* presents a historical and cultural framework for hip hop that extends to current or emerging artists, unearths the histories of important artists from outside hip hop's mainstream, and examines the varied and ever-changing forms of the music.

Each of our twenty-four profiles features in-depth coverage of the artist's life and work, highlighting the artist's influence in making hip hop music and culture what it is today. The profiles are supported by several sidebars that place the icons within cultural and historical context. The sidebars highlight such issues as hip hop's homophobia, vegetarian rappers, hip hop and Islam, the mafia, horror films, fashion trends, musical innovations such as turntable scratching and digital sampling, legal issues, and hip hop's culture of death. There are certain consistent themes to the sidebars, such as regional scenes (Houston, Memphis, and Canada), and hip hop's intersections with other musical forms (rock, jazz, blues, and metal). Each profile also includes a discography and list of resources for further research. Broad in scope and distinctive in detail, *Icons of Hip Hop* is an excellent resource for the student or casual listener as well as the true hip hop head.

—Mickey Hess

Courtesy of Photofest.

Ice Cube

David J. Leonard

As a member of N.W.A., and then as a solo artist, Ice Cube sat at the fore-front of gangsta rap. His lyrical brilliance and affected gangsta identity built the popularity of gangsta rap and West Coast hip hop. Speaking to and for disempowered and disenfranchised youth, Cube used the platform provided by hip hop to blow up, all the while giving voice to what was going on in the hood, from drug dealing and gang banging to police brutality and impoverished, jobless families. Equally important, Cube helped facilitate hip hop's emergence as a news bureau of sorts, often describing his work as that of a street reporter. Cube's career also mirrors hip hop's history in that Cube has faced significant opposition and condemnation from mainstream America. In fact, Cube, both as a member of N.W.A. and as a solo artist, has been at the center of a significant level of controversy because of his lyrical treatment of police brutality, black-Korean relations, women, and gays and lesbians. Yet even with his career characterized by controversy, Cube has emerged as possibly the most successful artist to cross over to the mainstream, not only as a rapper but as an actor, filmmaker, writer, and television executive. In fact, Cube symbolizes the life span of hip hop, having grown up to a point where he can make family films and television shows for the FX network, even as he continues to produce hip hop albums.

Although one view of Ice Cube's career sees him leaving behind hip hop for the allure of mainstream acceptance, another perspective sees Cube's career as a rags-to-riches story in which he uses music to rise out of the same social conditions he describes in his lyrics. The life and times of Cube is a story of hip hop, a complex narrative of inclusion and exclusion, progressive and reactionary agendas, crossover appeal and mainstream demonization, performed identities and keeping it real, and of course the continuity of poverty, despair, and cultural resistance. Hip hop is Ice Cube and Ice Cube is hip hop not just in abstract terms, but in its stories and development as a fundamental American cultural institution.

Born in 1969, O'shea Jackson came into the world in the aftermath of the Watts Riots and amid struggles over community control within South Central Los Angeles and other black communities throughout the nation. Insulated from the streets by his parents, Jackson's childhood was relatively uneventful. His parents, Hosea (a machinist and groundskeeper at the University of California, Los Angeles) and Doris (a hospital clerk) were loving and dedicated parents, who went to every length to both protect and empower young O'shea, giving him just enough freedom to develop as an independent thinker without sacrificing discipline and safety. His parents were not alone; his older brother, Clyde, who would eventually rename O'shea Ice Cube because of his coolness around girls, served as a protective force in his life: "He was there. He kept me on the right track. You don't realize that till you see other people who grew up without fathers and how their lives turn out" (McIver 12). Often excluding his mother from such praise while handing most of it to his father and brother, Cube has celebrated the discipline and guidance provided by these men, especially as South Central Los Angeles became more and more violent. The combination of shrinking social services, declining job opportunities, and an increasingly powerful police state during the 1970s resulted in a less than idyllic neighborhood. Gangs and drugs slowly infiltrated South Central, causing an even greater loss of jobs, social services, and police presence. In such an environment, O'shea's parents did everything to protect him, while still allowing him to be a kid who played football and basketball, and roamed the neighborhood. In fact, his childhood mirrored a typical narrative for American children, as he explored the spectrum of offerings available to him in South Central Los Angeles, even as increasing levels of violence and shrinking investment in children's programs limited his play spaces. Yet his parents did not respond to the changes in his community with fear and overprotection. Instead they allowed Cube to explore the streets, contributing to his sense of self and community, something that would motivate him for years to come. Ice Cube's childhood established an important foundation for his music career, instilling in him an immense amount of confidence and respect for family and school (although he would often eschew these values in his lyrics).

Ice Cube's career took him from novice high school rapper to controversial cultural figure, to hip hop icon, to major Hollywood player. No matter the project before him, Cube manages to express his social consciousness in his art; family, friends, the hood, racism, misogyny, police brutality, and education all, at different times and with varying degrees of potency, take center stage in Ice Cube's productions. After Cube completed grammar school, the Jackson family faced the difficult decision of where he would attend middle school. Violence and shrinking funds in Los Angeles public schools created uncertainty in the family. After learning that Randy, Cube's best friend, would be attending Hawthorne Christian School, which was located in the Valley some twenty miles east of downtown Los Angeles, the Jacksons decided to reunite the boys at Hawthorne. While crucial in Cube's own persona and artistic development, the experience was certainly not a positive one. Besides the lengthy commute that many black children experienced with busing, Cube's educational experience thrust him into an environment of gang rivalries. It exposed him to increased violence and stress, as his classmates included Bloods and Crips from rival gangs, brought to the same schools through busing. The experience taught Cube a lot about American race relations and how busing sought to bring together black and white students but did so without regard for the safety, educational development, and personal well-being of the students, particularly the black students. It also dramatically impacted Cube in terms of his interest in school, given the lack of respect afforded to students within this chaotic environment. The violence, the lessons about race, and his experience crossing borders and seeing other parts of Los Angeles all had a profound effect on Cube's outlook and philosophies, some of which can be seen in his lyrics. The experience turned Cube off school, and his parents removed him from Hawthorne, choosing to enroll him at William Howard Taft High School, located in Woodland Hills, a place where he would discover his passion for music alongside a revitalized focus on school and education.

ICE CUBE AND THE EMERGENCE OF WEST COAST GANGSTA RAP

As he entered Taft, Ice Cube was listening to everything from "Rapper's Delight" to Grandmaster Flash's "The Message," the music of Afrika

Bambaataa, Kurtis Blow, Run-DMC, DJ Kool Herc, and so many other East Coast rappers. Rap was emerging as a voice for the underclass. Serving as vehicle of empowerment and communal bonding, hip hop became a form of cultural resistance and empowerment for black youth throughout the United States. Inspired by the music and his burgeoning friendships with several classmates at Taft, Cube would find his voice in hip hop. In 1983, Cube penned his first rhyme during a typing class. Discussing the newest cuts from Run-DMC, his classmate Kiddo challenged Cube to an impromptu battle of their own. As they each sat down to write their own lyrics, to settle once and for all who could pen the dopest rhymes, Cube transformed himself from a listener of hip hop, someone who found voice and empowerment in the artistry of others, to a practitioner, an artist who used rap to illuminate, educate, pontificate, and of course give voice to his and his friends' anger, dreams, and frustrations.

Although he hadn't yet developed the rhyme skills for which he would become known, Cube remained focused on developing his game. After hearing the outcome of Cube's battle with Kiddo, Tony Wheatcob, a Taft classmate who, as Sir Jinx, would become a successful rap producer, proposed a collaboration. Cube and Jinx put a tape together in Jinx's garage, and throughout high school they would continue to write and perform their music, all the while devloping their hip hop skills (Chang 299).

By 1986, a hip hop scene had emerged on the West Coast, and once again Jinx would play an instrumental role in Cube's development. He introduced Cube to his cousin, a young man from South Central named Andre Young, who was performer and producer with World Class Wreckin' Cru, an up-and-coming hip hop group in the LA scene. Upon their introduction, Cube and Andre, aka Dr. Dre, began hanging together (Chang 300). After Dre heard one of Cube's raps, he invited him on a shopping trip. He also introduced Cube to his party scene, inviting him to the numerous parties he gave at a local roller rink. One night Dre alerted Cube that he and Jinx should prepare to perform at the next roller rink party. This was just the break they needed: Cube and Jinx found the right mix of comedy, serious lyrical content, and cussing to reach the audience, building on this singular party to a blossoming place in Los Angeles's hip hop scene.

In addition to hanging with Dre and performing at his parties, Cube formed his own group at Taft—the Stereo Crew. Selling over fifty tapes and known throughout the community, Stereo Crew put Cube on the local hip hop map. Their songs "Getting Sweated" and "She's a Skag," were both relatively popular among high school kids in the area. However, Stereo Crew would not last. After their breakup, Cube would join forces with Sir Jinx and Kid Disaster to form CIA—Cru in Action. Although still in high school, CIA possessed quite a following, even releasing a Dre-produced single on vinyl, which contained several notable songs: "My Posse," "Just 4 the cash $," and "Ill-legal."

Simultaneous to Cube's rise within the local hip hop scene, a young drug dealer and entrepreneur who went by the name of Eazy-E emerged on the scene in Compton, California. In 1986, their paths would cross, after Dre asked Eazy-E, whom he had met previously, for a $900 loan to post bail (he had been arrested because of a series of unpaid traffic violations). Eazy agreed to give Dre the money if he agreed to produce for a label he was developing, one he would call Ruthless Records. Even though their working relationship grew out of necessity, it quickly blossomed, with Eazy-E providing Dre with unlimited support and near autonomy. Dre would soon discover HBO (Home Boys Only), a New York–based rap group whose skill impressed Eazy and Dre enough to offer them a record deal. Unfortunately, neither HBO nor Dre and Eazy-E had writing skills, making the production of a single difficult. Dre suggested that Ice Cube's lyrics could deliver a hit for HBO, and authored "Boyz N the Hood," a song about violence and gang life in American ghettos. The members of HBO did not see its merits, but Cube, Dre, and Eazy all loved it. When HBO refused to record the song, they severed ties with Ruthless Records and left Eazy-E in a difficult position: a song, but no artist; studio time paid for but no one to record. Desperate, given the potentially damaging financial effects of not using the studio time, Dre offered another solution: Eazy, despite being a rap novice, should record the song himself, being the truest embodiment of a boy from the hood. After much persuading from both Cube and Dre, Eazy relented, agreeing to record "Boyz." Cube, Eazy, and Dre initially sold the single out of the trunks of their cars until Macola Records, who released the single, agreed to distribute it as well. The popularity of the song convinced Eazy-E to request additional songs from Ice Cube, who delivered "8-Ball," a track on Old English 800 malt liquor, and "Dopeman," a tale about a neighborhood crack dealer.

N.W.A. IS BORN

Although Cube, Dre, and Eazy were each committed to their own groups, the success of "Boyz," coupled with some difficulties each were facing (both Dre and Cube felt somewhat exploited by Lonzo Williams, the producer for both World Class Wreckin' Cru and CIA), made them think about forming a new group. As they came together to record these new songs, they were now joined by MC Ren, DJ Yella, Arabian Prince, and the D.O.C., all friends of Cube and Dre, resulting in the formation of N.W.A.—Niggaz with Attitude. This lineup lasted until 1988, when Arabian Prince and The D.O.C. went solo, leaving the group with its now-classic five-man lineup of Dre, Ice Cube, MC Ren, Eazy-E, and DJ Yella. Cube would later recount the unceremonious founding of N.W.A. and the process of naming the group in the following way: Traveling to the studio, Eazy and Dre informed Cube that the time had come to officially form their own group, leaving behind their various other projects. Wondering what to call themselves, Dre and Eazy came up with a name that would capture the essence of their identity and music: Niggaz with Attitude. And just like that, N.W.A. began, West Coast rap had arrived, and Cube and the rest of the group would forever change the landscape of hip hop, the music industry, and America's cultural terrain.

After his initial success in the rap game, Ice Cube would continue his education, graduating from Taft and then heading to college. His wandering mind—which tended to fixate on his own music and had greater interest in the histories of Public Enemy, Grandmaster Flash, and LL Cool J than those offered in class—impacted his studies. Hosea Jackson, however, cared little for his son's emerging music career, offering a stern hand and significant discipline as to his educational focus. In "Doin Dumb Shit," Cube would later rap about his lack of focus and his teenage difficulties, again crediting his father with keeping him on track. He told listeners that while he almost did not graduate, he ultimately decided to "fuck the dumb shit, cause pops'll fuck me real good." Because of his parents' disciplinary approach and emphasis on education, Cube not only graduated high school but went on to earn a bachelor's degree in architectural drafting at age twenty-one. Cube often praises his parents for instilling this passion for learning and teaching, a love and life's work that is evident with his determination in school and with his artistry (McIver 39–40).

In fact, Cube attributes both his perseverance with music and his respect for education to his parents. In 1987, despite the immense success of "Boyz" and an N.W.A. summer tour, Cube decided to take a break from N.W.A. so that he could attend the Phoenix Institute of Technology in Arizona, where he studied architectural drafting and design. Cube realized that nothing was guaranteed within the music industry, especially for a hip hop artist from South Central Los Angeles, a fact his parents emphasized over and over again. Given the media backlash against hip hop and constant wondering when the bubble would burst just as it had for disco, Cube agreed, feeling it was unlikely that he could make a career with music. After a year, Cube had successfully completed the program, receiving a degree in architectural drafting and design, which was perfect timing given the emerging success of N.W.A.

During that year at school, on vacations in California, Eazy had contacted Cube in hopes that he would write the lyrics for several songs that would appear on E's debut album, *Eazy-Duz-It*, which ultimately proved to be a tremendous commercial success. Although a solo album, the success of *Eazy-Duz-It* not only elevated the place of West Coast hip hop, putting Eazy and the other members of the N.W.A. on a national map, but demonstrated the market potential of N.W.A. In summer 1988, after returning from Arizona, Cube wrote "A Bitch Is a Bitch," which would become the fourth single released by N.W.A. Controversial to say the least, "A Bitch Is a Bitch" defended male descriptions of women as bitches. The success of this song in the clubs and the surrounding controversy convinced Macola Records that the time was ripe to release N.W.A.'s first album: *N.W.A. and the Posse.* The album, which featured "Boyz N the Hood," "8 Ball," "Dopeman," "A Bitch Is a Bitch," and several other tracks, was relatively successful as a club album, particularly within black clubs on the West Coast, yet the lack of radio play due to its language (*niggas* and *bitches*) and fears about its promotion of violence limited its success nationally.

Through 1988, N.W.A. continued to grow, leading Ice Cube to focus more attention on a career in hip hop. Joined by MC Ren during that year, N.W.A. was ready to take the hip hop world by storm with the release of its second album, *Straight Outta Compton.* Changing the face of hip hop and American music in general, *Straight Outta Compton* marked the arrival of West Coast hip hop, gangsta rap, N.W.A., and Ice Cube on the American cultural landscape. Within three months of release, *Straight Outta Compton* had gone triple platinum, a feat rarely achieved by any artist, ultimately selling over 3 million copies. Its effect on the music industry was not limited to its financial success in that it served as evidence of the long-term profitability of hip hop. Moreover, more than any other album, it brought hard-core gangsta rap with an overtly political message into the American mainstream.

The image and agenda of the album is set in the first moments of the title track, in which Ice Cube announces that he is a "crazy motherfucker" with a "sawed off," making it clear that N.W.A.'s music would bring listeners into America's most dangerous ghetto, a place defined by Uzi-packing gangstas, brutalizing cops, the dopeman, violence, and other unseemly realities that American culture tended to ignore, deny, and pathologize. It in turn offered a counternarrative to the dominant representations and discourse, from that of the news media to the reports of politicians like Daniel Patrick Moynihan; it chronicled the good, the bad, and the ugly, as any street reporter would do. In songs like "Straight Outta Compton," and "Gangsta Gangsta," N.W.A. sought to force America to deal with or reconcile its immense problems and reflect on its contradictions. Ice Cube described the album as an attempt to give voice to the streets, to explain the basis of communal anger (McIver 53). Through Cube's powerful lyrics, N.W.A. would introduce America to poverty, drive-bys, drug dealing, police brutality, and sadness; since most Americans feared places like Compton and made judgments without seeing, N.W.A. forced them to look and listen through their airwaves. No song embodied their desire to give voice to the underclass and its anger better than "Fuck tha Police."

Chronicling the brutality and daily occurrence of police abuse, "Fuck tha Police" documents the sordid and racist history of the LAPD and the daily experience of brutality faced by black youth. Cube tells listeners that "young nigga got it bad 'cause I'm brown," yet the song provides ample specifics: black cops being just as guilty as white cops in terms of brutalizing black youth; the ubiquity of racial profiling, and the daily police searches that resulted from black youths fitting the stereotype of a drug dealer or a criminal, and even the occurrence of police murders. While common and accepted knowledge within much of the black community, such criticism and condemnations of police officers, admired and revered in much of America, prompted a powerful backlash. Police officers throughout the country refused to work at N.W.A. concerts, while the FBI sent a letter to the members of N.W.A. condemning the song for its promotion of violence and overall disrespect for both the rule of law and law enforcement officials. Not surprisingly, Cube scoffed at such criticism, making clear that it was the police who were guilty of disrespect and promoting violence within the black community. Although Eazy-E tended to brush off these criticisms with claims that the group and its fans didn't care if the album or any of its songs offended the police or the FBI, Ice Cube defended his lyrics and their music by invoking the truthfulness and authenticity of experience behind the music. If their music offended people, it was not the fault of N.W.A., since the words merely described the reality of their world. Such a defense wasn't limited to the outcry over "Fuck tha Police," but extended to criticisms that NWA glorified gangsta violence and promoted misogyny and homophobia. For example, through the media and in a published conversation with bell hooks, a black feminist cultural critic, Cube questioned the basis of accusations of misogyny, claiming that his use of the term *bitch* did not describe all women but those scandalous and devious women whom he had met during his lifetime. Yet Cube also recognized then and most certainly in later interviews that the lyrical description of women and gays and lesbians reflected where he, and N.W.A., were when he was nineteen years old.

Straight Outta Compton left a lasting mark on the American cultural landscape, shifting the balance of power in hip hop from the East Coast to the West Coast and bringing the ghettos of a post–civil rights America and the stories of its gangsta residents to white suburban America. This success and popularity reflected the power and brilliance of Cube's lyrics as well as the phatness in N.W.A.'s beats; moreover, it showed the pleasure derived from their lurid stories of murder, mayhem, violence, and brutality. Most significantly, the success of N.W.A. with *Straight Outta Compton* reflected the dialectics of their marketing strategy, one that emphasized the truthfulness and authenticity of their music and those popular discourses that reduced blackness, particularly young black males, to images of criminals, deviants, drug dealers, and murderers. In other words, the power of Cube's lyrics and of course Cube himself with his perpetual scowl and endless swearing reflected their realness, a fact emphasized by N.W.A. and embraced by listeners.

GOING SOLO

In 1989, as Ice Cube and N.W.A. went on tour, Cube's commitment to the group began to wane. During that summer, he began a friendship with

Pat Charbonet, a publicist with Priority Records. During one of their many conversations about N.W.A.'s future and the endless possibilities for the group, Charbonet asked Cube how royalty payments were split between the group members and their manager, Jerry Heller.

Unable to answer these questions and concerned where the money was going, Cube requested a meeting of the band to discuss finances, especially any arrangements between Heller and Eazy-E that gave a larger perecentage to Eazy. At the meeting, Heller, whom Eazy advised to attend, offered each member a new contract along with a $75,000 signing bonus. Everyone but Ice Cube signed that day; Cube, already skeptical, told Heller and Eazy that he wanted to consult a lawyer. After meeting with both a lawyer and an accountant, Cube was advised never to sign the contract for a number of reasons, all of which demonstrate the lack of fair compensation in the deal: The *Straight Outta Compton* tour had grossed $650,000, of which $130,000 went to Heller and only $23,000 went to Cube. Although he had written half the tracks on *Straight Outta Compton*, he was only paid $32,000 for his work on the album. The terms of the new contract offered Cube a large cash bonus up front, yet still mimicked these past arrangements for royalties, which in Cube's estimation was neither fair nor equitable.

In addition to the royalty structures, the contract established a relationship between Cube and Ruthless Records but made no mention of Cube being a full member of N.W.A. To Cube, there was little choice but to leave the group (he would later sue Heller and settle the case out of court). Although Cube faced some teasing from other members of N.W.A., who questioned his sanity for turning down $75,000 and made jokes about how he wanted to go solo like the Arabian Prince (whose career had not been successful), he left N.W.A. on relatively good terms. In fact, immediately after his departure, he contacted Yella, Dre, and the others about working with him on his solo album, all of whom declined because they were busy working on Eazy's second album. In the end, this was a blessing in disguise, resulting in Cube's teaming up with the Bomb Squad, an East Coast group who had worked with Public Enemy, and the Da Lench Mob, a group from Southern California, to produce his debut album. His decision to produce the album in New York and join forces with an East Coast crew opened up many opportunities for Cube, neutralizing some of the disrespect that many West Coast artists faced from those on the East side.

AmeriKKKa's Most Wanted was released on May 16, 1990, to much fanfare and critical acclaim. The genius of *AmeriKKKa's Most Wanted* rests not just with Cube's ability to give voice to America's underclass and offer counternarratives, political commentaries, and powerful stories, but through the introspection, self-reflection, and his ability to provide listeners with multiple perspectives, some of which illustrated his own contradictions and shortcomings. For example, in "You Can't Fade Me," Cube tells how he got a girl pregnant; scared, he wonders if he should give her the money or abort the baby with a "kick to the tummy." He neither endorses nor rationalizes sentiments, using the song to question and problematize his own thoughts. Yet the power of Cube's lyrics exists in the next line, where he demonizes the consequences of domestic violence. Notwithstanding this newfound self-awareness, the misogyny evident during the N.W.A. years was on full display with "Get Off My Dick and Tell Yo Bitch to Come Here." Yet, with this album he offers something more with "It's a Man's World," a duet with his cousin Yo Yo (Yolanda Whitaker) in which she chastises Cube for his misogynist and sexist views of women. Still, Cube's focus on state violence, on the effects of police brutality within his community, mass incarceration, and poverty remained his trademark. In "Endangered Species," he laments the lack of concern for police brutality and cop killings, noting the absence of justice within America's ghettos. To him, the police exist "to serve, protect and break a nigga's neck." The consistency of Cube's anti–police brutality stance and his efforts to give voice to the underclass alongside the album's complexity and self-reflection embodies the greatness of *AmeriKKKa's Most Wanted*. *Spin* magazine called the album a masterpiece, and *The Source* awarded it the much-coveted five microphone rating. Despite limited radio play, the album spent several weeks on the Top 20 Billboard charts. Its success and his formation of Street Knowledge Productions (with Pat Charbonet) seemed to indicate that Cube had successfully left N.W.A. behind, moving on to a solo career without the proverbial public spats, yet it would be clear that his ties to N.W.A. would be difficult to sever.

In November 1990, members of N.W.A. appeared on *Pump It Up*, a hip hop TV show hosted by Dee Barnes, to promote their new album, *100 Miles and Runnin'*. During the course of the interview, its members dissed Cube, dismissing questions as to whether they would miss him. Shortly thereafter, Cube appeared on the show, offering similar insults and disparaging commentary about N.W.A. Worse, the producers of the show decided to edit the two interviews to create a single package that would overemphasize the battle and the mutual dislike between Cube and NWA. Despite the warning by Barnes that it was not a good idea, the producers went ahead with its airing, adding fuel to a smoldering fire with close-up shots of Yella crushing an ice cube with his shoes juxtaposed with Cube mocking the title of their new album as evidence of their failure, their lack of manhood, and fear of Cube: In his absence, they were 100 miles away and running. Their appearance on *Pump It Up* resulted in significant media coverage, especially following Dre's assault of Barnes and a more public battle between Cube and members of N.W.A., particularly Eazy-E. Still, Cube paid little mind to his former bandmates, focusing on his own personal and professional development, both of which became evident with the release of *Death Certificate*.

For Ice Cube, 1990 was a year of transition: from posse member to solo artist, from apprentice to master and mentor, from lyricist to artist and producer, from vocal misogynist to an individual with more enlightened views toward women. Amid these transitions and transformations, Cube also found greater knowledge regarding history and politics, much of which came as a result of his introduction to the Nation of Islam. His exposure to the teachings of Malcolm X, Elijah Muhammad, and Louis Farrakhan inspired not only personal reflection but education and consciousness-raising efforts within Cube. In fact, he began to read about black history and the writings of black nationalist thinkers, which had a tremendous influence on him. He began to question his own motives and almost obsession with making money, fame, and partying, challenging himself to refocus and use his artistry and platform for a greater good. The emphasis of Black Nationalism, the formation of a separate Black Nation, spiritual rejuvenation, reparations, and community control within the Nation of Islam resonated with Cube. Although he never officially joined the NOI, partly out of fear of how membership would affect listener perceptions and also because of ideological and political differences, his conversations with Louis Farrakhan and other ministers from the NOI as well as his investment in his spiritual development manifested in his artistry, maybe most evident with *Death Certificate*.

Released October 29, 1991, Cube's second solo album brought him together with Da Lench Mob and his old pal Jinx. Seizing the momentum of *AmeriKKKa's Most Wanted* and the press from *Boyz N the Hood*, *Death Certificate* was an immediate success. It entered the Billboard charts at number two and would eventually go platinum, an amazing feat given its overly political tone and the limited investment Priority Records had made in promoting the album. *Death Certificate*, which attempted to intervene in the state of emergency facing black America, was divided between the death side, a mirror of the horrors of inner-city life, and the life side, "a vision of where we need to go." Challenging the fetishizing of gangsta life and the sensationalism that often surrounded the representations of inner-city life—which he was certainly guilty of—*Death Certificate* speaks to the political and artistic maturation of Ice Cube. The album even included several spoken-word pieces serving as interludes, most of which were inspired by the words of the NOI ministers. The influence of the NOI and Cube's more radical politics are visible throughout the album, with tracks like "The Wrong Nigga to Fuck With," "I Wanna Kill Sam," "True to the Game," and "Steady Mobbin'."

Unfortunately, the message of these songs and the power of the album would be subsumed by the controversy surrounding "Black Korea" and "No Vaseline." Although only a forty-five-second track, "Black Korea" sparked immense controversy. It chronicles the treatment he and others within the black community face from Korean shopkeepers, who, he states, view all African Americans as potential criminals who deserve little respect and tremendous suspicion. The effort to bring this issue into public consciousness was challenging enough, but promises of retribution with threats of violence and arson if they didn't "pay respect to the black fist" elicited outrage.

Interestingly and more revealingly, it was "No Vaseline" that prompted the largest controversy and backlash. "No Vaseline" offers a response to N.W.A.'s dissing of Cube, which included his being called a Benedict Arnold in *Efil4zaggin*. The song begins with a challenge to N.W.A.'s hardness and even their blackness, noting how they moved "straight outta Compton" and had lost their edge, having appeared in an R&B/pop music video (Michel'le), certainly not a sign of being a Nigga with an attitude. Cube also uses the song to accuse N.W.A. of turning its back on the black community, calling Eazy-E out for attending a Republican fund-raiser. Worse, Cube dedicates much of the song to blasting Jerry Heller, who he says is screwing the group out of its money. The song takes aim not only at Heller but at the illegitimacy of N.W.A. as a hip hop group with a white male pulling the strings. Ice Cube points out the irony of calling your group Niggaz Wit Attitude while having "a white Jew tellin' ya what to do."

The accusations of homophobia and anti-Semitism that resulted from the release of "No Vaseline," combined with the controversy concerning "Black Korea," had a considerable impact on Ice Cube and the reception of *Death Certificate*. The backlash wasn't limited to the press. The anti-gang group Guardian Angels, who compared Cube to David Duke, unsuccessfully pressured MTV to ban Ice Cube videos from its rotation. The Simon Wiesenthal Center and the Southern Christian Leadership Conference called for a ban of sales from retailers. Camelot Music store did ban sales of *Death Certificate*, while Oregon passed a law making it illegal to display Ice Cube's image inside its stores. In the United Kingdom, Island Records (Priority's UK distributor) removed both "No Vaseline" and "Black Korea" from its version of the album. St. Ides also dropped Cube from its ad campaign for its malt liquor. (see sidebar: St. Ides).

St. Ides

David J. Leonard

Attempting to capitalize on the popularity of hip hop and its connection to malt liquor, solidified by N.W.A.'s "8-Ball" and numerous rap videos that showed artists sipping their favorite brew, St. Ides hired Ice Cube as one of its spokespeople in the late 1980s. Joining King Tee, the Geto Boys, EPMD, Snoop, and Nate Dogg, Cube did not merely endorse Ides by appearing in commercials but helped produce several songs that would be used throughout the campaign. The most notorious or infamous of these songs and videos had Cube rhyming St. Ides malt liquor with "Get your girl in the mood quicker." With such lyrics, along with the controversy surrounding the release of *Death Certificate*, Ice Cube and St. Ides faced massive public criticisms for the ad campaign. The U.S. Surgeon General and the New York State Consumer Protection Commission publicly criticized the commercials. The U.S.

Bureau of Alcohol, Tobacco and Firearms and the New York State Attorney General's Office levied fines against St. Ides. Additionally, Korean grocers throughout the nation, in response to "Black Korea," called for a national boycott of Cube's beer of choice. In December 1991, the *Wall Street Journal* named the St. Ides campaign as one of the worst advertising campaigns of the year. Feeling the heat, St. Ides quickly severed its relationship with Ice Cube. Yet the damage was already done. G. Heileman Co., the national brewing company that had created St. Ides, disavowed any connection to St. Ides and its maker, McKenzie River. The commercials were eventually banned altogether, which ironically made Ice Cube increasingly uncomfortable with the commodification and commercialization of hip hop, especially toward the sale of beer. In fact, he argues that the scene near the end of *Boyz N the Hood*, in which Doughboy pours out a bottle of Ides, is not just about his character paying respect to the dead but reflects Cube's own desire to wash his hands of his relationship with Ides and the advertising industry's exploitation of hip hop.

Although accusations of racism, anti-Semitism, and homophobia would stick with Ice Cube for several years, these media scandals propelled sales of *Death Certificate*, and boosted Cube's fanbase in the mainstream. In summer 1992, Perry Farrell asked Ice Cube to join his Lollapalooza Tour. The annual tour was primarily a showcase for alternative rock bands, but had featured Ice T and his heavy metal band Body Count in its inaugural 1991 tour. In 1992, Cube played the main stage along with rock bands Ministry, the Red Hot Chili Peppers, Soundarden, and Pearl Jam. While Lollapalooza allowed him some on-stage posturing (he had members of his posse hold fake guns through the set), he also made light of his gangsta image by using a water gun to cool off the crowd. It had been a long six months for Cube, given the immense backlash spawned by the release of *Death Certificate* and the media pressures that surrounded his music and cinematic careers, yet the success of the album and his increasingly evident crossover appeal marked the beginnings of Cube's surge within popular culture.

On April 29, 1992, Los Angeles erupted into riots following the acquittals of Lawrence Powell, Timothy Wind, Theodore Brisenio, and Stacey Koon, whose videotaped beating of Rodney King brought the issue of police brutality into the national consciousness just as Cube's previous album had done on a smaller scale. Both these events, along with the criticism he faced with *Death Certificate* and the shooting of Latasha Harlins impacted Cube in the long term, and in the short run with the release of *The Predator* (see sidebar: Hip Hop and the LA Uprising).

Released November 17, 1992, *The Predator* illustrates Cube's array of talent, demonstrating to the world that he was as much a political orator and social commentator as he was a rapper and an actor. Commercially, *The Predator* was a tremendous success. It was the first hip hop album to enter the

Hip Hop and the LA Uprising
David J. Leonard

The 1991 Los Angeles uprising, not surprisingly, had a dramatic effect on West Coast hip hop. As a music that sought to elucidate the happenings within America's inner cities and give voice to the black underclass, the fact that South Central Los Angeles was on fire, and that its black and brown residents were affected, would alter the direction and reception of hip hop.

Before the fires were even put out, media critics and politicians had already blamed hip hop for the lawlessness, the violence, and even the riot itself. Ice Cube took the brunt of this criticism, having rapped about a potential riot in "Black Korea." Additionally, songs on *The Predator* explored the anger over the beatings of Rodney King, leading some to claim that he was causing anger within the black community. Cube saw things otherwise, claiming that he merely expressed the sentiments of blacks in South Central Los Angeles prior to the riots. Had white America been listening to his music, he argued, it could have seen the uprising coming long before the verdicts. Not buying his claims about having the pulse of LA's underclass, media and politicians continued to blame hip hop for inciting the riots.

Cube, and others, responded not just to these critics but to the riots themselves just as you would expect: through their lyrics. Leaving behind the commonplace gangsta fairy tales of early 1990s gangsta rap (at least for a few months), the post-riot landscape saw extensive commentary on the Los Angeles uprising. In addition to "We Had to Tear This Motherfucker Up," Cube used *The Predator* to explain what happened on April 29, 1992, including several news-like interludes and even more references in various songs. Likewise, he collaborated with Kam in the production of "Get the First," a single released by Mercury Records to raise money for the Brotherhood Movement, an organization that was working to rebuild South Central Los Angeles. Similarly, Paris and Public Enemy each released albums that commented on the LA uprising, making clear that amid the political blame game, conversations about how to rebuild, and the ubiquitous questions about why LA happened, hip hop had some answers; some that white America might not want to hear but would have little choice given the popularity of artists like Ice Cube.

Billboard charts at number one; it would eventually secure this spot on the R&B charts as well, a feat that had last been done by Stevie Wonder, when *Songs in the Key of Life* topped both charts more than fifteen years before. The commercial success of the album did not merely reflect Cube's popularity, his ability to tap into the predominant questions of the day while capturing the anger of many (black) Americans, but elucidated the aesthetic and sound quality available on *The Predator*. Abandoning the bass-dominated traditions of gangsta rap, Cube blended together the sounds of funk, psyche-delic, and soul with the traditional sounds of hip hop. The Los Angeles uprising not only marked a shift toward even more political and social commentary with hip hop, which certainly was evident with *The Predator*, but a change to the sound as well, one that would guide the maturation of hip hop for several years to come.

The foundation song for *The Predator*, one that captures the political and aesthetic qualities or ethos of the album and its time was "We Had to Tear This Motherfucker Up." It chronicles the trial of the four LAPD officers and its aftermath, making clear as to why "we" (literally and lyrically) had to tear "this motherfucker up." Powerful in itself, juxtaposed with "It Was a Good Day," a song that imagines a perfect day in South Central, Cube offers immense insight into the despair felt by many African Africans. Sampling the Isley Brothers' "Footsteps in the Dark" and the Morent's "Come on Sexy Mama," two soulful R&B songs that enhance Cube's lyrics and style, "It Was a Good Day" offers a perfect counter to the anger and frustration in "We Had to Tear This Motherfucker Up." On this (good) day, as opposed to April 29, 1992, everything goes right: Cube's narrator eats a perfect breakfast, balls at the court with the fellas, has sex with his girlfriend, and chills with his homies. Most important, there is no death, no murder, and no cops ("No helicopters looking for murder"). Yet Cube makes clear that this dream is almost laugh-able, concluding the song by asking what he was thinking, transitioning into "We Had to Tear This Motherfucker Up." Like the metaphor of life and death offered with *Death Certificate*, these two songs capture the essence of *The Predator*: anger and hope; despair and possibility. *The Predator* seemed to be the culmination of Ice Cube's development as a solo artist. It was less controversial than his earlier solo albums, but just as socially relevant.

Ice Cube released his follow-up album, *Lethal Injection*, on July 12, 1993. Concerned about talk of his selling out and losing his gangsta roots, Cube sought to create an album that highlighted his G-funk style, his newfound mainstream style, and of course his well-known gangsta political commen-tary. For example, "You Know How We Do It," a commentary on the East Coast–West Coast feud within hip hop shows Cube's talent for in-the-mo-ment political and cultural commentary. "Down 4 Whatever" also makes clear that Cube is hip hop as he battles K-Dee in an old-school microphone battle session, in which he announces his preparedness to make records and revolution. "Ghetto Bird" is a classic Cube cut, which continues his effort to give voice to the experiences of the black underclass and their daily reality with police violence. To him, this was embodied by his return to underground street hip hop, with hard-core themes of police brutality, militarization, sur-veillance (ghetto birds = helicopters), and state violence. He graphically de-scribes the sights and sounds of ghetto birds patrolling the night, rapping, "They make the neighborhood seem like Saigon." Although each of these songs shows a return to his hard-core roots, "Cave Bitch" follows suit, almost serving as the ultimate piece of evidence that he hasn't sold out. Here he raps about white women and black men, more specifically how marrying blonde white women had become a status symbol for black male celebrities. Cube sought to demonstrate this outside the mainstream in hip hop, while illustrating the varied reactions of critics to his description of white women and black women as bitches. Critics who had made little of his description of black women as bitches denounced him in this case. However, "Cave Bitch" would be Cube's last blatantly misogynistic song.

The album was not a total reversal of styles, as Cube remained true to his more mainstream sound as well. With "Bop Gun," an eleven-minute epic with a contribution from George Clinton, Cube replicates the funky sound of previous albums. Cube also uses this album to focus on love, dispelling the criticism that he and hip hop were nothing but anger. To him, the album represents a lethal injection of truth (the mirror into society and self) and love (McIver 136). Reconciling street cred with marketability, *Lethal Injection* is yet another example of how Cube in particular, and conscious artists in general, attempt to work the system to both get their message out and avoid falling by the mainstream's wayside. Lackluster reception by critics is only one characteristic of an artist's competency; an artist's intentions are equally important, as Cube's career in Hollywood can attest.

A NEW BEGINNING

The 1993 release of *Lethal Injection* would mark the beginning of Ice Cube's five-year hiatus from making solo albums. During this period, he would produce and supply the lyrics for several albums, including Kam's *Never Again* and Da Lench Mob's *Guerillas in the Mist*. He additionally collaborated on several projects, joining Mack 10 and WC to form the Westside Connection, which recorded the immensely popular single "Bow Down." He also contributed to the soundtracks from *Dangerous Minds* ("The World Is Mine") and *I Got the Hook Up* ("Ghetto Vet") and joined with Snoop Dogg and Mack 10 to produce "Only in California." He also released *Bootlegs and B-Sides* (1994), a compilation of innovative remixes of some of his most popular songs, and *Featuring . . . Ice Cube*, a collection of his collaborative projects, and participated in the 1998 Family Values Tour with Korn and Limp Bizkit. Yet for all intents and purposes, his solo rap career had come to a standstill. The early and mid-1990s saw Ice Cube's focus turning away from hip hop music to an emerging ghettocentric imagination within Hollywood. Whereas rap music proved to be one of the strongest genres of expression for the black underclass during the 1970s and 1980s (as well as one of the few opportunities to make it big in the entertainment industry), Hollywood, which sought to capitalize on the popularity of N.W.A., Public Enemy, and Run-DMC, emerged as a powerful space for hip hop during the 1990s. Cube, perhaps more than any others, would use these opportunities to propel his own career

Ice Cube would release two more albums—*War and Peace Vol. 1 (The War Disc)* (1998) and *War and Peace Vol. 2 (The Peace Disc)* (2000), both sophisticated examinations of war, peace, violence, calm, death, and life. Because Cube had lost his fan base to a certain degree and was seen now, both albums were unable to match the success of the early 1990s. Moreover, the world of hip hop had changed, with bling, sex, parties, and excess being predominant themes of hip hop at the turn of the century—a change Cube was unwilling to accept. Cube claimed that the changes in hip hop reflected an obsession with fame and money making and an absence of consciousness raising and communal empowerment. His focus on movies resulted from hip hop losing its way within the mainstream; to him, there was no place in hip hop for a voice of politics and opposition. Although Cube's own growth as an artist and hip hop's changes certainly pushed him into virtual retirement, it was his success in Hollywood that facilitated his transformation from rapper to actor.

WELCOME TO HOLLYWOOD

Ice Cube's acting career began as a natural extension of his place in hip hop, as Hollywood merely sought to capitalize on the popularity and authenticity of hip hop artists to sell its projects. In 1988, John Singleton, then a junior majoring in film writing at the University of Southern California, approached Cube, telling him that he was developing a script that documented the experience of black youth in South Central Los Angeles; he hoped Cube would act in the film. Cube did not hear from Singleton again until 1990, when he asked Cube if he wanted to read for the part of Doughboy, the character Singleton had written with him in mind. Despite Singleton's immense confidence and determination to cast him in *Boyz N the Hood*, Cube's transition to acting was neither easy nor natural. His first reading was a disaster, leading Singleton to inquire if Cube had read the entire script. Learning that he had only read his part, Singleton sent him home, asking him to return several days later and only after he had read the entire script, at which time he was offered a role in the film.

Cube plays Doughboy, partly a stereotype of young black males—angry, violent, hypersexual, criminally minded, lazy—and otherwise a complex, innovative character. Cube's performance gives Doughboy depth, complexity, and humanity. He masterfully plays a foil to Tre (Cuba Gooding Jr.) and Ricky (Morris Chestnut), both of whom seek to transcend the limitations of inner-city life. Likewise, Doughboy contributes to Singleton's overarching argument about black fathers and parents in general, as they relate to black pathology. Without a father in his life, as opposed to Tre, who benefits from the wisdom of his father (played by Lawrence Fishburne), Doughboy falls into a life of criminality and degradation that ultimately leads to his own death. Besides mirroring his ideology as it relates to the importance of black fathers as protectors and educators, Cube's contribution to *Boyz* transcended his bringing Doughboy to life: He wrote and recorded the film's soundtrack; he gave legitimacy to the film's message and tone given his South Central roots; and his popularity and connection to hip hop contributed to the media buzz and the film's immense box office success. Still, *Boyz* and Singleton's faith in Cube did a lot for his career, further elevating him into the mainstream. Up to this point, his popularity had been very much connected to his place in N.W.A., his celebrity within black youth culture, and his voice and lyrical genius, yet following the release of *Boyz N the Hood* his face and artistry entered the national consciousness. While enhancing his rap career, the success and critical acclaim that came with *Boyz N the Hood* provided additional opportunities for Ice Cube within Hollywood, next with the production of *Trespass*.

Released on Christmas Day 1992, *Trespass* sought to capitalize on the success of *Boyz N the Hood*, *New Jack City*, and *Menace to Society*, as well as the popularity of hip hop, casting Ice Cube alongside Ice-T. While the film received mixed reviews, some of which criticized its deployment of racial stereotypes (white heroes versus black villains/criminals), Cube's performance was universally praised. Just as with *Boyz*, reviewers praised his ability to bring complexity and depth to an otherwise stock and racially flat character. Moreover, the reviewers tended to offer praise for Cube's growth as an actor, marking his entry into Hollywood not so much as the story of a rapper who acts, but as an artist who possesses multiple talents, which include making music and movies.

Despite the box office and critical success Cube experienced in his first two films, he faced a relatively bumpy future in the years immediately after the release of *Boyz N the Hood*. His next two films—*The Glass Shield* and *Higher Learning*—while certainly more reflective of his politics, were universally panned, failing to meet box office expectations as well. Both films were criticized for their over-the-top depictions of race and their focus on white-on-black racism. Although Cube's supporting performances illustrate his growth as actor—in *The Glass Shield*, in which he plays an innocent man arrested and charged with a crime by the racist Los Angeles Sheriff's Department, and in *Higher Learning*, where he plays Fudge, a campus radical who counsels Malik (Omar Epps) and other black students on the realities of race and resistance on a post–civil rights college campus—he could not escape the criticism of these films (although several reviews did describe him as exceptional). Still, his work in these films further solidified his place in Hollywood, opening up opportunities for greater artistic control.

At the same time Cube was achieving greater control of his film work, he made peace with N.W.A, the group he had left because he wasn't given equal compensation for his lyrics and vocals. (see sidebar: N.W.A. Reunion). He met with Eazy-E shortly before Eazy's death from AIDS in March, 1995. The former bandmates put their grudge to rest, and Ice Cube put this part of his musical past behind him just as his debut as a screenwriter was about to make him a bigger movie star. *Friday*, which was written by Ice Cube and DJ Pooh, was released on April 26, 1995. Marketed with slogans like "A lot can go down between Thursday and Saturday," *Friday* was a surprising comedic success. In fact, critics and moviegoers alike seemed shocked by Cube's successful turn to comedy, given his place in the American consciousness as angry, militant, and always serious and scowling. Perhaps to highlight this shift from the typical Ice Cube image, his character Craig wears the same clothes in *Friday*'s opening scene as Doughboy wore in his final scene in *Boyz N the Hood*. Craig is a relatively conservative Los Angelino, whose unjust firing from his underpaying job leads him to spend his Friday chillin' with Smokey (Chris Tucker). Cube uses *Friday* to build on the narrative offered in "It Was a Good Day," chronicling the goodness in chillin' with one's homies even on those days marked by the most heartache and injustice. More than

N.W.A. Reunion
David J. Leonard

Ice Cube left N.W.A. in 1989 over contract disputes, and he and the group recorded several songs dissing each other until Dr. Dre became unhappy with the N.W.A. contract terms as well, and left the group to form Death Row Records in 1991. Dre's departure marked the end of N.W.A, and he and Eazy-E continued the war of words in their subsequent releases. With such public animosity between group members, an N.W.A. reunion seemed unlikely, but in 1994, Dre reunited with Ice Cube to record "Natural Born Killaz," and in 1995, Ice Cube and Eazy-E put their beef to rest during a meeting at Tunnel, a popular New York City nightclub. Less than three months later, Eazy-E died from AIDS, yet the truce that he and Cube had struck during this meeting would have lasting effects on Cube, N.W.A., and hip hop as a whole. In 1998, Ice Cube and Dre invited their former bandmate MC Ren to record two new N.W.A. tracks: "Hello" was included on Ice Cube's *War & Peace: Volume Two*, and "Chin Check" was featured on the soundtrack to Ice Cube's film *Next Friday*. Neither song featured N.W.A's fifth member, DJ Yella, and Snoop Dogg replaced Eazy-E on "Chin Check." Although a planned full-length reunion album never happened, Ice Cube, Dre, Yella, and Ren, joined by Snoop, Nate Dogg, and other N.W.A. associates, came together for an N.W.A. reunion concert on March 11, 2000. While these collaborations never amounted to a full-fledged N.W.A. reunion., the fanfare generated once again reminded the hip hop world of the power of unity and the legendary status of the original gangstas of hip hop.

the movie itself, which received many positive reviews, Ice Cube stole the show as both a writer and a comedic actor. Review after review heaped praise on Cube for his humor, his talents as a writer, and his growth as an actor. He would receive similar critical praise, although not at the same level, following the release of *The Players Club* in 1998, which he wrote, directed, and produced (he also has a small part in the film). *The Players Club* tells the story of Dina Armstrong (Lisa Raye), who turns to stripping following an argument with her father, that results in her leaving home with her son. Hoping to make a film that touched upon the southern black strip club industry and the complexities and difficulties facing young black women, and explored the sacrifices people make to better themselves in the long term, Cube wasn't satisfied with a role as writer and producer, deciding to go behind the camera as the director, despite having no training. Having a vision and clear understanding of where the picture needed to go required him to take on the responsibility of directing.

He was able to hold to his vision, delivering a film that spoke to those issues while also being commercially viable (despite a small budget and limited release, it amassed $20 million at the box office). However, the film wasn't so well received by critics, who once again questioned Cube's gender politics. To many, the film seemed to glorify stripping, ostensibly celebrating the sexualization of black women's bodies. Though these reviews lacked depth, it seemed that Cube had not outrun the criticism that had defined his early years in hip hop. While opportunities increased with his heightened creative power, Cube remained outside the Hollywood mainstream. All that would change with the release of *Three Kings*.

Debuting in September 1999, *Three Kings* was an immediate hit with audiences and reviewers alike, something new given the responses to the Gulf War in the early 1990s. The movie starred George Clooney (Archie Gates) and Mark Wahlberg (Troy Barlow) along with Ice Cube (Chief Elgin). For Cube, beyond being part of a successful and politically progressive (in his mind at least) film, *Three Kings* provided him the opportunity to grow as an actor, revealing his talents beyond gangstas and black-theme films. Whether in his ability to deliver a character that was both tough and vulnerable, or the ease with which he meshed with Clooney and Wahlberg, reviewers and others in Hollywood paid notice to his performance specifically. What seemed to shock reviewers the most and probably opened the most doors was the fact that Cube, the one-time face of gangsta rap in Hollywood, with ease played a soldier, one who was deeply religious and spiritual no less. Delivering a wonderful performance in a film described as a masterpiece by Roger Ebert and a classic by several others, *Three Kings* further elevated Cube's acting career, resulting in increased opportunities in mainstream films, including *Ghosts of Mars* (2001) and *XXX: State of the Union* (2005).

Even with Cube's success as a prominent supporting actor among Hollywood's elite and the opportunities to participate in blockbuster films, he remained an active member of a black Hollywood contingent. In 2000, he wrote, produced, and starred in *Next Friday*; then in 2002, he also wrote, produced, and starred in both *All About the Benjamins* and *Friday After Next*. That same year, he starred in the immensely popular *Barbershop*, with Cedric the Entertainer and Eve. Cube once again defied expectations and stereotypes, playing Calvin, a relatively conservative barbershop owner, who spends most of his day wondering how he can live the American Dream with his wife and trying to control his hip hop clientele and employees. Despite playing a character that was a mere shadow of his hip hop beginnings, it was clear that he couldn't outrun his past. As they would again with the release of *Are We There Yet?* (2005), fans and critics alike questioned if Cube had sold out, if the allure of Hollywood had forced Cube to abandon his hardness, his politics, and his willingness to keep it real. Interestingly, Cube and others have continually argued that his importance in *Barbershop* and his contributions to the film have often been devalued because of widespread contempt for hip hop and fears over continued distaste for him by audiences. For example, Cube has long noted how Oprah and others invited Cedric the Entertainer and Eve and not him to promote the film, which demonstrates that neither he nor hip hop had been fully accepted in the mainstream. Despite this and similar rejections, the contributions of Ice Cube to the American cinematic landscape demand recognition, as Cube continues to add controversy with a conscience to the realm of popular culture.

ICE CUBE'S IMPACT AND LEGACY

In "True to the Game," Ice Cube laments the practice of black artists and other celebrities selling out upon crossing over, leaving behind the artistry and community that allowed them to "blow up." Ironically, his career path and choices have been subjected to similar criticism. His virtual disappearance from the rap game, his performance in films such as *Barbershop* and *Are We There Yet?*, have raised questions of his commitment to hip hop and its gangsta/political roots. For example, many have criticized him for his performance in *Barbershop*, not so much because he trades in his khakis and AK-47 for business attire and a set of clippers, but for playing a character, Calvin, who buddies up with the police and shows a propensity to celebrate bootstrap individualism. Likewise, others have wondered how Cube can claim to be a voice of the underclass, doing movies about the black middle class.

Jeff Chang and other hip hop critics have thoroughly discounted such accusations as both simplistic and reactionary. Rather, he and others see Cube's career as an allegory for hip hop, elucidating the powerful ways in which hip hop and the American cultural landscape have matured over the last twenty years. Likewise, Cube is quick to challenge these criticisms, noting that just because his worldview has changed doesn't mean he is selling out the community. In his estimation, he has merely matured and grown as a person and artist. Moreover, he and others (Ludacris, 50 Cent) are quick to point out that denunciations of him for selling out are ridiculous given the continued demonization and criticism faced by hip hop. Just because he makes movies with George Clooney and Mark Wahlberg, just because his albums have gone triple platinum or he is able to produce or direct various projects, doesn't mean that he or other black hip hop artists have made it. Racism and the widespread demonization of black youth preclude full acceptance of Ice Cube or hip hop in general from the mainstream. From Bill O'Reilly and Lynne Cheney to C. Delores Tucker and Oprah Winfrey, whom Cube has described as disrespectful, distant, or hostile to hip hop artists, many continue to see hip hop not only as outside the mainstream of America but as a dangerous pollutant to its cultural fabric. If still not mainstream, it is certainly difficult to accuse Cube of selling out.

In 2006, Ice Cube coproduced and helped created the controversial FX show, *Black. White.*, which brought a black and white family together to experience an alternative racial reality through the use of makeup. For Cube, this show created an environment of forced engagement and dialogue for both the show's participants and its viewers. Although some saw it as further evidence of Cube's fall/ascension into the American mainstream, the show itself and its intent follow in the footsteps of the vast majority of his works: It sought to provoke conversation, offer commentary on contemporary racial issues, and made no attempt to avoid controversy; it was classic Ice Cube. Whether with "Fuck Tha Police," "We Had to Tear This Motherfucker Up," "Cave Bitch," *Boyz N the Hood*, *The Player's Club*, *Three Kings*, or *Barbershop*, Ice Cube's career has been a story of controversy, of public outrage and redemption, of his using art and popular culture to foster self-reflection and conversation, and his performing different identities in different instances, not only showing his own growth but illustrating the shifting cultural landscape that sought different identities within him at different moments in American history.

See also: Dr. Dre and Snoop Dogg, Public Enemy

WORKS CITED

Chang, Jeff. *Can't Stop Won't Stop: A History of the Hip-Hop Generation.* New York: Picador, 2005.
Cheney, Charise. *Brothers Gonna Work It Out: Sexual Politics in the Golden Age of Rap Nationalism.* New York: New York University Press, 2005.
McIver, Joel. *Ice Cube: Attitude.* London: Sanctuary, 2003.

FURTHER RESOURCES

Boyd, Todd. *Am I Black Enough for You: Popular Culture from the 'Hood and Beyond.* Bloomington: University of Indiana Press, 1997.

Boyd, Todd. *The New H.N.I.C.: The Death of Civil Rights and the Reign of Hip-Hop*. New York: New York University Press, 2002.

Neal, Mark Anthony, and Murray Foreman. *That's the Joint! The Hip-Hop Studies Reader*. New York: Routledge, 2004.

Orr, Tamra. *Ice Cube*. New York: Mitchell Lane, 2006.

SELECTED DISCOGRAPHY

N.W.A.

N.W.A. and the Posse. Priority, 1987.
Straight Outta Compton. Priority, 1989.

Ice Cube

AmeriKKKa's Most Wanted. Priority, 1990.
Kill at Will. Priority, 1990.
Death Certificate. Priority, 1991.
The Predator. Priority, 1992.
Lethal Injection. Priority, 1993.
War and Peace Vol. 1 (The War Disc). Priority, 1998.
War and Peace Vol. 2 (The Peace Disc). Priority, 2000.
Laugh Now, Cry Later. Lench Mob Records, 2006.

Courtesy of Photofest.

Dr. Dre and Snoop Dogg

David Diallo

In his 2005 album *The Documentary*, Compton rapper the Game establishes his gangsta stance by affiliating himself with West Coast producer Dr. Dre and rapper Snoop Dogg (together they are mentioned thirty-five times). Such name dropping in rap songs is meant to legitimize an artist's position through his or her connections with iconic artists, in this case Snoop Dogg and Dr. Dre, undisputed icons of West Coast gangsta rap. Jay-Z uses a similar technique in his song "Change Clothes," where he defines his high-ranking status in East Coast rap through a comparison to Snoop Dogg's importance in the West. In "Flowin' on the D-Line," Digital Underground's rapper Shock-G expresses his ruthlessness toward women through a direct allusion to Dr. Dre's notorious physical assault on Dee Barnes, *Pump It Up*'s TV host. (On January 27, 1991, Dr. Dre got into a physical confrontation with the presenter after she presented an unfavorable segment on N.W.A. on her Fox TV rap video show.)

The success of tactical name dropping is highly dependent on the interpretive skills of the listener, for such links are ineffective when the listener cannot identify the artists named. The widespread references to Dre and Snoop Dogg in rap lyrics, then, indicate their importance as icons of hip hop. Dre and Snoop have established their iconic positions through a history of musical innovation. Dre was a founding member of N.W.A., who developed a new sound and propelled West Coast gangsta rap to national attention. After that group broke up in 1991, Dre introduced Snoop Dogg, a new MC whose unique slang and laid-back lyrical flow brought a new vocal style to fit with Dre's G-funk (gangstafied funk) production.

Artistic innovations aside, Dr. Dre and Snoop Dogg's ties to the streets and their conventional celebration of a gangsta hedonism greatly contributed to their high-ranking status and helped establish them as major forces in the music industry. Dre and Snoop's biographies follow a gangsta rap course that takes them out of the streets and into the studio. In gangsta rap, issues of authenticity, credibility, and legitimacy are integrally linked to the streets of the ghetto and their social practices. As the sociocultural matrix of rap music, ghetto streets remain, three decades after rap hit the mainstream, its paradigmatic habitat. In this respect, a catchphrase like "keepin' it real" literally means representing, realistically or through hyperbolic gangsta narratives, the symbolic forms of the ghetto. The final battle that opposes Eminem's character B. Rabbit and Papa Doc in the movie *8 Mile* offers striking evidence of the importance of this social and symbolic space. Rabbit defeats and humiliates his opponent by exposing his middle-class origins; Papa Doc went to private school and comes from a good home, so therefore he is not keepin' it real by posing as a gangsta in his lyrics. This strategy of exposing middle-class backgrounds is prevalent in hip hop. In one well-known example, Craig G defeated freestyle champion Supernatural in a battle after he emphasized his opponent's inappropriate geographical origin; Craig G was from New York, the birthplace of hip hop, whereas Supernatural was originally from Indiana. Similarly, the career of rapper Vanilla Ice abruptly ended when his claim of being from the streets was challenged by factual evidence that he had in fact experienced a middle-class upbringing and had never been involved in crime.

Recent releases and record sales confirm the current dominance of ghetto rap, an assortment of heterogeneous rap productions signifying streets of the ghetto, most particularly with labels like G-Unit, Roc-A-Fella, or Aftermath, whose artists generally glorify a criminal lifestyle and street corner activities (drug pushing, organized crime, pimping). This institutionalization of rap music as street/ghetto music is crucial to understanding the central status of both Dr. Dre and Snoop Dogg. The power struggle that animates rap music is undeniably dominated by ghettocentric orientations. Through a logic of inclusion and exclusion, the rap artists who develop street themes in their music, and who are somehow related to the streets, hold considerable symbolic capital. They are (according to the slang of the time period) dope, fresh, or gangsta, while rappers with no connection to the streets are generally wack, lame, or wanksta. Accordingly, if lyrical references to Dr. Dre and Snoop Dogg imply symbolic capital, these rappers' association with the streets is equally important.

DR. DRE

Andre Romel Young was born on February 18, 1965, in Compton, a city of the Los Angeles metropolitan area that would become, twenty years later, as important as the South Bronx in the geography of rap music (see sidebar: Compton). In fact, before the commotion caused by Ice-T's "Six N the Morning" and N.W.A.'s album *Straight Outta Compton*, California rap had very little echo outside local venues like Radiotron or the Eve After Dark. One of the most prominent contributors to the electro rap scene was the World Class

---

Compton
David Diallo

Like many other black ghettos, Compton, a city of the Los Angeles metropolitan area, went through the post-sixties transformation that turned communal ghettos into hyperghettos, disadvantaged areas characterized by organizational desertification and informal economy. Yet it symbolizes the aftermath of the political urban patterning of racial and class exclusion like few other places. In rap discourse, Compton, an emblematic place, is to West Coast rap what the South Bronx is to the seminal New York rap scene. The mutual success of N.W.A. and Dr. Dre firmly established the city as a symbolic space expressive of Los Angeles gang banging. Subsequently, the emblematic status of CPT (Compton) and its vicinities has been extensively referred to by local rappers (and filmmakers) in their expressive forms. Rappers like Compton's Most Wanted, Tweedy Bird Loc, Above the Law, WC and the Maad Circle, Boo-Yaa T.R.I.B.E. or the Game have drawn on the symbolic gangsta connotations attached to Los Angeles's newfound legitimacy in rap to enhance their credibility. Their glorification of a criminal lifestyle was emulated nationwide by groups like the Geto Boys or Detroit's Most Wanted. Almost twenty years after the release of *Straight Outta Compton*, Dr. Dre remains the leading representative of Compton. Throughout his career, he has consistently emphasized his ties to the place and has been greatly influential in establishing Compton as a highly evocative gangsta signifier through his recurrent use of "City of Compton"—a sample from Ronnie Hudson and the Street People's *West Coast Poplock.*

Wreckin' Cru, a DJ group managed by ex-break dancer Lonzo Williams. Williams' DJs were extremely popular during the first half of the 1980s and packed venues like the Sports Arena or the Convention Center with thousands of poppers and lockers (aka b-boys or break dancers) from South Central, Compton, and Inglewood. Andre started his producing career as a member of this group in 1984. He had developed an interest in music from a young age, and, encouraged by a music-loving mother, spent hours practicing his skills on turntables and mixing tables. Onstage, Dre wore a costume, including a stethoscope, and perfomed as "Dr. Dre," an homage to NBA superstar Julius "Dr. J" Irving.

Thanks to his performances with the World Class Wreckin' Cru and on KDAY, a local radio station, which, under the notable influence of Greg Mack, supported several local acts, Dr. Dre soon attained local celebrity status. As a result, he appeared regularly on shows like *Traffic Jam* and *Mixmasters*, a Saturday night all-star show where DJs from local crews mixed live and played their own productions. In 1984 he released "Surgery" on Macola Records, a local label owned by Don MacMillan. This title, based on his doctor persona, exploited his "beat surgeon" gimmick through a clinical arrangement of connotative samples ("Records! Mixer! Turntables!" replaced Scalpel! Forceps! Defibrolator!). The following year, World Class Wreckin' Cru released *World Class*, its first album. The reasonable success of this album, along with that of other Los Angeles–based electro rap musicians (*On the Nile* by Egyptian Lover, *Rockberry Jam* by the L.A. Dream Team, *Naughty Boy* by Uncle Jam's Army) rapidly stirred the interest of major record companies. The group was signed on CBS/Epic and in 1987 released *First Round Knock-Out*. This release put the Los Angeles rap scene on the map and, with its California imagery, clearly distinguished West Coast rap from East Coast rap. While rap music had diversified in New York and was no longer exclusively party music, the Los Angeles rap scene had principally exalted partying and hedonism over electronic melodies. This idiosyncratic aspect of the Angelino musical scene is loosely portrayed in *Breakin'* and *Breakin' 2*, two low-budget movies that presented a Hollywood version of the visual gimmicks, outfits, and Jheri curls that prevailed at the time. This imagery would radically change with Ice-T's 1986 single "Six N the Morning" and with Dr. Dre's next group, Niggaz with Attitude.

In 1986, Dre had started collaborating with Eric Wright (Eazy-E), an ambitious young drug pusher eager to launch his rap label, Ruthless Records. Wright, though he believed in the commercial potential of the new and scandalous gangsta themes developed by Ice-T in "Six N the Morning," had no serious connections in the music business (see sidebar: Eazy-E) . In contrast, Dr. Dre benefited from solid experience and considerable social capital in the fast-growing LA rap scene. He especially had connections at Macola Records and at Audio Achievements, the studio where he recorded with the World Class Wreckin' Cru, which would help Wright achieve his artistic and financial ambitions in the lucrative business that rap music was becoming. Their first release was "Boyz N the Hood." This street manifesto, on which Eazy-E rapped lyrics written by O'shea Jackson (Ice Cube) over Dr. Dre's production, laid the foundations of their N.W.A. collaboration to come. Ruthless Records, owing to the decisive entrepreneurial skills that Eazy-E had developed pushing drugs, independently sold more than 200,000 copies of "Boyz N the Hood." In the wake of this success, Eazy-E, with the help of his manager Jerry Heller, a long-established music executive, launched Niggaz with Attitude, a rap group that rapidly became, with the vernacular appeal of its exaltation of ghetto lifestyle and Dr. Dre's skillful production, a national musical sensation that would give its members an unparalleled status in rap.

The first significant release of Ruthless Records produced by Dr. Dre was its founder's solo effort, *Eazy-Duz-It* (1987). It was followed the next year by

---

Eazy-E
David Diallo

Folklore research on orality in black ghettos has established the importance of toasts—violent and obscene oral narratives recounting the exploits of "Ba-ad Niggers." In 1987, when Eazy-E (Eric Wright) founded Ruthless Records and N.W.A., he musically and parochially adjusted the themes and narrative structure of these long-standing heroic tales and paved the way for much of what would subsequently be labeled gangsta rap. As a former drug pusher, Wright fruitfully applied to the music industry the commercial skills that he had been developing on the streets and turned Ruthless into a foremost label. His early releases became underground hits with virtually no support from radio, the press, or MTV. In 1991, however, the label's maximizing business tactics led to financial disagreements between N.W.A. members. Dr. Dre's bitter departure ignited a vivid feud with Ruthless. Eazy-E riposted to the merciless attacks that Dre had launched on *The Chronic* through his 1993 EP *It's On (Dr. Dre) 187um Killa* on which he exhibited a ridiculing photograph of Dre taken during his World Class Wreckin' Cru days. Even though Ice Cube and Dr. Dre, who had been the principal creative forces in the label, had left Ruthless, Eazy-E's entrepreneurial skills helped him to maintain healthy record sales, mostly through lucrative groups like Above the Law and Bone Thugs-N-Harmony. He was thirty-one years old when he died on March 26, 1995, ten days after having been diagnosed with AIDS.

---

one of the most important albums in hip hop history, N.W.A.'s first official release, *Straight Outta Compton* (1988). By the end of 1987, even though Don MacMillan, willing to cash in on the increasing appeal of the self-proclaimed world's most dangerous group, had opportunistically released *N.W.A. and the Posse,* a compilation of Macola-distributed N.W.A. EPs ("Boyz N the Hood," "Dopeman," "8-ball," and "A Bitch Is a Bitch"), *Straight Outta Compton* was the first official album of the group. The commercial success of this highly controversial album paved the way for much of what would be termed gangsta rap in the 1990s. On this record, N.W.A. carried on the glorification of the activities of local gangs inaugurated on *Eazy-Duz-It* and emphatically put Compton on the map, owing greatly to its outrageous lyrics and to Dre's rumbling sonic production on the opening tracks, "Straight Outta Compton," "Fuck Tha Police," and "Gangsta Gangsta." *100 Miles and Runnin'* (1990), the group's second LP, released after Ice Cube's departure, was a ghetto variation of the slave narrative motif that presented soon-to-be-generic hyperbolic gangsta narratives. In spite of its obscene and violent content, it reached the twenty-seventh place on the Billboard Top 200 (*Straight Outta Compton* had ranked thirty-seventh the previous year). In 1991, N.W.A.'s final release, *Efil4zaggin* (Niggaz4Life spelled backward) entered the charts at number one and established rap music (with the parallel success of rap groups like Public Enemy and 2 Live Crew) as the new defiant musical expression. If, conforming to N.W.A.'s trademarks, this album contained larger-than-life violence (on "Appetite 4 Destruction" and "One in a Million") and pornography (on "She Swallowed It"), even both (on Dr. Dre's gory "One Less Bitch"), its generic gangsta themes were enhanced by sepulchral moods that distinctively differed from N.W.A.'s previous releases. This inclination toward gothic sonorities, prominent keyboards, and heavy beats would lead to the crafting of Dr. Dre's signature sound.

In 1989, Dr. Dre had single-handedly produced the D.O.C.'s first LP, *No One Can Do It Better.* Hitherto he had jointly produced Eazy-E and N.W.A.'s albums with fellow World Class Wreckin' Cru member DJ Yella. On this album, Dre displayed the range of his experienced production and provided the D.O.C. with an assemblage of slow and fast rhythms on which the skilled Texan MC delivered his resourceful lyrics. This noteworthy collaboration is representative of what would be Dr. Dre's later approach to rap music: a polished production designed for a distinctive lyricist with concrete ties to the streets. His subsequent collaborations with Snoop Dogg, Xzibit, Eminem, 50 Cent and, more recently, the Game, testify to its particularity. Exhibiting versatility, Dre also produced his wife's eponymous R&B album, *Michel'le* (Ruthless, 1989). On this record, Michel'le, a former chorus member of the World Class Wreckin' Cru who had already featured on *No One Can Do It Better,* sang urban romances on her husband's electronic melodies. Its single "No More Lies" became the best hit single in the label's history (seventh place on the Billboard charts). Later on, Dr. Dre would successfully repeat a similar ground shifting with Mary J. Blige (on *No More Drama*, MCA, 2002, and its hit single "Family Affair") and with Eve's crossover hit featuring Gwen Stefani ("Let Me Blow Ya Mind," 2001).

In 1987, financial and artistic disagreements ended Dre's collaboration with Lonzo Williams's entertainment-formatted group. Similar financial issues would end Dre's partnership with Eazy-E's Ruthless Records after the 1991 release of their final album, *Efil4zaggin*. After Ice Cube's departure and the D.O.C.'s serious car accident, Dr. Dre was the key creative force on the label. He had significantly participated in the production of all its major releases (*Supersonic, Eazy-Duz-It, Straight Outta Compton, No One Can Do It Better*, Above the Law's *Livin' Like Hustlers, Michel'le*), but considered that he had not been rewarded satisfactorily. In 1991, he left Ruthless at the peak of its popularity and cofounded Death Row Records.

Dr. Dre's new partner was Marion "Suge" Knight, a determined ex-gang banger turned bodygard who, inspired by Ruthless's achievements, was equally eager to succeed in the music industry. With Dick Griffey, an influential label owner (he was at the head of SOLAR, the Sound of Los Angeles Records), Dr. Dre and Suge Knight launched Death Row Records, a label that would rapidly become the first-ranking black-owned business in America and would top the U.S. charts half a dozen times between 1992 and 1996.

In 1992, Dr. Dre released "Deep Cover," his first solo EP on Sony and SOLAR. Its gothic sonorities, combined with Colin Wolfe's prominent bass line, clearly bore the signature sound Dre had introduced in *Efil4zaggin*. It also marked the debut of newcomer Snoop Doggy Dogg, a young MC from Long Beach who contributed to a great extent to the success of the producer's first album, *The Chronic* (1992). This multiplatinum album, which showcased several local MCs (Nate Dogg, Daz) was the second milestone of rap music produced by Dr. Dre. It forcefully introduced his patented G-funk sound, a transformation of P-funk's substantial catalogue into gangsta rap, and decisively affected mainstream hip hop. Its celebration of a gangsta lifestyle, particularly on the hit singles "Nuthin' but a G Thang" and "Let Me Ride," with their parochial idiosyncrasies and sociolect, greatly influenced the subsequent rap productions, locally and nationwide, and firmly consolidated Dr. Dre's emblematic status.

Even though he had been prolific at Ruthless Records, producing or collaborating on the seven releases of the label (in five years), Dr. Dre only produced two albums between 1993 and 1996, *The Chronic* and Snoop Dogg's debut album, *Doggystyle*. He nonetheless produced a few tracks for Death Row soundtracks and upcoming artists, most notably Lady of Rage's ego trip "Afro Puffs" in 1994 and 2Pac's "California Love," a highly successful title (on which Dr. Dre sampled Ronnie Hudson and the Street People's "West Coast Poplock" and Roger Zapp's "So Ruff, So Tuff") that blatantly symbolized his long-standing effort to establish California as a serious rival to the New York seminal rap scene. Due to various artistic disagreements and to the culture of terror that Suge Knight had transplanted from the violent world of street gangs to Death Row, Dr. Dre left the label in 1996 to create his own company, Aftermath Entertainment.

Dr. Dre's important achievements and his longevity had granted him high status in the rap industry. His collaborations with street-oriented groups like N.W.A., whose "Boyz N the Hood" figuratively expressed the worldview of many young blacks trapped in ghettos, with Snoop Dogg and 2Pac, two rappers who epitomized a hedonistic gangsta lifestyle, and, more recently, with record-selling rappers Eminem and 50 Cent, decisively conferred unfaltering credibility on him. On 2Pac's "California Love," Dre justified his legitimacy by drawing listeners' attention to his longevity in rap and reminded them that he had been in it for ten years. He would subsequently reiterate this self-referential strategy to signify his authenticity. He emphasized it on the opening of *Dr. Dre Presents . . . The Aftermath* (1996), the first release of his new label, and even more notably on its song "Been There Done That." Eminem did it in his place on "Guilty Conscience," the third single of his successful and controversial *Slim Shady* LP, and reiterated on the chorus of "Forgot About Dre," on *Chronic 2001*, the sequel to Dre's first album where this motif is extensively developed (particularly on "The Watcher," "Still D.R.E.," "Forgot About Dre"). Most importantly, as he proclaims on "Still D.R.E.," Dr. Dre stayed close to the streets and successfully produced underground sensations and respected battle rhymers with an indisputable street credibility like Xzibit (*Restless*), the Game (*The Documentary*), Eminem, and 50 Cent, whose respective albums *The Marshall Mathers* LP and *Get Rich or Die Tryin'* are two of the best-selling rap albums of all time.

Even though Dr. Dre's status derives from the representations, in his productions, of his sociogeographic origins, he nevertheless holds an important symbolic status in the nationwide field of rap music. He collaborated without prejudice with artists from both coasts (in 1997 on *The Firm*, a project that featured New York rappers like Nas and Foxy Brown, or in 1996 with Blackstreet on the hit single "No Diggity"), incidentally challenging the East Coast–West Coast enmity so hyped in the news. The focus on the spatial (the hood/the streets) being, in rap music, as important as the local (Compton, California), Dr. Dre's idealization of the criminal lifestyle that distinguished the streets of Los Angeles in the late eighties spoke instinctively to young blacks of both coasts. This street-oriented discourse undeniably helped establish him as a major force in the music industry.

SNOOP DOGG

Though Dr. Dre became famous as a key member of N.W.A., the group that would determinedly epitomize gangsta rap, he was never involved in gangs. In contrast, Snoop Dogg (Calvin Broadus) unambiguously draws his credibility as an original gangsta (OG) from his criminal feats. Eazy-E, however, would dispute Snoop's criminal background by calling him and Dre "studio gang-stas" on his 1993 EP *It's On (Dr. Dre) 187um Killa* (see sidebar: Studio Gangsta). Eazy's criticism aside, Snoop emphasizes his gang affiliation and criminal involvement as a key part of his credibility. Snoop was born on October 20, 1972, and grew up in Long Beach, California with his brother and his mother, who originally hailed from Mississippi. The number of

---

Studio Gangsta
Elijah Lossner

The term *studio gangsta* came into popular use among rappers during the early 1990s. It was used to describe rappers who portrayed themselves as gangsters in their lyrics but in reality had never been directly involved with crime or street gangs. Many believe the term was first used in Los Angeles during the late 1980s and began popping up in the song lyrics of popular West Coast rappers in the early nineties.

One of the first rappers to use this term was Oakland rapper Spice 1. The first two words on his 1993 album, *187 He Wrote* are "studio gangsta" (187 is the Los Angeles police code for homicide). On another song, "All He Wrote," he questions how many rappers who say they are gang banging are really doing it. Spice 1 goes on to list many of the rappers he thinks are real gangsters (he never mentions any rappers he thinks are studio gangstas). That same year, rap icon Eazy-E released an EP, *It's On (Dr. Dre) 187um Killa*, in which he calls into question the credibility of his former N.W.A. bandmate Dr. Dre. On Eazy's song "Real Muthaphuckkin G's," guest rapper B.G. Knock Out calls Snoop Doggy Dogg and Dr. Dre "studio gangstas" and "actors." The EP's liner notes feature a picture of Dr. Dre in his days with the 1980s dance group World Class Wreckin' Cru, in which Dre is wearing lipstick, eyeliner, and a sequined jumpsuit.

As gangsta rap gained popularity during the early 1990s, it seemed that everyone wanted to rap about crime and murder. Murder was what was selling and many talented rap artists felt the pressure to conform to the violent lyrics in order to survive. The market was overflowing with artists claiming to be gang bangers, provoking many established and respected gangsta rappers to do some housecleaning. Thus the term *studio gangsta* became a very popular way for rappers to call their colleagues into question. If an artist was considered a studio gangsta by his peers, or worse by consumers, then it could very well spell disaster for his career. There is much resentment among rappers who consider themselves real gangstas of the ones whom they perceive as fake.

The appeal of gangsta rap seems to rely strongly on the assumption that what is being said in the lyrics is actually occurring, or at least has occurred in that artist's life. The importance of authenticity in gangsta rap lyrics is unlike any other genre. The seriousness about claims of murder and drug dealing automatically provokes questions of legitimacy. Which rappers are really doing the things they proclaim in their lyrics? Which rappers are just exploiting the success of this genre?

---

female-headed households more than doubled between 1960 and 2000, and this type of household saw particular growth in ghetto communities. Correspondingly, rappers regularly describe his household in their lyrics (for example, in Jay-Z's "December 4th," Obie Trice's "Don't Come Down," Goodie Mob's "Mama"). The Broadus family lived on the east side of Long Beach, on Twenty-first Street. In conformity with rap and hip hop's emphasis on the sociogeographic origins of rappers, Snoop devoted a song to this street on his album *Murder Was the Case* in 1994 ("21 Jump Street"). This association with the neighborhood, an inherent characteristic that emphasizes hip hop's connection to the social practices of youth gangs, frequently comes out in Snoop Dogg's lyrics and biography. For example, a large number of his songs mention "the LBC," a reference to Long Beach City, the Long Beach Crips, or to Long Beach, California.

Nicknamed "Snoop" by his mother because of his resemblance to Charles Schultz' well-known comic strip character, Snoopy, Calvin rapidly became a member of the Rolling 20s, a street gang affiliated with the Crips. He consistently draws on the symbolic value of this prominent gang for street credibility throughout his musical career. For instance, in one of his hit singles, "Drop It Like It's Hot" (2005), he hints at his allegiance to this gang by keeping a blue flag hanging on the left side of his back (the Crip side). During his gang banging years, Snoop had quite a few brushes with the law and spent several months behind bars. He was in and out of jail for the three years after he graduated from high school. Such experiences were far from unusual at that period. According to the U.S. Census Bureau, one third of the black males between eighteen and twenty-nine, and up to 80 percent in disadvantaged inner cities of large urban centers, were either in prison or on probation. In parallel to his criminal activities, Snoop had developed an interest in rap music. This practice, like sports and the entertainment industry in the past, was becoming a legitimate means to earn money and gain social status for many young black males living in the ghetto. Like many other youngsters, Snoop was making homemade rap tapes and was part of a rap group. With his friends Nathaniel Hale (Nate Dogg) and Warren Griffin (Warren G), he formed 213 (they reunited in 2004 to release the album *The Hard Way* on Doggy Style Records). This name, which referred to a Los Angeles area code, explicitly pointed to their habitat. In spring 1992, Dr. Dre, who had detected Snoop's distinctive laconic drawl on a tape of the 213 that Warren G, his stepbrother, had given him, invited the young rapper to feature on "Deep Cover." The premise of this song—the brutal murder of an undercover cop—was not unfamiliar to Snoop. He had formerly done time in prison for trying to sell crack to an undercover police officer. Through this song, he seized the opportunity to figuratively take revenge by committing "187"—the LA police code for a homicide—on a fictional undercover cop. "Deep Cover" led to numerous successful collaborations between Dr. Dre and his new protégé. In the wake of "Deep Cover," Snoop Dogg appeared on *The Chronic*'s first single and biggest hit, "Nuthin' but a G Thang," on eight other songs of the album ("Lil' Ghetto Boy," "Stranded on Death Row," "The Day the Niggaz Took Over") and on the hit single "Dre Day."

After this promising debut, Snoop's short career took an ominous turn in August 1993. While recording his own debut album with Dre, Snoop Dogg was arrested in the shooting death of a member of a rival gang and remained caught up in legal procedures for nearly three years. He was driving the car from which McKinley "Big Malik" Lee, his bodyguard, shot Philip Wolde-marian, a young rival gang banger. Under California law, Snoop, even though he was behind the wheel and did not wield a gun, was equally responsible and liable to the same sentence. Although this case was effective publicity for his upcoming album, Snoop was facing a very severe sentence, especially because of his criminal past In November 1993, he released *Doggystyle* and sold approximately 800,000 copies in a week. The album, benefiting from the hype about Snoop, which had started on "Deep Cover" and gone sky-high on *The Chronic*, entered the charts at number one, establishing a record that only 50 Cent's *Get Rich or Die Tryin'*—another Dr. Dre production—would top a decade later, and greatly contributed to the takeover of West Coast G-funk. Its singles "What's My Name?" and "Gin and Juice" reached the Top 10 and the album stayed in the charts for the several months, during which a public debate raged over Snoop's murder trial and his violent and sexist lyrics. Within a few months, he had become a household name, owing his instant notoriety as much to the heavy rotation of "Nuthin' but a G Thang" and "Dre Day" videos in 1993 and "What's My Name" and "Gin & Juice" in 1994 as to a series of news reports of his trial that blended legal reports and excerpts of his songs or videos. This dissolution of fiction into reality caused a media mael-strom over rap music and its violent criminal imagery that would greatly contribute to the enduring stigmatization of this mode of expression. Gangsta rap consequently became the focal point of a public debate about violence and censorship, with Snoop Dogg often used as the epitome of violent and mis-ogynistic musicians. *Newsweek* magazine, on the front page of its November 29, 1993, issue presented a picture of Snoop Dogg captioned with the ques-tion: "When Is Rap 2 Violent?" Similarly, while the rapper was touring in England in the spring of 1994, London's tabloid *Daily Star*, supported by a Tory representative, pleaded for the government to throw the rapper out of the country with the front-page headline: "Kick This Evil Bastard Out!"

The heated debate around Snoop's greatly publicized trial was nonetheless good publicity for Death Row. In 1994, Dr. Dre directed *Murder Was the*

Case, a short film about the fictional murder of Snoop Dogg. The nineteen-minute film works almost as an extended music video for the *Doggystyle* song "Murder Was the Case" that called attention to Snoop's pending court case and his gangsta persona. Both the song and the film presented the murder of Snoop Dogg's character rather than portraying him as a killer. The film's soundtrack debuted at number one. It included a remix of the original "Murder Was the Case" and showcased label mates such as Tha Dogg Pound and DJ Quick. It also marked the reunion of Dr. Dre and Ice Cube on "Natural Born Killaz," a song named after Oliver Stone's controversial film. After this soundtrack, Snoop Dogg spent the following months preparing for his lawsuit, which finally went to trial in late 1995. Thanks to the defense of Death Row's legal representative, David Keller, an expert in criminal courts, and to Death Row's financial backing, Snoop Dogg was officially acquitted on self-defense grounds in February 1996 and could resume his career on better terms. He would nevertheless have to wait another year to release his second album. In October 1995, Suge Knight had signed rapper Tupac Shakur on Death Row and Snoop Dogg was no longer the label's leading light. In addition, because of the label's commercial strategy to release low-cost, highly profitable soundtracks (*Deep Cover, Above the Rim, Murder Was the Case, Gang Related*), solo projects were frequently postponed. This strategy, even though it was financially profitable, drained Death Row of some of its promising artists (both Warren G and the D.O.C. had left the label in 1994). In November 1996, Snoop Dogg finally released his second album, *Tha Dogg-father*. By that time, the appeal of Death Row's gangsta rap had begun to fade, dragged down by the violent murder of Tupac Shakur and the racketeering indictment of Suge Knight. Dr. Dre had left Death Row earlier that year, so Snoop coproduced *The Doggfather* with Dat Nigga Daz and DJ Pooh. Even though his distinctive flow was no longer enriched by Dre's G-funk sound, the album sold approximately 2 million copies, half as many as quadruple-platinum *Doggystyle*.

In 1998, frustrated by Death Row's strong-arm business methods, Snoop Dogg left Death Row and California to relocate to Baton Rouge, Louisiana, and sign with Master P's label, No Limit. Snoop appeared on most of the label releases that year and the next. Between 1998 and 2000, the rapper fulfilled No Limit's heavy release schedule and recorded three solo albums, *Da Game Is to Be Sold Not to Be Told* in 1998, *No Limit Top Dogg* in 1999 (featuring appearances by Dr. Dre, Warren G, and Nate Dogg), and *Dead Man Walkin'* in 2000. In 2000 he also released *Tha Last Meal* (Priority/ Capitol Records), on which he developed a laid-back pimp persona that somehow deviated from his hard-core gang-banging debut. In 2002 Snoop Dogg effectively reinforced his star status in rap music with the successful release of his album *Paid tha Cost to Be da Boss,* which featured the hit singles and videos "From tha Chuuuch to da Palace" and "Beautiful." He would subsequently secure this status in the following years, most notably with his album *R&G (Rhythm & Gangsta): The Masterpiece* in 2004 and its hit single produced by the Neptunes, "Drop It Like It's Hot." In the meantime, Snoop Dogg had prominently appeared on Dr. Dre's *Chronic 2001*, most notably on its hit singles "Still D.R.E.," which marked his reunion with Dr. Dre, and "The Next Episode." His enduring success had also opened the doors of an entertainment industry determined to cash in on the appeal of his nonchalant personality. Between 1998 and 2004, he appeared in no less than eighteen films (including *Baby Boy*, *Training Day*, *Bones*, and *The Wash* in 2001, and *Starsky and Hutch* and *Soul Plane* in 2004) and hosted his own sketch comedy show on MTV (*Doggy Fizzle Televizzle*), in addition to producing and directing music videos for himself and other artists. Similarly to Dre, with whom he periodically works, mostly to feature on albums of newcomers (Xzibit, Eminem), Snoop Dogg maintains a firm street credibility in rap music. Even though these two musicians have considerable wealth and no longer live in the ghetto, they have managed to sustain their emblematic ties to its streets. For instance, Snoop Dogg, like many other rappers (P. Diddy with Sean John, the Wu-Tang Clan with Wu-Wear, 50 Cent with G-Unit Clothing), developed his own brand of street wear (Snoop Dogg Clothing Company). In 2000 he also reinforced his connection to Long Beach by launching his own label, Doggystyle Records (formerly Dogghouse), after years of self-described "servitude" at No Limit and signed local talents like former Crip members Tha Eastsidaz (gangmates Tray Dee and Goldie Loc) and former Death Row artists.

Dr. Dre and Snoop Dogg's status in rap music stems, in part, from their ties, actual or symbolic, to the streets of the ghetto. It derives from a street credibility, which, in Snoop Dogg's case, unquestionably offsets his tricky participation in a series of television commercials for T-Mobile during the 2004 Christmas season or in projects likely to harm his legitimacy in rap. This credibility, however significant, does not fully explain the prestige attached to these musicians. This high regard is equally justified by the vernacular specificity of the themes and the motifs that they developed in their music: a larger-than-life phallocentric hedonism attached to a criminal lifestyle.

WINE, WOMEN, AND SONG "GANGSTAFIED": DR. DRE AND SNOOP DOGG'S HEDONISM

The proverbial formula "wine, women, and song," a shortened expression of a German epicurean adage credited to Martin Luther, is widely acknowledged in the English language. Many folk songs, particularly drinking songs, abound with references to it. Student songs celebrating a carpe diem frame of mind greatly helped to popularize this phrase. If not with this specific triad, with a corresponding ensemble of motifs (wine, men, and song for gay men; wine, women, and Porsches, etc.). A variant of this secular axiom is at the core of Dr. Dre and Snoop Dogg's discourse. Even though these rappers articulate an imagery that hyperbolically reproduces the criminal activities of hustlers, they equally celebrate their pleasure-seeking practices in their party rhymes. In one skit on Eminem's *Marshall Mathers* LP, an uncompromising record executive explains to the rapper why Dr. Dre's records are so successful. He argues that Dre is rapping about "big-screen TVs, blunts [hollowed-out cigars refilled with marijuana], 40s and bitches." This gangsta adjustment of Luther's proverb constitutes the fundamentals of the hedonism that figures so largely in Dr, Dre and Snoop Dogg's party rhymes. These rappers express flamboyantly a gangsta lifestyle epitomized by criminal activities, a celebration of wealth and consumption, and a distinctive phallocratic hedonism. They regularly glorify illegal money and the luxurious lifestyle it offers. Based on a carpe diem motto, Dr. Dre and Snoop Dogg's recreational activities are characterized by three forms of pleasurable indulgence: alcohol (several brands appear recurrently in their lyrics); drugs, generally marijuana (under various denominations, the most current being *chronic*); and exaggerated sexual debauchery. These practices, generally combined, as the aphorism DNA (drugs 'n' alcohol) testifies, are particularly expressive of the gangsta mentality that guides the pleasure-seeking practices of Dre and Snoop's gangsta personas.

As Eminem's fictional record executive notes, a certain imagery of debauchery prevails in Dr. Dre and Snoop Dogg's music. In "Pass It, Pass It," for instance, Snoop Dogg explains that smoking weed is part of what he calls a gangsta philosophy. Marijuana is invariably presented as the drug of choice of these musicians and is glorified in most of their albums. The titles and illustrations of *The Chronic* and *Chronic 2001*, whose covers respectively reproduce the logo of a rolling paper brand and a ganja leaf, unambiguously confirm this assertion. Dr. Dre exalts its consumption in almost all his tracks and recommends smoking it every day on "The Next Episode."

In expressing a ritualistic consumption of drugs and alcohol, Dr. Dre and Snoop Dogg's music develops a gangsta mentality that transgresses legal normative order and is resolutely in tune with ghetto hustler lifestyle, a style of fast and large living especially glorified by Snoop Dogg in numbers such as "Gin and Juice" and "Hennessy and Buddha." As several ethnographies have revealed, valorizing an immediate hedonism, rather than rationalizing the accumulation of durable goods that we find in the conventional economy, particularizes ghetto hustlers, who tend to dissipate their profits in flamboyant expenses (at the scale of disadvantaged inner-city areas). Hence the recurrences of prestigious brands of alcohol in Dr. Dre and Snoop Dogg's lyrics like Hennessy or Moët & Chandon. These brands are class markers of conspicuous consumption; they express a strategy of distinction and like guns are indexic gangsta signifiers. Through their consistent use, Dre and Snoop present symbolic personas in line with a gangsta lifestyle while valorizing practices and attitudes highly regarded by a segment of ghetto youth involved in

criminal activities, as well as by a sector of suburban youth who seek opposi-
tional forms of expression. In *A Personal Journey with Martin Scorsese
Through American Movies*, the film director describes the symbolic power
exerted by criminal imagery. Discussing his fascination for gangster films,
especially Howard Hawks's *Scarface* (1932), he affirms that even though
the main character of this movie was vicious, immature, and irresponsible,
his milieu was disturbingly attractive precisely because of its irresponsibility.
Roland Barthes gives a similar argument in *Mythologies* and justifies this
attraction by the fact that the world of gangsters, an irrational poetic universe, is the last refuge for fantasy. By putting an emphasis on criminal or
socially disapproved practices in their lyrics, Dr. Dre and Snoop Dogg position themselves on the margin of the legal system and explicitly assert a
gangsta mentality with a compelling symbolic resonance.

The social acknowledgment and respect young blacks of the ghetto earn for
their masculinity is an achieved status they establish through their sexual
prowess. Sexual activity not only enables an assessment of an individual's
masculinity, it determines the esteem that his peers have for him. As Charis
E. Kubrin, leaning on the ethnographic observations of Elijah Anderson,
explains, the more women with whom a young man has sex, the more esteem
he accrues among his peers. This value system is regularly reproduced in the
misogynist lyrics of both Dr. Dre and Snoop Dogg. Rap music is often singu-
larized, as the controversy around 2 Live Crew's *As Nasty as They Wanna Be*
revealed, for its misogynist representations of social and sexual relations
between men and women. This incontestable aspect, identifiable in Dr. Dre
and Snoop Dogg's catalog, is generally expressed as part of a valorization
of a gangsta lifestyle characterized by a strong emphasis on virility. The
graphic and humorous circumstances these rappers communicate regularly
depict relations between gangstas and women that invariably result in sexual
intercourse. Lyrically, Dr. Dre and Snoop Dogg's status, apart from their
physical and verbal expressions of violent temper, has been built on their lack
of respect for women. Such sexist attitudes are consistent with a conception of
masculinity that apparently prevails in the ghetto. French sociologist Pierre
Bourdieu has shown that the attachment to a set of attitudes and behaviors is
considerably determined by the structural conditions of their social milieu.
The assertion of attitudes attached to virility and physical strength, for instance, characterizes individuals who can only count on their physical skills to
work or fight. Similarly, the assertion of an exacerbated virility among young
ghetto dwellers may be viewed as a reaction to a set of social restrictions that
have altered the social role and status of men among ghetto residents. Postures expressing ideas of prestige, distance, superiority over outsiders, toughness and style, postures that have caused a schism between the young black
men who adopt them and women, correspond to a set of dispositions shaped
by specific social constraints (racial stigmatization, low socioeconomic status).
Snoop Dogg and Dre's strategies to adopt hypermasculine postures that

suggest distance, irony, or superiority are therefore figurative reproductions of a practical rationality produced by the conditions of existence of the black ghetto. It is interesting to point out that a similar set of hypermasculine postures characterizes calypso, a Caribbean musical expression which emanates from a social group that had to face forms of structural domination similar to the ones with which a sector of urban black youth is confronted today. Accordingly, the theatrical representations of virile, sexist, and phlegmatic attitudes presented in the lyrics of Dr. Dre and Snoop Dogg correspond to the exaggeration that characterizes rap music and ghetto orality. Such emotional posturing is epitomized by Dr. Dre and Snoop Dogg's collaboration on Dr. Dre's song "Fuck You," in which they express, in a stylized manner, the most salient aspects of a masculine ideal that is assumed by many young blacks living in the ghetto.

The mentality expressed by Dre and Snoop's gangsta personas principally rests on the triad of sex, alcohol, and drugs. Such an array, if it has been studied in other expressions and other social groups, reveals, in the music of Dr. Dre and Snoop Dogg, particularities inherent in the characteristics of the social relations of the ghetto. Luther's adage, updated by the rockers in the seventies who celebrated "sex, drugs, and rock and roll," finds its rap counterpart in the gangsta amendment "sex, drugs, and gangsta rap," a sentiment expressed in a majority of Dr. Dre and Snoop Dogg's lyrics.

MIDAS TOUCH: DR. DRE'S SIGNATURE SOUND

In an interview with the British newspaper the *Guardian* (February 20, 2004), leading rap producer Pharell Williams, though he was, at the time, behind 20 percent of the most-played rap and R&B songs on British radio stations, reverently referred to Dr. Dre as the Darth Vader of rap production and humbly compared himself to a mere storm trooper. In "We Ain't," a song from the Game's album *The Documentary* on which he features multiplatinum-selling rapper Eminem, declares that only Dre can judge him for his mistakes, putting the producer on the same level as God.

Dr. Dre undeniably owes such a celebrated status to his contribution to rap music and to the innovations of his production. It is important to underscore that Dr. Dre, in contrast to a musician like Kanye West who presents himself as both a rapper and a producer, is first and foremost a producer. Throughout his career, for instance, he has generally had an accomplished lyricist writing his lyrics—Ice Cube while they were under the N.W.A. banner, then the D.O.C. on *The Chronic*, and more recently, Jay-Z on "Still D.R.E." Unlike Snoop Dogg, who derives some of his status from his rhyming skills, his distinctive flow, and his personality, Dr. Dre derives his prestige from his invention, first with N.W.A., then with his patented G-funk, of a signature sound (and a universe) expressive of LA gang banging that would be regarded as typically Californian. An additional look at his biography is necessary to understand the crafting of what would become this signature sound.

Like most producers who were making rap in the early eighties, Dr. Dre was heavily influenced by the seminal single "The Adventures of Grandmaster Flash on the Wheels of Steel" and rap pioneer Afrika Bambaataa's "Planet Rock." The impact of these New York rap records is manifest on Dr. Dre's first productions. Its first electro rap single, "Surgery" and his contributions to *First Round Knock-Out* ("Cabbage Patch," "He's Bionic," "House Calls") are characterized by similar synthesizers à la Kraftwerk, fast 808 beats, multi-layered electronic sounds, and outer space imagery. Similarly, his first post–World Class Wreckin' Cru productions resembled the synchronic minimalist sonic architecture of avant-garde East Coast rap, most notably Run-DMC's and the Bomb Squad's. By the mid-eighties, most rap producers shifted from the robotic aesthetic conveyed through synthesizers and TR 808 beatboxes to the raw aesthetic obtainable with samplers. This shift is noticeable on all Dr. Dre's productions for Ruthless (1986–1991), ranging from "We Want Eazy" and "Fuck the Police," on which he sampled James Brown's "Funky Drummer," to "Straight Outta Compton" or the D.O.C.'s "The Formula," on which he sampled soul artists from the late sixties and early seventies, Wilson Pickett and Marvin Gaye respectively. With the sampler, Dr. Dre could revisit the musicians that had strongly influenced him during his formative years and use some of the records that he had been buying from Steve Yayo's, a well-known record dealer from the Roadium, a former drive-in located in Gardena which was, in the middle eighties, a sort of Mecca for hip hop deejays of Southern California (similar to the Amoeba store in San Francisco honored on the cover of DJ Shadow's album *Endtroducing*). If the funky breakbeats and dynamic syncopated rhythms of Dre's Ruthless productions were somewhat similar to the sonic montage of Public Enemy or Boogie Down Productions, *Efil4zaggin,* his last production for the label, was heading in a different musical direction that would lead to the crafting of what is regarded as his signature sound. This sound, characterized by prominent bass lines, heavy keyboards, and laid-back melodies (as opposed to rapid prosaic breakbeats) was appreciably influenced by the Bay Area sound introduced by Digital Underground on *Sex Packets* (Tommy Boy, 1990). These self-proclaimed *Sons of the P* had been among the firsts (with producer Teddy Riley) to amend P-funk melodies composed by George Clinton's musicians (Parliament Funkadelic) with slow beats and prominent synthesizers to narrate their extravagant ghetto narratives. Their distinctive approach to rap music would be the foundation of Dr. Dre's G-funk, a conversion of Clinton's P-Funk into slow-rolling melodies that significantly depended on prominent bass lines, synthetic symphonies, and the exaltation of a parochial gangsta lifestyle (see sidebar: The Sampler).

This sound, though it was perceptible at times on *Efil4zaggin* (notably on "Alwayz into Somethin'") would ripen on Dr. Dre's Death Row productions.

The Sampler
Shamika Ann Mitchell

A sampler is an electronic musical instrument that records and stores audio samples, generally pieces of existing recordings, and plays them back at a range of pitches and speeds. The term sampler is also sometimes used to refer to instruments (keyboards in particular) that store and play back samples, but are incapable of recording them.

There is a significant debate about the value of using live instrumentation for hip hop musical production versus gathering samples from recorded material. Depending on aesthetic tastes, either process is suitable; however, the overall opinion is that the sample needs to sound vintage, worn, recycled. Achieving sampling's initial popularity around 1986, many DJs utilized the breakbeat or drum solo from other songs as the foundation for new beats, often looped or segmented. The breakbeat, which is the catalyst for the break dancer, is considered the song's climactic moment. Since hip hop's early years, countless DJs have pursued the quest to find the perfect breakbeat. DJ Afrika Bambaataa's 1982 release *Looking for the Perfect Beat* highlights the breakbeat and its musical significance. The actual process of digging through crates and boxes of long-forgotten vinyl records for break-beats is akin to treasure hunting. Those DJs who find rare and obscure beats guard their sources closely; legendary DJs such as Grandmaster Flash, Kool Herc, and Afrika Bambaataa were known to remove the labels from their vinyl records.

The cost of sampling has become an obstacle for artists on a shoestring budget; sample clearance fees can absorb a substantial proportion of one's recording budget. Furthermore, because of copyright permissions, lawsuits regarding either unpaid sampling fees or samples used without permission are abundant in the legal system, and the penalties for copyright infringement can be high.

While there are many DJs (who later became producers) who have used the technique of sampling, several have established themselves as leaders in the field. DJ Marley Marl is considered a pioneer in this arena because of his discovery of the drum sound sample: others include Rick Rubin's efforts fusing classic rock tunes on several Run DMC songs; DJ Pete Rock's ability to masterfully utilize classic soul samples; Prince Paul's production on De La Soul's seminal album *3 Feet High and Rising*, which introduced samples from folk and country music; and Teddy Riley's ingenuity, which led to the pro-liferation of the New Jack Swing sound in both hip hop and R&B genres during the 1990s. Also, producer Jermaine Dupri is often hailed as an inno-vator in the field. Other noteworthy producers are Timbaland, DJ Scratch, the Neptunes, Swizz Beatz, Alchemist, Just Blaze, and Kanye West. Still, the two DJs-turned-producer who are most lauded as iconic figures are Dr. Dre and DJ Premier. Interestingly, representation by women in the DJ-producer role is virtually nonexistent; aside from Missy Elliott and Salt-N-Pepa's Spinderella, few women have ventured into these musical roles.

Further Resources

Schloss, Joseph G. *Making Beats: The Art of Sample-Based Hip-Hop.* Middletown, CT: Wesleyan University Press, 2004.

Though "Deep Cover," with its prominent bass line, resumed *Efil4zaggin*'s sinister atmosphere and minor sonorities, Dr. Dre's G-funk sound definitely matured on his first solo album, *The Chronic*. This album, which lyrically exalted a gangsta lifestyle epitomized by hedonistic party rhymes, firmly established Dr. Dre's musical interpolations of the 1970s funk canon ("Atomic Dog" on "Knee Deep," Donny Hattaway's "Little Ghetto Boy" on the eponymous title, or Leon Haywood's "I Wanna Do Something Freaky to You" on "Nuthin' but a G Thang"). The use of interpolation, a technique that consists of hiring studio musicians to play segments in the studio instead of sampling a song, significantly developed after several rap producers had to face numerous lawsuits about copyright issues (interpolation allows producers to secure the rights to sheet music without having to pay royalties to use the sound recording) Dr. Dre, who admits never having been comfortable with the sampler, had started using this technique and collaborating with studio musicians on *First Round Knock-Out* (on "Cabbage Patch").

In the wake of *The Chronic*, many rappers emulated Dr. Dre's G-funk. Local rappers somehow affiliated with him embraced his patented sound and released albums that captured the musical (and lyrical) expression of LA gang banging that he had instituted. Warren G with his album *Regulate … G-Funk Era* (1994), Tha Dogg Pound (Dat Nigga Daz and Kurupt) with *Dogg Food* (1995), Ruthless's Above the Law with *Black Mafia Life* (1993), and the Maad Circle with their album *West Up* (1995) offer representative illustrations of this trend. Nevertheless, the impact of Dre's G-funk sound was not restricted to California. MC Breed's album *The New Breed*, produced by the D.O.C. and featuring Warren G, and Scarface's *The Diary* (1994) adapted G-funk to, respectively, Atlanta and Houston.

For nearly four years, G-funk, with its typically Californian aesthetic, dominated hip hop and significantly influenced the imagery of rap music as we know it today. A new gritty style of East Coast production took hold around the same time, with Wu-Tang Clan's *Enter the 36 Chambers* (1993), Mobb Deep's *Infamous* (1995), and Nas' *Illmatic* (1994) creating sparse, rough and rugged soundscapes that cleary differed from Dre's multi-layered melodies. This stark difference between East Coast and West Coast style set the stage for the East Coast versus West Coast beef, in which Death Row was a prime player. Dre's sound became the sound of the West Coast. His productions, for Snoop Doggy Dogg (*Doggystyle*), Blackstreet ("No Diggity"),

2Pac ("California Love"), and various soundtracks (*Friday*'s "Keep Their Headz Ringin'"), productions that consistently glorified street corner activities, insensitive sexual intercourse with frivolous women, and a flamboyant lifestyle, were massive hits. They fashioned a rupture with the dynamic funk and political activism that somewhat prevailed at the time and established rap, which had principally been dance oriented, as automobile music (Dr. Dre maintained that he played some of his demos in his car to make sure they sounded right). The success of his hit single "Let Me Ride" and of the "Still D. R.E." video greatly contributed to the valorization of the car as a central symbol of rap music. The recurrence of cars in the lyrics of rappers and in their videos, as well as the success of the MTV show *Pimp My Ride*, hosted by Xzibit, another Dr. Dre protégé for whom the producer used samples of hydraulic systems and bouncing lowriders (on his album *Restless*), confirm the pronounced relationship between automobiles and rap.

The solid production that Dr. Dre subsequently crafted for Eminem, Xzibit, or 50 Cent were as responsible as the skills of these gifted lyricists for keeping him at the top of the charts. They exhibited a vast array of high-pitched pianos or harpsichords (on Xzibit's hit single "X" and Eminem's "Guilty Conscience"), bells and string orchestrations (on *The Documentary*'s "How We Do"), laid-back melodies, heavy beats, synthesizer sounds (on 50 Cent's hit single "In da Club" and, more recently, on *The Documentary*'s "Westside Story"), or clean electric guitars (on *2001*'s "Xplosive," Eve's "Let Me Blow Ya Mind"), with which Dr. Dre both retained the eerie atmosphere introduced on *Efil4zaggin* and refined his recognizable signature sound.

This distinctive sound, whether it is supported by prominent kick drums or old-school 808 beats has guaranteed Dr. Dre, through multiple collaborations with major artists (Jay-Z, Mary J. Blige, Ice Cube, 2Pac, etc.) and multiplatinum sales (Eminem's *Slim Shady* and *Marshall Mathers* LPs, *Chronic 2001*, 50 Cent's *Get Rich or Die Tryin'*), an unfaltering (and repeatedly recalled) potent symbolic status both in rap discourse and in the field of the production of this music.

THE SNOOP DOGG PERSONA

The prestige and influence of Snoop Dogg in rap are as palpable as those of his mentor Dr. Dre. His famous use of a slang device (originally created by rapper E-40) that consists of substituting an "izz" or "izzle" sound for a syllable has been adopted by several rappers, the most prominent being Jay-Z on his hit single "H.O.V.A." and Ludacris (on Chingy's hit single "Holidae Inn"). In the same way, he popularized a dog(g) motif that would be taken up, simultaneously or subsequently, by many other rappers (Nate Dogg, Tha Dogg Pound, Doggy's Angels, Cypress Hill's Sen Dog, [Lil'] Bow Wow). Like Dr. Dre, if Snoop Dogg owes some of his importance in rap to his ties to the streets and to his exaltation of its social practices, he equally derives his status from his aesthetic distinctiveness.

Snoop Dogg's flow, like Dr. Dre's signature sound, is distinctively recognizable. When Dr. Dre invited him to feature on "Deep Cover," the typical rhyme style was characterized by a fast and emphatic delivery, inspired by groups like Das EFX, which concentrated predominantly on the rhythm. On "Deep Cover," Snoop Dogg introduced a distinctive languid flow that, with its musicality, differed somewhat from the paradigmatic vocal style. Snoop Dogg, like many young blacks from the ghetto, had developed his effortless-sounding MCing on street corners and during his frequent sojourns in jail. The ritual emulation that singularizes these social spaces, accurately portrayed in Kevin Fitzgerald's documentary *Freestyle: The Art of Rhyme* (2004), helped him develop a distinctive type of debonair rhyming that would sway Dr. Dre and significantly contribute to the success of their subsequent collaborations (*The Chronic*, *Chronic 2001* with its hit singles "Still D.R.E." and "The Next Episode"), not to mention Snoop's countless featurings on further releases produced by Dr. Dre (Lady of Rage's "Afro Puffs," Eminem's "Bitch Please II," and Xzibit's "DNA").

Snoop Dogg developed a symbolic persona of his own that greatly contributed to his success. Even though he circumstantially changes aliases, according to the role-playing function of rap, and introduces himself either as Snoop Eastwood/Mister 187 (on "Deep Cover" and "Who Am I [What's My Name]?"), Mr. Dizzle (on his MTV show), or Bigg Snoop depending on the themes developed in his songs, his Snoop Doggy Dogg persona is primarily presented. The recurrence of this dog motif, in Snoop's lyrics as well as those of Sen Dog from Cypress Hill, which expressed a similar hedonistic criminal mind, clearly established it, at least in West Coast rap, as a substitute for the long-standing monkey (a key character in various toasts—violent and obscene oral narratives—such as Pool-Shooting Monkey, Party-Time Monkey, and some versions of the Signifying Monkey) as the animal personification of ghetto hustlers. This assertion finds an expressive illustration in the "Who Am I (What's My Name)?" video in which pool-shooting gangstas digitally morph into dogs. Snoop Dogg equally exploited this motif on several occasions throughout his career. For example, he drew extensively on its prolific lexical field. He titled his first album *Doggystyle*, a term that, with its double entendre, simultaneously conveyed sexual innuendo and enlightened listeners on his rhyming style. The noteworthy cartoonlike artwork of this LP, realized by Joe Cool (Darryl Daniel), would considerably influence the design of rap albums (Virginia rappers from the Clipse used a similar visual aesthetic on their LP *Lord Willin'*). His second album, *Tha Doggfather*, through an intertextual technique that literary theorist Michael Riffaterre calls ungrammaticality—an orthographic anomaly referring to a preexisting textual reference —symbolically blended his dog persona with the criminal imagery of *The Godfather*, Mario Puzo and Francis Ford Coppola's mobster trilogy.

This functional dog motif, with its pronounced sexual connotations, is also instrumental in the affirmation of his pimp persona, Bigg Snoop, through which he usually expresses a symbolic supremacy over women (irreverently referred to as "bitches" in the sociolect of the ghetto). The pimp (or mack) possesses an important social status in the streets of black ghettos where the term, used as an adjective, commonly means sharp or beautiful. In rap music, the pimp is a functional representation that enables rappers to synthesize important components of the lifestyle of gangstas, in particular the invariable money, sex, drugs, and alcohol. If terms like *gangsta, hustler, pimp,* or *thug* are generally interchangeable in the criminal discourse of rappers, they generally favor a pimp persona when they wish to emphasize their sexual and economic exploitation of women. Rap scholar Eithne Quinn has accurately analyzed this proliferation of pimp imagery in rap lyrics.

Snoop Dogg's pimp persona, through present in his early albums, has become more apparent in his latest releases under the notable influence of his new guide, Bishop Don Magic Juan, an actual retired pimp who allegedly gave up pimping years ago when he became a Christian. This deliberate adoption of a marketable pimp aesthetic, with its long mink coats, coordinated satin suits, and scantily clad women, capitalized on by blaxploitation films, is especially marked on his albums *Paid tha Cost to Be Da Boss* (and its singles "From tha Chuuuch to da Palace" and "Beautiful") and *R&G (Rhythm & Gangsta): The Masterpiece.* Snoop Dogg's praised pimp aesthetic, resting on his charismatic personality and his quick sense of humor, precisely exemplifies the attitudinal and discursive expressions of masculinity mentioned earlier, expressions that do not correspond to a "cool pose" or a "code of the street," as sociologists Majors and Billson and Elijah Anderson have argued respectively, but to a practical rationality shaped by the social restrictions which have altered the roles and socioeconomic status of black lower-class men living in ghetto communities. Bigg Snoop, Snoop Dogg's pimp persona, precisely exemplifies the allegorical compensation of an inferior status through what Eithne Quinn calls a pimp "lifestylization," a fabulous representation of pimp lifestyle and iconography. Besides, he conforms to the basic rules of the pimp game described in the novels of Iceberg Slim and Donald Goines. Physically, he habitually presents himself as a sharp and expensively dressed hustler reminiscent of the blaxploitation films of the early seventies (as in 50 Cent's "P.I.M.P." video, for example). As for his moral fiber, he totally despises women, as he indicates lyrically on his pimp anthems "I'm Threw with You" and "Can You Control Your Hoe"—both on *R&G (Rhythm & Gangsta): The Masterpiece*—and visually in *Snoop Dogg's Doggystyle* and *Hustlaz: Diary of a Pimp,* two pornographic productions in which, with the smooth and laid-back tone of voice symptomatic of the pimp, he expresses no other interest in them than a monetary and functional one.

Snoop Dogg undeniably owes a part of his appeal to the fact that his gangsta personas, especially this pimp character, differ slightly from the aggressive thug attitude that, with its frequent glorification of muscular bodies and armed or physical brutality, prevails in the ghetto and its representations. His tall and svelte figure and his nonchalant drawl are closer to the characteristics of pimps, whose power resides chiefly in their phlegmatic and verbal skills, than to these of violent and sturdy gangstas who, as formulaic rap videos testify, commonly parade their physical strength.

Dr. Dre and Snoop Dogg, thanks to the cultural and social capital necessary to succeed in the field of rap music production, and to their artistic peculiarities, hold a prominent and steadfast status both in this field and in rap discourse. With his G-funk, Dr. Dre crafted a sound expressive of LA gang banging and found a perfect representative with Snoop Dogg, a distinctive MC who pioneered or familiarized a unique style and language on which several rappers now trade. Their numerous collaborations with equally celebrated artists and producers helped them to remain major forces in a highly competitive field where status is intimately linked to record sales and street credibility.

See also: Ice Cube, Eminem, Kanye West, Tupac Shakur

WORKS CITED

Anderson, Elijah. *Code of the Street: Decency, Violence, and the Moral Life of the Inner City*. New York: W.W. Norton, 1999.

Bourdieu, Pierre. *Questions de sociologie*. Paris: Editions de Minuit, 1984.

Kubrin, Charis E. "Gangstas, Thugs, and Hustlas: Identity and the Code of the Street in Rap Music." *Social Problems* 52. 3 (2005): 360–378.

Majors, Richard and Billson, Janet. *Cool Pose: The Dilemmas of Black Manhood in America*. New York: Lexington, 1992.

Quinn, Eithne. "Who's the Mack?: The Performativity and Politics of the Pimp Figure in Gangsta Rap." *Journal of American Studies* 34 (2000): 115–136.

FURTHER RESOURCES

Burton, Richard D. E. *Afro-Creole: Power, Opposition and Play in the Caribbean*. Ithaca: Cornell University Press, 1997.

Dr. Dre 2001. Official Dr. Dre Web site. www.dre2001.com.

Evil, Pierre. *Gangsta Rap*. Paris: Flammarion, 2005.

Forman, Murray. *The 'Hood Comes First: Race, Space, and Place in Rap and Hip-Hop*. Middletown, CT: Wesleyan University Press, 2002.

Mieder, Wolfgang. "Wine, Women and Song: From Martin Luther to American T-Shirts." *Folk Groups and Folklore Genres*, Ed. Elliott Oring. Logan: Utah State University Press, 1989: 279–290.

Snoop Dogg and Davin Seay. *Tha Doggfather: The Times, Trials, and Hardcore Truths of Snoop Dogg*. New York: William Morrow, 1999.

Wacquant, Loïc. "Scrutinizing the Street: Poverty, Morality, and the Pitfalls of Urban Ethnography." *American Journal of Sociology* 107.6 (2002): 1468–1532.

22

SELECTED DISCOGRAPHY

N.W.A., *Straight Outta Compton*. Ruthless, 1989.
N.W.A. *Efil4zaggin*. Ruthless, 1991.
Dr. Dre, *The Chronic*. Death Row, 1992.
Snoop Dogg, *Doggystyle*. Death Row, 1993.
Dr. Dre, *Chronic 2001*. Aftermath, 1999.
Snoop Dogg, *Tha Last Meal*. Priority Records, 2000.
Xzibit, *Restless*. Sony, 2000.
Snoop Dogg, *Paid tha Cost to Be da Boss*. Doggy Style Records, 2002.
The Game, *The Documentary*. Aftermath, 2005.
Various Artists, *Up in Smoke Tour*, DVD. Eagle Vision, 2000.

Courtesy of Photofest.

Nas

Susan Weinstein

Nasir Jones, born September 14, 1973, entered the rap scene at what many consider to be the end of the genre's golden age. Between 1988 and 1993, old schoolers were still producing classic work while a younger generation was infusing a variety of new styles and perspectives. Run-DMC and the Beastie Boys continued to produce beat-heavy party music. Meanwhile, tougher voices were beginning to be heard with the introduction of gangsta rap (e.g., Schoolly D's "P.S.K. (What Does It Mean)," Ice-T's "Six in the Morning," N.W.A.'s *Straight Outta Compton*) and hard-hitting political rap (e.g., Public

Enemy, Paris). A collection of artists known as the Native Tongues Posse took an Afrocentric focus, with artists including A Tribe Called Quest, De La Soul, and Queen Latifah delivering lyrics full of black pride, references to the motherland, and a playful spirit. Musical experimentation had always been a feature of hip hop, and shifts in lyrical focus were accompanied by a broadening of musical influences. With *The Chronic*, Dr. Dre created the G-funk sound, in which often-harsh images and language were accompanied by irresistible seventies-style horns and bass. Meanwhile, many Native Tongues artists incorporated jazz rhythms and instrumentation on their tracks.

Young Nasir Jones took it all in. His classrooms were the parks, stoops, and street corners of New York's Queensbridge housing projects, the largest public housing structure in North America. Here, he interacted with members of the Juice Crew, including DJ Marley Marl, MC Shan, and Intelligent Hoodlum. The variety and richness of rap's golden age combined with Queensbridge's hip hop heritage and its often violent streets in the young Nas to produce his universally lauded first album, *Illmatic*. If Nas's career had ended with *Illmatic*, he would have been ensured a notable place in hip hop history. Yet his career continues, and it is the details of that career that make him an undeniable icon. Nas's attention-grabbing debut was followed by bigger-selling follow-ups that drew less critical praise, then an artistic comeback driven by one of hip hop's legendary beefs. Through it all, Nas has maintained a consistent commitment to lyrical and musical experimentation.

CHILDHOOD INFLUENCES

Nasir bin Olu Dara Jones (*bin* means *son of*) comes by his musical talent honestly. Nas has music in his genes. His father is the jazz trumpeter, guitarist, and singer Olu Dara (born Charles Jones III), and Dara's father and grandfather were both singers in Natchez, Mississippi, where he was raised. Nas added to his musical lineage a raw intelligence, an impressive vocabulary, a gift for keen observation, and a remarkable ability with rhyme, imagery, and narrative. Olu Dara made his living traveling the world with various jazz ensembles, yet although Nas's parents divorced when he was twelve, the child visited Dara in his Harlem home regularly. During these visits, the two would waste little time getting down to making music. Nas was playing the trumpet by age four, and the two might also jam on the drums or guitars Dara had around the house. While Dara was, and continues to be, a strong personal and artistic influence on his son, Nas's lyrics make clear that it was his mother, Ann Jones, who provided her children with a sense of stability, self-worth, and love. The fact that Nas had positive relationships with both of his parents, and was constantly encouraged and supported by them, probably explains a good deal about Nas the man's own relative stability, responsibility, and equilibrium. Nas lived with his older brother, Jabari (aka Jungle, a member of rap group the Bravehearts, who have appeared on several Nas songs) and his mother. His father was often on the road playing music, leaving Ann Jones as the boys' primary caretaker. Nas refers to the strain this put on his mother in the song "Poppa Was a Playa" from *The Lost Tapes* (2002).

Nas's artistic tendencies appeared early. Along with his childhood interest in music, he also wrote short stories and created his own comic books. By early adolescence, he had taken to educating himself, studying African history and the Bible and perusing books at the library to collect new vocabulary for his rhymes. Nas's trademark complexity was already present at this early point in his life. He was reading, writing, and learning about Five Percenter beliefs at the same time that he was starting to smoke marijuana, commit petty crimes, and sell drugs under the name "Nasty Nas," one of the many aliases he would use as a rapper. He dropped out of school in early ninth grade, around the time his parents split up. His problems with school are briefly recounted in the 2004 song "Bridging the Gap," in which Nas raps about spending classroom time drawing caricatures of his teachers and writing rhymes, and having his father called to school when he got in trouble. Like a number of other rappers (e.g., dead prez in "They Schools," Kanye West in "We Don't Care," and Masta Killa in "School"), Nas would later make the point in his lyrics that though he loved learning, much of the school curriculum seemed irrelevant to him as a young, poor, urban, black male.

During his early adolescence, Nas became deeply enmeshed in all aspects of hip hop culture. He joined a b-boy posse called Breakin' in Action (B.I.A.), dancing under the name Kid Wave, which was also the name he tagged on walls as a graffiti writer. He rapped with a crew called the Devastatin' Seven. He briefly aspired to DJing, inspired by the example of fellow Queensbridge native and hip hop legend Marley Marl. Nas's partner in crime during these years was William "Ill Will" Graham, who lived in the apartment directly above him. In Will's bedroom, the two would play with rhymes and beats, Will playing the DJ with his turntables and mixer. In 1992, the same year that Nas got his first record contract, Will and Nas's brother Jabari were both shot after a Queensbridge party. While Jabari recovered from his leg injury, Will's wounds proved fatal. Losing his best friend had an intense effect on the young Nas, who has honored Will's memory through ubiquitous shout-outs on songs and through the name of his publishing imprint, Ill Will Records. Nas has said that as a youngster, he viewed the experiences he was having and seeing in Queensbridge as a movie; there is an undeniable narrative quality to the timing of both his signing and Will's death, which together seem to mark the end of the artist's childhood.

MAJOR LABEL RELEASES

There are certain stories that every long-term hip hop fan knows: how Kool Herc kicked it all off by setting up his speakers in a Bronx park, how Sylvia

Robinson of Sugar Hill Records went searching for local rappers to capitalize on the new craze, and how Suge Knight bailed Tupac out of jail and signed him to Death Row Records. In the same vein is the emergence of Nas on the New York scene. The fifteen-year-old newcomer had been introduced to Queens-based Large Professor, who was part of a group called Main Source and whose grand moniker belied the fact that the busy producer was only seventeen years old and still attending high school while producing songs for the likes of Eric B. & Rakim and Kool G Rap in his home studio. Nas spent time at Large Professor's home, taking in the production process and occasionally recording his own rhymes when a scheduled rapper didn't show up. When it was time for Main Source to record its debut album, *Breaking Atoms*, Large Professor invited Nas to contribute a verse on the song "Live at the Barbeque." The album was well received; fans and critics alike were particularly excited about Nas's guest verse.

Meanwhile, Def Jam artist 3rd Bass was breaking up (see sidebar: 3rd Bass). The group's two white MCs, Pete Nice and MC Serch, both would record solo albums. Serch also moved into a new career as a producer and was

---

3rd Bass
Susan Weinstein

While the white, Jewish Beastie Boys had established a successful career in the primarily black world of rap during the mid-eighties, 3rd Bass came along at a time when Afrocentrism—of both the warm-and-fuzzy and militant varieties—was becoming a central trope of the genre. Respected for their skills, the group was nonetheless targeted by the intensely political group X-Clan, who accused 3rd Bass's record company of trying to pass the group off as black. How to racially categorize a group that is two thirds white (MC Serch and Pete Nice) and one third black (DJ Richie Rich) is itself an intriguing question that reveals the fundamental flaws of racial thinking. 3rd Bass were themselves sensitive to the racial politics of rap, and they recognized Vanilla Ice's hip hop posturing and false claims to ghetto credibility as problematic. Their second album, *Derelicts of Dialect*, features the song "Pop Goes the Weasel," which directly targets Vanilla Ice in order to distance the group from his co-optation of rap.

3rd Bass worked closely with established black artists such as producer Prince Paul (of De La Soul and Stetsasonic fame), and up-and-coming group KMD. KMD's Zev Love X (who would later perform as the masked rapper MF DOOM) provided a guest verse for 3rd Bass's first single "The Gas Face," the video for which features prominent black artists like Erick Sermon of EPMD. Aligning themselves with established hip hop artists, 3rd Bass used the song to criticize MC Hammer for being a pop crossover.

3rd Bass was MC Serch (born Michael Berrin), Prime Minister Pete Nice (born Pete Nash), and DJ Richie Rich (born Richard Lawson). Signed to Def

Jam soon after the Beastie Boys left the label in 1988, 3rd Bass targeted the Beasties on the well-received *Cactus Album*. The Beastie Boys issued a delayed response on "Professor Booty" (from 1992's *Check Your Head*). While the Beastie Boys don't mention 3rd Bass by name, MCA's verse appears to take on the group as a whole and specifically mock Serch's dancing ("Dancing around like you think you're Janet Jackson"). After two albums, 3rd Bass disbanded, with Nice and Rich continuing to record and perform together. Serch put out one solo album before turning his focus to production.

3rd Bass is regularly acknowledged by aspiring white rappers as a positive model. D12 member Proof (DeShaun Holton), who as Eminem's onstage hype man knew something about the potentials and pitfalls facing white rappers, said of Serch, "He was there before the struggle of even today's top artists. He had to fight. 3rd Bass and the Beastie Boys showed that hip hop can show racial harmony" (Garner).

Work Cited

Garner, Curtrise. "Serch and Destroy." *Detroit Metro Times*, 16 April 2003. 7 July 2006. http://www.metrotimes.com/editorial/story.asp?id=4797.

Discography

3rd Bass. *Cactus Album*. Sony, 1989.
3rd Bass. *Cactus Album Revisited*. Def Jam, 1990. (Remix EP)
3rd Bass. *Derelicts of Dialect*. Def Jam, 1991.
MC Serch. *Return of the Product*. Def Jam, 1994.
Prime Minister Pete Nice and Daddy Rich. *Dust to Dust*. Def Jam, 1993.

looking to work with new artists. Serch drove to Queensbridge to find Nas, the rapper behind that "Live at the Barbeque" verse. When Serch discovered that Nas was still unsigned, he called a representative at Sony Records, who offered Nas a contract. Serch invited Nas to contribute a song to the soundtrack he was producing for the movie *Zebrahead*; this song, "Halftime," became the soundtrack's first single and appears on Nas's acclaimed first album, *Illmatic* (1994).

Illmatic earned its place in hip hop history by being the first album ever awarded five microphones out of five from *The Source*, at the time the premier rap magazine. The first track is more aural montage than song. "The Genesis" starts off with the sound of an elevated train and an almost-inaudible voice rhyming beneath it. Over these sounds, a snatch of dialogue, two men arguing. In this brief montage, Nas tells us everything he wants us to know about him. The train is shorthand for New York; the barely discernible rap is, in fact, his "Live at the Barbeque" verse; and the dialogue comes from *Wild Style*, one of the earliest movies to focus on hip hop culture. Each of these is a point of genesis. New York for Nas as a person, "Live at the Barbeque" for Nas the rapper, and *Wild Style*, symbolically at least, for hip hop itself. These are my roots, Nas was saying, and he proceeded to demonstrate exactly what those roots had yielded.

Illmatic's impact comes from its particular combination of theme and artistry. The setting is New York City: its streets, jails, and low-rent apartments. Fittingly, the first full song on the album is "N.Y. State of Mind." The title seems an ironic reference to older, more romanticized views of the city, but Nas sounds respectful when he refers to earlier songs of the same title by Frank Sinatra and Billy Joel (Nas would release a new song of the same name on his mixtape *Carry the Cross Vol. 1*, which would feature a sped-up sample of the Billy Joel song). While "N.Y. State of Mind" fills listeners' heads with images of violence and drugs, Nas's New York is not all dark. The album moves back and forth between experiences of pain and pleasure, frustration and nostalgia. This dialectic is at work as we move from the first track's image of the city as "a maze full of black rats trapped" to the second song's promise to the residents of those mazes that "the world is yours." The latter phrase is used in the film *Scarface,* where it resonates with the promise of material wealth but also with the implied warning that an uncontrolled ambition may ultimately lead to destruction, as it did for Tony Montana, aka Scarface. *Illmatic*'s success lies in these layers of irony and contradiction. Nas's braggadocio is on display here, but so is a love for home ("Memory Lane"), a fierce commitment to friends ("One Love"), and stark, painful images of the symptoms of urban poverty. A little girl gets shot in the head, a mother cries for her jailed son, a young man fills himself so full of drugs that he doesn't know if he's shot any of the children he remembers seeing during his criminal rampage.

The other thing that sets *Illmatic* apart is the production. Although MC Serch was the executive producer of the album, five different producers worked on various songs. Large Professor, Pete Rock, Q-Tip of A Tribe Called Quest, DJ Premier of Gang Starr, and L.E.S. each contributed production work to the album. Despite the then-unusual decision to use multiple producers, the album has a consistent sound. Powerful beats combine with horns on one song, with a marimba on another. "It Ain't Hard to Tell" samples Michael Jackson's "Human Nature." On "Life's a Bitch," rapper AZ contributes an accomplished opening verse, and Olu Dara plays the song out with a bittersweet solo. The result of so much talent coming together for one ten-track LP could hardly have resulted in anything less striking than *Illmatic*. For better and for worse, Nas had set a nearly impossible standard for everyone, himself included, to live up to.

The Nas albums that followed outsold *Illmatic*, even as their reception was clouded by comparisons to Nas's debut. *It Was Written* (1996), Nas's second album, went double platinum. It was generally well received by critics, went to number one on the charts, and had hits with "If I Ruled the World," featuring Lauryn Hill, and "Street Dreams," which samples the Eurythmics' hit "Sweet Dreams (Are Made of This)." Nas continued his lyrical innovation with the song "I Gave You Power," a narrative about a gun told from the gun's perspective. "Affirmative Action" and "The Set Up" feature members of the Firm, Nas's Dr. Dre-produced group that included Foxy Brown, AZ, and Cormega (rapper Nature would replace original member and former Nas associate Cormega, who was mentioned on *Illmatic*'s "One Love" after he and Nas had a falling out). The Firm would release its one full album in 1997, then disband after disappointing sales. The production on *It Was Written* was smoother and less gritty than *Illmatic*. Nas went with one producer, the production team of Trackmasters Entertainment. The album sold well, produced hit songs, and garnered Nas many new fans, even as *Illmatic* diehards began what would be an ongoing murmur of concern about Nas's stylistic departure from his classic debut.

1999's *I Am . . .* came next, again going double platinum. DJ Premier and L.E.S., two of the producers from *Illmatic*, returned and contributed several songs, as did Trackmasters, who produced *It Was Written*. "Nas Is Like" and "Hate Me Now" (featuring Puff Daddy) were both released as singles. The Premier-produced "Nas Is Like," the first single from the album, samples lines from *Illmatic* as the rapper runs through a long list of similes. "Hate Me Now" is an angry, insistent response to the criticism Nas had experienced after the success of his first album. In the song, Nas attributes to envy the complaints that he had sold out or was chasing success in too calculated a fashion: "It's a fine line between paper [money] and hate." While Puff Daddy was a curious choice for a guest appearance (even then, Puff was more entrepreneur than rapper), Nas says that he was motivated to collaborate with Puffy as a gesture to the memory of Biggie Smalls, the flagship artist on Diddy's Bad Boy label until his death. The other guests are more fitting: DMX and Scarface each make an appearance, adding their lyrical facility and street-based perspectives to "Life Is What You Make It" and "Favor for a Favor," respectively. Originally, *I Am . . .* was supposed to be a double album. However, much of disc two was bootlegged (an early case of MP3 leaks), so only disc one was released. This wasn't the only drama surrounding the album; in the video for "Hate Me Now" both Nas and Puffy originally appear on crucifixes. Puff Daddy had second thoughts about the scene and asked that it be cut, but the wrong edit was sent to MTV, which aired it in its entirety. As a result, Puff Daddy and his bodyguards barged into the office of Nas's manager, Steve Stoute, attacking him and, at one point, hitting him over the head with a champagne bottle. Stoute sued, and the case was settled out of court.

Nastradamus, also released in 1999, is widely considered to be Nas's artistic low point. It sold well, but its quality reflects the fact that it was written and recorded in only four months, after Nas decided not to include the bootlegged *I Am . . .* songs on the album (some of these songs were finally released on 2002's *The Lost Tapes*, a compilation of Nas's previously unreleased material). Nas has acknowledged that this album was a departure from his other work, saying, "*Nastradamus* was just me experimenting, into some dark world, I don't know what" (Jones, *Video Anthology*). Nas's rhyming skills remain strong, but some of the sung choruses on songs such as "Nastradamus" lack energy. The music on several of the songs verges on easy listening-style jazz. The single "U Owe Me," featuring R&B singer Ginuwine and an electronic dance beat, provided perhaps the best ammunition to date for critics and fans who feared that Nas was sacrificing artistry for popular success. The album didn't lack talented producers: DJ Premier and L.E.S. were on board once again, as was Timbaland, who has since made his reputation producing hits for Missy Elliott, among others. Dame Grease, who produced one song on *I Am . . .* , produced four cuts here. The album opens and closes with performances by spoken word poet Jessica Care Moore, although the ethereal musical accompaniment distracts from Moore's words, much as the music and production do throughout.

By the time Nas's fourth studio album came out, much had changed. His relationship with the mother of his daughter was in trouble, and his own mother had been diagnosed with cancer. To top it off, Jay-Z launched a lyrical attack with "The Takeover" from his album *The Blueprint*. Combined, the result of these challenges was to bring Nas back to top form. Released toward the end of 2001, *Stillmatic* was heralded by critics and fans alike as the follow-up to its namesake that they had been waiting for since 1994. Once again, *The Source* awarded a Nas album five mics, although other reviews didn't necessarily reach that level of praise. Despite the negativity of Jay-Z's attack, it seemed to have gotten Nas's juices flowing. He matches his rival song for song, with biting attacks on "Ether" and "Got Ur Self a Gun," which borrows its music from HBO's hit mob show *The Sopranos*, and which Jay-Z's next Nas dis, "Supa Ugly," would sample. He also used the album to address beefs with old neighborhood friends: "Destroy and Rebuild" takes aim at Prodigy of Mobb Deep and at former associate Cormega. In this song, Nas reworks Boogie Down Productions' old Queensbridge-knocking Juice Crew dis song, "The Bridge Is Over" (see the Roxanne Shanté essay for more on the BDP/Juice Crew beef) and turns it into a chorus about cleaning house in Queensbridge. Also on this album is the single "One Mic," in which each verse builds in intensity until Nas is screaming out the words, only to be undercut by the quiet, almost tender refrain.

God's Son (2002), Nas's next release, reflects an artist sobered by the death of his beloved mother, Ann Jones. Nas returns to her again and again throughout the disc, culminating with the song "Dance," a simple, heartfelt expression of a son's love and loss. "Made You Look," the first single, features a driving loop under Nas's relentless delivery; the chorus is a playful insistence on the power of words. It begins with the sound of a gunshot; several voices shout in unison, "They shootin'," to which Nas responds,

"Ah, made you look." This brief exchange is a reminder that speech is not an alternative to action, but at its most forceful, is itself a form of action. This perspective reflects and perhaps explains the manner in which Nas has conducted his various professional beefs, which is always to keep the battles verbal. The album produced Nas's biggest single to date with "I Can," a motivational song for children built around the melody of Beethoven's "Für Elise." Also tucked away on *God's Son* is a hint of the political turn Nas would take on his next release, the song "Revolutionary Warfare," which, however, features a much more overtly political verse from guest artist Lake, who name checks sixties Black Power leaders Bobby Seale and Huey Newton.

That political sensibility becomes central on disc one of 2004's double-CD *Street's Disciple*, which features songs like "American Way" and "These Are Our Heroes," which takes to task black actors and athletes whom Nas accuses of being disconnected from their roots and culture. Disc two reflects yet another development in Nas's personal life, this time his marriage to R&B singer Kelis, to whom he devotes several songs. Nas also takes the unusual step of singing on this disc, on a song for his daughter Destiny. Listening to this song, one can't help but be reminded of Eminem's "Hailey's Song," on which the Detroit rapper sings to his own daughter. There are two standout songs on disc two, "Thief's Theme," on which Nas raps over the driving rhythm of Iron Butterfly's rock classic "In-a-Gadda-da-Vida," and "Bridging the Gap," Nas's duet with his father (see sidebar: Hip Hop and the Blues).

Hip Hop and the Blues
Susan Weinstein

"Bridging the gap from the blues and jazz to rap," Nas rhymes on a 2004 song featuring his father, jazz trumpeter Olu Dara. The gap Nas names in his song is more an issue of awareness than of musical reality. In fact, the blues predict rap in style, subject matter, and attitude. Like rap, the blues is a form powerfully inflected by the working-class experience. Because of this, both the blues and rap have, in their times, been the targets of criticism by middle-class African Americans who view the themes of overt sexuality, alcohol, drugs, and crime as at best unproductive and at worst reinforcing of stereotypical images of blacks as hypersexual and uncontrolled.

Born in the rural south before spreading to the cities, the blues reflected both country and urban realities. Performers' lived experiences with work, love, and sex provided the basic subject matter for the blues, which is, like rap, primarily a genre of personal narrative. Female performers were often overtly sexual, expressing through both lyrics and delivery a power and desire starkly at odds with middle-class notions of femininity. Female rappers like Lil' Kim and Trina are clear descendants of such women.

Both blues and hip hop have also infused new vocabulary—or, sometimes, new meanings for old words—into the English language. Much blues lingo—for example, *mojo, creeping, jive, boogie,* and even *rock,* which was first used as a musical reference in blues—has now become so much a part of American English that we no longer recall the words' origins or early connotations.

Further Resources

Davis, Angela. *Blues Legacies and Black Feminism: Gertrude "Ma" Rainey, Bessie Smith, and Billie Holiday.* New York: Vintage, 1998.

Through form and content, "Bridging the Gap" draws connections among the many movements in African American music. As striking as the song is artistically, however, it is also unique because it depicts a functional relationship between a black father and son, something rarely represented in hip hop songs. The song, and the publicity that accompanied it, focus on this relationship. Nas says the absence of fathers from the lives of many black youths was a motivation for the song: "We had to make this record as an example for the kids whose fathers were either shot down in the street or taken down by the prison systems or drugs" (Foster 50), to show them that there are other models that these youths can follow with their own children.

The duo's performance of "Bridging the Gap" on the 2005 *VH1 Hip Hop Honors* broadcast captured the power implicit in the song and provided additional visual layers. The performance featured Nas striding the stage while Olu Dara leans on a stool, playing his horn and singing his blues refrain. Nas is dressed for the occasion in a dark suit, yet still sporting his trademark off-kilter baseball cap. Father and son play off each other, exchanging glances, Olu Dara at times appearing to sing directly to Nas, the two exchanging the line "You're the greatest" to each other during one refrain (see sidebar: The Father Figure in Hip Hop). Equally striking is the moment when Nas walks over to the corner of the stage, above which are seated the show's honorees. He looks up at them, and we see KRS-One and Chuck D out of their seats, rocking to the music, KRS-One with a broad smile on his face. In the midst of rapping, never missing a beat, Nas lifts his cap and offers a formal bow to his predecessors.

VIDEOS AND COVER ART

Nas came of age as an artist at a time when the music video had already come into its own as both an art form and a potent commercial force. Consistent with the trajectory of his music, Nas's videos started out low-tech, grainy, and local, and became progressively slicker in look and theme before turning back

---

The Father Figure in Hip Hop
Mickey Hess

Naughty by Nature's "Ghetto Bastard" opens with scripted dialogue between a doctor and nurse in a maternity ward. The nurse informs the doctor that there is no father to include on a newborn's birth certificate, and the doctor describes the situation as "not a shame, a problem." Hip hop lyrics are full of stories about absentee fathers, from Ghostface Killah's "All That I Got (Is You)" to Tupac's "Dear Mama," to Kanye West's "Hey Mama," to 50 Cent's verse on the Game's "Hate It or Love It," which includes the line, "Daddy ain't around, probably out committing felonies." These songs tend to celebrate the mother's strength in raising her kids alone, and to present the father as weak for abandoning his responsibility. Nas's collaboration with his father Olu Dara on "Bridging the Gap" is unusual in a music genre where many stars may have little to no relationship with their fathers.

Many of the same rappers who discuss growing up without a dad also depict themselves as caring and responsible fathers. Ghostface, who, on "All That I Got (Is You)," describes his father packing up and moving out when Ghost was six years old, brings his own son onstage to perform with him in concert footage from the DVD *Put It on the Line*. The Game's video for "Hate It or Love It," which opens with 50 Cent's verse about his absentee dad, ends with the Game holding a baby. Will Smith and Eminem have dedicated songs to their children, and Wu-Tang Clan frequently features their children in skits between songs, and have recently, in the cases of Ghostface Killah and GZA, helped their sons launch their own rap careers.

---

toward simpler settings and styles. Along the way, Nas collaborated with top directors, often using his videos to reinforce his central grounding in hip hop culture and his ongoing commitment to home.

Two of the three *Illmatic* videos, and some from *It Was Written*, were filmed on location in the Queensbridge Projects. On the DVD commentary accompanying the video for "If I Ruled the World," Nas mocks this early tendency, saying, "I had to like get my head together, smack myself one day, say listen, stop shooting the videos in your projects, you gotta stop one day, because every video was seeming the same." At the same time, this early positioning is important in establishing Nas as an artist firmly grounded in the hood's apartments, parks, streets, and corners. The videos for "One Love," "Half-time," "Nas Is Like," and "The World Is Yours" in particular provide visual references for the world that Nas describes in so many of his songs.

Illmatic's "It Ain't Hard to Tell," directed by Ralph McDaniels of TV's *Video Music Box*, became Nas's first official video. Using three different New York settings, the video portrays a young, chip-toothed rapper onstage in a small Manhattan club, hanging with friends on Coney Island, and performing

at a hip hop landmark. This last is the park that served as the final scene for
the movie *Wild Style*, which as mentioned above was one of the earliest
movies to portray New York hip hop culture and which Nas drew on in
the opening cut of *Illmatic*, "The Genesis." The rapper says that being able
to shoot on the stage at the park was "real serious for me."

The "One Love" video continued the connection to *Wild Style* through the
history of its director, Fab 5 Freddy, who appeared in the movie and was one
of the earliest hip hop promoters (he is name checked by Debbie Harry in her
band Blondie's 1980 punk-rap song "Rapture"). The video was shot on location in Queensbridge and at a prison in New Jersey, where Nas brought his
friends to portray inmates shooting baskets and staring out of jail cells. The
brief opening scene of the video resonates with stories that early friends, and
Nas himself, have told about the nascent artist; we see Nas leaning out of an
apartment window, watching as a young man is chased down and arrested by
several police officers. The scene presents Nas as primarily an observer and
chronicler of street life, witnessing the traps in which so many of his peers
were being caught and using his lyrical ability and intellect to contextualize
these lives for listeners.

The video for *It Was Written*'s "If I Ruled the World" provides a segue
from the early, gritty, street-style Nas to the more refined and worldly artist
he was in the process of becoming. This video marks the beginning of an
ongoing collaboration with video director Hype Williams, who would also
direct "Street Dreams" and "Hate Me Now," and who would direct Nas and
rapper DMX in the feature-length movie *Belly*. We once again encounter Nas
in his Queensbridge Projects, but the clothing of Nas and his crew (AZ and
Cormega of the Firm are featured) now sports designer labels, and Lauryn
Hill, who provided the chorus for the song, is shown singing while riding
through the streets of New York, standing up in the sunroof, the colors and
speed providing a polished sensation different from the earlier videos in which
Nas and his crew roam the city on foot, blowing into their hands to ward off
the deep cold of a New York winter.

By the "Street Dreams" video (also from *It Was Written*), Queensbridge is
nowhere in sight. This time, the setting is Las Vegas, and we see the most
conceptual treatment yet of a Nas song. The plot is borrowed directly from
Casino, Martin Scorsese's Vegas crime drama starring Robert DeNiro, Shar-
on Stone, and Joe Pesci. Frank Vincent, who appeared in the movie, also
appears in the video, and Nas credits Vincent with coaching him on his
performance.

By the time Nas's third album, *I Am . . .* was released, the backlash against
the artist was in full swing. Nas responded with the song "Hate Me Now,"
which would serve as the basis for one of his most notorious videos. If the
video for "Street Dreams" was high concept, then the one for "Hate Me
Now" was literally biblical in scope. The video featured Nas rapping while
hanging on a cross. Prior to the shoot, Nas had gotten a tattoo reading *God's*

Son across his stomach, which made his comparisons of himself to Jesus Christ even bolder. Puff Daddy, who is featured on the song and in the video, originally also appeared hanging on a cross. After Puff Daddy changed his mind, his crucifixion was later cut from the video, which now begins with a disclaimer noting that "thousands upon thousands" were crucified in ancient times and ends by saying that "Nas believes in the Lord Jesus Christ and this video is in no way a depiction or portrayal of his life or death." Commenting on the video, Nas stands by it as "a great video," while acknowledging that "a lot of mess followed it" (Jones, *Video Anthology*).

By *Stillmatic*, Nas was working with new video directors, and the results were striking. The video for "One Mic" features Nas sitting in an empty room on a simple chair for the hook; by the end, he is marching through a riot among locals and police in what appears to be an unnamed African town (apartheid-era South African townships come to mind), though in fact the scenes were shot in Los Angeles due to time constraints and unrest in the planned African locations. "Got Ur Self a Gun" features reenactments of the events leading up to the murders of both Tupac and Biggie, with Nas sitting in for each. To Nas's way of thinking, the video was an homage to two artists whose loss he was still mourning, and a way of preserving their memories. The idea came from director Benny Boom, and Nas admits that he himself was at first "real hesitant" about doing it, but "then I was like, nah, I'm gonna rep for them. They deserve that. I'm gonna acknowledge them as one of their disciples, and them one of my disciples, and we're the same family" (Jones, *Video Anthology*).

For *God's Son*'s "Made You Look" video, Nas returned to the New York streets and to street style. Working again with Benny Boom, the two created a very different video from "Got Ur Self a Gun." While the quality of production is high, the feel is old school. Sporting khaki jacket and hat and a single chain, Nas raps in shifting settings; old English-style tags identify each neighborhood: Brooklyn, Queens, Harlem, the Bronx. Local stars turned up for the shooting; among others, Fat Joe appears standing in front of a mural of his close friend, deceased rapper Big Pun, whom Nas references in the song's lyrics. These scenes are interspersed with black-and-white concert footage of Nas performing in a small club, the audience surrounding him, waving their hands and jumping up and down in time to the beats.

While Nas's videos are stylistically diverse, his other main visual medium, the album cover, has been almost uniform in its imagery. All of Nas's solo albums prior to *Street's Disciple* feature a single photograph of the rapper on the cover; indeed, among these albums, all but *God's Son* feature a picture of Nas against a Queensbridge backdrop (albeit, in the case of *I Am . . .*, a pharaohed-out version)—*God's Son* shows Nas against a simple blue background. *Street's Disciple* departs from this tradition by presenting a version of the last supper, with Nas posing as every character in the scene. This isn't the first time Nas has posed as Jesus (as mentioned above, he appears on the cross in the video for "Hate Me Now"). Here, though, the iconography suggests that Nas is both Christ and Judas, as well as everyone in between. For the artist who proclaimed on his first public verse, "When I was twelve, I went to hell for snuffin' Jesus," who tattooed the words *God's Son* on his stomach and years later used the phrase as an album title, the image makes sense.

ARTISTIC INFLUENCES

The esteem with which fans and critics hold Nas's skills as a rapper is reflected in the fact that the artist to whom he is most often compared is Rakim, who secured his legendary status while recording as half of the duo Eric B. & Rakim from 1987 to 1992. It is hard to find a list of top ten MCs that does not include Rakim. Old-school rapper Kool Moe Dee puts Rakim at number two of all time in his book *There's a God on the Mic: The True 50 Greatest MCs* (number one is reserved for Melle Mel, who rapped with Grandmaster Flash and the Furious Five and delivered the genre-changing lyrics on that group's "The Message"). Like Nas, Rakim comes from musical stock. He is the nephew of blues legend Ruth Brown. He is credited with nothing less than revolutionizing lyrical style through both the complexity of his rhymes and the tone and style of his delivery. When other rappers were shouting their verses, Rakim's voice remained deep and cool. Interestingly, while Rakim is universally considered one of the greatest MCs in hip hop history, the content of his rhymes has relatively little to do with that reputation. In his heyday, Rakim rapped primarily about his own skills, but he did it more poetically than perhaps anyone before him. On *Street's Disciple*, Nas paid direct homage to the master on the song "U.B.R. (Unauthorized Biography of Rakim)," referring to Rakim's calculated rhyme style and crediting him and Eric B. with "invent[ing] a new sound."

Of course, Nas didn't need to look as far as Rakim's native Long Island for models. Queensbridge was full of them when he was growing up. Marley Marl was, and his Juice Crew were a New York staple for Nas's generation of hip hoppers. In the late seventies and early eighties, Marley was playing parties in the park and honing his skills in an internship with experienced producer Arthur Baker. In 1984, he became the record-spinning sidekick to Mr. Magic, host of *Rap Attack*, a now-legendary New York radio show airing on Friday and Saturday nights. At the time, Kurtis Blow was rap's star producer, but playing Blow's pop- and synth-tinged records on the air made Marley want to rebel. Off the air, he began producing his own records in his sister's Queensbridge living room, developing a gritty sound that diverged from Blow's clean productions. He also pioneered the drum sample (looping drum segments from old records to create the beats for new songs), which provided him an alternative to the clean drum machine sounds being used at the time.

Marley Marl needed MCs to record songs that would showcase his new techniques. He organized the Juice Crew, who in short order would put Queensbridge on the hip hop map. The original members were Roxanne Shanté, MC Shan, Biz Markie, and Big Daddy Kane, with Kool G Rap & DJ Polo, Craig G., Tragedy (aka Intelligent Hoodlum), and Masta Ace joining later. Under Marley's production, Shanté recorded "Roxanne's Revenge," the legendary response to U.T.F.O.'s boy-brag song "Roxanne, Roxanne." Meanwhile, MC Shan recorded "The Bridge," which would start a style war with the South Bronx's Boogie Down Productions, also known as KRS-One and DJ Scott La Rock. Biz Markie would become known as rap's class clown, while Big Daddy Kane developed a smooth, upscale image that won him many female fans.

It makes sense that of the four original Juice Crew MCs, Nas would gravitate primarily to MC Shan, who had the most straightforward style (at least among the males of the crew). In addition, the story of "The Bridge" puts Nas's continual repping of Queensbridge into historical hip hop context. Now that the term *regional* in hip hop refers to areas of the country or the world, the neighborhood representing of New York rappers is a shout-out to the old days and the now-legends who started it all.

The other major Juice Crew influence Nas cites was a later addition to Marley Marl's stable. Intelligent Hoodlum, aka Tragedy Khadafi, performed primarily political raps such as "Arrest the President" and "No Justice, No Peace." Tragedy's lyrics reflect the kinds of unusual vocabulary and creative rhyming that are common to Nas's rhymes. Unknown to Tragedy, a young Nas used to look over his shoulder as he would sit outside in the neighborhood writing in his rhyme book; during the recording of "Da Bridge 2001," Nas told Tragedy that he remembered how Tragedy would put slashes at the end of each written line. Perhaps most telling of Tragedy's influence on Nas as a young artist is the fact that the title of his first album is taken from a song on the *Intelligent Hoodlum* LP. In "The Rebel," Tragedy flows, "Forget ill, I get illmatical."

In late 2000, Nas produced an album representing the best of Queensbridge hip hop, called *QB's Finest*. "Da Bridge 2001" features an all-star cast in an update of the MC Shan/Marley Marl song "The Bridge." Nas's version features Capone, Mobb Deep, Tragedy, Nature, MC Shan, Marley Marl, Cormega, and Millennium Thug. Here, Nas takes the opportunity to bring his generation of artists together with the generation that, to a large extent, spawned them.

In turn, Nas has either influenced or directly supported countless artists. Once he gained a level of attention and success with the release of *Illmatic*, Nas immediately began contributing guest verses to the albums of other up-and-coming New Yorkers, including fellow Queensbridge natives Mobb Deep and close friend AZ. He rapped on Juice Crew member Kool G Rap's "Fast Life" on the album *4, 5, 6*, and Wu-Tang Clan member Raekwon's "Verbal Intercourse" from the album *Only Built 4 Cuban Linx*, becoming the first non-Wu-Tang member to appear on one of their albums. Nas has supported his brother Jabari's (aka Jungle's) group Bravehearts, appearing on their 1998 debut album and including them on the 2001 collection *QB's Finest*. In the late nineties, Nas created the Firm, with old friends AZ and Cormega (AZ contributed a verse to "Life's a Bitch" from *Illmatic*; Cormega is name checked on "One Love" from the same album) and new discovery Foxy Brown. When relations between Nas and Cormega soured, the latter was replaced by school friend Nature. While the Bravehearts connection has lasted, the Firm disbanded amid unenthusiastic reception of their solo album.

Identifying Nas's artistic descendants is more difficult—Nas has joined Rakim and KRS-One as standard points of comparison any time a new rapper emerges who demonstrates an unusual gift for combining meaningful subject matter and lyrical innovation. Eminem is among Nas's artistic descendants; he has acknowledged his artistic debt to Nas on several occasions, including in the song "Till I Collapse" from his 2002 release, *The Eminem Show*, where he ranks Nas at number eight on his list of MCs, putting himself just behind him at number nine. Eminem reiterated and expanded on this list in accepting his Grammy for Best Rap Album on February 23, 2003, saying that these MCs "inspired me to bring me where I am today, 'cause honestly, I wouldn't be here without them." Reflecting a mutual admiration, Nas invited Eminem to produce the song "Carry the Cross" on *God's Son*; Nas also contributed a song to the Eminem-produced *8 Mile* soundtrack.

KINGS OF NEW YORK

It was inevitable that the three breakout rappers of mid-nineties New York would be compared to one another. Nas released the first album of the three, but Notorious B.I.G. and Jay-Z soon followed, outselling Nas if not outshining his critical reception. In 1997, Jay-Z alluded to the competition on "Where I'm From," saying that locals "argue all day about who's the best MC: Biggie, Jay-Z, or Nas?" After Biggie's murder that same year, the question became which of the two survivors would claim the crown.

The story of how competition turned to beef is complicated, but worth recounting given that beefs often go on and the flames are fanned by the fans and the media, long after most everyone has forgotten why they began. In this case, the origin of the beef was not with Jay-Z but with his protégé Memphis Bleek. Bleek's song "Memphis Bleek Is" from his debut album appeared to mimic Nas's "Nas Is Like." Nas responded by including a song on *Nastradamus* with the same title as another Memphis Bleek song, "What You Think of That?" In it, Nas takes a line that Jay-Z delivered on Bleek's song and turns it back on Bleek as a challenge. Nas and Memphis Bleek exchanged another round of insults, Nas's on "Da Bridge 2001." This time, Nas attacked not only Bleek but many other Roc-A-Fella artists as well.

This is where Jay-Z got involved. At the 2001 Hot 97 Summer Jam in New York, he performed a new song called "The Takeover." It was primarily a Mobb Deep dis, with only one line about Nas. But when Nas responded with an underground song ("Stillmatic Freestyle") attacking Jay-Z and Roc-A-Fella, Jay revised "The Takeover." When it appeared on 2001's *The Blueprint*, the song took direct and extended aim at Nas.

The rest of the story is familiar to most rap fans. Nas responded with "Ether," a devastating attack that signaled a return to lyrical form by the artist and that appeared on his critically acclaimed 2001 album *Stillmatic*. Jay-Z came back with "Supa Ugly," in which, among other things, he claims to have slept with Carmen Bryan, the mother of Nas's daughter. Jay-Z's own mother reportedly said that this was in poor taste, and Jay-Z actually went on Hot 97 to offer a public apology to Carmen Bryan soon after (although Bryan herself has said that Jay's claim was true). Nonetheless, the argument about who had lyrically won the beef continued, so Hot 97 played both songs and asked fans to call in with their votes. "Ether" won over "Supa Ugly" 52 percent to 48 percent, but both artists and their followers have continued to debate the issue.

One continuing theme in the exchange between these two undeniably talented artists was a subject that is central to rap: realness or authenticity. Jay-Z broke into rap after a successful career as a drug dealer, basing most of his rhymes on a criminal career the validity of which few have questioned. Nas's artistic strength, conversely, has often been the main point of attack by his detractors. His role in the projects was more that of observer than participant, at least in terms of heavy-duty crime and violence. Yet his lyrics paint rich pictures of street life, often using the first person to relate these tales. For listeners who understand the literary practice of writing fictional characters in the first person, Nas's representations are unproblematic. For rap fans to whom artist and art are assumed to be one and the same, however, Nas's first-person narrations appear to be a blatant case of fraud. Nas has never spent much time addressing this criticism, perhaps assuming that enough fans and critics understand that a defense is unnecessary. While Jay-Z has certainly fed the Nas-as-fake-gangsta flames, one suspects that Jay-Z is, in fact, one of those who understand. Strategically, he has attacked Nas on the grounds of realness when it served his purposes to do so, while at other times expressing respect for Nas's lyrical craft.

As both artists' places in hip hop history have become secure, the need for continued beef has diminished. In 2005, the beef was officially put to rest when Jay-Z invited Nas onstage during his *I Declare War* show; following that public reconciliation, Jay-Z used his new position as president of Def Jam Records to sign Nas to a four-album deal. Nas describes the latest turn in his relationship with Jigga as yet another way to break new ground: "How many people get over war? Any time you can squash a beef and move on, you lead by example" (Barrow 83).

LITERARY TECHNIQUES

Nas has been consistent in demonstrating a gift for rhyme and rhythm, for complex but accessible song construction. When fans of the genre insist that rap lyrics are simply poetry performed to a beat, they are referring to the kinds of literary techniques (metaphor, alliteration, rhyme, allusion) that appear throughout Nas's work.

Rap is an intensely intertextual and self-referential form. In other words, rappers often refer to other rappers, to other rap songs, and to the history of hip hop in their lyrics. Partly, this probably grows out of the competitive elements of the discourse. When a writer is trying to launch or respond to an attack, it makes sense to refer to things that have been previously said about him or her, to reference an opponent, even to compare the present battle to others that have come before. At the same time, it makes sense that rap is intertextual because literary genres generally are intertextual. Contemporary novelists regularly reference biblical stories, Shakespearean plots and characters, mythological figures, popular songs, and so on. Poets make nods, often indirectly, to one another's work or take a line from one poem and build an entirely new piece around it. As a literary genre, then, it would be odd for rap lyrics not to use this strategy.

Nas most regularly borrows text for new songs from his own work. He often returns to his professional beginnings in these references. As we have seen, this tradition began with his first full album, which starts out by playing part of his "Live at the Barbeque" verse. "The Message," the first song on *It Was Written*, follows this pattern by featuring lines from *Illmatic*, its immediate predecessor (the song's title also references the classic single "The Message," by Grandmaster Flash and the Furious Five). The references to the artist's moment of professional origin, in particular, continue to pop up throughout Nas's career. Some examples: the phrase "street's disciple," the first two words from Nas's "Live at the Barbeque" verse, appears in *Illmatic*'s "It Ain't Hard to Tell," and then, a decade later, becomes the title of his 2004 double album. Similarly, *Street's Disciple*'s "Thief's Theme" takes its name from a phrase on *Illmatic*'s "The World Is Yours." "The World Is Yours," in turn, becomes a line on both *It Was Written*'s "If I Ruled the World" and *Stillmatic*'s "Got Ur Self a Gun."

References to movie characters, musicians, and local New York celebrities abound in Nas's lyrics as well. *Illmatic*'s "Memory Lane" mentions Lorenzo "Fat Cat" Nichols and Ken "Supreme" McGriff, two of the major crime figures in Queens when Nas was growing up. Pappy Mason, who brought down an era of Queens drug business by murdering a New York City police officer, appears in "The World Is Yours" from the same album. One can't be sure whether it was a romanticization of these local figures that led to Nas's affection for mob movies like *Scarface* and *Casino*, and to his adoption of the nickname Nas Escobar (after Nicaraguan drug lord Pablo Escobar), or whether the larger-than-life cinematic portrayals of the mob world made local criminals seem more glamorous than they actually were. Either way, references to both fictional and real-life gangsters are ubiquitous in his work. Nas also draws on novelistic influences: "Black Girl Lost," from *It Was Written*, takes its title from a book by early seventies pulp writer Donald Goines, a popular source of references for so-called gangsta rappers in particular.

A particularly curious recurring reference in Nas's lyrics is to Mahatma Gandhi, leader of the peaceful resistance to British colonial rule in India. Sometimes the allusion is to the movie rather than the historical figure, as when Nas describes "watching Gandhi 'til I'm charged" on "The World Is Yours." On *God's Son*, he returns to the revolutionary pacifist twice. In "Book of Rhymes," Nas quotes one of his own unfinished verses: "Gandhi was a fool, Nigger, fight to the death"; he then casts doubt on his commitment to this statement by dismissing the rhyme as "weak" (see sidebar: book of rhymes). On "Revolutionary Warfare," he is more reflective: "I'm thinking Gandhi was a fool, but chronic's a fool." He follows this by saying that he's

---

Book of Rhymes
Mickey Hess

The book of rhymes, rhyme book, or pad and pen has itself become a hip hop icon, making appearances in the lyrics of songs from Nas, A Tribe Called Quest, the Beastie Boys, and many other artists. Nas's "Book of Rhymes" takes the listener through a series of unused rhymes, scraps from Nas's journal that have not been used in his lyrics. The book of rhymes appears in hip hop music videos, films, and album covers as a visual representation of an MC's dedication to writing rhymes. The cover art for Masta Ace's *A Long Hot Summer* depicts Ace sitting on his front stoop, notebook and pen in hand. In *8 Mile*, Eminem pens his battle rhymes on a city bus. In the music video for "I Try," bullies steal a book of rhymes from a young Talib Kweli, and later return the book because they are so impressed with the writing. The rhyme book also appeared on the MTV series *Made*, in which high school students write in to ask the network to help them fulfill their dreams of being athletes, musicians, or socialites. In one episode, a Minneapolis teen, The Blizzard, is sent to New York to meet Ghostface Killah, who shows him a stack of composition notebooks and tells him to "write every day."

The RZA's *Wu-Tang Manual* features a page copied from one of Ghostface's rhyme books. The handwriting conveys a sense of urgency and at the same time recalls the graffiti writing that preceded MCing in hip hop's formative years. Similarly, in the video for Del the Funky Homosapien's "Catch a Bad One," viewers can see pages from Del's rhyme book. The primacy of paper and pen among MCs reminds fans that hip hop is a writing culture, very much based on the power of the written word. Eschewing computers and word processing software, MCs carry notebooks in which they can jot their rhymes on city buses and in the streets. Seeing handwritten pages from these rhyme books personalizes the writing even further.

just "thinking out loud," suggesting that he's not yet quite ready to trade his beloved marijuana for civil disobedience. The fact that he introduces such an uncharacteristic symbol in his lyrics and continues to muse on it over time in the presence of his audience suggests an intellectual openness and engagement that Nas is inviting his listeners to share.

One of the most common literary techniques in rap is the metaphor (simile is included under this category). It's difficult to find songs in the genre that don't incorporate metaphor, even if they are often somewhat obvious or clumsy. Nas doesn't overload his songs with this technique, but when he does use metaphor, it is often particularly original or clever: "like Malcolm X catching the jungle fever" ("Halftime"), "Made me richer than a slipper made Cinderella" ("One Time 4 Your Mind").

The literary technique Nas most strongly excels in is the one that would seem to be most pedestrian: rhyme. However, while many rappers struggle to come up with one good rhyme for each bar, Nas regularly tosses off a series of them within a single line. Along with his confident delivery, it is this skill that stands out on his earliest recordings. The first lines in the first song on his first album threaten to overwhelm the listener with the sheer quantity and quality of rhyme and near-rhyme. This kind of virtuoso performance reveals an artist reveling in his talent, while simultaneously putting listeners on notice that they are in for something new and exciting.

Nas's formal inventiveness, which would reemerge throughout his career, is first on display in *Illmatic*'s "One Love," a song composed solely of letters written to a friend in jail. Several years later, Eminem would employ a similarly striking use of the epistolary form in "Stan." Nas explains that the title of the song came from Bob Marley's famous song of the same name, which in turn echoed the ubiquitous street salutation "one" (similar to "peace") used around Nas's neighborhood. He had a number of friends in jail at the time and was receiving letters from them detailing their experiences there. Another unique lyrical form appears in *God's Son*'s "Book of Rhymes," in which we hear the rapper standing in the studio, flipping through the pages of one of his old notebooks (we even hear the shuffle of the paper as the pages turn), performing snatches of half-finished lyrics and then commenting on them to himself and his producer (well-known hip hop producer the Alchemist). *It Was Written*'s "I Gave You Power" plays with point of view, offering the first-person narrative of a gun. Young Noble, a close friend of Tupac Shakur's, claims that this song was the inspiration for Tupac's "Me and My Girlfriend," which uses a similar conceit. "Rewind," from *Illmatic*, is a revenge narrative told in reverse, including backward dialogue and actions (e.g. "I vomited vodka back in my glass with juice and ice").

NAS'S IMPACT AND LEGACY

One of the debates critics and fans alike indulge in when it comes to Nas is whether any of his subsequent albums achieved the seamless artistry of *Ill-matic*. Ironically, every album after *Illmatic* surpassed it in terms of sales, but none received the kind of unanimous admiration of that first release. What it does to someone to know that he may have achieved his artistic peak with his first work is something only such an artist can know. In Nas's case, it seems to have led to frustration and freedom in more or less equal measures. As he matures, the freedom appears to be winning out, particularly now that his beef with Jay-Z is behind him. There will always be rappers trying to start beef with Nas because of the attention it brings them, but Nas's attitude seems to be that between the evidence of his own body of work and his success against an artist of Jay-Z's caliber, he doesn't need to prove himself by rising to every verbal assault aimed his way. In addition, time has served to lessen expectations that Nas will someday make another *Illmatic* and has simulta-neously seen critics and fans reconsidering the merits of his other albums.

Nas is a hip hop icon both in spite of and because of his ups and downs. He matters because his songs ooze hip hop in subject, attitude, style, and skill. One is tempted to see Nas as a lived, if compressed, version of rapper Com-mon's classic hip hop allegory, "I Used to Love H.E.R." Like the female stand-in for hip hop in that song, Nas started in the streets, rapping out of "a love for the thing" (to quote Mos Def, another accomplished rap lyricist); his lyrics move from gritty narratives to Afrocentricity and conscious themes to God, bitches, and bling, sometimes within one song, with marijuana wind-ing a pungent trail in and around it all. At the end of "I Used to Love H.E.R.," Common pledges to take his world-weary love back to her roots. Nas has never needed a musical savior, though; part of the fascination of his career is that he has the depth of talent to return to top form even after several artistically uneven releases. This means that until he hangs up his mic for good, no one who knows their hip hop history will ever count Nas out.

Nas is also a part of the small group of rappers on whom academia has turned an approving gaze. Since his artistic emergence, Nas has been some-thing of a scholar's darling, referenced regularly in books and articles explor-ing the ideological and artistic implications of black youth culture. Given Nas's attention to African history, the term *griot* is particularly apt. Griots are nomadic West African poets and storytellers, oral historians who were traditionally attached to a particular royal family. They go from town to town recounting their patrons' histories and exploits, and are thus the appointed keepers and disseminators of cultural knowledge. Applying the term to a rapper like Nas may be partly inadvertently ironic, since he recounts the stories not of the high and mighty but of the dispossessed.

In an era in which *rapper* has become almost synonymous with *entrepreneur*, Nas stands out as an artist who is first and foremost committed to his craft. He has been criticized for not capitalizing on his reputation by branching out into other businesses, like so many of his peers. On *Illmatic*'s "The Genesis," Nas says to his friends, "When it's real, you're doing this with or without a record contract." That love of music and lyrics remains at the core of Nas's work, and it is what makes him a hip hop icon.

WORKS CITED

Barrow, J. "Broken Silence." *Scratch* 2.9 (2006): 80–83.
Foster, S. "Bridging the Gap." *Ave Magazine* 2.5 (2004): 48–54.
Jones, Nasir. *Video Anthology, Vol. 1.* Sony, 2004.
Kool Moe Dee. *There's a God on the Mic: The True 50 Greatest MCs.* New York: Thunder's Mouth Press, 2003.

FURTHER RESOURCES

Brown, Ethan. *Queens Reigns Supreme: Fat Cat, 50 Cent, and the Rise of the Hip-Hop Hustler.* New York: Anchor Books, 2005.
Cowie, D. "Nas: Battle Ready." *Exclaim*, 2004. http://www.exclaim.ca/index.asp?layid=22&csid=1&csid1=3163.
Jones, Nasir, perf. *Belly.* Dir. Hype Williams. Live/Artisan, 1998.
Jones, Nasir, perf. *Made You Look: God's Son Live.* Sony, 2003.
Jones, Nasir, perf. *Video Anthology Vol. 1.* Sony, 2004.
Jones, Nasir. *Slave to a Page: The Book of Rhymes.* New York: ReganBooks, 2006.
Light, Alan. (Ed.). *The Vibe History of Hip-hop.* New York: Three Rivers Press, 1999.
Margena, C. "Nas." *Ebony Man* 12.8 (1997).
MTV. Greatest MCs of All Time: #4 Rakim. MTV. http://www.mtv.com/bands/h/hiphop week/2006/emcees/index8.jhtml.
Nas Homepage. 7 July 2006. http://www.streetsdisciple.com.
Nas. Lyrics. The Original Hip Hop Lyrics Archive. 7 July 2006. http://www.ohhla.com/YFAnas.html.
Rapcentral.co.uk. "Nas Timeline: A Full Career Timeline of His Life and Career." 29 March 2006. http://www.rapcentral.co.uk/nasTimeline.html.
Spirer, Peter. *Beef* (video). Image Entertainment, 2003.
Toure. "Nas Stands Tough." *Rolling Stone* 814 (1999).
VH1. *Nas: Driven* Web site. http://www.vh1.com/shows/dyn/driven/89048/episode-about.jhtml.

SELECTED DISCOGRAPHY

Individual Studio Releases

Illmatic. Sony, 1994.
It Was Written. Sony, 1996.

I Am ... Sony, 1999.
Nastradamus. Sony, 1999.
Stillmatic. Sony, 2001.
God's Son. Sony, 2002.
Street's Disciple. Sony, 2004.

Remixes, Compilations, and Side Projects

From Illmatic to Stillmatic: The Remixes. Sony, 2002.
The Lost Tapes. Sony, 2002.
Nas and Ill Will Records Present QB's Finest. Sony, 2000.
Nas, Foxy Brown, AZ, and Nature Present The Firm: The Album. Sony, 1997.

Wu-Tang Clan

Jessica Elliott and Mickey Hess

Wu-Tang Clan is a group of nine MCs that formed in Staten Island in the early 1990s. The structure of the group was unprecedented. RZA's goal was to build a team of nine generals, a group of nine artists who stood on equal footing and who could each succeed at solo careers, but who were bound together by loyalty to the Clan. The RZA, the GZA, Ol' Dirty Bastard, Inspectah Deck, Raekwon the Chef, Ghostface Killah, Method Man, Masta Killa, and U-God burst onto the hip hop scene with a raw new sound that redefined New York hip hop and reaffirmed New York City as the center of the hip hop universe. In the early 1990s, West Coast producer Dr. Dre had created a new sound that he called G-funk in tribute to George Clinton's group Parliament Funkadelic (P-Funk), but with a distinct gangsta attitude. Dr. Dre's work on N.W.A.'s *Efil4zaggin* (1991) and his own album *The Chronic* (1993) had shifted attention to the West Coast's new, laid-back style of hip hop.

In 1993, a new label, Loud Records, released twelve-inch singles from Wu-Tang Clan and Mobb Deep, two groups that along with Nas and

Notorious B.I.G. would reestablish New York City as the center of hip hop. Loud's first seven releases included four singles from Wu-Tang and one solo twelve-inch, "Heaven & Hell," from Raekwon. Wu-Tang's new, sparse, sound would help reaffirm that New Yorkers not only invented hip hop music but remained innovators as well. With gritty beats and versatile rhyme styles from nine different MCs, Wu-Tang changed hip hop music, hip hop style, and hip hop business. Wu-Tang Clan is significant in that the group was able to ink an unprecedented contract that allowed each of them free reign to record as solo artists with any label of their choosing. It was by diversifying and expanding that the Wu would take over the record industry. Yet no matter how successful these solo careers have been, the nine members have remained true to Wu-Tang Clan for life and have rejoined forces to release four full-length Wu-Tang Clan albums: *Enter the Wu-Tang (36 Chambers)* (1993), *Wu-Tang Forever* (1997), *The W* (2000), and *Iron Flag* (2001). Since the death of Ol' Dirty Bastard, who suffered a cocaine-related heart attack in a New York City recording studio in 2005, Wu-Tang Clan has yet to release a new album. As solo artists, however, Wu-Tang members continue to be productive and innovative.

Wu-Tang Clan's financial savvy has become so legendary in the world of hip hop that Dave Chapelle, on Comedy Central's *Chapelle's Show*, invited RZA and GZA to guest star in a sketch called "Wu-Tang Financial." The sketch parodies television commercials for financial planners, and features RZA and GZA sitting in a corporate boardroom, giving accounting advice to well-dressed white businesspeople: "You gotta diversify your bonds, nigga." RZA and GZA learned the secrets of the music business the hard way. The Wu-Tang saga began when hip hop artists and cousins the Genius (now GZA) and Prince Rakeem (now RZA) found themselves signed to unsatisfactory record contracts. Rakeem changed his name to RZA and began working on a new crew of MCs that would bring a new style to hip hop. Wu-Tang Clan would make him famous for his signature sound: His use of organs, violins, and operatic singing, along with samples of kung fu, blaxploitation, and gangster films, made him unique among producers. The name Wu-Tang Clan is borrowed from a kung fu film about a group of martial arts students who rebel against their teachers, and was transformed by the group into an acronym for Witty Unpredictable Talent and Natural Game. The name is a significant comment on Wu-Tang's approach to making music. Like the young martial artists in the film from which they took their name, Wu-Tang Clan broke with tradition to create a new style all their own.

Naming is very important to the mythology Wu-Tang Clan has built around itself. Wu-Tang lyrics draw from martial arts films, comic books, and gangster movies. Members of the group take on multiple names that often reference these influences. RZA, for instance, also goes by Bobby Steels (combining the name of Black Panther revolutionary Bobby Seale with the wheels of steel, a slang term for turntables), the Abbot, and Bobby Digital.

Method Man calls himself Johnny Blaze, Ticallion Stallion, Hot Nikkels, the MZA, and John-John McLane (a name he borrows from Bruce Willis's character in the *Die Hard* films). Other Wu names include Ironman, Lucky Hands, Golden Arms, Lex Diamond, and Noodles. While recording their second album, *Wu-Tang Forever*, group members took on Italian Mafia names and called themselves collectively the Wu-Gambinos.

Wu-Tang's debut album, *Enter the Wu-Tang (36 Chambers)*, contained samples of radio interviews the group had done. Raekwon and Method Man took turns introducing the group members: first, the RZA, the head of the organization. RZA's production combined gritty SP-1200 beats with ethereal violins, piano, and singing, lending a new operatic sound to music he had made on a classic machine. The GZA, the genius. His lyrical wordplay and complicated rhythms would influence Method Man and Inspectah Deck, MCs whose internal rhymes (like Deck's "Socrates' philosophies and hypotheses") and extended metaphors (like Method Man's "bust shots at Big Ben like we got time to kill") would raise the art of rhyming to a new level. Ghostface Killah added high-pitched, urgently delivered vocals. Ol' Dirty Bastard added a gruff, barked delivery and a level of unpredictability to their songs and performances but would shift into soulful wails within these same verses. Method Man also had several unique and distinctive rhyming methods. The singing styles that ODB and Method Man brought to their vocals influenced later artists such as Nelly and Cee-Lo. U-God's deep voice and Masta Killa's laid-back delivery rounded out the group.

Wu-Tang built choruses around call-and-response chants that sounded almost military ("Clan in da Front" in particular) and were often developed from the question-and-answer format of the Five Percenters' Infinity Lessons. Much of Wu-Tang's slang derives from the Five Percenters as well. They often refer to each other as "God," to their mothers as "Old Earth," and to the "mathematics" and "knowledge" they seek to achieve and to convey to their listeners. RZA's involvement with the Five Percenters during his childhood led him to his wider interests in religion, numerology, and strategy, which form the backbone of the Wu-Tang philosophy. Outside RZA's studies in religions ranging from the Nation of Islam to Buddhism to Christianity, his other influences range from martial arts to Sun Tzu's *The Art of War* to the game of chess.

Although most of the members of Wu-Tang Clan have become successful artists in their own right, each solo album includes at least one track that features other members of the clan, as well as close affiliates Capadonna, Tru Masta, Sunz of Man, Popa Wu, and Killah Priest (now calling himself Priesthood), many of whom have released their own solo albums as well. After the success of solo albums from Method Man, Ol' Dirty Bastard, GZA, Raekwon, and Ghostface Killah, Wu-Tang Clan reunited to record *Wu-Tang Forever*, a double album that showcased the group's excess as much as its loyalty. RZA's production added a new level of theatrics to what had originated as a stripped-down sound. Wu-Tang released an epic, six-minute music video for "Triumph," directed by Brett Ratner, who directed *X-Men: Standoff* and the *Rush Hour* trilogy. Ratner brought his special effects expertise to the project; the video opens with Ol' Dirty Bastard leaping from a skyscraper, and Inspectah Deck rhyming while clinging to the side of the same building. Such excess was justified; *Wu-Tang Forever* was highly anticipated by fans, and debuted at number one on the *Billboard* albums chart.

Even after the death of founding member Ol' Dirty Bastard in 2004, Wu-Tang Clan continues to build a hip hop dynasty through new solo albums, film scores, movie roles, book deals, and collaborations with new artists outside the clan. In a radio interview included on *Enter the Wu-Tang (36 Chambers)*, a reporter asks a young Raekwon and Method Man what their ultimate goal is for the group. Raekwon lists bringing a new sound to hip hop through styles that people have never before heard. Method Man, who also describes how he wants to build a sustainable career and give his children the things he couldn't afford growing up, best sums up his goals in one word: domination. With a career spanning over twelve years at the top of the hip hop game, Wu-Tang Clan has made that happen.

RZA

RZA (pronounced "rizza") is short for razor, and refers to the sharpness of RZA's rhymes, beats, and business savvy. The name also mimics the sound of turntable scratching to stutter a vocal track ("rizza rizza Rakeem"). In 1991, before the official formation of the Wu-Tang Clan, RZA (Robert Diggs), recording as Prince Rakeem, released two singles through Tommy Boy Records: "Ooh, I Love You Rakeem," and "My Deadly Venom." He'd produced these two songs on the advice of his label, but neither song fared well in the industry. So, when RZA, GZA, and Ol' Dirty Bastard formed Wu-Tang Clan, RZA wanted to have control of the group's production decisions. This amount of control was unconventional in the music industry, so RZA declined offers from several different labels before finally signing a contract with Loud Records in 1993. In his book, *The Wu-Tang Manual*, he claims that their deal "changed the way hip-hop artists negotiate, the way deals are structured; it changed the whole rap game" (76).

His plan was to negotiate not only for the present, but also for the future, attributing this strategy to his love of chess. He promised the group that, if they would give him five years, he would ensure their success not only as a group but as solo artists. During that time, he produced Wu-Tang's first group album and all of the group members' solo albums. The release of the group's second album, *Wu-Tang Forever*, marked the end of his five-year plan. He'd provided the success he'd promised and afterward wasn't as fully involved in each member's individual projects.

During these fateful five years, the RZA became one of the hardest working producers in the music industry. After *Enter the Wu-Tang* was released, RZA recorded with a second group, Gravediggaz, a horror-theme hip hop group consisting of RZA, Prince Paul, Frukwan, and Too Poetic. The Gravediggaz released three albums, though RZA stopped working with the group after their sophomore album, 1997's *The Pick, the Sickle, and the Shovel*. The group is notable because their debut album, 1994's *Six Feet Deep*, was a collaboration between RZA and Prince Paul, two of hip hop's most revered producers. At the time of the album's recording, Prince Paul was known for the unique sound he had created on albums such as De La Soul's *3 Feet High and Rising*, and RZA, until then a relatively unknown artist, was beginning to get attention for the new sound he brought to the Wu-Tang's debut album. Gravediggaz were also pioneers of a hip hop subgenre, horrorcore (see sidebar: Hip Hop and Horror).

Hip Hop and Horror
Danielle Hess

Horror in hip hop traces its roots back to the Geto Boys' *We Can't Be Stopped* (1991), the cover of which features a graphic photograph of Bushwick Bill on a hospital gurney, surrounded by fellow Geto Boys members Willie D and Scarface. Bushwick was hospitalized after forcing his girlfriend to assist in his suicide attempt. In the photograph, Bushwick's eye is swollen and bleeding from a bullet wound. *We Can't Be Stopped* also featured the song "Chuckie," named after a character from the horror film series *Child's Play.*

"Chuckie" was written by horrorcore pioneer Ganxsta Nip, whose debut CD *South Park Psycho* (1992) was shrouded in controversy when it was found in the tape deck of a teenager who killed a police officer. The first song on the album was "Horror Movie Rap," which sampled the *Halloween* soundtrack. Other pioneers include Insane Poetry, unique for combining images of horror with reality to create a socially conscious rap that often outlines the struggles of black America, and Esham, whose album *KKKill the Fetus* (1993) encourages drug-addicted pregnant women to abort their fetuses.

While there is much debate over who coined the term *horrorcore*, it was not until the 1994 release of the Flatlinerz' *USA (Under Satan's Authority)* and Gravediggaz' *Six Feet Deep* that the term hit the mainstream. While most horrorcore album sales are lackluster, groups like Insane Clown Posse, Twizted, and Necro have achieved substantial sales.

In production, the theme music from horror films can provide a dramatic backdrop for MC vocals. The Beastie Boys and Busta Rhymes both have used the score from the classic horror flick *Psycho*. The *Halloween* theme song has been sampled by Dr. Dre, the No Limit Records group Tru, and Project Pat, along with Ganxsta Nip. Other hip hop artists feature horror movies prominently in their music. Metabolics and Mr. Dead use samples from old horror movies to add to themes of Armageddon and death.

With hip hop's love of horror and many rappers' desire to become actors, it is only natural that several hip hop artists have played roles in horror films. Snoop Dogg played the title character, a 1970s player who returns from the dead, in *Bones*. Redman was gutted on a kitchen table by Chucky's bride, Tiffany, in *Seed of Chucky*. Busta Rhymes played a smarmy reality TV producer in *Halloween Resurrection*. In *Halloween H20*, LL Cool J plays a security guard with dreams of becoming a romance novelist. LL plays an instrumental role in killing Michael Myers, which is unusual in a movie genre known for killing off all African American characters first.

Aside from his production work with Wu-Tang, the Wu solo albums, and Gravediggaz, RZA recorded his own solo album, 1998's *RZA as Bobby Digital in Stereo*. Bobby Digital was one of RZA's pseudonyms, and, in the album, he raps as the personality this pseudonym portrays, a futuristic MC from outer space. This is a technique RZA adapted from Kool Keith, who, after his group Ultramagnetic MCs broke up, recorded a solo album under the name Dr. Octagon, a gynecologist from Jupiter. RZA's Bobby Digital persona utilized this same outer space theme, one that would also be used for Deltron 3030, a collaboration between Del the Funky Homosapien and Dr. Octagon producer Dan the Automator, who would later work with Prince Paul in the group Handsome Boy Modeling School. Kool Keith, known to be unpredictable, lampooned RZA's Bobby Digital persona by releasing an album as Robbie Analog. In 2001, RZA released his second album, *Digital Bullet*, a follow-up Bobby Digital album.

In 1999, RZA started composing movie soundtracks. His first soundtrack was for Jim Jarmusch's *Ghost Dog: The Way of the Samurai*, a film that featured a chess-playing martial artist in New York City. It was right up RZA's alley, and, in addition to the soundtrack, he had a small role in the film. From there, he composed the soundtracks for *Kill Bill*, *Blade: Trinity*, and *Soul Plane*. He and GZA played themselves in a skit in Jarmusch's *Coffee and Cigarettes* (2004), and RZA and several other Wu members played themselves in the 2003 movie, *Scary Movie 3*.

RZA's first solo album as RZA, *Birth of a Prince*, was released in 2003, and featured longtime Wu affiliate True Master. That same year, RZA produced *The World According to RZA*, an album for which he recruited MCs from several European countries. Many of the vocals are not in English, and RZA's production showcases the vocal talents of European hip hop artists. The album was followed up with the 2004 DVD of the same title, which consists of documentary footage of RZA's travels, as well as a live concert in Germany with Euro rap stars Xavier Naidoo, Curse, Afrob and Seko.

In 2005, the RZA published *The Wu-Tang Manual*, his guide to everything important about the group. This book was unprecedented; no other hip hop artist before him had published such a detailed guide to a group and its music. In the book, RZA gives a short overview of each member in the group, but overall it revolves around his personal beliefs and experiences as a member of the Wu-Tang Clan. RZA speaks about the things that influenced both the group- and business-oriented mentality that ultimately led to the group's success. Some of these influences were spiritualism, martial arts, comics, chess, the Mafia, movies, and capitalism. He dedicated a chapter to explaining each element and how it led to Wu-Tang's ideals.

RZA explains the many influences that were important to the formation of the Wu-Tang Clan as well as to himself as an artist. RZA discusses his spiritual influences from the Five Percenters and the Nation of Islam (see sidebar: Islam and Hip Hop under Eric B. & Rakim) to Buddhism and other East Asian religions. While it was ultimately his spirituality that led to his dedication to his group members, RZA cites chess as what made him excel in his five-year plan. He explains that he used to play chess with the old men on Wall Street, and that chess taught him to think ahead and to strategize, leading him to develop and negotiate Wu-Tang's legendary contract with Loud Records.

The first half of the book is dedicated to explaining these group influences while the second half focuses primarily on their music. In "Book Three," RZA prints lyrics from nine different Wu-Tang songs and, in sidebars, explains exactly what those lyrics refer to. The fourth book focuses on producing, sampling, MCing, and performing live.

Other elements of *The Wu-Tang Manual* include six pages of slang term definitions, the histories of several comic books, Mafia films, and kung fu movies, and a thorough explanation of Supreme Mathematics. When RZA introduces an element that he cites as a group influence, he gives the information necessary for his readers to put that influence into context. He annotates the lyrics to several Wu-Tang songs, offering explanations of phrases used by his band mates and commenting on their unique rhyme styles.

GZA

GZA (Gary Grice) is the oldest of the three cousins (RZA, GZA, and Ol' Dirty Bastard) who formed Wu-Tang Clan. Before Wu-Tang formed, GZA was the first of its future members to release a solo album, *Words from the Genius* (1991), which featured the minor pop-rap hit "Come Do Me." The album had disappointing sales, and many of the decisions about it were made by his label, Cold Chillin'. GZA's displeasure with his label eventually led to the formation of the Wu-Tang Clan and the contract that gave the nine members more control over their music. On his song "Labels," GZA calls out specific hip hop record labels for misleading and mistreating hip hop artists. RZA opens the track with spoken dialogue, urging young rappers to "read the labels" or else be poisoned.

GZA was born and raised in New York City. When rap music was still in
its infancy, GZA was traveling around New York, performing in rap battles.
He took his two younger cousins with him to these battles and encouraged
their interests in rap music. In *The Wu-Tang Manual*, RZA explains that
GZA was the one who taught him about two things: MCing and Supreme
Mathematics. RZA studied under GZA and later taught Ol' Dirty Bastard
what he had learned. This spiritual aspect became a large part of what the
Wu-Tang Clan would stand for.

In 1994, GZA recorded "I Gotcha Back," a single from the movie soundtrack *Fresh*. In 1995, he released his first solo album since the formation of
the Wu-Tang Clan. GZA's solo album, *Liquid Swords*, extends Wu-Tang's
metaphor of the tongue as a sword. The album cover depicts GZA cutting the
head off an opponent over a chessboard. The back cover of *Liquid Swords*
listed the songs out of order, their titles worked into a paragraph-length story.
This technique, along with the carefully placed samples from martial arts
movies, may indicate that GZA intends the album to tell a consistent story
and that he is complicating any attempts to skip from track to track with no
regard for narrative consistency. Ghostface would later list his songs out of
order on the back cover of *Bulletproof Wallets*.

Liquid Swords opens with a lengthy sample from the film *Shogun Assassin*.
The same movie dialogue would later be heard in Quentin Tarantino's *Kill Bill
2*, as Beatrice Kiddo watches *Shogun Assassin* with her daughter. After the
initial sample of dialogue from *Shogun Assassin*, GZA's *Liquid Swords* shifts
into the title track's organ sample and its chorus, which GZA chants along
with RZA: "When the MCs came, to live out their name . . . " *Liquid Swords* is
GZA's solo classic, yet it showcases RZA on the title track, Method Man on
the steady-paced "Shadow Boxin'," and RZA, Killah Priest, and Ghostface
Killah on "4th Chamber," which samples one of Prince's guitar riffs. Wu-Tang
solo albums tend to include guest appearances from other members of the
group, both to show solidarity and to enhance the quality of the music.

Since *Liquid Swords*, GZA has continued to be active in recording. In 1999,
he released his third solo album, *Beneath the Surface*. His fourth solo album,
Legend of the Liquid Sword, was released in 2002. *Legend of the Liquid
Sword* contained a track titled "Uncut Material" that was the first Wu-Tang
song that was produced exclusively by GZA. Both albums sold well and were
well received by his fans and critics. In 2004, GZA released a greatest hits
album, *Collection of Classics*. The same year he announced that his son,
Young Justice, was preparing to release his debut solo album. Young Justice
had been featured on the intro to *Legend of the Liquid Sword* and had later
released a cover of GZA's "Killa Hills 10304." The second generation of Wu-
Tang appears to be on the horizon: Ghostface Killah's son delivers a live verse
on his father's 2006 DVD, *Put It on the Line*.

In 2005, GZA released an album, *Grandmasters*, a collaboration with DJ
Muggs, a producer best known for his work with Cypress Hill, House of Pain,

and Funkdoobiest, as well as his own group Soul Assassins. Muggs's signature sound borrows the high-pitched horns and vocals first used by the Bomb Squad, who produced albums for Public Enemy and Ice Cube. Muggs's production on *Grandmasters* brought this style to meet with Wu-Tang's finest MCs. Along with GZA, Raekwon, RZA, and Masta Killa provide verses on the album. Cypress Hill's Sen Dog joins in as well, delivering a verse in Spanish. GZA is rumored to be a large part of Raekwon the Chef's upcoming solo album *Only Built 4 Cuban Linx II*. He is currently working on his sixth solo album through his new deal with Babygrande Records.

OL' DIRTY BASTARD

Ol' Dirty Bastard (Russell Jones) was so named because "there ain't no father to his style," Method Man explains on *Enter the Wu-Tang*. Dirty's vocal style was unprecedented in hip hop, lying somewhere between Al Green's soulful cries and Rick James's funky wails, combined with gruff hip hop grunts and growls that were 100 percent ODB. Like Method Man, Dirty both rapped and sang his verses, alternating between the two even within one line. This technique is evident in his Wu-Tang and solo vocals, as well as in his guest appearances on Mariah Carey's song "Fantasy" and on Pras's "Ghetto Supastar," which revised the Kenny Rogers–Dolly Parton duet "Islands in the Stream." Dirty ends the song by mimicking Kenny Rogers's wails on the original.

Ol' Dirty was RZA's cousin from Brooklyn, and he used to ride the train to RZA's mother's home in Staten Island so he could rhyme and watch kung fu movies with the rest of the crew. RZA, GZA, and Dirty formed a group called All in Together Now that would lay the foundation for the collective that would become the Wu-Tang Clan. Wu-Tang's debut, *Enter the Wu-Tang*, included the second track, "Shame on a Nigga," which introduced Ol' Dirty Bastard to the world. His staggered rhyme style featured fragmented phrases and onomatopoeia: "You wanna get gun? Shoot. Blow!" Dirty was the second Wu-Tang member to release a solo album, and the first member to embark on a solo tour (in 1998). Although all nine Wu-Tang members have given themselves several nicknames, Ol' Dirty's were often the most outrageous and caught the attention of music journalists. He called himself Osirus, Dirt McGirt, Ason Unique, and Big Baby Jesus. Dirty even changed his voice from one line to the next on his debut album, *Return to the 36 Chambers: The Dirty Version*. On his hit single, "Shimmy Shimmy Ya," the entire second verse was flipped backward.

With these vocal styles and his often X-rated subject material, Ol' Dirty Bastard was the most outrageous member of the Wu-Tang Clan. *The Dirty Version* begins with a long spoken-word track in which Dirty complains about getting gonorrhea from a woman, then going back to the same woman and getting burned again. After the group's first album became a hit, he famously took MTV cameras with him as he rode in a limousine to pick up his welfare check. He would reference this lifestyle on Wu-Tang Clan's "Dog Shit": "Got bills but still grill that old good welfare cheese." Dirty, like the other members of the Wu-Tang Clan, strived to get out of the poverty he'd lived in as a child. He was raised in Brooklyn on public assistance, and he fathered his first child as a teenager. In opposition to the glamorous lifestyles portrayed by Bad Boy Records artists Puff Daddy and Notorious B.I.G., who claimed to have risen from poverty to strike it rich in the music business, Dirty's debut album cover featured a re-creation of his food stamp card.

Ultimately, it was Dirty's mentality of keeping one foot in the ghetto that would lead to his early death. As a hip hop superstar, Dirty remained addicted to heroin and spent time in prison for weapons possession and drug offenses. In prison, his health was bad. He needed dental work, and fellow inmates jumped him and broke his leg. He missed the recording of Wu-Tang's third group album, *The W*. Ol' Dirty's problems with substance abuse became a topic for his rhymes. He guest starred on Tha Alkaholiks' "Hip-hop Drunkies," and uttered lines in his own lyrics like "I get the cocaine, it cleans out my sinuses." The antics that Dirty wrote into his lyrics were killing him in real life. The charges for which he was arrested included one in 1997 for failing to pay over a year's worth of child support on three of his alleged thirteen children. The three children were those that he shared with his wife, Icelene. In other arrests, Dirty was charged with assault (1993), shoplifting (1998), carrying drugs (1999), and even wearing a bulletproof vest (1999). California had recently enacted a law stating that it was illegal for a convicted felon to wear a bulletproof vest. Dirty was one of the first arrested under this law.

Ol' Dirty's arrests and antics only added to his legend. In October 2000, he escaped while being transported from a drug treatment center to the Los Angeles Criminal Courthouse. He remained a fugitive for nearly a month before he made a surprise appearance onstage with Wu-Tang Clan at New York's Hammerstein Ballroom. The concert was the release show for Wu-Tang's new album *The W*. RZA announced Ol' Dirty as a special guest, and he joined the Wu-Tang Clan to perform "Shame on a Nigga" before fleeing the venue. He was arrested five days later signing autographs for fans outside a McDonald's in south Philadelphia.

In February 1998, during one of the most memorable weeks of his career, ODB interrupted country singer Shawn Colvin's acceptance speech at the Grammy Awards ceremony. Climbing, uninvited, onto the stage, Dirty complained about losing to Puff Daddy in the category of Best Rap Album. Earlier that week he had announced that he was launching a clothing line, My Dirty Wear, and he had pulled a four-year-old girl from a burning car. Although he left the scene before police arrived, Dirty seemed to offer a veiled reference to his act of heroism in his impromptu speech, uttering the mysterious line, "Wu-Tang is for the children." His heroism was unfortunately overshadowed by his performance at the Grammys, which added to his image as an unpredictable, unstable rap artist.

Ol' Dirty started a trend of rappers acting out at awards shows. He connects with a similar feat pulled by MCA of the Beastie Boys at the MTV Music Awards, and preceded the infamous brawl at the 2000 Source Awards, in which Bone Thugs-N-Harmony rapper Krayzie Bone was injured, and the 2004 Vibe Awards, during which G-Unit's Young Buck stabbed a man in defense of Dr. Dre. These antics are parodied in Aaron McGruder's comic and television show *The Boondocks*, in which rappers often throw chairs at each other, and the character Eat Dirt is a caricature of Ol' Dirty Bastard.

After his release from prison in 2003, Dirty capitalized on becoming a caricature of himself. He played himself in skits on *America's Next Top Model* and MTV's *Video Music Awards*. Before his death, the men's network Spike TV filmed the first season of an Ol' Dirty Bastard reality show called *Stuck on Dirty*, in which a contestant was required to remain within ten feet of the rapper as he went through his daily life. The series has never aired, although Spike, with the blessing of Ol' Dirty's mother and his manager, has announced plans to run it in the future.

Though he is most known for *Return to the 36 Chambers*, Dirty's second solo album, *Nigga Please*, was much anticipated, and was his hip hop tribute to funk and soul. The cover art features Ol' Dirty wearing a 1970s-style track suit and sporting a long, curly wig. The sound is very different from the raw, gruff vocals of his debut album. The RZA produced only two tracks, and Wu-Tang affiliates True Master and Buddah Monk contributed mixing and production to three more, but the bulk of the album's production was done by the Neptunes: Chad Hugo and Pharrell Williams. The Neptunes' production made Dirty's sound more club friendly. He covered a Rick James song, "Cold Blooded," adding his own vocal flair over interpolations from James's original and new beats produced by the Neptunes. The hit single "Got Your Money" featured hip hop singer Kelis, who later married Nas and scored hits of her own with "Milkshake" and "Bossy." Even over the cleaner production style of the Neptunes, Dirty's lyrics remained gritty and included references to tossed salads (prison slang for analingus) and cocaine.

Dirty's third solo album, *The Trials and Tribulations of Russell Jones*, was released in 2002 while he was locked up in the Clinton Correctional Facility doing prison time and undergoing drug rehabilitation. The album was pieced together from scraps of material Dirty had recorded in the studio. In a prison interview with William Shaw, Dirty made clear that he had no part in making the album, and had not even seen the track listing or cover art.

Ol' Dirty Bastard signed to Roc-A-Fella records in 2003. On November 13, 2004, he collapsed and died in a New York City recording studio, two days before his thirty-sixth birthday, of a cocaine overdose. His death came just as two other Wu-Tang members, Ghostface Killah and Raekwon the Chef, were returning to the drug stories they had told in their earlier albums.

Even with his drug problems, Dirty was hard at work in the studio in the months preceding his death. While an official Roc-A-Fella album has yet to surface, some of his final recordings have been released by other labels, on the compilation CDs *Osirus: The Official Mixtape* and *Rest in Peace, Dirt McGirt*.

RAEKWON THE CHEF

Raekwon the Chef (Corey Woods) was given his nickname for three reasons. First, he liked to cook, and he often cooked for the other members of the Wu-Tang Clan. Second, in the Wu-Tang martial arts movies upon which the group based much of their ideology, one of the best fighters was a pudgy figure named the Chef. The final reason Raekwon was called the chef, according to RZA, was because of his flavor or style. Early on, he was the most fashion-conscious member of the group, although soon other Wu-Tang Clan members worked with him to found Wu-Wear, a new clothing line. Raekwon was also the most fluent and creative member in slang. In *The Wu-Tang Manual*, RZA asserts that Raekwon's first solo album, *Only Built 4 Cuban Linx*, "has the most slang ever in hip-hop" (21). The album title itself means "made for those in the know." RZA's book features a six-page glossary of Wu-Tang slang, much of it invented by Raekwon.

Raekwon has the honor of being the first MC heard on Wu-Tang's breakout single "C.R.E.A.M.," which brought them to MTV airplay. The track opens with spoken dialogue between Raekwon and Method Man, then launches into Raekwon's verse: "I grew up on the crime side, the New York Times side." After recording *Enter the Wu-Tang (36 Chambers)*, Raekwon stayed with Loud rather than seeking another label to release his debut single, "Heaven and Hell" in 1994. His first solo album, *Only Built 4 Cuban Linx*, was released in 1995, and it went gold within three days. The album plays like a movie from beginning to end, each track seeming to follow the previous one seamlessly, the songs woven together by samples from Italian Mafia films. *Only Built 4 Cuban Linx* is Raekwon's album, but the album cover states "guest starring Tony Starks (Ghost Face Killer)." The cover of this album was the first time that Ghostface had shown his face to the world, having previously worn a mask in all of the group's appearances. Ghostface appears on the album almost as much as Raekwon, rhyming on twelve of the eighteen tracks, and in most songs they trade verses. In the album, the two MCs take on many alter egos and comic book personas, including Raekwon's Lex Diamond. The single "Verbal Intercourse" also features Nas Escobar, an alternative persona of Nas.

Only Built 4 Cuban Linx was one of the first hip hop albums to use Mafia themes (see sidebar: Hip Hop and the Mafia). In *The Wu-Tang Manual*, RZA calls Raekwon a "master criminologist" (21). In "Incarcerated Scarfaces," Raekwon expresses respect for the Mafia. He scorns black people who get

Hip Hop and the Mafia
Mickey Hess and Jessica Elliott

On the music video for the song "Appetite for Destruction," gangsta rap group N.W.A. borrowed its imagery from another type of gang, the Italian Mafia. The video, shot in black and white, mimicked the style of classic Mafia films. The N.W.A. members dressed in suits, rather than the black baseball caps, sagging jeans, and plaid jackets they had sported in other videos to assert their association with LA gang culture. They shot tommy guns instead of the AK-47s and nine millimeters they so often brandished in their videos, press photos, and album covers. This mafia imagery was also adopted by Kool G Rap, Notorious B.I.G, Ill Bill, Scarface, and several other artists. While street gang imagery remains prevalent in gangsta rap today, with Snoop Dogg often throwing gang signs in his videos, N.W.A.'s video set the stage for a new wave of criminal imagery tied less to street gangs than to the organized crime of the Mafia. Even as he maintains his gang allegiance in videos, Snoop has embraced Mafia imagery as well; his album *The Doggfather* played on Francis Ford Coppola's *Godfather* films.

Wu-Tang Clan is another group that adopted new Mafioso personas as the Wu-Gambinos for their second album *Wu-Tang Forever*. This album picked up on the Mafia imagery that featured prominently in Raekwon the Chef's solo album, *Only Built 4 Cuban Linx*. On that album, Wu-Tang members Raekwon and Ghostface Killah referenced Mafia figures in their lyrics and samples, presenting the gangster as a ruthless but glamorous underdog figure who got rich through crime. In the song "Incarcerated Scarfaces" from his album *Only Built 4 Cuban Linx*, Raekwon the Chef expresses his respect for Mafia members with the line, "Word up, peace, incarcerated Scarfaces." The film *Scarface*, which tells the story of fictional Cuban-born mafioso Tony Montana, is a favorite of Ghostface Killah and Raekwon. The film is also widely sampled by artists like Ill Bill. The figure of the Mafia don carries more wealth than the figure of the street thug, and as hip hop became big business, several artists started to promote themselves as dons who enjoyed the spoils of crime while removed from the streets.

money and forget where they came from, stating, "Guess who's the black Trump?" This is a reflection on his success as an artist who earned his money by staying connected to his time growing up in the projects. The song references the film *Scarface*, in which Tony Montana (played by Al Pacino) rises from low status as a Cuban immigrant to Mafia don.

Despite this focus on staying true to his roots, Raekwon appeared to turn his back on the Wu-Tang Clan in producing his second solo album, *Immobilarity* (1999). Between his first and second solo albums, Raekwon had appeared with fellow Wu-Tangers in the film *Black and White* and worked with the rest of the group on the second Wu-Tang Clan album,

Wu-Tang Forever. When it came to recording *Immobilarity*, though, Raekwon became impatient with RZA's busy schedule and his own place in line among the other members of the clan. So instead of waiting for RZA's production and signature sound, Raekwon chose to use other producers, many of whom had just gotten into the field but hadn't yet made names for themselves. Several tracks were produced by Triflyn, a member of American Cream Team, a new group assembled by Raekwon. Further asserting his independence, Raekwon avoided Ghostface's guest star role on *Immobilarity*. Ghostface wasn't featured on a single track, but Method Man and Masta Killa did make one appearance each. *Immobilarity* is almost exclusively MCed by Raekwon, with the exception of the two verses by Method Man and Masta Killa, and cameos by American Cream Team and Big Bub.

Raekwon's first album, *Only Built 4 Cuban Linx*, relied heavily on Mafia themes and drug-dealing scenarios and became a classic in the subgenre of cocaine rap. Yet without RZA's production, Raekwon's commercial success faltered in his subsequent albums. *Immobilarity* and *The Lex Diamond Story* established more distance between Raekwon and Wu-Tang Clan, but they made less of an impact commercially, leaving many listeners to wonder if RZA's work in the studio formed a key part of Raekwon's appeal as an MC. Raekwon reunited with the Wu-Tang Clan in 2000 and 2001 to make the albums *The W* and *Iron Flag*, and even though he had worked with outside producers, *Immobilarity* did not signal a rift between Raekwon and Ghostface. Raekwon appeared on tracks on Ghostface's solo albums *Ironman* and *Bulletproof Wallets*, and Ghostface appeared on two tracks from Raekwon's third solo album, 2003's *The Lex Diamond Story*, which tells the story of Raekwon's comic book character alter ego.

Raekwon spent 2006 producing three mixtapes: *Vatican*, *Da Vinci Code: Vatican Mixtape V2*, and, with DJ Thoro, *Heroin Only*. He also appears on an Ill Bill mixtape released that same year. Listeners speculate that these tapes contain rough versions of songs that will eventually be released on Raekwon's forthcoming fourth solo album, *Only Built 4 Cuban Linx II*, which promises production from RZA and Dr. Dre as well as an appearance by Ghostface. Raekwon promises that this *Cuban Linx* sequel will be a return to the style of his debut album, and the music for which he is most respected. He released rough versions of several new tracks in 2006 on his *Vatican* and *Vatican II* mixtapes. Raekwon released these mixtapes in limited quantity on his own Ice Water Records, in order to build hype for his new album. A release date for *Only Built 4 Cuban Linx II* has not been announced.

GHOSTFACE KILLAH

Ghostface Killah (Dennis Coles) wore a mask in the photos included in *Enter the Wu-Tang* and in each video from the clan's first album. The rumor was that he had warrants and didn't want to be recognized by the authorities, but his image created a new feature of hip hop, the secret identity. The secret identity and mask would be picked up by underground artist MF DOOM, who would later collaborate with Ghostface on his 2006 album *Fishscale*, and on Cartoon Network's *Dangerdoom* album, for which Ghostface and MF DOOM recorded "The Mask." Ghostface grew up reading comic books and alternatively calls himself Tony Starks, the billionaire whose secret identity is the superhero Ironman (see sidebar: Hip Hop and Comic Books). Ghostface Killah revealed his face to the world on the cover of Raekwon's album *Only Built 4 Cuban Linx*.

Hip Hop and Comic Books
Mickey Hess and Jessica Elliott

Ghostface Killah borrowed the Marvel character Ironman for the title of his debut album. In keeping with Ghostface's fascination with secret identities (he wore a mask in all the publicity photos taken for Wu-Tang Clan's first album), he often calls himself not only Ironman but Tony Starks, the billionaire who secretly fights evil as Ironman.

Ghostface is not the only Wu-Tang member to create a comic book hero (or villain) identity. RZA's comic book personality is Bobby Digital. Raekwon's is Lex Diamond. RZA explains the relationship between rappers and comic book characters in *The Wu-Tang Manual*, saying that growing up with a single parent in the projects, kids often want to imagine a powerful, protective second self. They read comic books and want to find the superhero within. Clark Kent was a completely different person than Superman, just as Tony Starks is a completely different person than Ironman, and Bobby Digital is a completely different person than RZA. Bobby Digital was RZA's public way to be the person he grew up as rather than the rap star.

In 1999, the Wu-Tang Clan developed its own comic book series. In it, each member is portrayed as his comic book persona, and each member had a say in his character. Method Man appears in the series as MZA, Ol' Dirty Bastard as Osirus, and U-God as Golden Arms. This trend of MCs borrowing identities from comic books extends beyond Wu-Tang Clan. Deltron 3030, an alter ego of Del the Funky Homosapien, is a futuristic rap superhero. MF DOOM borrows both his name and disguise from Marvel Comics' Dr. Doom. DOOM, one of underground hip hop's hottest MCs and producers, has become a Wu affiliate as well as an honorary member of Spitkickers, the collective consisting of De La Soul, Talib Kweli, A Tribe Called Quest, Dave Chappelle, and many other entertainers. DOOM has worked with RZA on a track for Think Differently's *Wu-Tang Meets Indie Culture*, and produced tracks for Ghostface's *Fishscale*.

Further Resources

Drumming, Neil. "The Nerd Behind the Mask." *Village Voice* 46.32. 14 August
   2001.
Goedde, Brian. "Behind the Iron Mask: MF DOOM Faces Art's Volatility." *The
   Stranger*. 16 August 2001. 9 September 2002. http://www.thestranger.com/
   2001-08-16/music3.html.
Singer, Marc. "Black Skins and White Masks: Comic Books and the Secret of Race."
   African American Review 36.1: 107–119.

Ghostface's first solo album, *Ironman*, introduced the superhero persona he
borrowed from Marvel Comics. This album's standout single was the pensive
"All That I Got (Is You)," a tribute to Ghostface's mother, who kept her large
family together after Ghostface's father left home when his son was six years
old. Like Tupac's album *Strictly for my N.I.G.G.A.Z.*, Ghostface's *Ironman*
shifts from a tribute to his mother to songs that disrespect women, including a
revenge fantasy on an ex-girlfriend. In other songs, the album continues the
samples of blaxploitation films and gangster films like *Scarface* that had begun on *Only Built 4 Cuban Linx*.

Ghostface's second album, *Supreme Clientele*, marks his maturation as an
MC. Working closely with RZA as well as producers DJ Premier and the
Beatnuts, Ghostface delivers an album full of complex wordplay. The use of
horns on songs like "Apollo Kids" and *Ironman*'s "260," a track built around
a sample of horns from an Al Green song, makes his urgent vocal delivery
sound more dramatic. From buying sneakers from a street vendor ("Apollo
Kids") to jumping off ledges ("Ghost Deini") to dissing Sony Record Executive Tommy Mottola ("Cherchez la Ghost"), Ghostface shows his range of
topics and styles.

By 2006, Ghost had matched RZA's level as the most productive member
of the Wu-Tang Clan, and he remains one of the most inventive. Ghostface is
now working with a crew called the Theodore Unit, which includes up-and-
coming MC Trife da God. In 2005 and 2006, Ghost appeared in a series of
MTV2 commercials called "The World According to Pretty Toney," where he
spoke about such topics as stretching his dollars to buy food in his younger
days. Ghostface appeared on a 2005 episode of MTV's *Made*, in which
Blizzard, a sixteen-year-old hopeful MC visits Ghost in the recording studio.
Ghost shows him a stack of notebooks and encourages him to write every
day. This advice fit with Ghost's own agenda. Between 2004 and 2006, he
released two full-length solo albums, *The Pretty Toney Album* and *Fishscale*,
as well as a Theodore Unit album and a Ghostface and Trife da God album,
each of which featured Ghostface's vocals and production work.

On 2006's *Fishscale*, Ghostface worked with producers Pete Rock, MF
DOOM, and J Dilla. Dilla died from a lupus-related illness before *Fishscale*
was released, and shortly after the release of his own album, *Donuts*.

Dilla, only thirty-three years old, was part of Slum Village and the production team the Umma, which first gained fame for its work on the Pharcyde's *Bizarre Ride II the Pharcyde* and A Tribe Called Quest's fourth album, *Beats, Rhymes, and Life*. His production relied heavily on samples of sixties and seventies funk, soul, and R&B, and added a new level of dramatics to Ghostface's music. Pete Rock, producer and half of the group Pete Rock and CL Smooth, created an upbeat club hit and mixtape favorite with his track for Ghostface's "Be Easy." *Fishscale* is named for a form of pure, uncut heroin, the title indicating that Ghostface was returning to his roots with raw, straight-ahead rhymes and beats. Aside from providing a metaphor for his music style, *Fishscale* also returns to the stories of drug trafficking for which Ghostface was known on Raekwon's *Only Built 4 Cuban Linx* and his own *Ironman*.

METHOD MAN

Method Man (Clifford Sparks) also goes by Johnny Blaze, Ticalian Stallion, and Mef. He spent his childhood between his father's home on Long Island and his mother's home on Staten Island, where he'd meet fellow members of the Wu-Tang Clan. Method Man went on to become one of the most recognizable members of the group, in part because of the track titled "Method Man" from *Enter the Wu-Tang*. The song stands out on Wu-Tang's debut album as a radio-friendly alternative to the darker, grittier sound of the rest of the album. Adapting the chorus from Hall and Oates's "Method of Modern Love," Method Man begins his song chanting "M-E-T-H-O-D *Man*." This single established Method Man's potential to cross over to the pop charts while maintaining his hip hop credentials with Wu-Tang. As one of the most radio-friendly members of the group, Method Man is careful never to stray too far from the dark, gritty production for which RZA and Wu-Tang are known. His first solo album, *Tical*, returns to this sound and relies heavily on beats produced by RZA.

Method Man was the first Wu-Tang member to release a solo album after the group's debut, *Enter the Wu-Tang*. Taking advantage of the flexibility of the group's record contract with Loud, he signed as a solo artist to the legendary Def Jam label. Ghostface Killah would follow his bandmate to Def Jam with 2004's *The Pretty Toney Album*, after working with a series of other labels. As a breakout solo artist, Method Man emphasized that he remained a member of Wu-Tang Clan. The cover of his debut album featured the Wu-Tang logo's W flipped to form an M. This visual consistency with the Wu-Tang logo would continue with GZA's solo album and later with Raekwon and Masta Killa. As the first solo album from a Wu-Tang member since the group officially formed, *Tical* featured Method Man's fellow Wu-Tang members prominently. One track, "Meth vs. Chef" featured a studio rhyme battle between Method Man and Raekwon. The message was clear: Method Man had not left Wu-Tang to pursue a solo album. Instead, his solo album was an extension of the Wu-Tang Clan's overall musical project.

In keeping with the Wu-Tang's focus on taking New York City rhyme styles new places and Method Man's own "mad different methods," *Tical* begins with the line "I got styles, all of 'em sick." *Tical* celebrates Method Man's love of marijuana and his loyalty to his girlfriend. In the music video for "All I Need," Method Man robs a convenience store to steal a box of tampons for her. *Tical* had platinum sales, and its single, "Bring the Pain," just missed reaching Top 40 status. Method Man released a second single, "I'll Be There for You/You're All I Need to Get By," which featured R&B singer Mary J. Blige. The song made it into the pop Top 5 and gave Method Man major commercial exposure. As a Def Jam artist, Method Man began to work with Redman, a loud, funny MC from Newark, New Jersey. Redman was discovered by Erick Sermon of EPMD, and rhymed with Sermon's Def Squad, a group of three MCs (Sermon, Redman, and Keith Murray), who scored a hit with their cover of Sugarhill Gang's "Rapper's Delight." In November 1994, Def Jam released Method Man's *Tical* and Redman's *Dare Iz a Darkside* one week apart.

On the Wu-Tang Clan's live DVD, *Disciples of the 36 Chambers*, Redman joins Method Man onstage to perform "Da Rockwilder." In 1995, Method Man recorded the single "How High" with Redman, and it made it into Billboard's Top 20. In 1999, Redman and Method Man collaborated to release an album, *BlackOut*, which showcased how well their rhyme styles and senses of humor fit together. In videos, the duo dressed up like the Blues Brothers and like Beavis and Butthead. Redman and Method Man went on to work together on a film, *How High*, and a short-lived television sitcom, *Method and Red*. *How High* is a college film in the tradition of *Animal House*, and the cinema format allowed Method Man and Redman to showcase their irreverent drug humor farther than the Fox Network censors could allow on *Method and Red*.

Method Man's acting skills are not limited to comedy. After the release of Wu-Tang's group album *The W*, Method Man spent a lot of time trying to launch his acting career. His first major acting role was in Hype Williams's 1998 film *Belly*. In 2001, Method Man played a character on the HBO series *Oz*. In 2003, he played himself alongside other Wu members in *Scary Movie 3*. In 2004, he had roles in *My Baby's Daddy*, *Garden State*, and *Soul Plane*.

Method Man released his second solo album, *Tical 2000: Judgement Day*, in 1998. This album features both a variety of guest rappers and producers and skits between songs. *Tical 2000: Judgement Day* focuses its songs and lyrics on the Armageddon that many people believed would occur at the turn of the millennium. In the album's cover art and the music video for the title track, "Judgement Day," Method Man borrows futuristic, postapocalyptic images from sources such as the *Mad Max* film trilogy to present a world destroyed by war and disease. The album, like so many Wu-Tang albums, begins with a lengthy spoken narration in which Method Man describes the bombs, pestilence, and death that set the scene for the songs on his album. Songs like "Perfect World," featuring Lisa "Left Eye" Lopes of TLC fame, extend this theme of a world destroyed. Even with the dark themes that drive the album, Method Man also maintains the humor for which he became known on Wu-Tang's debut album and in his acting career. The album features several skits with celebrity guests such as Chris Rock, Janet Jackson, and Donald Trump.

Method Man's third solo album, *Tical 0: The Prequel*, was released in 2004. Though he had recorded twenty RZA-produced tracks for the album, Def Jam decided to include only one of those on the final copy. Though this album contained the successful single, "What's Happenin'," featuring Busta Rhymes, it was not well received by his fans. Meth later complained that Def Jam had too much influence on the album's direction. It had a commercialized sound and featured guest rappers Missy Elliott, P. Diddy, and Ludacris. Method Man's fourth solo album, *4:21 . . . The Day After*, was released in 2006.

INSPECTAH DECK

Inspectah Deck (Jason Hunter) is one of the less prominent solo members of the Wu-Tang Clan, yet his verses on the group's albums are some of the more memorable. Deck got his nickname because of his quiet and thoughtful demeanor. He was a part of all of the Wu-Tang group albums, but he was featured more prominently in the group's first two albums, MCing in hit singles "C.R.E.A.M." and "Protect Your Neck." His verse begins "Triumph," the epic first single from Wu-Tang's highly anticipated sophomore album, *Wu-Tang Forever*. Deck's line, "I bomb atomically," which opens that song, initiates one of the classic rhymes associated with Wu-Tang Clan.

Deck was born in Brooklyn but grew up in Staten Island, where he attended school with some of the other members of the Wu-Tang Clan. He lived in the Park Hill projects at 160, an address that comes up in many Wu-Tang lyrics, often pronounced "one-six-ooh." In *The Wu-Tang Manual*, RZA explains that 160 was the best place to get weed in Staten Island. Anyone who smoked would go to 160 to get their weed, and this is where Deck lived. He had just been released from prison when the group started recording their debut album.

Deck, along with U-God and Masta Killa, was one of the last three group members to release a solo album. His album, *Uncontrolled Substance*, was originally scheduled for release in 1995 but was not actually released until 1999. However, besides working on the group albums, Deck was featured on many of the other members' solo albums, including Raekwon's *Only Built 4*

Cuban Linx and GZA's *Liquid Swords*. Inspectah Deck is both an MC and a producer. He produced the track "Visionz" from the Wu-Tang Clan's 1997 album *Wu-Tang Forever*. He also produced most of his first solo album, *Uncontrolled Substance*, which heavily featured other Wu-Tang members. It was well received and made it into the Top 5 on the R&B music charts. It was completely different from most of the other Wu-Tang solo and group albums in that its style was influenced by 1970s funk. When Deck released his second solo album, *The Movement*, in 2003, he moved away from the funk style and created an album that would be better accepted commercially.

In between his first and second albums, Deck helped to produce some tracks and MC some verses in GZA's *Beneath the Surface*, RZA's *Bobby Digital in Stereo*, and Method Man's *Tical 2000: Judgement Day*. Additionally, he played himself in the 1998 movie *Black and White*. Though it was attributed to the entire group, he produced and MCed the song "Let Me at Them" from the soundtrack for the 1995 movie *Tales from the Hood*.

MASTA KILLA

Masta Killa (Elgin Turner) was the only member of the Wu-Tang Clan who wasn't an MC before the group was formed. He was the last of the nine members to join Wu-Tang, and he narrowly beat out Killah Priest to record a verse for *Enter the Wu-Tang*'s "Da Mystery of Chessboxin'." At the time the album was produced, he was in prison, so that was the only song in which he appeared on Wu-Tang's debut. However, after he was released from prison, he contributed to all of the Wu-Tang albums that followed. Within the Wu-Tang Clan, a group dedicated to dominating the record industry, Masta Killa provides fewer vocals than any of the other members.

Masta Killa also was the last of Wu-Tang's nine members to release a solo album. As a comment on his laid-back approach to making the record, he titled his debut album *No Said Date*. On the title track, a voice asks Masta Killa when his album is dropping, and he replies "No said date." This album finally debuted in 2004, more than a decade after the release of Wu-Tang's first group album. Masta Killa's vocal style matches his approach to his career. Out of Wu-Tang's nine MCs, his delivery is most laid-back. Standing in stark opposition to Method Man's energy, Ghostface and RZA's urgency, or Ol' Dirty Bastard's frenzy, Masta Killa's vocals take on a very casual sound. His subject matter and fashion style are also distinctive within the group. While he isn't the oldest member of the clan—GZA was born in 1966, three years earlier—Masta Killa often comments on his age in lyrics, in lines like "I was rollin', showing my age, unshaven" and on "D.T.D.," where he says, "Got the old man feeling twenty-three."

Aside from Wu-Tang releases, Masta Killa has been involved in a lot of projects in the music industry, collaborating with Afu-Ra, Bounty Killer, and

---

Vegetarian Rappers
Danielle Hess

Vegetarianism is not a subject typically paired with hip hop. However, there are over a dozen rappers and producers who refuse to eat meat, including Andre 3000, Jeru the Damaja, Common, Prodigy of Mobb Deep, KRS-One, and Wu-Tang Clan's Masta Killa and RZA. Many hip hop stars such as Ice Cube follow Islamic dietary guidelines that omit pork from their diets, and Muslim rappers Mos Def and Q-Tip are entirely vegetarian. The dead prez song "Be Healthy" boasts the health benefits of vegetarianism and speaks out against the poor lifestyle decisions made in black America regarding food and drink.

Russell Simmons, cofounder of Def Jam and a hip hop producer and impresario, is a vegan who is a member of PETA's campaign against Kentucky Fried Chicken and has been very vocal against slaughterhouses and factory farms. Simmons provided some of his favorite recipes for vegan versions of the soul food staples hush puppies, ribs, hoppin' John, and sweet potato pie for the spring 2000 issue of *PETA's Animal Times,* a magazine mailed to their members. While serving as the founder and manager of his hip hop clothing company Phat Farm, Simmons was asked to design new uniforms for McDonald's to boost their image. He immediately issued a press release noting that he would never work with the fast-food restaurant since it is against his vegan lifestyle. Ironically, Phat Farm Shoes did market a line of leather goods while under Simmons's management.

Public Enemy. In the film industry, he played himself in the 1999 film, *Black and White.* In 2006, Masta Killa joined forces with PETA (People for the Ethical Treatment of Animals), creating advertisements explaining his stance against eating meat and wearing fur. His vegetarianism extends to his lyrics as well; on fellow vegetarian RZA's song "Grits," Masta Killa touts Morningstar veggie bacon (see sidebar: Vegetarian Rappers).

U-GOD

U-God (Lamont Hawkins) was the eighth Wu-Tang member to release a solo album. *Golden Arms Redemption*, released in 1999, was an album, like those of RZA, Raekwon, and Ghostface, that was written as his comic book personality, Golden Arms. U-God was in jail for drug possession during most of the recording of *Enter the Wu-Tang (36 Chambers)* but was released in time to be included in the recording of two tracks: "Protect Your Neck" and "Da Mystery of Chessboxin'." His verse sets off "Chessboxin'" with U-God's signature growl: "Raw I'mma give it to ya." This gruff delivery made him a prominent MC on the group's second album, *Wu-Tang Forever.* In the video for "Triumph," U-God rhymes while hanging by one arm from a burning tree.

On one track from *Wu-Tang Forever*, "A Better Tomorrow," U-God raps about how his son was accidentally shot and injured. In his lyrics, U-God expresses remorse for his own actions that he felt contributed to his son's injury. With 2001's *The W*, U-God shone on a remix of "The Jump Off," a song that featured all of the Wu-Tang members except for Ol' Dirty Bastard. As U-God's verse begins, RZA fades out all the music except for the sparse drumbeat that forms the backbone of the track. U-God's rhythm over nothing but drums recalls earlier days of MCs rhyming over breakbeats or drum machines, and RZA's technique of dropping out the horns and guitar show-cases the uniqueness of U-God's flow.

In *The Wu-Tang Manual*, RZA asserts that U-God is known for his temper. In 2004, U-God engaged in a very public battle with RZA over royalties. Their disagreement was aired over the radio, and RZA later claimed that U-God had started the argument as a publicity stunt. However, U-God later went on to record the album, *Ugodz-Illa Presents: The Hillside Scramblers*, with four other MCs. He also released a DVD, *Rise of a Fallen Soldier*, that documented his complaints against RZA and the Wu-Tang Clan.

U-God and RZA eventually reconciled their disagreements, and U-God went on tour with Wu-Tang in the summer of 2004. In 2005, he released his second solo album, *Mr. Xcitement*. Soon afterward, he again started a dispute with RZA but resolved it in time to be a part of Wu-Tang's Ol' Dirty Bastard memorial tour in 2006.

THE WU SAGA CONTINUES

Wu-Tang's legacy is built not only from the vocal talents of its nine MCs and the innovative production of RZA but from a business model that centers on the strength of the collective. Hip hop is a very collaborative form, with groups often including the terms clique (often spelled "click" in hip hop circles), clan, crew, squad, camp, unit, and posse in their names. Collectives such as Marley Marl's Juice Crew, 50 Cent's G-Unit, Buckshot's Boot Camp Click, Outkast's Dungeon Family, Michael Watts's Swisha House, and Del the Funky Homosapien's Hieroglyphics center on a tight-knit group of artists, bound together by a common hip hop aesthetic.

The 2001 hit "The Jump Off" proved that Wu-Tang Clan still could pro-duce a posse cut. Although Ol' Dirty Bastard was in prison at the time of the recording, Inspectah Deck references him in lyrics, suggesting that the group will send half the song's profits to their incarcerated bandmate. Dirty also is absent from the back cover photo of Wu-Tang Clan on *The W*. RZA, posed in the middle of the shot, holds a black bandana with his cousin's hip hop initials: "ODB."

On July 17, 2004, Wu-Tang Clan recorded a live concert in San Bernadino, California, for the DVD *Disciples of the 36 Chambers*. This was the first show that all nine Wu-Tang members had come together for in seven years, and it would prove to be the group's last. Outside the stadium, fans were surprised to learn that Ol' Dirty Bastard would perform on stage with Wu-Tang. He had begun to skip out on concert appearances with the group, and in an interview featured on the DVD, RZA says that while ODB had wanted to remain in his hotel room, other group members encouraged him to perform. In the concert footage, Ol' Dirty Bastard was visibly deteriorating. He had been out of prison for just over a year. He was wearing his new Roc-A-Fella Records shirt, and he spent most of the concert sitting down. At times he appeared exhausted, confused, and disoriented. Unlike the other Wu-Tang members, the DVD features no interviews with Ol' Dirty, who died less than four months later. Ghostface Killah pays tribute to ODB by performing his "Shimmy Shimmy Ya" in concert footage included on the 2005 Ghostface and Trife da God CD and DVD *Put It on the Line*, released by Ghost's own Starks Enterprises label.

Wu-Tang's legacy is secured with their mainstream sales and their underground credibility. In 2005, Dreddy Kruger produced *Wu-Tang Meets Indie Culture*, a CD that paired Wu-Tang MCs with artists from the world of underground hip hop, including MF DOOM and Del the Funky Homosapien. Members of the Wu-Tang Clan have been highly successful, both as a group and as solo artists, but it hasn't been without struggle. After making an abrupt exit from their tour with Rage Against the Machine in 1997, the group was sued by a record store employee who alleged that four members of the group had beaten and robbed him after an August concert in Illinois. During the same tour, they were charged when, after asking people to get on stage, people rushed onto the floor, and many attendees were hurt. These charges were later dropped. In 1998, the group was sued by a dancer who was hired to appear in one of their videos. She claimed that members of the group made derogatory comments about her and held her against her will. In 2000, the group was sued by their lawyer for breach of contract after they failed to pay the legal fees that accrued during the lawsuit brought by the dancer. Then there were the many legal problems for the individual group members, particularly Ol' Dirty Bastard.

In 2005, the Wu-Tang Clan regrouped to create a new album, their first since Ol' Dirty Bastard's death. Though they recorded a few songs, the album was cancelled, or postponed, due to scheduling conflicts. It's been reported that some of the tracks they recorded will be included on Raekwon's *Only Built 4 Cuban Linx II*. In 2006, Wu-Tang Clan grouped together to form a tour, also the first without Ol' Dirty Bastard. The tour lasted less than two weeks in February 2006, and it was dedicated in memory of Ol' Dirty Bastard. The group wanted to celebrate ODB's life and prove that, even though they'd lost one of their members, they were still connected as a group. A part of the proceeds of the ticket sales from the tour were donated to ODB's family. In an interview with Shaheem Reid of MTV News, Raekwon explained that he thinks ODB would have wanted the group to continue working together in order to make a living. "At the end of the day," he said, "the show must go on."

See also: The Geto Boys, Nas

WORKS CITED

Reid, Shaheem. "Raekwon Linx up with Busta, RZA; Wu-Tang Dedicate Tour to ODB." *MTV News.com.* 11 January 2006. http://www.mtv.com/news/articles/1520591/20060111/wutangclan.jhtml?headlines=true.
RZA. *The Wu-Tang Manual.* New York: Penguin, 2004.
Shaw, William. "Portrait of an Artist in Jail." *The Guardian.* 22 March 2002. http://www.guardian.co.uk/friday_review/story/0,3605,671387,00.html.
Wu-Tang Clan. *Disciples of the 36 Chambers.* DVD. Sanctuary, 2004.

FURTHER RESOURCES

Masta Killa. http://www.mastakilla.net.
Wu-Tang Clan. *Legend of the Wu-Tang: The Videos.* Loud, 2006. http://www.sonymusic.com/labels/loud/wutang.
Wu-Tang Corp. The Official Site of the Wu-Tang Clan. http://www.wutangcorp.com.

SELECTED DISCOGRAPHY

Wu-Tang Clan

Enter the Wu-Tang (36 Chambers). Loud/Columbia, 1993.
Wu-Tang Forever. Loud/Columbia, 1997.
The W. Loud/Columbia, 2000.
Iron Flag. Loud/Columbia, 2001.

Method Man

Tical. Def Jam, 1994.
Tical 2000: Judgement Day. Def Jam, 1998.
Tical 0: The Prequel. Def Jam, 2004.
4:21 . . . The Day After. Def Jam, 2006.

Inspectah Deck

Uncontrolled Substance. Loud, 1999.
The Movement. Koch, 2003.

Raekwon

Only Built 4 Cuban Linx. Loud, 1995.
Immobilarity. Loud, 1999.
The Lex Diamond Story. UMvd, 2003.
Vol 1: The Vatican. Ice Water, 2006.
The Da Vinci Code: The Vatican Mixtape V2. Ice Water, 2006.

GZA

Liquid Swords. Geffen, 1995.
Beneath the Surface. MCA, 1999.
Legend of the Liquid Sword. MCA, 2002.
GZA and DJ Muggs. *Grandmasters.* Angeles, 2005.

Masta Killa

No Said Date. Nature Sounds, 2004.
Made in Brooklyn. Nature Sounds, 2006.

RZA

RZA as Bobby Digital in Stereo. Gee Street, 1998.
Digital Bullet. Koch, 2001.
Birth of a Prince. Sanctuary, 2003.
The World According to RZA. EMI/Virgin, 2003.

Ol' Dirty Bastard

Return to the 36 Chambers (The Dirty Version). Elektra, 1995.
Nigga Please. Elektra, 1999.
Osirus: The Official Mixtape. JC, 2004.

Ghostface Killah

Ironman. Sony, 1996.
Supreme Clientele. Sony, 2000.
Bulletproof Wallets. Sony, 2001.
The Pretty Toney Album. Def Jam, 2004.
Fishscale. Def Jam, 2006.
More Fish. Def Jam, 2007.
Ghostface Killah and Trife da God. *Put It On the Line.* Starks Enterprises, 2005.
Theodore Unit. *718.* Sure Shot, 2004.

U-God

Golden Arms Redemption. Priority, 1999.
Mr. Xcitement. Free Agency Media, 2005.

Courtesy of Photofest.

Tupac Shakur

Carlos D. Morrison and Celnisha L. Dangerfield

Rapper. Actor. Poet. Dancer. Thug. Rival. Change agent. Icon. No one can deny the complexities of the late Tupac Amaru Shakur. While he was respected by many for his thug anthems, he was equally loved and hated for his lyrics about women (some inspiringly positive, others dreadfully negative), his willingness to speak his mind, and his ability to share his lived experience through the eloquent imagery evident in his music, in his poetry, and even in his movie roles. Tupac lived a life that exemplified contrast and, even in death, the contradiction that is Tupac Shakur continues to raise questions and fuel debates about his actions and choices in life. After his death, Tupac has managed to increase his fan base as loyal listeners have shared his music with others and introduced a new generation to Tupac through his poetry and his posthumous music releases.

There is something about Tupac that lives on. His murder could not destroy his music, and that truth lies in the fact that he became bigger than the East Coast–West Coast feud he helped to create (see sidebar: East Coast versus West Coast), bigger than his music and his personal style, even bigger than

---

East Coast versus West Coast
Carlos D. Morrison and Celnisha L. Dangerfield

Although Tupac was born and raised on the East Coast, he had strong allegiance to the West Coast. In fact, in many ways he became the face of the West Coast with songs such as "California Love" and "To Live and Die in L. A." In addition, Tupac managed to become the unofficial representative of Death Row Records (especially after the departure of superproducer Dr. Dre). It should not have been a surprise then that a feud between Tupac and Biggie would evolve into a feud between Death Row Records and Bad Boy Records, and eventually create a binary split between hip hop music on two coasts. While rivalries among hip hop artists have been a part of the culture since its inception in the 1970s, none captured more attention than the East Coast–West Coast feud that began as a personal beef between Tupac and Biggie. Many speculate that the media coverage played a large part in hyping the growing feud, but in any case, the East Coast–West Coast feud would be felt by hip hop heads worldwide.

On November 30, 1994, Tupac was shot five times at a New York recording studio. He publicly blamed Biggie Smalls and Bad Boy Records for the shooting. The two record labels, Bad Boy and Death Row, were thrown into conflict as a result. This feud escalated after Suge Knight taunted Sean (Puffy) at the Source Awards in August 1995. Biggie added fuel to the fire with the song "Who Shot Ya," while Tupac retaliated with "Hit 'Em Up" and "Bomb First (My Second Reply)."

On September 7, 1996, Tupac was shot several times as he rode in a car with Suge Knight in Las Vegas; he died seven days later. About six months later, on March 9, 1997, Biggie was shot and killed in California. Both murders remain unsolved, and numerous theories have surfaced about what happened to each of the slain rappers. Some propose that Biggie had something to do with Tupac's death, while others believe that someone from Tupac's camp killed Biggie as payback.

While the East Coast–West Coast feud ended with the death of two grand contributors to hip hop, one of the positive legacies that remain from the feud is the determination to keep other artists from trudging down that same negative path. Since the days of the feud, artists such as JaRule and 50 Cent and Nas and Jay-Z have had beef, but they have managed either to squash their differences or, at the very least, confine their squabbles to the lyrics of their songs.

Further Resources

Bruno, Anthony. "Gangstas." Court TV Crime Library. 2005. Courtroom Television Network LLC. http://www.crimelibrary.com/notoriousmurders/celebrity/shakurBIG/index.html.

Court TV Crime Library. "East Coast vs. West Coast." Court TV Crime Library. 2005. Courtroom Television Network LLC. http://www.crimelibrary.com/notoriousmurders/celebrity/shakurBIG/2.html.

hip hop. How else can one explain how a dead man can release eight albums and sell millions after his passing? This unusual feat has put him in the ranks of deceased stars who inspire conspiracy theories and a belief that, like Elvis, Tupac still lives. Although it has been ten years since his death in Las Vegas, Nevada, Tupac lives on as a mythic figure in the minds and hearts of hip hop heads worldwide. While some simply viewed him as a one-sided individual, in reality Tupac—especially as analyzed after his death—has proven to be a compartmentalized being that, when studied in totality, demonstrates a life filled with contradiction. Through an exploration of his formative years, his contributions to hip hop, his influence on society at large, and the contradictions in his nature that made his name a household word, one gets a glimpse of the factors that have led to his iconic status in popular culture.

TUPAC SHAKUR: THE FORMATIVE YEARS

While Tupac would later claim allegiance to, and love for, the West Coast, his earlier life centered on the East Coast. Tupac was born in Brooklyn, New York, in 1971 to Afeni Shakur, who, at the time of her son's birth was a member of the Black Panthers. She named him "after an Incan chief, *Tupac Amaru* [which] means 'shining serpent,' referring to wisdom and courage. *Shakur* is Arabic for 'thankful to God'" (Powell 22). As a young man, Tupac lived in a poor, female-headed household. He was exposed to crime and criminals, even within his own household. Yet despite the challenges he faced, at the age of twelve Tupac began to work with a New York acting guild. The young thespian would continue to sharpen his acting skills when the family relocated to Baltimore, Maryland, in 1986.

The family moved to Charm City because of the promise of better job opportunities for Afeni Shakur. While living there, Tupac attended the Baltimore School for Performing Arts, where he developed a greater appreciation for the arts, poetry, ballet, and jazz. He continued to hone his skills as an actor and was exposed to great literature including the work of William Shakespeare. Tupac was highly driven and showed promise at the school. He also developed a lasting friendship with another young student and budding thespian, Jada Pinkett. Both Pinkett and Shakur were highly driven, very opinionated and passionate about their work to the point that they often bumped heads. Nevertheless, Shakur and Pinkett developed an admiration and respect for each other's talents and abilities that would have a lasting effect on their lives. Jada would go on to work on the television series *A Different World* and star in several movies, including *Jason's Lyric* (1994), *Set It Off* (1996), *The Nutty Professor* (1996), *The Matrix Reloaded* (2003), *The Matrix Revolution* (2003), and *Collateral* (2004). She married actor-rapper Will Smith in 1997; the couple have two children and are raising Will's son from a previous marriage. Jada is now a member of the music group Wicked Wisdom and serves as an executive producer for the sitcom *All of Us*, a show loosely based on the experiences of her family.

Even though Tupac thrived at the performing arts school, he was unable to finish his training due to mounting concerns at home. Although Afeni Shakur moved to Baltimore to find stable employment and support her children, her battle with drug addiction created great tension between her and Tupac. The mounting violence on the streets of Baltimore also contributed to Tupac's inability to stay focused on his work and to stay out of trouble. Given the severity of the situation, it was now time for Shakur to leave Baltimore and the East Coast. Yet the events that precipitated this move would be revisited later in his life as content for some of Tupac's songs. In work such as "Dear Mama," Tupac dealt with his childhood poverty and his mother's drug addiction. However, Tupac's deep respect for his mother's achievement in raising two kids on her own, and without the benefit of much money, surpass the negative memories of his mother. In fact, "Dear Mama" is a tribute to her and a testament to her strength. In the song's lyrics, Tupac tells his mother "You are appreciated" (see sidebar: The Mama Complex).

The Mama Complex
Carlos D. Morrison and Celnisha L. Dangerfield

Even the hardest gangsta rapper could rhyme about shooting someone fifty times and still show reverence for his mama on the next track. Yes, the mama complex is in full effect. She is often the only woman that a rapper may seem to care about, for in the face of adversity the mother figure often stands as the only representation of security, order, and strength. It is no secret that African American households are disproportionately headed by single females. Often, African American women find themselves in situations where they must be both mother and father. The struggles that the African American mother must endure to ensure that her children's needs are met are apparently never forgotten. All of the attention is thus given to the mother-head and she becomes an eternal symbol of love.

The lyrics to Tupac's "Dear Mama" support the notion love for one's mother can supersede the hard knocks experienced during childhood and can even be used to pay tribute for the good that came as a result. Tupac states that he can never pay her back for her struggle in raising him. The children also recognize that the absence of the African American male in the family household puts a strain on the mother. When the mother overcomes these stresses, it seems that her children take pride in her. In his song "Hey Mama," Kanye West (2005) thanks his mom for all of her support in spite of the stressful situations she had to endure in his upbringing. The mother holds an important role in the hip hop community because she represents strength, persistence, and courage, values embraced by even the hardest thugs.

Tupac left Baltimore and headed to Marin City, California, in the Bay Area, to live with Linda Pratt, wife of Black Panther Elmer "Geronimo" Pratt. Nicknamed the Jungle, Marin City is an impoverished community across the bay from Oakland where Tupac began to sell drugs and learn even more about the streets. Tupac arrived in Marin City at the height of the crack cocaine explosion of the late 1980s and early 1990s, a period of death and destruction to the lives of a multitude of young people living in the urban areas of California. The crack cocaine explosion paralleled the rise of hip hop in the Bay Area. As a result of the onslaught of drug- and gang-related violence, rappers and songwriters responded to the urban crisis in a variety of ways. Drugs and gangs were becoming common topics for songs such as the crossover hit, "The Ghetto." This song from Too $hort's 1990 release *Short Dog's in the House* painted a gloomy and dark picture of urban America. R&B artist Tony! Toni! Tone! went a step further with their 1988 song "Little Walter," a ballad about a drug dealer shot when he opened his door. With this new surge of West Coast hip hop, artists and groups like MC Hammer, Ant Banks, Capitol Tax, and Digital Underground became famous in the late eighties and early nineties. Although Hammer and Digital Underground were more focused on dance music and party music than exposing social conditions, Tupac drew material for his music from the poverty, drugs, and crime he witnessed in California. He would later use his lyrics to speak to the raging drug scene in Marin City and in the poor black communities across the country.

THE WORLD WILL NEVER BE THE SAME: ENTER TUPAC SHAKUR

Tupac got his start in the music industry with Digital Underground (DU), one of the most eccentric hip hop acts of the early nineties. The group, which consisted of main members Shock-G, MC Humpty Hump, Money-B, and DJ Fuze, also included a bizarre host of revolving group members such as DJ DOT, Esenchill, Dungeon Squad, Saafir, and Big Money Otis. The group's sound blended samples of Parliament/Funkadelic, Bootsy Collins, and Jimi Hendrix to create classic singles such as "The Humpty Dance" and "Doo-wutchyalike," which were included on their 1989 Grammy-nominated album *Sex Packets*. These self-proclaimed "Sons of the P," as they would title their second full-length album, were the inheritors of the P-Funk tradition. They scored another hit with *This Is an E.P. Release* in 1990. The album included the hit "Same Song," which introduced the world to Tupac Shakur.

Tupac recorded his first verse for "Same Song," which was also featured on the *Nothing but Trouble* soundtrack, but he began his career with Digital Underground as a roadie and dancer. The role of dancer can serve as a point of entry into the music business for some hip hop artists (e.g., the Pharcyde and Jennifer Lopez). This strategy certainly worked for Tupac, who worked as a dancer for only about a year. This helps explain why even though he enjoyed being able to "clown around with the Underground," as he rhymes in "Same Song," Tupac had more to say and could not remain in the shadow of DU. He decided to venture out as a solo artist, but Atron Gregory, Tupac's manager at the time, was unable to convince Tommy Boy Management that he had what it takes to be an independent, financially viable artist. Interscope Records, however, signed Tupac and financed his debut album.

Interscope Records released *2Pacalypse Now* in 1991; it was the boost Tupac needed to propel him out of the shadows of DU and into the realm of hip hop stardom. The album included songs such as "Rebel of the Underground," Trapped" (featuring Shock-G), and "Young Black Male." However, it was "Brenda's Got a Baby" that truly caught the attention of the hip hop community. In the song, Tupac's Brenda is a dope fiend who gives up her newborn for drugs and sex and is later found dead. The song is a powerful testament of the grittiness of life in urban America, which Tupac witnessed in Baltimore and later in Marin City.

2Pacalypse Now reached number thirteen on the R&B charts and was certified gold in 1995. However, the lyrics on the album became the center of a national debate. Vice President Dan Quayle brought attention to the album during his bid for reelection, noting inappropriate lyrics, specifically Tupac's comments about killing cops on "Soulja's Story." Tupac was not the first rap artist to let his fantasies of revenge on police officers play out in lyrics. N.W.A. got the FBI's attention with "Fuck tha Police," Paris recorded "Coffee, Donuts, and Death," and perhaps most infamously, Ice-T's heavy metal group Body Count was boycotted by a Texas police group after they released the single "Cop Killer." Body Count ultimately was forced to remove the song from their album.

Tupac's notoriety grew with the release of his second album, *Strictly 4 My N.I.G.G.A.Z.* (1993), his third, *Thug Life* (1994), and his fourth, *Me Against the World* (1995). Yet it was Tupac's 1996 album, *All Eyez on Me,* that sparked his rise to iconic status. This record would become hip hop's first double CD, with twenty-eight cuts, including "California Love" and "How Do U Want It." The album finished number one in the R&B and pop category and was certified platinum seven times. It was with the release of this album that Tupac became a major player at Death Row Records, the label founded by West Coast gangsta rap legend Dr. Dre, and former gang member and NFL player Marion "Suge" Knight.

The prison imagery conjured by the name Death Row fits Tupac when one considers his numerous run-ins with the law. Tupac was accused of shooting two police officers in Atlanta, but the charges were dismissed. He served time for assaulting directors Allen and Albert Hughes. However, one of his most significant cases came in the form of sodomy and sexual abuse charges in November 1993. Tupac and his friends were accused of sexually assaulting a twenty-year-old woman. The woman alleged that she had consensual sex with Shakur before the incident in question, but when she went to visit his hotel room for the second time, she was sexually abused by members of Tupac's entourage. Even though Tupac maintained that he was asleep when the incident occurred, Tupac was formally accused of sexual abuse and sodomy and tried in a court of law. On November 31, 1994, the day before the jury would deliver its verdict, Tupac was shot five times in the lobby of a Manhattan recording studio. The next day, against his doctor's orders, Tupac arrived at the courthouse bandaged and in a wheelchair. He was found guilty of sexual abuse, and served eleven months in jail. It was while he was serving time for this crime that the album *Me Against the World* was released. In October 1995, his case got an appeal and he was released on bond through money supplied by Suge Knight, with the condition that Tupac sign to his label, Death Row.

Less than a year later, on September 7, 1996, Tupac would be shot five times in a drive-by shooting as he rode in a car with Knight. He died seven days later, on September 13, 1996.

C. DELORES TUCKER: TUPAC'S CENSORSHIP NEMESIS DURING HIS LIFE AND AFTER DEATH

One of the most vocal opponents of Tupac Shakur's gangsta rap lyrics was C. Delores Tucker, the founder and chair of the National Congress of Black Women and the first black woman to serve as Pennsylvania's Secretary of State (1971–1977). Tucker and Dan Quayle were critics of Tupac's music, particularly the controversial album *2Pacalypse Now,* which was released in 1991. While Tupac billed the recording as a socially conscious album that addressed the plight of young black males in America, political leaders and law enforcement officers denounced the album for its violence against the police. The fury over the album increased after it was reported that the song "Soulja's Story" allegedly inspired a young man to kill a Texas state trooper. This incident led former Vice President Quayle to suggest that the album "has no place in our society." Pac would later sample Quayle's statement on his follow-up, *Strictly 4 My N.I.G.G.A.Z.,* where he dedicates the songs "Point the Finger" and "Souljah's Revenge" to responding to his critics.

In 1994, criticism of Tupac Shakur and other gangsta rappers' lyrics would culminate in congressional hearings on gangsta rap in Washington, D.C. Tucker, along with conservative Republican William Bennett and U.S. senators Joseph Lieberman and Sam Nunn, began a four-year crusade to rid society of a genre of music they deemed to be "pornographic smut." Snoop Doggy Dogg's *Doggystyle* and Dr. Dre's *The Chronic* came under heavy scrutiny by Tucker and her cohorts during the hearings sponsored by the Committee on Energy and Commerce's Subcommittee on Commerce, Competitiveness, and Consumer Protection. Tucker was particularly critical of Tupac, and Tupac responded in kind in his lyrics. Nearly a year after Shakur's death in 1996, Tucker filed a defamation lawsuit against Tupac's estate accusing the slain hip hop artist of slander, invasion of privacy, and emotional stress. Nevertheless, the lawsuit was thrown out by U.S. District Judge Ronald Buckwalter in 1999; the judge wrote that while the statements were inappropriate, they did not qualify as slander (see sidebar: Hip Hop and Censorship).

Hip Hop and Censorship
Jessica Elliott

In 1985, after her purchase of Prince's album *Purple Rain,* Tipper Gore, wife of then-Senator Al Gore, cofounded the Parents' Music Resource Center (PMRC). They were responsible for the laws that required parental advisory warnings on records that were deemed inappropriate for young listeners.

By 1990, the Recording Industry Association of America (RIAA) announced that it had created a uniform parental advisory sticker that would appear on the covers of albums with explicit content. More hip hop albums received parental advisory stickers than any other music genre—some albums being labeled with warnings for no apparent reason. In the same year, *Newsweek* published an article called "The Rap Attitude" (Adler and Foote). Appearing as a cover story, this article was more editorial than news report, and mostly represented its authors' views on rap music. While references were made to certain rock and roll groups, overall the article focused on classifying rap music as a negative influence promoting anger, stereotyping, and disrespect for authority.

The amount of attention drawn to rap music in 1990 by both the PMRC and *Newsweek* preceded the arrest and trial of Miami's 2 Live Crew. In June, a Florida judge declared that the group's album *As Nasty as They Wanna Be* violated obscenity laws. No other record in American history had drawn such a charge. Laws immediately went into effect that prohibited the sale of the album, and, later that week, three members of the group were arrested for performing songs from the album live at a local concert.

2 Live Crew was ultimately acquitted, and some jurors were even reported to have laughed during the hearing when excerpts from the group's album were played (Anderson 29). Yet the 2 Live Crew decision did not dissuade the PMRC from their attempts to censor hip hop, and the PMRC isn't the only group to promote such censorship. Dr. C. Delores Tucker, a feminist advocate against rap music, claimed in the 1990s that the lyrics in many hip hop songs both promoted violence against and were derogatory toward African American women. Her anti-rap activities included buying shares in Time Warner so that she could attend the shareholders' meeting and protest the company's production of hip hop albums. In 1994, she protested outside of the NAACP after they nominated Tupac Shakur for an Image Award.

Dr. Tucker and her husband, William Tucker, filed a lawsuit against the estate of Tupac Shakur for remarks made about her on his album, *All Eyez on Me*. Shakur's lyrics were a rebuttal of Dr. Tucker's protest of his Image Award nomination. In addition to Dr. Tucker's claims that statements in the album were slanderous and defamatory, Mr. Tucker took part in the lawsuit by claiming that Shakur's lyrics resulted in Dr. Tucker's lack of interest in sex. Dr. Tucker planned to use money from her lawsuit to pursue further censorship of hip hop music, but the court ruled in favor of Shakur's estate.

Works Cited

Adler, Jerry, and Jennifer Foote. "The Rap Attitude." *Newsweek* 19 March 1990: 56–59.

Anderson, Charles-Edward. "2 Live Crew Acquitted." *ABA Journal* 76.12 (1990): 29.

Horwitz, Carolyn. "C. DeLores Tucker Sues Tupac's Estate." *Billboard* 16 August 1997: 18.

Further Resources

Gilmore, M., and A. Karl. "The Year in Music." *Rolling Stone* 13–27 December 1990: 13–16.

The two songs on *All Eyez on Me* that mentioned Tucker were "How Do U Want It" and "Wonder Why They Call U Bitch." In "Wonder Why They Call U Bitch," Tupac discusses the promiscuity and gold-digging that, from Tupac's vantage point, leads certain women to be rightfully labeled bitches.

Furthermore, Tupac suggests that these women should instead get an education so that they can become financially independent. C. Delores Tucker's name is mentioned only at the end of the song. Notably, Tupac never calls her a bitch, but rather attempts to explain to Tucker why some women, but not all, are considered bitches. Gines asserts that "Tucker misunderstands Tupac; he is criticizing the unequal exchange of sex for money. He isn't attempting to reduce all women to bitches and hos" (94). Thus, it seems that Tucker had mistaken Tupac's social commentary, albeit vulgar, for an attack on her person.

However, in the song, "How Do U Want It," Tupac does in fact attack Tucker by calling her names and saying that she's out to "destroy a brother." Here, Tupac is employing a rhetorical strategy used by black revolutionists called vilification, which is "the use of harsh language against a single conspicuous leader of the opposition with the intent of belittling [her] before the community" (Smith 12). Having inherited a black revolutionary ethos from his mother, Afeni, it is not surprising that Tupac would use such a tactic in his lyrics to attack a woman who sought to censor his life's work. Gines further posits that what we also see in the lyrics of this song is "Tupac evoking the image of the *emasculated Black woman* who, despite any merits in her position is always . . . trying to pull brothers down" (96).

TUPAC THE ACTOR

With sexual abuse charges looming, other court cases pending, and even in the midst of a bicoastal feud, Tupac managed to appear in several films during his short life. By the time of his death, he had starred in *Juice* (1992), *Poetic Justice* (1993), *Above the Rim* (1994), *Bullet* (1996), and *Gang Related* (1997). His last film was *Gridlock'd* (1997), which was released posthumously. Unlike many rapper-turned-actors, Tupac actually had training in dramatic performance. Tupac saw opportunities to act as more than a way to make money. Producer Preston Holmes, who worked with Tupac on the movies *Juice* and *Gridlock'd*, has suggested that Shakur was interested in getting black youths in particular to read and think critically about societal issues affecting them. However, this notion is juxtaposed with the fact that Tupac was kicked off the film *Menace II Society* because of an altercation with the directors, Allen and Albert Hughes. His contradictory nature becomes evident early on in that while he wanted to enhance the critical thinking skills of moviegoers, he could not maintain the self-control to stay out of a fight with the film's directors.

In many ways, Tupac's acting roles beg the question, "Does art imitate life?" His characters often possessed many of the same characteristics he did, or lived lives that were very similar to his earlier years. In analyzing Tupac's first movie role, one gets a clearer sense of how Tupac used his acting career to reinforce the image he created initially through his music. His first movie role was Bishop, in the movie *Juice* (1992). *Juice* was the story of four young teens: Bishop, Q, Raheem, and Steel. The teens from Harlem, New York, skip school one day only to find that one of their old friends has been killed in a shootout at a bar. After learning of this tragic incident, Bishop tells his friends that they have no "juice" or respect. In order to get respect, the four teens rob a corner grocery story and Bishop shoots and kills the store clerk for no apparent reason. After the shooting of the store clerk, the four young black males run into an alley where Raheem tells Bishop to give him the gun. A fight breaks out between Bishop and Raheem, and Raheem is shot and killed. Since the other youths know what happened, Bishop seeks to get rid of them also.

From this synopsis of the movie, one can see that Tupac's stage identity as an outlaw or thug played out in the movie roles he landed. In *Tupac: Resurrection*, Tupac states, "Bishop is a psychopath; the character is me, I'm Bishop. Everybody got a little Bishop in them" (85). Moreover, Bishop is the quintessential thug who embodies the nihilism that exists in many urban communities in America. In his book *Race Matters,* Cornel West posits that nihilism is "the lived experience of coping with a life of horrifying meaninglessness, hopelessness, and (more important) lovelessness" (4).

The streets of Harlem are a place where young black males such as Bishop learn to negotiate their survival among a variety of social vices such as illegal drugs and drug-related shootings, gang violence, illicit sex, and carjackings. In order for Bishop, as well as Q, Raheem, and Steel, to survive the streets of Harlem, they must embrace what social scientist Elijah Anderson calls the "code of the streets, which amounts to a set of informal rules governing interpersonal public behavior, including violence" (82). Anderson further suggests, "The rules prescribe both a proper comportment and a proper way to respond if challenged. They regulate the use of violence and so allow those who are inclined to aggression to precipitate violent encounters in an approved way" (82).

One of the informal rules on the streets of Harlem in the movie *Juice* is that those who are deemed vulnerable, such as a shop clerk, can and will be subjected to violence and may be killed in order for kids to earn respect. This was the case with Bishop and the store clerk. By killing the store clerk, Bishop's own sense of selfhood was affirmed in his own eyes. Another informal rule is that if a person is challenged, he must avenge himself and his honor. This was also the case between Bishop and Raheem; Raheem attempted to try Bishop by taking his gun. This was deemed by Bishop as an attack on his person, the rationalization being that Bishop's gun was an extension of himself. In the end, the killing of Raheem serves two purposes: Bishop's honor is restored and juice (respect) granted—that is, on a societal level; and Bishop's friends learn that he is not to be messed with, which in turn also grants him additional juice among his peers.

Tupac's role as Bishop in *Juice* is powerful because the character he plays is only an extension of the outlaw/thug identity portrayed in his lyrics. Thus, both Bishop and Tupac lived by the Thug Life mantra. In explaining the complex relationship between Tupac the rapper and Tupac the actor, Tupac stated, "I am real. The lyrics might be a story or they might be real. But I stay real. Even when I am playing a character I'm really a character at the same time. There is nothing fake" (*Tupac Resurrection* 85). There should be no question that Bishop and all of Tupac's other characters possess some of his own qualities. Undoubtedly, it was his realness that led him to be cast in so many movies where his thug qualities took center stage.

Tupac's acting career gave him the ability to work with notable actors and directors such as James Belushi, Thandie Newton, Samuel L. Jackson, Regina King, Janet Jackson, and John Singleton. While he never starred in a movie with his former classmate actress Jada Pinkett, their love for acting would serve as one of the links that catapulted their relationship to deeper levels. Despite physical distance after Tupac's move to California, incarceration, and whatever could have potentially ruined their bond, their friendship would stand the test of time and continue until Tupac's murder.

LITERACY AND THE DEBUNKING OF ANTI-INTELLECTUALISM IN RAP MUSIC

A major contribution that Tupac made to hip hop culture involved his role in countering the notion that illiteracy is commonplace within the hip hop community (Dyson 99) and enhancing the plausibility of an intelligent thug. For many, prior to Tupac's entry into the hip hop game, the idea of the intelligent thug was an impossibility, the thinking being that surely thugs do not read and have ideas rooted in deep philosophical thinking. Tupac changed this.

The importance of literacy in Tupac's life was inherited from his mother, Afeni Shakur. As a Black Panther during the 1960s, Afeni read the literary works of Langston Hughes, Toni Morrison, James Baldwin, and August Wilson. She also read classical works such as Shakespeare's *Hamlet* and *Macbeth*. Like his mother, Tupac was an avid reader and believed that knowledge and learning were critical to the intellectual growth and development of an individual or a people. Since the aforementioned works were in Tupac's environment at an early age, the writers and their works had a tremendous effect on the man, his song lyrics, and his poetry.

In addition to inheriting a love for reading from Afeni, Tupac was also influenced by Leila Steinberg, a cultural critic whom Michael Eric Dyson describes as Shakur's "literary soul mate" (92). Steinberg, a writer and producer in the music industry, conducted multicultural educational programs and afterschool workshops in the public schools of Marin City and Oakland, California. She first met Shakur in 1989 during an afterschool workshop on writing, literature, and performance. Impressed by his love for learning as evidenced during these workshops and programs, Steinberg invited Tupac into her home for further study. The two spent many hours reading and critically reflecting on the works of various writers from a variety of disciplines. Tupac read historian William Styron's *The Confessions of Nat Turner,* as well as George Orwell's cryptic novel, *1984.* In addition, Robert M. Pirsig's *Zen and the Art of Motorcycle Maintenance,* Sun Tzu's *Art of War,* Niccolo Machiavelli's *The Prince,* and Jack Kornfield's *Teachings of the Buddha* were also part of Tupac's reading list.

Tupac also read works in the African American literary canon. For example, Tupac read Alex Haley's *The Autobiography of Malcolm X* and *Roots,* Maya Angelou's *I Shall Not Be Moved* and *I Know Why the Caged Bird Sings,* Richard Wright's *Native Son,* W.E.B. DuBois's *The Souls of Black Folks,* Assata Shakur's *Assata: An Autobiography,* and Nathan McCall's *Makes Me Wanna Holler.* Tupac was as eclectic in his approach to literature as he was in his approach to knowledge and learning. His love for reading and ideas were influenced and heightened by his interest in a variety of topics including history, spirituality, philosophy, feminism, politics, and education. In addition to reading various literary works, Tupac also participated in weekly writing circles conducted in Steinberg's home, where he developed his skills as a literary artist and poet. One of the first poems that he wrote there was "The Rose That Grew from Concrete." This particular poem would later have a lasting impact on hip hop culture and in academia as it would be the lead poem in a book of poetry written by Tupac and compiled by Steinberg after his death. The collection *The Rose That Grew from Concrete* was published by Pocket Books in 1999. Other poems in the book include "Life Through My Eyes," "The Shining Star Within!," "Black Woman," "I Know My Heart Has Lied Before," "2 People with 1 Wish," "The Sun and the Moon," "The Promise," and "Nightmares." Out of Tupac's poetry flows the very heart of a man that is complex and deeper than could ever be determined by listening to his rap lyrics alone. In poems like "Jada," he speaks about his platonic love for his dear friend Jada Pinkett, and in "UR Ripping Us Apart!!! (Dedicated 2 Crack)," Tupac not only speaks to his hurt over his mother's struggle with crack but also demonstrates his view of Afeni Shakur as his hero, weakened as she may have been. The complexity that is Tupac becomes increasingly apparent as his sometimes misogynist lyrics are contrasted with his odes to women in some of his songs and poetry. Today, colleges and universities across the country are using Tupac's collection of poetry in their literature courses. The University of California at Berkeley, Harvard University, and the University of Washington are but a few of the schools that have created classes that study Tupac's work from an intellectual perspective, dissecting the writings that influenced him as well as highlighting how Tupac's writings and lyrics have influenced others.

Both reading and writing informed Tupac's critical consciousness. In his lyrics, hints of Tupac's reading list emerge. In some cases, the references are obvious, such as in the example of Shakur assuming the name of Makaveli and foreshadowing his own death on the album, *The Don Killuminati: The 7 Day Theory*. The album was an homage to Niccolo Machiavelli, a military theorist, playwright, historian, and diplomat who spoke of staging one's own death in his book, *The Prince*. So while in some cases the listener could clearly identify the inspiration for Tupac's lyrics, the listener may not have been as aware of his influences in cases like references to the writings of Shakespeare. There is no doubt, though, that Tupac was very inquisitive and he not only analyzed the ideas of others but processed them and (re)presented them in his music.

Tupac's intellectualism had a profound impact on his rap lyrics. He was interested in using the power of rap music to educate as well as entertain members of the hip hop community. As a result of his position on educating others, his love for reading, learning, and knowledge ultimately translated into two lasting contributions to hip hop culture: Tupac further shattered the notion that hip hop culture is anti-intellectual, and Tupac encouraged youths in the culture to read and think critically: "Tupac's profound literacy rebutted the belief that hip-hop is an intellectual wasteland. [Shakur] helped to combat the anti-intellectualism in rap, a force to be sure, that pervades the entire culture" (Dyson 99). Tupac's influence can be seen today in the thought-provoking lyrics of hip hop artists such as Erykah Badu, Common, Jill Scott, and Kanye West. These artists all evoke thoughtful consideration of their lyrics. For example, in the song "Bag Lady," Erykah Badu encourages women to consider the negatives that come with bringing along baggage from past relationships. Hip hop producer/recording artist Kanye West brings attention to the mining and sales of conflict diamonds in the song "Diamonds from Sierra Leone."

Tupac wanted the hip hop community to become knowledgeable and informed. He clearly understood the power of ideas and the ability of those ideas to have great influence over others. He earnestly understood that the ideas expressed in Machiavelli's *The Prince,* for example, could, despite the passing of time, have a lasting impact on the hip hop nation. He proved this to be true with the posthumous release of the film *Gridlock'd*, and the album *The Don Killuminati: The 7 Day Theory.*

DON KILLUMINATI: THE SUPPOSED MUSICAL CONCLUSION TO THE LIFE OF TUPAC SHAKUR

Tupac's assault on anti-intellectualism in hip hop stands as a lasting contribution to the culture. However, it would be his release of *The Don Killuminati: The 7 Day Theory* that would further solidify his icon status. Produced by Tyrone "Hurt M Badd" Wrice and Darryl "Big D" Harper, the album was recorded in August 1996 at Los Angeles's Can-Am Studios. Twenty songs were initially recorded during the sessions; however, only twelve songs, such as the hip hop classics "Hail Mary," "Toss It Up," and "To Live and Die in L.A." made the cut. Released November 5, 1996, the album went to number one on both the R&B and pop charts. It was later certified platinum five times. It would be the last album recorded by Tupac before his death, and demonstrated a marked improvement of his rhyme styles from early in his music career. His rhyme style, which had earlier incorporated an upbeat tempo on songs like Digital Underground's "Same Song" and his own "If My Homies Call," was now slowed down. The keyboards, synthesizers, and bells used in those early songs were replaced with stringed instruments to give *Don Killuminati* a darker and less pop sound. On "Hail Mary," Tupac elongates syllables to draw out words like "me" and "see" at the end of each line of the chorus. His voice sounds slower and deeper, almost anticipating the sluggish, slurred speech that Houston's DJ Screw would later popularize in his screwed and chopped mixtapes.

Tupac's last album is controversial for several reasons. To begin with, it was made during the height of the East versus West Coast tension and during internal conflicts at Death Row. Second, the album was released as the first of several posthumous records. What made this even more controversial is the fact that it was this album that introduced Tupac as his alter ego, Makaveli, a truth that would serve as the catalyst for the "Tupac is alive" conspiracy theory. Finally, this album marked Tupac's return to making social and political commentary.

While the Makaveli album did extremely well once it was released, it was recorded amid a great deal of strife and controversy between East Coast and West Coast rappers, as well as the strife and controversy at Death Row Records. The East-West conflict between Tupac and New York rapper and Bad Boy recording artist Christopher Wallace, better known by those in the hip hop community as Notorious B.I.G., had been boiling over for months. Each of these rappers took turns disrespecting the other on their albums and in person. Moreover, New York rappers, particularly Biggie Smalls, were still brooding over Shakur's "Hit 'Em Up" anthem, which suggested that Tupac had sex with Biggie's estranged wife, R&B artist Faith Evans. Tupac's song had been in response to Biggie's "Who Shot Ya," a song Tupac interpreted as comments about him being shot, and the suggestion that Biggie was involved in the shooting. This growing feud gave Tupac, the Outlawz (Shakur's friends and family members who debut on the Makaveli album), and music producers Wrice and Harper a sense of urgency about the making of *Don Killuminati*; it took only seven days to make. Some of those close to the making of the album, and some of his staunchest fans, believe that Tupac sensed that his life was going to be cut short; he worked feverishly with the understanding that in all likelihood, he was running out of time.

In addition to the East-West conflict, there were also internal rivalries at Death Row Records that were created as a result of artistic differences and inflated egos. Dr. Dre, Death Row's in-house producer, left the company in part because of differences with Tupac, including Tupac's suggestion that Dre did nothing more than take credit for the hard work of others. In addition, Tupac was highly critical of Dr. Dre's decision not to testify in court on behalf of Snoop Doggy Dogg in his murder trial.

Despite tension inside and outside of Death Row Records, Tupac became even more driven and determined to produce an album that would have a different sound and feel than his previously released *All Eyez on Me*. The recording sessions that took place in the Can-Am studios would, in the end, yield an album with far-reaching impact, especially after Tupac's death.

DON KILLUMINATI AS SOCIAL AND POLITICAL COMMENTARY

Tupac's *Don Killuminati* is a very dark, passionate, and intensely dramatic work that captures the rapper at his best. For Tupac, the album heralds a return to the social and political commentary that he became known for in previous recordings. In the song, "Bomb First (My Second Reply)," Tupac goes on the attack by dissing his East Coast rivals such as Nas, Jay-Z, Puffy, and Biggie Smalls. "Bomb First (My Second Reply)" is a song about a street soldier or "capo" (Tupac) maintaining respect in the face of his enemies by fighting them lyrically. Undoubtedly, Tupac's street credibility was greatly enhanced in the eyes of fellow West Coast thugs for the barrage of comments that he directed toward his East Coast adversaries.

In the song, "White Man'z World," Tupac also provides a sociological critique of black life behind prison bars. While writing to his mother and sister from prison, Tupac discusses the complexities of both prison life and street life, and he reflects on the challenges of being black in a world that doesn't seem to care about the plight of the urban poor. Moreover, the song addresses such political issues as reparations, Black Nationalism, and class.

In "Life of an Outlaw," Tupac and the Outlawz, Death Row's up-and-coming rap group, provide strong social commentary on the daily struggles and hardships of an outlaw on the streets of urban America. The rappers paint a gritty picture of what it means to be a minority caught up in a web of street violence, retaliation, and nihilism. Moreover, the song demonstrates that the political nature of the outlaw is "ride or die." This kill-or-be-killed mentality is revealed in the strategic and calculating choices the outlaw makes to survive in the urban killing fields or war zones of America.

In "To Live and Die in L.A.," Tupac shows love and admiration for the "city of Angels." While there are differences, the song is reminiscent of Tupac's "California Love." Socially, the song describes the people of Los Angeles and discusses their lived experiences in the city. Politically, the song makes reference to the LA rebellion of 1992 and Governor Pete Wilson's conservative practices.

Yet the most popular (and socially significant) song on *Don Killuminati* is "Hail Mary." In the song, Shakur, assuming the alias of Makaveli, paints a dark and gloomy picture of society's thugs contemplating a nihilistic existence and shrouded in religious symbolism—the same religious imagery also present on the track "Blasphemy." "Hail Mary" became an instant classic in hip hop culture. "Hail Mary" was one of Tupac's favorites, and the song had a lasting effect on him. Tyrone "Hurt M Badd" Wrice recalls Tupac's reaction to "Hail Mary": "'Pac was loving every song. But when they played *that* song, he just went through a thing. . . . He threw his hands up in the air like he ruled a nation" (Matthews 112). Digital Underground still covers "Hail Mary" in concert as a tribute to their fallen friend.

The duress Tupac was facing inside and outside of Death Row Records served as a catalyst for the thought-provoking commentary on *Don Killuminati*. Tupac wanted listeners to think critically about the social and political conditions affecting black people and other people of color and their communities, and then work to change those conditions. Through "Hail Mary," Tupac also reminds the hip hop nation that their conditions are capable of changing, but a belief in God and an active prayer life (i.e., "Hail Mary full of grace") may be necessary in order to do so.

TUPAC'S *DON KILLUMINATI*: THE BEGINNING OF LIFE AFTER DEATH

One of the most significant contributions that Tupac's *Don Killuminati* album makes to hip hop culture involves the development of Shakur's alter ego, Makaveli, which in turn established the basis for theories that Tupac faked his death. The creation of the album, coincided with the development of a new identity for Tupac. Having read *The Prince*, Tupac saw utility in the thinking expressed by the fifteenth-century political strategist. Machiavelli was interested in using the thinking promulgated in *The Prince* to gain a political edge. In the rap game, Tupac understood that this same advantage could come by faking his own death or by outselling his competitors. In one of his last in-depth interviews, as an answer to questions about the album and why he chose to name himself after a fifteenth-century politician, Tupac stated, "It's not like I idolize this one guy Machiavelli. I idolize that type of thinking where you do whatever's gonna make you achieve your goal. I'm gonna change the rules in this rap game" (Marriott 125). Shakur was referring to the album *All Eyez on Me* in this interview, but the sentiment would evolve as he moved on to a new project. He used the philosophy espoused in *The Prince* to change the rap game through this album: It was hip hop's first double CD, and also hip hop's most expensive CD. Taking Tupac's cue, artists such as Wu-Tang Clan would subsequently release double albums. In 2006, GM Grimm would take things further to release a triple album.

However, raising the bar by releasing a double album belied the deeper impact of the political philosopher Machiavelli on Tupac. Thus, while *All Eyez on Me* changed the rap game concerning album structure and record sales, *Don Killuminati*, more than anything else, perpetuated the belief that Tupac Shakur had either anticipated his own murder or was in fact not dead. The symbolism that fuels these conspiracy theories is most obvious in the album's title and cover. In the cover art, the five holes in Tupac's crucified body match the exact number of bullet wounds that killed him. Because of the album's title, *Don Killuminati: The 7 Day Theory*, hip hop heads would come to believe that Tupac, after reading *The Prince*, wanted to gain a political edge in the rap game by faking his own death. Also of interest to fans was mysterious subtitle *The Seven Day Theory*; the number seven resounds in many statistics surrounding Tupac's death. Tupac died seven days after he was shot. He was twenty-five, and two and five added together equal seven. Similarly, Tupac's time of death was 4:03, which again adds up to seven. The theory that Tupac, having assumed his alter ego Makaveli, had faked his own death became widespread among hip hop listeners. Some speculated that the reason that his body was supposedly cremated was so that no one would be able to confirm his death by producing his body.

The rumors and various conspiracy theories that developed after Tupac's death have helped catapult him into icon status. Moreover, rumors and conspiracy theories have the ability to alter our perceptions of reality, thereby becoming our reality, ultimately becoming the truths by which we live. The hip hop community needed to believe that Tupac, who existed as a solid representation of a generation of hip hop heads, was indeed alive. To accept any other truth was to suggest that a generation of believers was also dead: "If he is dead, then we [the generation] are, or could be, dead. Keeping him from dying, insisting on his bodily persistence in a secret location, forestalls that realization" (Dyson 252). Nevertheless, the real meaning of *Don Killuminati* lies in its ability to suggest that a generation of hip hop heads is in fact alive, well, and critically astute because one of their own, Tupac Shakur, is still with them. He may be nailed to the cross as the CD cover suggests, but like Jesus, he is resurrected for a generation to see and believe.

In addition to the Makaveli CD cover, Tupac has been resurrected in a variety of ways within contemporary black popular culture. Various posters, movies, books, and magazines bear the image of Tupac, further enhancing the suggestion that he is still alive, especially since many of these artifacts were issued after his death. The volume of posthumous release from Tupac inspired a sketch on Comedy Central's *Chappelle's Show* in which a DJ announces and plays a new Tupac song in a club. As Dave Chappelle dances, he begins to notice that Tupac's lyrics are referring to events that occurred after his death, such as George W. Bush's presidency and the release of the video game *Grand Theft Auto: San Andreas*. By the end of the song, Tupac is describing and predicting that night's events in the club, as if he is watching the scene from beyond the grave. Beyond music, there is also a Makaveli clothing line and a performing arts center founded by Afeni Shakur that is dedicated to keeping her son Tupac's legacy alive. Further solidifying his icon status, a wax figure of Tupac was unveiled at Madame Tussauds wax museum in Las Vegas, Nevada, on April 5, 2006.

Don Killuminati: The 7 Day Theory played a major role in shaping Shakur's iconic status. The sociopolitical messages, the significance of Makaveli, and the foundation the album laid for the rumors that Tupac was alive contributed to the importance of the album in hip hop culture. In the context of the circumstances of Tupac's death, the album's lyrics and cover art seem to convey hidden messages through numerology. The message for hip hop heads seems clear: Tupac Shakur lives. The rumors are continually fueled by the reality that Tupac's murder remains unsolved.

THUG LIFE: SHAKUR'S IDEOLOGY

Another major contribution to hip hop culture that further crystallized Tupac as an icon is his Thug Life ideology. Tupac suggested that Thug Life was "not an image, it's just a way of life; it's a mentality. Part of being [a thug] is to stand up for your responsibility and say this is what I do [hustle, challenge authority, and engage in illegal behavior] even though I know people are going to hate me" (Dyson 112–113). Moreover, according to Tupac, Thug Life was also an acronym that stood for "the hate you gave little infants fucks everyone." The Thug Life ideology rests on several tenets: (1) thugs must ride or die; (2) thugs must be able to embrace death; and (3) thugs must embrace a nihilist attitude about life. These tenets were apparent in Tupac's life and surfaced in his lyrics as well.

The Thug Life ideology revealed in Tupac's lyrics and in his lifestyle paints a view of the world where characters such as the outlaw or ridah engage in illegal behavior, violence, and gang warfare in the killing fields of urban America. These urban warriors, many of them young black men, are often at war with their communities and with each other. The anthem that they carry into battle is ride or die, which essentially translates into retaliate, kill, or be killed. In songs such as "How Long Will They Mourn Me," and "Death Around the Corner," Tupac's Outlaw persona faces revenge and retaliation against his enemies. Ultimately, the goal of an outlaw is survival at all costs, and not just survival, but survival with an added tinge of pride; this pride stems from triumphing over your enemy—or continuing to ride. Part of Tupac's allure was found in the fact that he not only defeated death when he was shot five times in the studio, but he lived in spite of his apparent enemies, which led to a cockiness about life that somehow erased his fear of death. Even in death, Tupac is still riding as his legions of fans continue to support the theory that he is not dead.

Another important tenet of the Thug Life ideology suggested in the lyrics and lifestyle of Tupac Shakur is the unrelenting embrace of death. In Tupac's worldview, the ridah or outlaw has no fear of death; at times, he welcomes it as a way of escaping the urban war zones. Tupac, like his outlaw persona, had a preoccupation with death that was reflected in such songs as "Lord Knowz," "So Many Tears," "No More Pain," "Bury Me a G," and "If I Die 2Nite" (Morrison 193). Tupac's obsession with death was rooted in at least two factors that were prevalent in urban black America: suffering and nihilism. "The readiness to die is characteristic of the thug [ideology] as much because of the intensity of the suffering [Tupac] observed and endured [in the streets] as the belief that [he had] squared [himself] with God. Suffering—as misery and unhappiness, as pain and evil observed—was a constant theme in Tupac's work" (Dyson 212). The Makaveli album exists as a testament to the fact that Tupac no longer had a fear of death; rather, he embraced it with the mindset that death was certain, and his death would probably come very soon.

In addition to death, nihilism was another tenet of Tupac's Thug Life ideology. His preoccupation with death was rooted in nihilism. On the streets, an outlaw or ridah doesn't care about his life or the life of others; his or her actions are the results of living and surviving in the American killing fields. Tupac often displayed a nihilistic attitude by throwing up his middle finger at the camera; he also had a tattoo across his upper back that said, "fuck the world," which further illustrates his nihilistic mentality, as well as his disregard for the media and their (re)presentation of his life, his behavior, and his music. This truth underscores the fact that not only did Tupac use his music and poetry to teach and speak out, but his very body became a canvas through which he espoused his beliefs, however grim they may have been at times.

Tupac's Thug Life ideology had a big impact on hip hop culture. To be thugged out, or even to be in compliance with the notion of being a thug, was quite popular within the culture. Rappers of various persuasions wore clothing and tattoos displaying "thug life." Dress and style make a particularly important contribution to hip hop culture, and Tupac certainly influenced hip hop styles of dress during his lifetime. For him, Thug Life was a worldview not only to be embraced mentally but also worn physically. Tupac's thug image was very popular in hip hop culture and in the media, but before engaging in an in-depth discussion, one first has to come to a realization of how this idea of the thug life is personified. Tupac wore common artifacts that, when worn together, constitute a typology of a thug. A typology is a symbol or representation of something else. Tupac's thug typology is defined as a rigid nonverbal costume that represents thuggishness and the hard-core image of a gangsta rapper. Horn and Gurel suggest that a "clothing symbol stands for something beyond itself. Symbolism in dress is often unconscious, but a symbol used consciously can be more powerful" (310–311). Whether Tupac consciously tried to personify the thug typology or not, his style of dress and his influence cannot be ignored.

Not only did Tupac wear these common artifacts that construct his thug typology, but more important, his fans, homies, and other rappers also wore the clothing. These basic artifacts are: boots, jeans or fatigues, black leather jacket or vest, do-rag, and hooded sweater. Boots are a major artifact in the construction of the thug typology. Boots symbolize dominance and defiance. Those who wear boots don't just step on their enemies; they crush and smash them while waging war. Denim jeans are also a part of the thug image. Tupac's jeans symbolized toughness and durability. Rappers such as N.W.A., 50 Cent, and Bone Crusher have popularized the wearing of jeans and jean jackets in their videos. The strapped black vest, popularized by Tupac, also communicates thuggishness and durability, not only of the clothes, but, more important, of the wearer. The hooded jacket or sweater is a very important artifact in the thug typology because of the hood's ability to conceal the identity of the owner. Tupac hooded up in the movie *Juice* and his homies were likewise concealed on the cover of his *2Pacalypse Now* album cover. The hood, which is the most distinctive aspect of the jacket, allows the owner to hide himself from interlopers; it is a cloaking device. Moreover, the hood, symbolically, represents an aura of mystery, intrigue, and in some cases death. Specifically in the case of Tupac, this aura of mystery, intrigue, and death could be seen as a prelude to what would come later with the advent of his alter ego, Makaveli.

The black leather jacket, which traditionally was associated with white Western culture, has found its way into Thug Life and hip hop culture. Traditionally, the black leather jacket has been a symbol of rebellion and badness. The black leather jacket reinforces the thuggishness of the wearer just as the do-rag, which Shakur was known for wearing, reinforces the image of toughness and what it means to be hard-core. The specific use of black clothing becomes important when one considers that color is important in creating meaning. The color black meant a great deal to Tupac and to Thug Life devotees. It has the power to create mood and can also reinforce other symbolic images. Tupac, in his thugged-out black outfits, symbolized danger, seriousness of purpose, and intrigue. Tupac's thug typology was the perfect way to mask his sensitive and caring side from those who might try to do him harm because the color black has historically been associated with gloom, darkness, evil, and despair. Notably, Tupac managed to present the positive images associated with black, such as dominance, defiance, and sophistication.

At least two other artifacts that are not related to clothes further construct the thug typology for Tupac and those within hip hop culture that embrace his ideology: weed and the forty-ounce. These artifacts add a great deal of credibility to the wearer: "Befitting the outlaw character of the hard-core rapper, ingesting huge amounts of legal and illegal substances amounts to a ghetto pass and union card. Getting high is at once pleasurable and political: It heightens the joys to be found in thug life while blowing smoke rings around the constraints of the state" (Dyson 239).

Tupac's thug typology contributed greatly to hip hop culture. Not only could hip hop heads embrace Thug Life from an ideological standpoint, they could and did embrace it from the standpoint of fashion. Choosing an artifact, its color, and how to wear it is also a political act. Today, rappers such as 50 Cent have constructed their public image by immersing themselves in Thug Life ideology and presenting themselves as the model of what it really means to be hard or to be a thug. 50 Cent has even been criticized for trying to mimic Tupac in attitude, dress, lyrics, and lifestyle. He is just one example of the influence of Tupac's Thug Life ideology, but it can be seen in the images of other rappers such as Ja Rule, Lil Wayne, and Young Jeezy. Clearly, the ideology influenced more than just the minds and hearts of hip hop heads; it also influenced the way they dress and their overall style.

THE LEGACY OF TUPAC SHAKUR: EXISTENCE AS A CONTRADICTION

Tupac's life was filled with contradictions; he was a multifaceted individual to say the least. On the one hand, he embraced a revolutionary ethos inherited from his mother and uncle. Tupac had a strong desire to motivate change in the lives of his fans and in the community in which he lived. On the other hand, he truly embraced the whole Thug Life concept as an ideology, rather than as just a passing fad or phase. Tupac Shakur was a walking, breathing symbol of young black manhood existing in a contradictory state. In many ways, it was this contradictory state of existence that contributed to Tupac's iconic status.

In an examination of the competing realities of the life of Tupac Shakur, one finds that his complex existence was based in contradiction and carried over to his art forms. In songs such as "Unconditional Love," "Dear Mama," and "Keep Ya Head Up," Tupac's heart toward women becomes clear in his celebration of positive attributes and images of women. Still, it is impossible to deny that more often than not, Tupac wrote lyrics that were misogynistic and degrading to black women. Songs such as "I Get Around," "How Do U Want It," and "Toss It Up," as their titles suggest, present women as sex objects who exist mainly for the pleasure of men. He caught a lot of flack from the likes of C. Delores Tucker and others for such unwarranted sentiments. This again contrasts with much of his poetry, which provided significant insight into the more sensitive side of Tupac. The notion of contradiction, or more specifically double-consciousness, is reflected strongly in Tupac's lyrics, his poetry, and the tattoos on his body. While the notion of the contradiction existed before Tupac Shakur, the hip hop community, scholars of popular culture, and everyday lay people have become intrigued with the contradictions expressed in varied ways throughout Tupac's life. This has become especially true of scholars in the academy. Yes, it is a fair assumption that many people were initially interested only in analyzing his poetry, but in any thorough analysis, one must understand the context in order to take a true assessment of a person's work. Upon inspection of Tupac's childhood, his relationships, his education, and his artistic creations (i.e., music, poetry, and movies), one begins to see how Tupac's thinking and experiences influenced everything that he did.

When one takes into consideration the sum of his existence, Tupac Amaru Shakur emerges as hip hop's greatest iconic symbol. From the beginning, the hip hop community was intrigued by him. Tupac's love for reading, learning, and knowledge, as well as his commitment to destroying the notion that hip hop culture embraces anti-intellectualism is probably his greatest contribution to the culture. The creation of *Don Killuminati* as a concept album and ideology will forever haunt hip hop as members of the culture continue to search for Tupac's whereabouts. Moreover, the Thug Life ideology, style of dress, and so on will continue to perplex hip hop heads as they struggle to understand their own dualities embodied in their notion of self. Tupac's contributions did not provide all the answers facing rap music and hip hop culture; however, he did, through his lasting contributions, give hip hop culture enough questions to ask about a lifestyle that many have felt, and others continue to feel, so passionately about.

Surely, Tupac is representative of the common, impoverished, broken folk; he is a thug in every since of the word. Somehow though, he had an uncanny knack for communicating across race lines, social structure, and socioeconomic status. Very few can walk among thugs, yet be capable of building on the philosophy of political thinkers, and greater still, use these ideas to change hip hop forever. Tupac Shakur did just that. He made it acceptable to study hip hop as an art form. He brought hip hop to the forefront among the educational elite that represent academia. He made it possible that some individuals might look past the foul language and sexist remarks to truly understand the message behind a song or a poem. Tupac managed to make a huge impression in the twenty-five years of his life. More poignant is the realization that in the years since his death, people are still paying homage to his life, his music, his thoughtful insight into a world unknown to many and yet all too familiar to others.

See also: Notorious B.I.G., Dr. Dre and Snoop Dogg, Nas, Eminem

WORKS CITED

Anderson, Elijah. "The Code of the Streets." *Atlantic Monthly* May 1994: 81–94.

Dyson, Michael E. *Holler if You Hear Me: Searching for Tupac Shakur.* New York: Basic Civitas, 2001.

Gines, Kathryn T. "Queen Bees and Big Pimps: Sex and Sexuality in Hip Hop." *Hip Hop and Philosophy: Rhyme 2 Reason.* Ed. Derrick Darby and Tommie Shelby. Chicago: Open Court, 2005.

Horn, M., and L. Gurel. *The Second Skin.* Dallas: Houghton Mifflin, 1981.

Marriott, Rob. "Last Testament." *Tupac Shakur.* New York: Crown, 1997. 124–126.

Matthews, Adam. "Straight Spittin.'" *XXL* October 2003: 108–122.

Morrison, Carlos. "Death Narratives from the Killing Fields: Narrative Criticism and the Case of Tupac Shakur." *Understanding African American Rhetoric: Classical Origins to Contemporary Innovations.* Ed. Ronald L. Jackson II and Elaine P. Richardson. New York: Routledge, 2003. 187–205.

Powell, Kevin. "This Thug's life." *Tupac Shakur.* New York: Crown Publishers, 1997. 21–31.

Shakur, Tupac A. *The Rose That Grew from Concrete.* New York: Pocket Books, 1999.

Shakur, Tupac A. *Tupac: Resurrection.* New York: Atria Books, 2003.

Smith, Arthur L. "Strategies of the Revolutionists." *African American Rhetoric: A Reader.* Ed. Lyndrey Niles. Dubuque, Iowa: Kendall/Hunt, 1995.

West, Cornel. *Race Matters.* Boston, Massachusetts: Beacon Press, 1993.

FURTHER RESOURCES

Alexander, Frank, with Heidi Siegmund Cuda. *Got Your back: Protecting Tupac in the World of Gangsta Rap.* New York: St. Martin's Griffin, 2000.

Boyd, Todd. *Am I Black Enough for You: Popular Culture from the 'Hood and Beyond.* Bloomington: Indiana University Press, 1997.

Chuck D, with Yusuf Jah. *Fight the Power: Rap, Race, and Reality.* New York: Delacorte, 1997.

Datcher, M., and K. Alexander., eds. *Tough Love: The Life and Death of Tupac Shakur.* Alexandria, VA: Alexandria, 1997.

Davidson, Joe. "Caged Cargo." *Emerge* October 1997: 36–46.

Davis, Marcia. "The Blue Wall." *Emerge* November 1997: 43–49.

Dyson, Michael E. *Between God and Gangsta Rap: Bearing Witness to Black Culture.* New York: Oxford University Press, 1996.

Dyson, Michael E. *The Michael Eric Dyson Reader.* New York: Basic Civitas, 2004.

George, Nelson. *Hip Hop America.* New York: Viking, 1998.

Guy, Jasmine. *Afeni Shakur: Evolution of a Revolutionary.* New York: Atria, 2004.

HitEmUpRobbo. "The Meaning of 'The Don Killuminati.'" 18 February 2006. http://www.2pacworld.co.uk/killuminati.html.

hooks, bell. *Outlaw Culture: Resisting Representations.* New York: Routledge, 1994.

Hoye, Jacob, and Karolyn Ali, eds. *Tupac: Resurrection 1971-1996.* New York: Atria, 2003.

Rose, Tricia. *Black Noise: Rap Music and Black Culture in Contemporary America.* Hanover, NH: Wesleyan University Press, 1994.

White, Almond. *Rebel for the Hell of It: The Life of Tupac Shakur.* New York: Thunder's Mouth, 1997.

SELECTED DISCOGRAPHY

2Pacalypse Now. TNT/Interscope/EastWest, 1991.
Strictly 4 My N.I.G.G.A.Z. TNT/Inerscope/Atlantic, 1993.
Thug Life. Outta da Gutta/Interscope/Atlantic, 1994.
Me Against the World. Outta da Gutta/Interscope/Atlantic, 1995.
All Eyez on Me. Death Row/Interscope, 1996.

Albums Released Posthumously

The Don Killuminati: The 7 Day Theory. Death Row/Interscope, 1996.
R U Still Down (Remember Me). Amaru/Jive, 1997.
Greatest Hits. Interscope Records, 1998.
2Pac + Outlawz: Still I Rise. Interscope Records, 1999.
Until the End of Time. Interscope Records, 2001.
Better Dayz. Interscope Records, 2002.
The Resurrection. Amaru/Interscope Records, 2003.
Loyal to the Game. Amaru/Interscope Records, 2004.

Courtesy of Photofest.

Notorious B.I.G.

James Peterson

The Notorious B.I.G., also known as Biggie Smalls, was born Christopher George Latore Wallace on May 21, 1972. His mother, Voletta Wallace, was intermittently estranged from his father, Selwyn Latore, who was at least twenty years her senior. Voletta immigrated to the United States from the West Indian island of Jamaica. Selwyn was also from Jamaica, but migrated to the United States after living in London, where he kept his primary family during his courtship of Voletta Wallace and through Biggie's formative years.

Voletta Wallace was Christopher Wallace's primary caregiver and certainly the person who knew Biggie the best and the longest. Voletta's childhood in Jamaica consisted of humble beginnings informed by a powerful familial and communal set of ethics with deep, abiding aspirations to and appreciation for education and religious piety. As a little girl she dreamed of America through the imagery in travel brochures and *Ebony Magazine*. Once her opportunity to come to America presented itself, she quickly took advantage. When she arrived in the United States at age seventeen, the streets of New York City were a radical departure from the America she had envisioned from her home in Jamaica. "I was disappointed but still hopeful. I knew there had to be more in this big country. I just needed time, money and a plan" (Wallace and Mackenzie 19).

Voletta Wallace got herself a plan in 1969 when she came to America. It involved an indefatigable work ethic and an uncompromising commitment to economic independence. This plan did not include her relationship with Selwyn Latore. By 1971 she had decided to stay in the United States no matter what happened. In her first job, she assisted a psychiatrist for just eighteen dollars a day. She met Selwyn after being coaxed into attending a friend's party. She was immediately drawn to him because he showed flashes of the father figure she had missed from her upbringing in Trelawny, Jamaica. Selwyn whisked Voletta off her feet, wined and dined her; he showed her New York City in ways she had not previously experienced, and eventually Christopher Wallace was conceived.

After Wallace's birth, Voletta committed herself to the upbringing of her son. Selwyn was already married and ambiguous about his newborn son. He was essentially out of the familial picture during Wallace's toddler years. Voletta committed herself to contributing the energy and resources of at least two parents in order to raise her son. It wasn't long before her nurturing had a direct impact on the young Christopher Wallace. Voletta admits that her son earned the name Biggie even as a young boy because he was well fed in her household. "If I had it to do over again, that's one area where I would have done things differently. I would not have fed him so well. But during that time, the mindset was that the bigger the child, the healthier and happier he or she is" (Wallace and Mackenzie 51).

Biggie's mom also stressed education in their home, a two-bedroom apartment on Brooklyn's St. James Place between Fulton and Washington streets. If there was an undying conflict between them, the value and importance of traditional education would be the battleground. Because Voletta grew up in Jamaica where education was private and strict with physical disciplinary consequences, she attached great value to the public educational opportunities in the United States. When Biggie was just a toddler, Voletta also embarked upon her career as an early childhood educator, thereby underscoring her childhood experiences with education. Biggie, on the other hand, grew up in Brooklyn and although he did attend private school early on he eventually demanded to be in public school for social (and safety) reasons. It was not long thereafter that this conflict between mother and son over Christopher's commitment to his own education began to erupt. When Voletta was informed of Biggie's truancy and blatant disrespect of the educational process, she quickly challenged him. This confrontation played itself out repeatedly, especially during Biggie's high school years. From Biggie's perspective, he could make more as a garbage collector than as an educator. Thus his mom's insistence essentially fell on deaf ears. But this was only part of the reasoning behind Big Poppa's aversion to traditional education. According to his mother, Biggie was always an inquisitive and intellectually gifted child. But by the mid to late 1980s, Biggie's teenage years, Brooklyn was caught up in the crack cocaine epidemic that plagued much of urban America at that time. Substance abuse was not the challenge faced by Biggie or his mom, but the economic allure of the drug game was the centerpiece of the street life within which Biggie Smalls, the legendary freestyling MC, was to hone his skills and live the experiences about which he would spend his short career rhyming earnestly.

BEFORE HE WAS BIGGIE: THE FORMATIVE YEARS

Before Biggie became Biggie Smalls, he chose the name Cwest as his first MC moniker (see sidebar: Big Time MCs). He and his DJs, the Techniques, would meet after school and work on their craft. They would also meet with jazz

Big-Time MCs
James Peterson

At close to 400 pounds, Christopher Wallace called himself Biggie Smalls, an extraordinary oxymoron. Wallace's physical stature and his sensible marriage of that stature with his artistic designations (Biggie Smalls and eventually Notorious B.I.G.) follow a powerful and entertaining legacy of larger-than-life MCs who made similar decisions. As far back as the Fat Boys (circa 1985), oversized MCs have used their weight as a gimmick or for artistic capital. The Fat Boys made hit records and hip hop history by starring in the campy film *Disorderlies*. Heavy D hit it big with a single whose refrain reminded fans that "the overweight lover's in the house." Heavy D has since shed some pounds and parlayed his career as an MC into acting and producing.

Fat Joe, representing the Bronx like no other MC since KRS-One, has quietly become one of the most stable, long-lasting, and successful MCs in hip hop history. Fat Joe (aka Joey Crack/Don Cartagena) paired himself with an enormous and enormously talented MC by the name of Big Punisher, who passed away from complications having to do with his weight. Before his death, Big Pun sought medical treatment in an effort to shed some of the extra weight. Gone from the popular hip hop landscape but not forgotten is the enigmatic Chubb Rock, whose "Treat Me Right" single is a club classic. All of these Big MCs have made lasting impressions on their hip hop audiences by writing classic lyrics, selling millions of records, and challenging traditional conceptions of masculine body image and sex appeal.

---

saxophonist Donald Harrison, who encouraged all three of the boys to think beyond the postindustrial confines of their neighborhood. He allowed them to hone their craft on his equipment and he traded tidbits of knowledge about jazz in return for the same in rap and hip hop.

Biggie went to Westinghouse High School in Brooklyn, New York. Both Jay-Z and Busta Rhymes attended the same school. He dropped out of school at age seventeen, much to the chagrin of his mother, who is on record as stating that she and her son were not destitute or even poor by inner-city standards. Thus Biggie's affinity for street life and hustling did not derive from economic lack in his own home. Essentially, Biggie lived a double life as a teenager. In the home he was his mother's child, essential to her existence, polite, loving, respectful, and dearer to her than any other human being in her life. In the privacy of his room, or, better still, in the streets, on the corners, or in the basement studios of aspiring producers, he was Biggie Smalls, dreaming of becoming a rapper just like those superstars he was avidly reading about in *Word-Up Magazine*. LL Cool J, Run-DMC, and especially Big Daddy Kane were all powerful career and artistic influences on Biggie Smalls. But these dreams did not have the promise of the quick money crack trade, especially once Biggie realized that he could make even more money even faster if he trafficked his Brooklyn products in the South. It was in North Carolina that Biggie actually settled on the MC moniker Biggie Smalls. He came to this conclusion with one of his hustling partners, while they were hustling and watching Sidney Poitier and Bill Cosby's *Let's Do It Again*. Biggie Smalls was a gangster in the film and hence the appropriate fit. It is ironic and worth noting here that Biggie borrowed his name from a minor character in a hugely popular film from the 1970s. He eventually brought more popularity to this oxymoronic name than that character or even the film itself were able to achieve. Unfortunately, although he popularized the name Biggie Smalls, he did eventually have to forego it (due to legal complications) for the less-catchy Notorious B.I.G.

Biggie's DJs, the Techniques, didn't last long beyond the Harrison phase, but eventually a pair of DJs, DJ 50 Grand and DJ Mister Cee, worked together to create a demo tape for Biggie Smalls. 50 Grand was aware of Biggie's potential from a basement session where Biggie ripped some freestyles over classic breakbeats, including the breakbeat sampled for Big Daddy Kane's classic, "Ain't No Half-Steppin'." 50 Grand implored DJ Mister Cee (who was on tour with Kane) to listen to Biggie Smalls. 50 Grand knew that Biggie was destined to be big in the rap game. Mister Cee was skeptical at first, but once he heard the tape, he knew that a more professional demo would have to be created and he knew exactly who to give it to.

In the early 1990s, *The Source* magazine was considered a bible of hip hop culture. Its reputation for covering the culture and informing its broad readership was impeccable. At that time, a young man from Washington, DC, edited a now famous column titled "Unsigned Hype." Matteo Capoluongo or Matty C had already introduced several rap stars to the world through this small column in hip hop's most important journalistic venue. He felt so strongly about Biggie's demo that he actually played it for a young up-and-coming A&R guy named Sean Combs (see sidebar: Sean Combs and Bad Boy Records). Sean "Puffy" Combs, now known as "Diddy," needed no convincing when it came to Biggie's artistic potential. Biggie was exactly what Combs was searching for. Combs created Bad Boy Records as a home for hard-core hip hop with mass marketing appeal, and Biggie fit the bill perfectly. Combs

---

Sean Combs and Bad Boy Records
James Peterson

Sean Combs has changed monikers several times over the course of his extraordinary career as a promoter, A&R person, record executive, artist manager, recording artist, fashion designer, and music television star. But from Puffy to Puff Daddy to P-Diddy to Diddy, he has always been about an indefatigable work ethic and a natural penchant for success by all means necessary. After leaving Howard University without his degree, he returned to New York where he continued to promote parties and events. One such event at City College ended in disaster (nine people dead and dozens injured), when the venue was oversold and concertgoers became trapped and trampled as more fans tried to push their way inside the doors. But eventually Combs became Andre Harrell's star intern at Uptown Records. As he moved up the ranks at Uptown Records, he became more and more instrumental in the careers of some of the hottest up-and-coming acts in the music business, including Mary J. Blige and Jodeci. The brain child known as Bad Boy was a collection of slogans and some T-shirts at that time but as Combs began to take more credit for Uptown's success and aspire to running his own recording company, he was fired by his mentor and boss, Harrell, in the summer of 1993. Several tracks from *Ready to Die* had already been recorded. He was devastated by this, but his desire for success was (and still is) unmatched. He somehow brokered a meeting with Clive Davis, who promptly advanced him $1.5 million, total creative control, and distribution. Bad Boy was officially born. But the core executives—Combs, Harve Pierre, and Derric "D-Dot" Angelette (holdovers from the Howard University days)—had already been hard at work in Bad Boy's original studio and office, located in Diddy's mother's house. The support from Clive Davis merely helped to catapult the

Bad Boy brand into the stratosphere. After selling tens of millions of records with Biggie, Craig Mack, Total, 112, Mase, and himself, Combs went on to star in movies and TV shows, start clothing companies (Sean John and Bad Boy), and open a restaurant (Justin's).

---

immediately put Biggie on the remix for Mary J. Blige's hit single, "Real Love." This song was essentially Biggie's introduction to the world, although he had already appeared on a few lesser known singles and posse cuts (songs with multiple rappers on them). A rough and relatively unknown Biggie was a natural fit for the up-and-coming queen of hip hop soul. And even though "Real Love" aspired to be an upbeat love song, it ended up being a club banger, most certainly due to the sixteen-bar verse delivered by Biggie Smalls.

Technically speaking, Biggie's solo debut is a track titled "Party and Bullshit" on the 1993 soundtrack to the film *Who's the Man?*. Although this isn't the first time we hear Big, it is the first time that a solo recording of his enjoys a major release. "Party and Bullshit" is obviously an early Biggie recording; notice his higher-pitched, faster-paced vocals. However, the content of these rhymes, which essentially chronicle a night out partying, walks that ever-troublesome line between having a good time, drinking, rapping to women (i.e., the party), and having to deal with the sometimes violent realities of inner-city living (i.e., the bullshit). Hence, Big's narrator in "Party and Bullshit" is having a great night out but he also has "two .22s in his shoes" in case anyone is looking for trouble. There were two other collaborations that year. One was the "What's the 411?" remix with Mary J. Blige and the other was one of the earliest dance hall–hip hop collaborative concoctions, "Dolly My Baby." On "Dolly My Baby," Biggie coined one of his most famous and most often sampled lines: "I love it when you call me Big Poppa."

Even with this flurry of remixes, singles, and guest appearances, Biggie was still not satisfied with the pace of the cash flow from the music industry. He still didn't have any advance monies on the recording deal that was supposed to come to fruition through Puffy and Andre Harrell at Uptown/Bad Boy. To make matters worse, Big's ex-girlfriend, Jan, was pregnant with his first child. When he broke this news to his mother, Voletta Wallace reminded him that although he had been talking about this so-called record deal for weeks, no material evidence of such a deal existed. The pressures of impending fatherhood combined with the sluggish compensation schedule of the entertainment industry convinced Biggie that he better get his hustle back on in the streets for real. He returned to North Carolina because he was higher up on the hustler's food chain in Raleigh than in Brooklyn, but also because in North Carolina he thought his activities would not be subject to Puffy's or the label's scrutiny. He was wrong. When the various deal points were finally sorted out, Puffy contacted Biggie in North Carolina and expressed his disappointment in where Big was and what he was doing at that time. His record deal was in New York City waiting for him. This couldn't have happened soon enough. Biggie left for New York on a Monday morning and that Monday evening his illicit establishment in North Carolina was raided. He, of course, took this as a sign.

Back in New York with his low-level record deal in hand ($125,000 advance and recording budget) Biggie went to work on his first major label release, *Ready to Die*. It was fitting that one of the first tracks that Big worked on was "Party and Bullshit," produced by Easy Mo Bee. Easy Mo Bee was the last producer to work with Miles Davis and the first to work with Biggie Smalls on a solo record. Mo Bee is a touchstone for Biggie's impending iconic status. Surely, Easy Mo Bee, through the cheerleading efforts of Mister Cee, 50 Grand, Matty C, and others, was preconditioned to Biggie Smalls's greatness even before he was able to work directly with him.

There are, however, several lesser known contributing reasons to Biggie Smalls's status as an icon within hip hop culture. Some of these factors and reasons were in place even before he began work on his first major recording with Bad Boy/Uptown. Big's flow, voice, persona, and experiences—those things that constitute his artistic production—are at least partially a result of his upbringing and the various regions or neighborhoods with which he made himself familiar. First, he is from Brooklyn, New York, a borough with extraordinary cachet in the hip hop world. Even though hip hop started out in the Bronx, Brooklyn had, by the early 1990s, taken its place as the premier borough of New York when it came to hip hop culture. Some of this stems from the number of famous rap artists who hail from Brooklyn, but much of it also stems from Brooklyn's international reputation as one of the toughest, most culturally diverse cities in the world—especially when it comes to violent crime, drug dealing, and other illegal activities. So Biggie is from Brooklyn, an icon from an iconic town. But more lurks beneath this surface.

Although Biggie was born in Brooklyn, his Jamaican heritage is of extraordinary significance to hip hop. First, certain language undertones in his milky flow remind us of a peculiar Jamaican-Brooklyn patois. But more importantly, Biggie shares this heritage in common with the founding father of hip hop Culture, Clive Campbell, also known as the legendary DJ Kool Herc. Herc immigrated to the United States in 1967. He and his sister started throwing the first hip hop jams in the mid-seventies in the Bronx. This was the beginning of hip hop culture—Jamaican-born youth finding their voices and various outlets for artistic expression in postindustrial New York City. Although we never hear Biggie big-up Jamaica as his homeland (he was born in the United States, after all), it still must be acknowledged that his parental heritage and cultural domestic upbringing reflect that of the founding family of hip hop culture. This heritage informs his iconographic status almost invisibly, but the vocal influence is audible, especially early in his career (listen to the "Dolly My Baby" remix with Biggie, Puff, and Supercat, for example).

Once we combine his Jamaican parentage and Brooklyn upbringing with his hustling experiences in the South, then an accurate portrait of the artist as black American hip hop icon emerges. Although Biggie never actually lived in North Carolina, hustling crack anywhere other than where you live is probably the closest one can get to hard-core ethnographic investigation. Biggie's trips to North Carolina were most assuredly lucrative, but they must have also exposed him to southern black America, an extraordinarily representative group when one considers the folk experience so central to nearly all of hip hop culture's artistic narratives and historical legacies.

So Jamaican American, Brooklyn-bred Christopher Wallace returned from Raleigh, North Carolina, to officially begin his recording career as Biggie Smalls. The preproduction sessions for Biggie's first album literally took place in that very same bedroom in which he first envisioned himself as an MC. In his tiny bedroom in his mother's apartment, Big would sometimes have all of his boys jam-packed in for inspiration and general grimy creative energy. "The 'One Room Shack' that Biggie would later refer to in the song 'Juicy' was Wallace's bedroom—funky yellow walls, a bed, a chair, clothes and assorted junk all over the place, a TV with a VCR, and two big party-size speakers. It was in that room that Biggie Smalls, the rapper worked out his rhymes" (Coker 79). This room, along with his vast array of urban lived experiences, functioned as the incubator for *Ready to Die*, Biggie's classic debut album.

Ready to Die was released in September 1994. In order to fully understand the impact and significance of this momentous debut, we must also understand the state of hip hop at that time. Two years earlier, Dr. Dre had released *The Chronic*. This multiplatinum G-funk-inspired West Coast gangsta rap record crystallized the dominance of West Coast artists on the international rap landscape. New York City, the birth place and mecca of hip hop culture, hadn't produced a multiplatinum star in years. West Coast–style gangsta rap dominated the culture and industries of hip hop. "The final testament to the power of Biggie is the types of songs he made. He single-handedly shifted the musical dominance back to the East Coast. From 1991 to 1994, the West Coast style of rap was the dominant force in Hip-hop. Biggie, with the guidance of Puffy, used familiar melodic R&B loops, combined with his voice texture and rhyme skills, and caused a Hip-hop paradigm shift" (Kool Moe Dee 264). In many ways, the New York/East Coast audiences were given to believe that the center of the hip hop universe had shifted to Los Angeles. But "in just a few short years the Notorious B.I.G. went from Brooklyn street hustler to the savior of East Coast hip-hop" (Huey 359).

B.I.G. IN THE PLATINUM ERA

Ready to Die was East Coast rap's saving grace for many reasons. The cinematic intro to the album promised a fresh and gritty portrait of the urban underground hustler-turned-rap artist. The intro track on *Ready to Die* features snippets of four previously released songs with various voiceover skits corresponding with key moments in B.I.G.'s life. The first scene is B.I.G.'s birth, featuring an ironically proud pappa (who isn't in B.I.G.'s life too much beyond his toddler years) coaxing B.I.G.'s mother to "push!" The soundtrack for this portion of the intro interpolates snippets from Curtis Mayfield's classic "Super Fly," released during the year of B.I.G.'s birth, 1972. The second scene begins with Sugarhill Gang's "Rapper's Delight," the single that inaugurated hip hop culture in the mainstream music industry in 1979. The voiceover here is an argument started by B.I.G.'s father, who finds out that his son has been caught shoplifting. Of course he wonders profanely why neither he nor B.I.G.'s mom can control the youngster. Note here that according to Voletta Wallace, Christopher Wallace actually was a model child until his high school years, when the allure of the streets simply overwhelmed her domestic influences. This music snippet is important because it provides listeners with a sense of where B.I.G. was when "Rapper's Delight" (and by extension modern popular rap music) exploded onto the American pop cultural landscape. The third and most powerful scene features B.I.G. in a heated conversation with an anonymous crime partner. B.I.G. challenges his partner in crime to "get this money" just as they are about to rob a New York City subway train. The musical snippet for this scene is the classic single by Audio Two, "Top Billin'," released in 1987. As "Top Billin'" fades out and then back in, B.I.G.'s shouts, gunshots, and screams from his victim flesh out this scene. The final cinematic scene of the intro track features an exchange between B.I.G. and a prison CO. As B.I.G. is leaving prison, the CO claims that he will be back: "You niggas always are." The musical snippet for this scene is taken from "Tha Shiznit" on Snoop Dogg's debut album, *Doggystyle*, released in 1993. Even though this particular sample bears no credit to Snoop in the *Ready to Die* liner notes, listeners can actually hear Snoop rapping in the background of the final piece of B.I.G.'s cinematic introduction. Moreover, Snoop's *Doggystyle* was an important model for *Ready to Die* because of its extraordinary success and its ability to straddle the hard-core gangsta rap tensions and a lighter sensibility with popular mainstream appeal. In many ways, *Ready to Die* mirrors *Doggystyle* even more than *The Chronic*. The remainder of *Ready to Die* realizes the power and complexity of this four-part introduction.

Several hit singles were released from the album: "Juicy," "Big Poppa," and "One More Chance." Each of these tremendously successful singles employed similar formulas by Sean "Puffy/Diddy" Combs and the Bad Boy production team. "Juicy" interpolates Mtume's "Juicy Fruit" to perfection with a rap narrative that chronicles a Horatio Alger–like rise from the grimy streets of Brooklyn to ghetto superstar status as a rapper. Many of the lyrics from this song have gone on to an unofficial lyrical hall of fame, but at least the following line warrants repeating here: "You never thought that hip hop would take it this far." This line captures definitive aspects of B.I.G.'s lyrical appeal; a simple rhyme scheme betrays the complexity of the content. While "Juicy" is about B.I.G.'s unlikely rise to popularity, he is also very much aware of the fact that hip hop culture and rap music had by the early nineties stunned its critics and nay-sayers en route to becoming the world's most popular music. In many ways, B.I.G.'s career (big, black, ugly, and utterly lovable) mirrors that of hip hop in terms of early questions about viability and ultimately achieving rags-to-riches success. "Juicy" captures these themes perfectly. More than any other rapper, B.I.G. ushered in the platinum era of hip hop culture.

Hip hop's development can appropriately be broken down into several eras: First, the old-school era. From 1979 to 1987, hip hop culture cultivated itself, usually remaining authentic to its countercultural roots in the postindustrial challenges manifested in the urban landscape of the late twentieth century. Artists associated with this era included Grandmaster Flash and the Furious Five, the Sugarhill Gang, Lady B, Big Daddy Kane, Run-DMC, Kurtis Blow, and others.

Second, in the golden age, from 1987 to 1993, rap and rappers began to take center stage as the culture splashed onto the mainstream platform of American popular culture. The extraordinary musical production and lyrical content of rap songs artistically eclipsed most of the other primary elements of the culture (break dancing, graffiti art, and DJing). Eventually the recording industry contemplated rap music as a potential billion-dollar opportunity. Mass-media rap music and hip hop videos displaced the intimate, insulated urban development of the culture. Artists associated with this era included Run-DMC, Boogie Down Productions, Eric B. & Rakim, Salt-N-Pepa, Queen Latifah, De La Soul, A Tribe Called Quest, Public Enemy, N.W.A., and many others.

Third, in the "platinum present," from 1994 to the present, hip hop culture has enjoyed the best and worst of what mass-media popularity and cultural commodification have to offer. The meteoric rise to popular fame of gangsta rap in the early nineties set the stage for a marked content shift in the lyrical discourse of rap music toward more and more violent depictions of inner-city realities. Millions of magazines and records were sold, but two of hip hop's most promising artists, Biggie Smalls and Tupac Shakur, were literally gunned down in the crossfire of a media-fueled battle between the so-called East and West Coast constituents of hip hop culture. With the blueprint of popular success for rappers laid bare, several exceptional artists stepped into the gaping space left in the wake of Biggie and Tupac. This influx of new talent included Nas, Jay-Z, Master P, DMX, Big Pun, Snoop Doggy Dogg, Eminem, and Outkast.

B.I.G.'s seminal role in some of the most significant and powerful transitions in hip hop culture developed through the release of the incredibly popular singles from *Ready to Die*. Thus, the inaugural single, "Juicy," covers a dizzying array of transformations and transitions from B.I.G.'s life as a petty thief and hustler to his new life as a player, rapper, and finally an extraordinary storyteller. "Notorious B.I.G. is the all time greatest hard-core Hip-hop storyteller ever. Slick Rick is the overall king of storytelling, but for the rated-R, violent type of story, Biggie is the man" (Kool Moe Dee 263). Ironically, the singles from *Ready to Die* do not exhibit B.I.G.'s most compelling hard-core narrative abilities. He shows some glimpses, but most of the released singles are about flossing, partying, and sexing women.

"Big Poppa" garnered even more industry success than "Juicy," sampling the Isley Brothers' "Between the Sheets" perfectly (and almost in its entirety). Very few rappers can, as new artists, create singles that sample their own voices in the hook or refrain. B.I.G.'s voice was distinct enough and had been featured on so many singles even before his major label debut that the classic line from "Party and Bullshit"—"I love it when you call me Big Poppa"—almost instantly solidified "Big Poppa" as a mainstay on radio playlists and in club DJ repertoires. The classic Isley Brothers riff combined with B.I.G.'s classic rap aimed at women make this particular single a timeless testament to Biggie's power as an artist. "Another testament to Biggie's power was he was anything but your prototypical ladies man, and yet he made songs geared towards women, and had a huge female following" (Kool Moe Dee 264).

"One More Chance" solidified B.I.G.'s appeal to his women listeners more than either of the two previously released singles from *Ready to Die*. "One More Chance" samples the Jackson Five's "I Want You Back." The album version and the single version are almost completely different from each other in sound and content, at least with respect to profanity. "Released in the spring of '95, the 'One More Chance' remixes represented the apex of Biggie-mania in New York City. While Bad Boy's previous strategy with singles featured one side for the radio and one for the streets, 'One More Chance' covered all bases by including two somewhat different instrumentals to accompany Big's vocal track of entirely new (and somewhat sanitized) lyrics" (Coker 310). In order to fully appreciate the impact and significance of the single version of "One More Chance," the music video must be taken into account. "The video for the remix of 'One More Chance' was a star-studded 'damn I wish I was there,' old-school house party. From Kid Capri to Miami's own Luke, everybody was in this one. Mary J. Blige, Queen Latifah, Da Brat, the reggae artist Patra ... Total sang the hook 'Oh Biggie give me one more chance'" (McDaniels 335). The model, Tyson, Heavy D, R&B sensations Zhane and SWV, and of course Biggie's wife, Faith, all make appearances. The video is a mid-1990s house party how-to manual in visual form. And the fact that so many well-known female artists were willing to make cameos (especially considering the lyrics of the original) was a powerful affirmation of Biggie's irresistible sex appeal with women. The video also reifies for its viewers B.I.G.'s iconic status within the music industry itself. The people's champ was also the executives'. His mass appeal had micro impressions as well; at this point in hip hop history the Notorious B.I.G. was being crowned king both within the music industry and among millions of fans across the nation.

Although most of B.I.G.'s audience might associate *Ready to Die* with its overplayed radio-friendly club-smashing singles, the remainder of the album explores the much darker, somewhat less marketable themes of homicide and suicidal mentalities in the crack-infested inner-city environment. Consider the title track, "Ready to Die." It is almost as if certain songs like "Ready to Die," "Suicidal Thoughts," and "Everyday Struggles" are on a separate album from the singles "Juicy" and "Big Poppa." But it is all Biggie Smalls. "Ready to Die" chronicles the nihilistic inclinations of a crook who is trapped at the crossroads of lack and desire. This "crossroads of lack and desire" is originally connected to hip hop culture via Tricia Rose in *Black Noise* (1994), but the concept itself is crystallized in Houston Baker's *Blues Ideology and Afro American Literature: A Vernacular Theory* (1987). B.I.G.'s narrator obviously exists in a world where material wealth is ubiquitous; hence his undying desire. However, he lacks these resources and any legal means of obtaining them. The narrator on the album title track, "Ready to Die," captures the predicament of hundreds of thousands of inner-city youth who are jobless and alienated from social institutions like schools and churches; yet they must navigate one of the wealthiest nations in the world with little or no resources. They are therefore ready to die for the material assets that tease and evade them in a prototypical late capitalist society.

"Suicidal Thoughts" plays like a stream-of-consciousness rap in which B.I.G. contemplates taking his own life. In his suicidal reverie, B.I.G. explains why he prefers hell over a heaven filled with "goodie goodies" hanging out in a paradise where God's rules might be too strict. He does, in sincere tones, ask for forgiveness from his mother for being an evil son. But there is otherwise very little remorse in "Suicidal Thoughts." To B.I.G., death's call is comparable to the alluring call of crack cocaine for crackhead characters like Pookie from *New Jack City*—maybe the most famous cinematic crackhead for the hip hop generation. At one point in *New Jack City*, Pookie, played by a young, skinny Chris Rock, pleads with a dealer offering to trade sexual favors for a five-dollar vial of crack cocaine. Taking into account the manner in which B.I.G. dies, this analogy between crack/crack addicts and B.I.G. and death takes on an extraordinarily realistic tenor imbued with a sad seriousness of which most listeners in 1994 were hardly aware (see sidebar: Hip Hop's Culture of Death).

In "Everyday Struggles," Biggie's narrator exclaims that he doesn't want to live anymore. He hears death knocking at his front door. This song is the portrait of the low-level crack dealer, hustling to barely sustain himself on the violent streets of Brooklyn. Initially this narrator is barely surviving. He can't enhance his hustle through consignment with his supplier, and in general the community hates him. He contemplates taking his hustle out of state and finally starts to make some progress in the drug economy. The final verse

Hip Hop's Culture of Death
Carlos D. Morrison and Celnisha L. Dangerfield

Hip hop figures seemingly have a fascination with death. Artists boast about being shot or taking someone out. Bulletproof vests adorn the bodies of rappers in music videos, gunshots can be heard resounding on the tracks of CDs, and self-made prophecies of death are put to the rhythm of a beat and made to rhyme. Songs such as "Six Feet Deep," by the Geto Boys, "Gangsta Lean" by Dirty Rotten Scoundrels, "If I Die 2Nite," by Tupac, and "Goodbye to My Homies," by Master P featuring Silk the Shocker, Sons of Funk, and Mo B. Dick are dirges to the fallen soldiers in the killing fields of urban America. When gansta rap hit the mainstream, artists such as N.W.A. spoke of the atrocities that were commonplace in the hood. They gave many people a dose of reality. However, what was at first a verbal release of pain and anguish later became a trend.

For many artists in the gangsta rap era, in order to get signed, it became almost a necessity to have street credibility and a hard-core reputation. This included having bullet wounds, carrying guns, and wearing bulletproof vests. Rhyming about death and murder became fashionable, and the violence spilled out of the lyrics and into the streets, with the murders of Tupac, Biggie, Big L, Freaky Tah, and Fat Pat, and the attempted murders of 50 Cent and the Game.

While 1990s gangsta rap certainly elevated the level of attention to murder and gun violence in lyrics, old-school hip hop also had its run-ins with death. DJ Scott LaRoc of Boogie Down Productions was stabbed to death in an altercation, and Slick Rick was sentenced to prison for attempted murder in a drive-by shooting. Yet even with this history, to say that rap lyrics influence or cause violence is to ignore the statistics that tell us that physical violence and murder occur at alarming rates in impoverished neighborhoods, particularly among young African American men. Rappers who capitalize on real-life ghetto violence, however, may find themselves, even as major-label recording artists, not that far removed from the perils of street life. In the film documentary, *The MC: Why We Do It*, several MCs, including Rakim and Raekwon the Chef, speak of the dangers of promoting violence and death in lyrics; people may hear these rhymes and test their veracity by turning their guns on an MC on the street. For some artists, this lyrical theme of death serves as a way of selling more records. Many opponents, however, point out that a lot of the artists that talk about death and violence really don't live the life they rap about in their songs. However, in the case of Tupac Shakur and fellow rapper Notorious B.I.G., they certainly lived the lives they talked about in their songs. The question becomes whether their rap personas were true to their persons, or if offstage they grew into the personas they created in their music. The legends of Tupac surviving five bullets and 50 Cent surviving nine shots, including one to the face, make these rappers seem invincible on their records, and more hard-core than other artists; this hard-core image appeals to listeners. The music of the day represents the culture of the day and the current happenings within a society. Many rappers claim that they are confronted with death every day, but this situation is only heightened when violence, murder, and death become a point of marketing.

Further Resources

Bruno, Anthony. *Gangstas*. Courtroom Television Network LLC. 17 February 2006. http://www.crimelibrary.comnotorious_murders/celebrity/shakur_BIG/index.html.

of the song finds his crew surviving the perils of this violent underground economy even as he suggests that black criminals face limitations that white criminals (like John Gotti) do not. In the end though, even after some modicum of success, the refrain completes the song, and the struggle to live even with the desire to die for material wealth ultimately amounts to not living at all.

READY TO DIE: BIGGIE'S MUSIC AND HIS SHORT LIFE IN THE LIMELIGHT

Most of the tracks on B.I.G.'s debut album flip back and forth between two opposite themes. One theme is the celebration of success in the music industry. Partying, running through numerous anonymous women, and flashing (or flossing) newly acquired monetary resources dominate the content of these songs. On the opposite side of the spectrum, other songs are much more thematically aligned with album title. These rhymes reflect a pursuit of material sustenance and wealth that transcends relentlessness. These songs "express the futility of ghetto life in terms explicit and real enough to speak to the streets, but human enough to avoid myopia" (Mao 309). In each of these darker tracks, B.I.G.'s narrator is literally ready to die for material gain, but this preparedness is not glorified. It is not sexy or appealing. In fact, B.I.G. makes it clear that being ready to die for material things is, in many real-life cases, the equivalent of already being dead.

Ready to Die went on to sell millions of records. It was certified quadruple platinum on October 19, 1999. Along with several other debut albums from New York City artists (Nas's *Illmatic*, Wu-Tang's *Enter the Wu-Tang (36 Chambers)*, and Black Moon's *Enta da Stage*), *Ready to Die* recaptured the flag for East Coast hip hop. But most, if not all, of these artists avoided the ultraviolent pitfalls of overexposure that surely contributed to B.I.G.'s early and unfortunate death. "We nodded our heads in affirmation and then when

Biggie named his first album *Ready to Die* we all acted surprised when it happened. Word is bond, son. Plain and simple" (Williams 171).

Many artists with B.I.G.'s level of popularity would be criticized for taking nearly three years to release a sophomore album, but B.I.G. was extraordinarily busy between *Ready to Die* and the first of three posthumous releases, *Life After Death*. On the heels of the "One More Chance" remixes, B.I.G.'s Brooklyn protégées, Junior M.A.F.I.A. (featuring Lil' Cease and Lil' Kim), released *Conspiracy* on Undeas/Big Beat Records. Two powerhouse singles, "Player's Anthem" and "Get Money," "provide the prototypical soundtrack for ghetto fabulous aspirations; you can almost hear the Cristal bottles popping within their incessantly hooky productions" (Mao 314). *Conspiracy* has yet to be certified platinum, but the timing of the release of these two popular singles almost immediately following the last releases from *Ready to Die* further reinforced B.I.G. as the icon of hip hop culture. He also clearly targeted the heart of mainstream success in the music industry with as much relentless desire as those grimy narrators on the darkest *Ready to Die* tracks.

B.I.G. also had several minor single releases during that time. Some of these releases were live recordings (at the Palladium in New York and in Philadelphia) and or soundtrack singles (Def Jam's soundtrack for the concert film *The Show*). In 1995, DJ Mister Cee released the *Best of Biggie* mixtape. "Lovingly compiled (in near chronological order no less) with little intrusive or extraneous cutting by the man who gave Big his first significant break in the music business, it is an essential document of the first half of Biggie's career" (Mao 315). Again, this constant release of performances and singles provided audiences with a sense that B.I.G.'s artistry was boundless and that no matter how much we heard from him we still wanted to hear more. In 1996, B.I.G. collaborated with Jay-Z on "Brooklyn's Finest," a classic collaboration with his Brooklyn partner in rhyme. But probably the most important project that B.I.G. worked on (other than his own) was Lil' Kim's debut album, *Hard Core*.

There were a lot of women in B.I.G.'s short and extraordinary life. But very few of these women had a significant impact. His mother, Voletta, was, of course, a dominant force. She raised him and shaped his powerful personality in ways that only those engaged in strong mother-son relationships might appreciate. The mother of his first child, daughter T'yanna, was probably Big's first young love (Florence "Jan" Tucker). His only wife, Faith, was a whirlwind of love, drama, and mother of Big's only son, Christopher Wallace Jr. Yet among these powerful women who mothered children for him, Lil' Kim clearly had a special place in B.I.G.'s heart. Artistically she continues to take her cues from him (nearly ten years after his passing), but while he was alive they were able to pour all of their illicit affection for each other into one of the most powerful and sexually explicit albums ever released in hip hop (by either a male or female solo artist), Lil' Kim's *Hard Core*. Purely out of respect for the Wallace family, Kim Jones, and Faith and her new family, we should not make too much out of the love triangle: B.I.G., Faith, and Lil' Kim. But clearly they were all forced to wrestle with Big and Kim's indiscretions in some occasionally very public ways. In the music video for Junior M.A.F.I.A.'s "Get Money," B.I.G. and rap artist-model Charli Baltimore (another reported love interest of B.I.G.) act out a violent domestic disagreement between B.I.G. and a platinum blonde Charli Baltimore. Since Big was married to Faith and she at that time sported various platinum blonde hairstyles, the audience was invited to make the most obvious connections.

At the height of the East Coast–West Coast conflict, Faith made a record with Tupac Shakur and took a photo with him in the recording studio. This was all Tupac needed to start a vicious rumor that he had slept with Biggie's wife. Although Faith has categorically denied ever having intimate relations with Tupac, the public hashing out of these matters (between B.I.G. and Tupac, Kim and Faith, Faith and B.I.G., etc.) created one of the most volatile and potentially violent moments in hip hop and the music business in general. To B.I.G.'s credit, aside from the one-line jab at Faith on "Brooklyn's Finest" ("If Faith have twins she probably have two Pacs") and the video escapade with Charli Baltimore, he rarely responded to Tupac's incitement or any of his relentless dis records. He never responded negatively. Big clearly understood that because of his stature in the industry, any beef between him and Tupac could be blown completely out of proportion. He was, unfortunately, absolutely right.

On September 13, 1996, Tupac Shakur died in Las Vegas from multiple gunshot wounds incurred immediately following a Mike Tyson fight earlier that week. When B.I.G.'s biographer, Cheo Hodari Coker, asked him where he was when he heard the news of Tupac's death, B.I.G. responded: "I got home and it was on the news, and I couldn't believe it. I knew so many niggaz like him, so many ruff, tuff mother fuckers getting shot. I said he'll be out in the morning, smoking some weed, drinking some Hennessy, just hanging out" (Coker 167). In other interviews, B.I.G. was similarly shaken by Tupac's passing. It must have been even more unnerving that he had to finish his much-anticipated second album and promote this album amid rumors that he or his label, Bad Boy Records, had something to do with Tupac's unsolved murder. "You be thinking that when a nigga is making so much money that his lifestyle will protect him; that a drive-by shooting ain't supposed to happen. He was supposed to have flocks of security; not even supposed to be sitting by no window" (167).

By the time the fateful 1997 Soul Train Awards were approaching in early March, B.I.G. had spent over a month in Los Angeles finishing his album, shooting the video for the first single, "Hypnotize," and promoting his upcoming release. On Saturday, March 8, B.I.G. should have been in London, England, promoting *Life After Death*. Instead he decided to cancel the promo tour. He was having a good time in Los Angeles and he wanted a break from his rigorous recording schedule. His sense about all of the tensions surrounding

Tupac's unsolved murder, his rumored involvement, and his impending prominence across the hip hop landscape was extraordinarily positive. He felt as if he would make all of the haters love him. He knew that he had crafted an album that could appeal to a mass audience as well as various niches and regional pockets of the hip hop world. He was excited about how West Coast listeners would respond to "Goin' Back to Cali," B.I.G.'s ode to the west side. He had also achieved a newfound peace with God. He commemorated this peace with a tattoo on his inside right forearm. The tattoo took verses from Psalm 23 (e.g., "The Lord is my light and my salvation, whom shall I fear?").

On the night of March 8, just hours before B.I.G. was murdered, he and his entourage attended what was by most accounts the party of the century. *Vibe* magazine and Qwest Records sponsored an official Soul Train Awards after-party at the Petersen Automotive Museum. Since there were so many industry folk in town, as well as most of the key people from Bad Boy records, this after-party was essentially an unofficial release/listening party for *Life After Death*. The single, "Hypnotize," had already been released and the Bad Boy promotion machine was gearing up for its biggest project ever. As spectacular as this party was, it makes sense that it had to be shut down at 12:35 a.m. for being overcrowded. It was almost too good. As B.I.G. and the caravan carting his entourage exited the party, a car pulled alongside B.I.G.'s rented Suburban and seven forty-caliber nine-millimeter shots rang out (for a full, detailed account of this gruesome scene and the eerie events leading up to Biggie's murder, consult the film *Tupac and Biggie* or Cheo Hodari Coker's in-depth biography, *Unbelievable*). After the shooting, B.I.G. was rushed to Cedars-Sinai Medical Center, but he never regained consciousness. At 1:15 a.m. on March 9, 1997, Christopher George Latore Wallace was dead at the age of twenty-four.

BIGGIE'S IMPACT AND LEGACY

Christopher Wallace's funeral was equivalent to his stature in hip hop culture. As a beloved son of Brooklyn, he was afforded a funeral procession through the streets of his neighborhood. This procession was attended by tens of thousands of people who were emotionally charged and distraught with shock at the murder of Biggie Smalls. The fact that it was a drive-by shooting and that the shooting took place in Los Angeles, so far from home for his homegrown Brooklyn audience, enhanced the tension in the atmosphere even further. As the procession came to an end, the mournful silence in the streets was interrupted by the blaring sounds of Biggie's new single, "Hypnotize." Journalists and various people who were present claim that the crowd erupted in joy and pain. Unfortunately, there were several clashes with police and at least ten people were ultimately arrested, a sad ending to hip hop culture's most poignant memorial service. But for Biggie there was literally life after death.

In many ways, the posthumous album *Life After Death* picks up exactly where *Ready to Die* left B.I.G.'s growing audience. But instead of B.I.G. dying in a suicidal rut, he recovers from a violent trauma to grace us with two albums' worth of the most powerful and appealing rap music produced to date. Considering the fact that the album was released just weeks after B.I.G.'s murder, the introductory track is just as eerie as the album's title. B.I.G. has indeed experienced an extraordinary life through his musical career even after his brutal assassination. *Life After Death* features tracks that are specific to various subcommunities within hip hop culture. In order to fully appreciate B.I.G.'s fluidity in almost every vernacular rap style developed in the United States, you must actually listen to the album with a good sense of the developments in hip hop culture and rap music since 1997.

The "B.I.G. Interlude" is modeled directly after Schoolly D's classic gangsta rap song "PSK (Park Side Killers)," which is as much an ode to Philadelphia as "Going Back to Cali" is to California. On "Notorious Thugs," B.I.G. assumes the popular staccato style of the (at the time) most famous rap act to hail from the Midwest: Cleveland, Ohio's Bone Thugs-N-Harmony. Collaborations with R. Kelly, the Lox, Mase, 112, and Puffy's near-ubiquitous presence were, amazingly, not overdone. And B.I.G. did not disappoint his base audience. "Kick in the Door" and "Ten Crack Commandments" are pure DJ Premier-produced street bangers, while "Hypnotize" and "Mo Money, Mo Problems" blazed the radios and clubs for months. "Never has an artist attempted to please so many different audiences simultaneously and done it so brilliantly.... *Life After Death* was nothing short of a gangsta rap *Songs in the Key of Life*, the stylistically diverse Stevie Wonder double album that made listeners wonder if there was anything Stevie couldn't do" (Coker 262–263). Narrative structure and detail abound on "I Got a Story to Tell," "Niggas Bleed," and "Somebody's Got to Die." Songs like these make *Life After Death*, and Biggie's lyrical prowess in general, unparalleled in hip hop even now, ten years after his death. *The Source* magazine gave *Life After Death* a five-mic rating. The mic rating system is a long-standing barometer for hip hop albums. Although, unfortunately, this ratings system, along with *The Source* itself, has been called into question, very few fans challenged the five-mic rating on B.I.G.'s second album. Even those purists who did not like the fact that Brooklyn's native son was as close as any rapper had ever been to authentic universality had to at least appreciate such an exceptionally skilled effort on record.

Notorious B.I.G.'s second posthumous album, *Born Again*, was released in December 1999, almost three years after his murder. Unlike *Life After Death*, *Born Again* relied on previously recorded material, numerous guest appearances, and some production wizardry from Sean "Puffy/Diddy" Combs to make it whole. Guest appearances include Snoop Dogg, Eminem, Nas, Lil' Kim, Busta Rhymes, Redman, Method Man, Ice Cube, and Missy Elliott. Very few, if any, of these tracks stand out or grab the ears of listeners in the same manner as B.I.G.'s earlier work. "Dead Wrong," featuring Eminem, conjures nostalgia for the early preconflict days; here producers sport a classic verse from early in B.I.G.'s career, evidenced by the higher pitch in his delivery. Finally, though, *Born Again* was (and is) completely incapable of satisfying audiences' desire to hear more of their fallen hip hop icon. The album itself was super-saturated with guest appearances and, in light of the amount and variety of posthumous material being released on Tupac Shakur (a comparison impossible to avoid, considering the ways in which these two were connected in life as friends, enemies, and murder victims), *Born Again* cannot shine as a viable album in Biggie's repertoire.

On what should be the last full-length album headlined by the Notorious B.I.G., *Duets: The Final Chapter*, executive producers Sean "Diddy" Combs and others were able to somehow come up with a formula that is remarkably similar to the template for *Born Again*, but with more effective results. They combine verses from Biggie with mostly contemporary rappers (except for Tupac and Big Pun) over contemporary hip hop production. Either we as an audience of B.I.G. miss him more than ever or these are just better songs, stronger musical productions, and more authentic collaborations. One of the album's standouts is the track "Living in Pain" featuring Mary J. Blige, Nas, and Tupac. By any standards, this is a legendary all-star lineup of artists. This may be the best work that Mary J. Blige has provided for a Biggie Smalls track since his much earlier work on "Real Love." Blige's vocals perfectly capture the pain and mourning that we feel hearing these kinds of posthumously produced recordings even as she soulfully captures the pain and nihilism of violent inner-city living that has claimed the lives of two of the three MCs on this particular recording. "Living in Pain" stands out among hip hop culture's posthumously produced materials. Three of the greatest MCs of all time— Biggie, Pac, and Nas—contribute classic verses over a modulating operatic track produced by Just Blaze. It is a shame that these three were unable to collaborate when they were all alive, but Nas clearly understands the pain of the lost opportunity and the burden he bears to promote the legacies of both B.I.G. and Tupac even as he lives and continues to create more music in their shadows. Other tracks, especially "Hustler's Story" featuring Akon and the legendary Scarface, "Wake Up Now" featuring Korn, and even "Ultimate Rush" featuring Missy Elliott all help to lift this album well beyond the results of *Born Again*.

Ten years after B.I.G.'s murder, the case still remains unsolved. The story and the controversy surrounding the unsolved murders of both B.I.G. and Tupac continue to make headlines. In September 2002, a *Los Angeles Times* business reporter, Chuck Phillips, wrote a story that directly implicated B.I.G. in Tupac's murder. "The *Times* reported that on the night of Shakur's killing a Crips 'emissary' had visited B.I.G. in the penthouse suite at the MGM Grand Hotel in Las Vegas, where the enormous rapper promised $1 million on the condition that Shakur was killed with his gun" (Sullivan, "Unsolved Mystery," 140).

This article turned out to be so flimsy in terms of sourcing and actual new evidence that less than five days later Phillips published another article detailing proof provided by the lawyers of B.I.G.'s estate that B.I.G. had been in a recording session in New York City at the time that this alleged conspiracy to murder Tupac Shakur was taking place. Moreover, close friends of B.I.G. corroborated this and solidified that he was in New York, not Nevada, at those times. Still, the fact that the *Los Angeles Times* reported this thinly veiled attack on B.I.G.'s legacy and credibility was indicative of other major developments between the Wallace contingent and the city of Los Angeles.

Voletta Wallace hired attorney Perry Sanders to spearhead a wrongful death suit against the Los Angeles Police Department (LAPD). Although the case ultimately focused on the "deliberate indifference" of the LAPD with respect to the investigation of Biggie Smalls's murder, author Randall Sullivan and former LAPD detective Russell Poole had been piecing together one of the most extraordinary cases of police corruption and cover-up in history. Sullivan's book-length expose, *LAbyrinth*, details Russell Poole's comprehensive investigations into the Rampart scandal and its overlapping connections to the murders of Biggie Smalls and Tupac Shakur. The Rampart scandal involves various LAPD officers who were part of the CRASH unit, which focused on gang activities. Several officers from this unit have been implicated in various illegal activities, including everything from planting weapons on innocent victims to selling narcotics. Detective Poole's investigations revealed several incredible facts: (1) Certain CRASH officers were in league with the Bloods gang; (2) a few of these officers, including Ray Perez and David Mack, also worked for Marion "Suge" Knight and Death Row Records at the time of both murders; and (3) the powers that be in the LAPD, the *Los Angeles Times,* and possibly the city of Los Angeles itself were extremely reluctant to cooperate with Detective Poole when he was leading these investigations or to accurately and fairly report on these matters as information became available. Poole believes that David Mack, employed by Suge Knight, conspired with Amir Muhammed to assassinate Biggie. Muhammed was the alleged trigger man and David Mack provided the drive-by vehicle and helped to case the party and security for B.I.G. immediately preceding the actual hit.

All of this labyrinthine mess came to a head when the Wallace estate's civil suit was declared a mistrial. The judge ruled that a detective (Steve Katz) in the LAPD had deliberately concealed a tremendous amount of evidence in the Biggie Smalls murder case. She therefore concluded that the department was attempting to conceal David Mack's involvement in the case. Although she did not find in favor of the Wallace family, the court clearly judged against the nearly nine-year cover-up. "After the mistrial, Wallace's lawyers were contacted by a number of political figures in Los Angeles—worried that this lawsuit might bankrupt the city" (Sullivan, "Unsolved Mystery," 142).

Surely these legal maneuverings and mistrials will not be the lasting legacy of Christopher Wallace, aka Notorious B.I.G. In fact, generations of Brooklyn youth will know him better through the Christopher Wallace Foundation, managed by Voletta Wallace. The foundation's B.I.G. (books instead of guns) program provides support for students and schools in Biggie's neighborhood. Ultimately, this will be B.I.G.'s legacy: His impact on youth facing the same challenges he faced will sustain itself based on his short but incredible presence on the hip hop cultural landscape. "Biggie's legacy is different. Wallace's lasting imprint on hip hop is more musical than iconographic. He is a master of flow, of lyrical rhythm and technique—the Jordan to Rakim's Magic. While his catalogue of unreleased records isn't as large as Tupac's, the quality of many of the surviving freestyles is unsurpassed" (Coker 293).

See also: Tupac Shakur, Nas, Lil' Kim, Wu-Tang Clan

WORKS CITED

Baker, Houston. *Blues Ideology and Afro-American Literature: A Vernacular Theory.* Chicago: University of Chicago Press, 1987.

Coker, Cheo Hodari. *The Life, Death, and Afterlife of the Notorious B.I.G.* New York: Three Rivers Press, 2003.

Huey, Steve. "The Notorious B.I.G. (Christopher Wallace)." *All Music Guide to Hip Hop: The Definitive Guide to Rap and Hip Hop.* Ed. Vladimir Bogdanov, Chris Woodstra, Stephen Thomas Erlewine, and John Bush. San Francisco: Backbeat Books, 2003.

Kool Moe Dee. *There's a God on the Mic: The True 50 Greatest MCs.* New York: Thunder's Mouth Press, 2003.

Mao, Chairman. "If You Don't Know ... Now You Know: Discography." *Unbelievable: The Life, Death, and Afterlife of The Notorious B.I.G.* Ed. Cheo Hodari Coker. New York: Three Rivers Press, 2003.

McDaniels, Ralph. "Brooklyn's Finest: Videography." *Unbelievable: The Life, Death, and Afterlife of The Notorious B.I.G.* Ed. Cheo Hodari Coker. New York: Three Rivers Press, 2003.

Rose, Tricia. *Black Noise: Rap Music and Black Culture in Contemporary America.* Hanover, NH: Wesleyan University Press, 1994.

Sullivan, Randall. *LAbyrinth: A Detective Investigates the Murders of Tupac Shakur and Notorious B.I.G., the Implications of Death Row Records' Suge Knight, and the Origins of the Los Angeles Police Scandal.* New York: Grove Press, 2002.

Sullivan, Randall. "The Unsolved Mystery of the Notorious B.I.G.: The Murder. The Cover-up. The Conspiracy." *Rolling Stone.* 15 December 2005: 124–147.

Wallace, Voletta, and Tremell McKenzie. *Voletta Wallace Remembers Her Son, Biggie.* New York: Atria Books, 2005.

Williams, Saul. *The Dead Emcee Scrolls: The Lost Teachings of Hip-hop.* New York: MTV Books, 2006.

FURTHER RESOURCES

Biggie and Tupac: The Story Behind the Murder of Rap's Biggest Superstars. Lafayette Films, 2002.

Scott, Cathy. *The Murder of Biggie Smalls.* New York: St. Martin's, 2000.

SELECTED DISCOGRAPHY

Ready to Die. Uptown/Bad Boy Records, 1994.
Life After Death. Bad Boy Records, 1997.
Born Again. Bad Boy Records, 1999.
Duets: The Final Chapter. Bad Boy Records, 2005.

© AP Photo/Tammie Arroyo.

Lil' Kim

Aine McGlynn

On a warm July morning in 2006, Kimberly Jones was released from a Pennsylvania correctional facility after having served ten months of a 366-day sentence. This release would mark the launch of the latest version of the rapper's ever-changing public persona. July 3 would be the *next* first day in the epic narrative of the Notorious K.I.M. Just shy of her thirtieth birthday, and in just over a decade, Lil' Kim had established herself as an indelible icon in the temple of hip hop. Having shaken off the qualifying word *female* from any and all discussion of her skills, Kim stood shoulder to shoulder with the roughest, baddest, most gangsta rappers. With her fourth album, *The Naked Truth,* receiving critical acclaim, and her assertions that she was only just beginning to control her style, her image, and the way that she was marketed, Jones was poised to become Lil' Kim once again. Over the course of that July morning, Kimberly Jones shed her prison garb and once again assumed the mantle of Queen Bee. In a pristine white low-cut suit and shades, Lil' Kim walked beyond the prison gates to an awaiting silver Rolls Royce that sped her and her overjoyed mother back to the pampered life that the tiniest and most provocative member of hip hop's royalty was accustomed to.

In an effort to protect her bodyguard, Suif Jackson, who was accused of shooting a member of rapper Capone's entourage during a 2001 confrontation outside of hip hop's radio Mecca, Hot 97, Kim testified that she couldn't remember if Jackson had been present that day. Unfortunately for Kim, a security camera revealed that she had been standing beside Jackson moments before the shooting took place. Other members of her posse who were present that day copped plea bargains and cooperated with the prosecution, resulting in a twelve-year sentence for Jackson. Kim was the only one who refused to cooperate, and she was found guilty of obstruction of justice (see sidebar: Hip Hop and the Law).

Hip Hop and the Law
Aine McGlynn

Lil' Kim's year-and-a-day prison sentence is not unusual in the hip hop world. In fact, a little jail time can often increase a rapper's credibility and provide an excellent marketing opportunity. Released just eight days into her prison term, Kim's album *The Naked Truth* benefited from all the press that surrounded her impending prison term. 50 Cent has also served some time, as have Chi-Ali, Mystikal, and Tupac. Foxy Brown is currently awaiting trial on an assault charge; Snoop was acquitted of murder; Eminem has faced down weapons charges, and the new editor of *The Source* magazine, Dasun Allah, has faced charges. Popular music, from rock and roll to jazz and blues and even country and western, has always been considered rebel music. The lifestyle of a musician implies an element of subversion or counterculturalism. As a result, musicians are often uncompromising about their individual rights and often don't care about the law.

Hip hop, though, seems to have more than its share of outlaws. The argument has been made that you can take the thug out of the ghetto but you can't take the ghetto out of the thug. The mistrust of the law and the disrespect for authority that come with a legacy of harassment by the cops are not easily forgotten. Serving a jail sentence also becomes part of a rapper's narrative. It can bolster claims to authenticity and make the persona appear harder. Street credibility bolsters respect from the rap community while it also pads out the story that accompanies the press release for the latest album.

During Lil' Kim's prison term, she composed letters to her fans that emphasized how well she was getting along with her fellow inmates. She described the volleyball team that she joined and the cake that her new friends made for her "record release party." As a gift to Lil' Kim, one inmate fashioned a stiletto made entirely out of watermelon Jolly Ranchers. This is hardly the stuff of the stereotypical prison term. Kim failed to mention gangs, strategic allegiances, shanks, or days spent in solitary. Nonetheless, Kim served her time and her album did rather well, garnering her nominations for *Vibe*'s Album of the Year and BET's Female Rapper of the Year.

If nothing else, the steady stream of rappers to the courthouse raises attention to the culture of litigation and imprisonment that exists in America. The heavy-handedness of drug laws and controversial racial profiling have all led to stifling conditions both within overcrowded detention centers and for those trying to stay beneath the sweeping radar of law enforcement.

Never one to do anything without creating a media fuss, Kim decided to go to prison with all eyes focused on her. The press packets for *Countdown to Lockdown*, a BET reality show chronicling the last few days before Kim went to prison, promised viewers unprecedented access to the notorious life of Lil' Kim. Perhaps most shocking of all, the producers told viewers to watch as "her glam team starts to peel away all the layers of fabulousness that make Lil' Kim the celebrity she is, until she is stripped down to a bare Kimberly Jones. No weave, no makeup, no jewelry, Kim is dressed in a T-shirt with none other than Big Poppa's face on it" ("Lil' Kim: Countdown to Lockdown").

This unadorned woman is, they argue, the real Kimberly Jones; the Lil' Kim veneer is as easily peeled off and discarded as a false eyelash. However, the lines between persona and person are not as distinct as the press writers would have you believe: The insecurity and loudmouthed brashness of Kimberly Jones seep into every stunt that Lil' Kim pulls. Similarly, Kimberly Jones's rap persona, be it the Notorious K.I.M., Big Momma, or the ghetto royal Queen Bee, has changed Kimberly Jones. These personas are absorbed into her, leaving Kimberly Jones, from the outside at least, unrecognizable to her childhood self.

THE NOTORIOUS LIFE OF KIMBERLY JONES

Kimberly Jones was born in Brooklyn, New York, on July 11, 1974 Her father was an ex-marine corps officer and a strict disciplinarian who kept Kim, her mother, and her younger brother, Christopher, on a very short leash. Her family described her on VH1's *Driven* as a tough child, willing to tussle with anyone, but nonetheless not a tomboy. At a young age she pranced around in her mother's clothing, makeup, and shoes. Ruby Mitchell-Jones worked at high-end department stores. She loved fashion, a love that Kim developed early in life. As her fame grew, she translated that love into a style that was imitative of no one and that no one in their right mind would dare imitate (see sidebar: Hip Hop and Fashion).

Kim's talents were not nurtured by her father, with whom she butted heads to such an extent that the police were called several times to attend to their

---

Hip Hop and Fashion
Aine McGlynn

Hip hop has always been about style. Afrika Bambaataa, a pioneer of hip hop sounds, was also an early trendsetter for the hip hop aesthetic. His style choices were always bold and fiercely individual. He ushered in the hip hop artist as trendsetter. Run-DMC made popular the iconic hip hop look: jeans, track jackets, pristine white shelltoe Adidas sneakers, shades, and gold chains, and always a hat. Rappers and hip hop heads continue to riff on this look, wearing baggier jeans, diamond-encrusted chains, even whiter sneakers, a sports jersey of some description, and always a hat.

Hip hop has always intersected with fashion because rappers have always rhymed about the labels that they wear. Kangol hats topped most domes in the early eighties, and Missy Elliott still often sports the brand. Run-DMC's famous track "My Adidas" made pop culture icons out of the brand. Rappers have always tended to be a step ahead of popular trends and often anticipate those styles that find their way to the runway. It wasn't long before huge gold chains, doorknocker earrings, and athletic chic were incorporated into Karl Lagerfeld, Gucci, and Louis Vuitton runway shows. Recognizing the purchasing power of the hip hop audience, the fashion world was quick to catch on to the styles that rappers would rock in their videos and in performances. The watershed moment for the commercial intersection of fashion and hip hop occurred in a 1994 performance by Snoop Dogg on *Saturday Night Live*. Snoop came out clad in an oversized Tommy Hilfiger rugby shirt and overnight, Hilfiger became a brand that would be forever linked with the rap community. Tommy Hilfiger himself would win the title of Menswear Designer of the Year by the Style Council of America in 1995. For a label that had languished in relative obscurity, dressing prep-school kids for country club dances, the jump to the center of the street culture and aesthetic sent the company in a totally different direction.

Different regions of the country have contributed to the various styles that rappers rock. From West Coast Chicanos, the huge T-shirts and jeans; from the south, the gold and diamond grills that cover people's teeth; from New York, Afrocentric images of the continent, of Marcus Garvey, and T-shirts featuring the black, red, green, and yellow of African pride.

> More recently, the real sign that a rapper has made it is the decision to start his or her own clothing label. Jay-Z's Roca Wear, Puffy's Sean John, Outkast's Outkast line, and Russell Simmons's Phat Farm all trade on the personal styles of the rapper behind the label.

disputes. In her late teenage years, Kim picked up a kitchen knife and tried to stab her father during one particularly nasty argument. Her mother, having left her father, was living out of her car, and thus was in no position to assist Kim's aspirations of fame. At barely seventeen years of age, Kim left her father's home after being told that she was not welcome to move with him, his new wife, and her brother to their new house in New Jersey. Instead, Kim was left to her own devices in the rough Brooklyn neighborhood around Ryerson Towers. A teenaged girl without a family or a home to go to for help and support is compelled to do a number of things in order to survive. In interviews, her friends and family describe Kim as doing whatever she could to make ends meet. She ran errands for drug dealers, who delighted in having a pretty young female around. Though she never states it outright, the implication is strong that Kim had to prostitute herself.

Kim was hustling. She relied on the kindness of friends, crashing on couches here and there; but she still had her eyes focused on a career as a performer. She grabbed the mic at every basement party she found herself at, rapping, singing, sometimes just running her mouth over any record the DJ threw on the decks. She began to develop a reputation in the neighborhood, mostly because of her tiny frame, relentless energy, and surprising ferocity.

Right around this time, Christopher Wallace, aka the Notorious B.I.G., aka Biggie Smalls, was coming up out of the same Brooklyn neighborhood. Puffy Combs had been promoting Biggie with Uptown Records, and through appearances on other artists' tracks—namely Mary J. Blige, 2Pac, and Big Daddy Kane in the early nineties—the larger-than-most MC began to garner some attention. In the meantime, he had heard about Kim through the network of Brooklyn's hip hop hopefuls and introduced himself to her. She was shy at first, but he encouraged her to drop a few rhymes for him and, to his surprise, this under-five-feet-tall, sweet smiling girl could spit with an intensity that rappers twice her size could never muster. Kim and Biggie had an intense connection made of complex layers of lust and sexual energy, genuine love and affection, marketing strategies and showbiz realities, jealousy, money, and burgeoning fame.

In 1994, while his career was just about to blow up with the release of *Ready to Die*, Biggie's attention turned to building the careers of the Brooklyn rappers that he had come up with. He began Junior M.A.F.I.A. (Masters at Finding Intelligent Attitudes), a posse made up of Biggie's Brooklyn crew. Kim became Big Momma in the Mafia. She was described as Biggie's lieutenant, running the show with Big Poppa. Atlantic Records released 500 copies of "Player's Anthem" in 1994 to see what the street-level reaction would be. The track blew up, and a subsequent performance of it at Harlem's famous Apollo Theater announced Kim's arrival.

Biggie got a reaction when he rapped, but when Kim, the tiny woman standing next to his 300-plus-pound immensity, got up and matched his rhyme, crowds lost their minds. Biggie implied that he was going to set up Kim as the next big thing in hip hop. He introduced her to his mother as his artist and went about styling her to sell her own records, while also promoting his own career. Kim was to be his protégé, but he needed her help to invent a persona for himself. At street level, where their fame was biggest, it served Biggie to make this woman appear to be the most vicious sexual animal possible in order to position himself as her conqueror. They struck a remarkable pose together; the four-feet-eleven-inch woman and the 300-pound, six-feet-plus man styling themselves as a thugged-out Bonnie and Clyde.

The promotional posters for *Hard Core*, her debut album in 1996, featured Kim in a leopard print bikini, crouched down to the floor, legs spread wide. It was a poster that shocked Biggie's mother, who demanded to know what he was doing to her. Biggie remained insistent that it was her sex that would sell the album. And sell it did. The album debuted at number eleven on the Billboard 200 and number two on the rap chart. Three singles from the album went to the top of the rap chart, with "Not Tonight (Ladies Night)" earning her a Grammy Award nomination.

As Biggie acknowledged, as record producers proclaimed, as the fans at the shows realized, this woman could spit fire on the mic. This was evident in the listening. Up until this point, female rappers had rocked a groovy neo-soul line, or a Native Tongues pro-black, pro-woman style. MC Lyte was the rapper Kim was musically most reminiscent of. Lyte had represented Brooklyn with a similar intensity, but faded by the early nineties. Then, hip hop underwent a revolution when the center of creativity shifted from the East to the West Coast in the early nineties. Gangsta rap, characterized by misogyny and hypermasculinity, appeared to have no room for female MCs. Lil' Kim came along and changed all that, ushering in a new era of female rap for herself, Foxy Brown, Missy Elliott, Eve, Da Brat, and Trina; but in spite of her skills, Kim still had to prove herself with her body first. Her rhymes were an extra bonus. For Kim though, the rhymes were about the clothes, or lack thereof, and the style she rocked was about visually representing what she rapped about. She acknowledges this intersection of skimpy clothes and red-hot lyricism on the track "Single Black Female" from *The Notorious K.I.M.* She rhymes, "If I dress freaky that's my business."

Kim wasn't always so scantily clad. In the early days, she performed with Junior M.A.F.I.A. in fly Versace suits and furs, but with *Hard Core*, the clothes came right off. During the recording of the album, Biggie and Kim's relationship reached new levels of drama. Biggie married Faith Evans within weeks of meeting her. Some say the union was a marketing ploy to hype both their albums; this clearly did not sit well with Kim, a woman who had been loyal and devoted to Biggie, but who also challenged him, giving as good as she got. Their relationship was often violent, with Biggie reportedly dragging her across a hotel lobby by her hair one particularly nasty but not uncharacteristic evening, and Kim threatening to kill Biggie on several occasions.

After Biggie and Evans's marriage, Kim was relegated to the status of mistress. She wasn't Biggie's second in command, she was his second-string lover, one with whom he wouldn't have a child, leaving Kim to abort a pregnancy during the recording of *Hard Core*. Kim could never mother Biggie's children. She was his sexpot, a raunchy provocateur for rap fans to ogle while behind her back, Biggie and his male fans could share a sly moment of collective male sexual prowess.

With her album on the charts, her name on the lips of ghetto princes and princesses, and her tracks garnering critical and industry attention, it was clear that Lil' Kim was a legitimate hip hop success story. But her success was soon tainted by tragedy. In March 1997, Biggie was shot and killed leaving an event in Los Angeles. It wasn't long before a veritable satellite industry grew up around posthumous releases of Big's rhymes. Puffy rode Biggie's death to massive success for Bad Boy Records, including a huge tribute hit with "I'll Be Missing You," featuring Faith Evans. Kim, however, was not invited to star on the song, although she was devastated by Biggie's death. She had lost her lover, her collaborator, her mentor, and her friend. Evans got to release the lament for Big, while Kim, two years after his death, performed on the hyped party track "N.O.T.O.R.I.O.U.S." Though she couldn't be Biggie's wife, Kim could enact the true depth of their connection in her rhymes. While he was alive, Kim was styled to represent Big's sexual prowess. After his death, Kim was free to recoup him as her partner and reposition herself as his equal and his collaborator.

In the four-year gap between *Hard Core* and her follow-up album, *The Notorious K.I.M.*, rumors abounded that Kim's career was over. In spite of her attempts to assert herself as Biggie's equal, it was repeatedly suggested that Biggie had written all her rhymes and that he had coached her on every line on both the Junior M.A.F.I.A. tracks and her own album. One could understand the accusation, especially listening to "No Time," a hit track featuring Puffy, where Kim's delivery is reminiscent of the hard-hitting, bass-heavy staccato, grunts, and internal rhymes that were characteristic of Big's style. Big echoes in Kim's delivery on "No Time" when she says "butta leathers and mad cheddaz." Biggie's style of punctuating the beat with the rhymed word and his thick, lazy delivery are all evident on *Hard Core*. Given the fact that Big was determined to shape Kim's career to reflect his own authority as a hip hop mogul, his influence is unquestionably all over Kim's first album. Kim's 2005 album, *The Naked Truth,* suffers from a similar sort of parroted style. On "Quiet" the beat is reminiscent of Eminem's "Lose Yourself," while the escalating punctuated aggression of her rhyme style sounds like Eminem's as well. On "Durty" she mimics Sean Paul's dance hall delivery, and her single "Lighters Up" also rocks a reggae style.

After Biggie's death, Kim felt immense pressure to produce an album that would convince the hip hop audience of her skills as a writer and MC with her own individual style. Under the guidance of Puffy, who was still hard at work marketing Biggie's death for all it was worth, Kim was encouraged to shed still more clothes and to take her already raunchy lyrics to a whole new level. It was in this interim between the first and second albums that Kim began her dramatic transformation into the Lil' Kim who both aggravates and fascinates black feminists.

LIL' KIM'S PERSONAL FEMINISM

There are many, sometimes competing, definitions of feminism and feminists. bell hooks once said that feminism is about "talking back to essentializing discourses that have defined women in demeaning ways and pushing boundaries within an environment oppressive to women" (quoted in Guillory 29). Kim refused to be essentialized, to be lumped into a category of female rapper. Her desire was to be respected outright, as an MC with skills who didn't see being a woman as a handicap. Gangsta rap is notoriously hateful of women, and Kim's unabashed boasting about her skills, her body, and her ability to threaten men by her very femininity aligns her with hooks's definition of feminism—in theory. But Lil' Kim is never so easy to encapsulate.

Tricia Rose, in an interview with MC Lyte, defined feminism for the rapper. MC Lyte belonged to an older generation of female MCs who, along with the likes of Queen Latifah, resisted the label of feminism for fear that they would be seen as anti–black male. This is the choice that black feminism has always had to make, between two solidarities; one based on race, the other based on gender. Rose suggested to MC Lyte that feminism didn't have to be a dirty word, or necessitate the choosing of loyalties. A feminist, then, could be a woman who "wrote, spoke or behaved in a way that was pro-woman, in that she supported situations that were trying to better the lives of women" (176). The case could certainly be made that on tracks such as "I'm Human," where she intones that the new millennium will belong to women, Kim adopts a pro-woman stance. Nonetheless, Kim's relationship with feminism is more subtle and nuanced than either hooks's or Rose's definitions allow. The main trouble with their definitions in relation to Lil' Kim lies in the fact that both talk about a collective of women. Kim's feminism is about her specifically unique position as a woman, not about the plight of women generally. It is here that Kim stands apart from her female predecessors in the rap game, especially Queen Latifah.

Queen Latifah's music video for the song "Ladies First" is an example of the type of feminism that the mainstream can support and comprehend.

The video features Latifah rapping with images of South African women and children projected on a screen behind her. Latifah here is a benevolent queen, concerned with the plight of her weakest subjects and determined to align herself with their struggle so that they might benefit from her power. Kim, on the other hand, chose to adopt the moniker of the Queen Bee, the singular, lone female in a world of male drones who labor unquestioningly to ensure her comfort and survival. Their own survival depends on it.

The Queen Bee, both the one in the hive and the one who prances down red carpets, is also utterly self-centered. The only female whose life Kim is trying to improve is her own. This feminism, characterized by a woman who puts herself before any collective struggle, is influenced by the harshest, most self-centered dictums of survival in the capitalist market. The hip hop style of the gangsta, with which Kim most obviously aligns herself, rejects the morality of the black middle class. Gilroy calls this resistance to community uplift and the politics of racial solidarity "the ghetto-centric individualism of the poor" (266). For the poor, it is the self that must first be lifted up out of oppression. The community comes second.

For Kim, there were only a limited number of places at the top of the rap game, and her efforts were always directed toward securing her own place at that apex. There is no sense in Lil' Kim's music that she will make personal sacrifices for the good of the larger collective. For instance, in "Doin' It Way Big" on *La Bella Mafia*, in direct contradiction to Latifah's attempts to re-present for South Africans, Kim boasts that she gets her diamonds "straight out the Kimberly gold mine in Africa." Totally oblivious, or perhaps uncaring, about the history of horrendous labor practices in South African mines and the devastating environmental effects of the gold industry, Kim's boast is characteristic of the American individualism that places acquisition above political responsibility at every turn. Kim's song predated Kanye West's "Diamonds (from Sierra Leone)" (2005), which criticized hip hop stars for supporting the diamond trade.

Kim's individualist feminism is nonetheless realist. It embraces the truth of existing in a value exchange economy where each individual, male or female, is required to bring their goods to market to sell. Kim's feminism is defined by the fact that as a woman, she seeks to achieve the highest price possible for her single most precious and valuable product: her sex. A line in "Heavenly Father" on *La Bella Mafia* reveals Kim's price. Her manager remarks that if you want Kim, it will cost $75,000 and "that's just for conversation." Kim prices herself out of the range of your average prostitute, but her critics still easily make the comparison. Lil Kim's raunchy lyrics have been read as disparaging to women and as reducing women to sexual playthings, but Kim's feminism is about how she uses her own sexuality to secure the future that she wants for herself. In Kim's lyrics, her sexuality is a powerful tool necessary to her survival in the rap game. While male gangsta rappers often include sexual aggression in their boasts of how violent and threatening they can be, Kim boasts about her sexual abilities. In "Gimmie That" from her 2005 album *Naked Truth*, she boasts that she has the "tightest, rightest vagina."

The differences between the way men and women rap about sex are evident in Lil' Kim's collaborations with male artists. "Gimmie That" features Maino and Kim in a conversation about their sexual prowess and conquests. Maino claims he can dominate a girl and Kim insists that her body has the power to leave a man insane, spent, and ruined for any other woman. In the context of "Gimmie That," and in the larger context of hip hop and sex, both male and female MCs claim to hold the power in sex. On "Magic Stick," a track that Kim recorded with 50 Cent, both MCs refer to their genitals as magic. Kim is also known to adapt men's sexual slang for her own songs, such as "Suck My Dick" from *Notorious K.I.M.* In this song and "Not Tonight," Kim redefines rap's view of sex, making it first and foremost about the woman's pleasure. The competition between men and women on the microphone has become more and more explicitly sexual since the early 1980s beef that Roxanne Shanté started with the male MCs of the group U.T.F.O. This competition in itself is useful in that it sparks dialogue between men and women rappers, but when rappers' rhymes become obsessed with the quest for sexual dominance, they can risk giving listeners a dangerous impression: Listeners can begin to associate hypersexual aggression with black men and women, which is a dangerous racial stereotype.

KIM'S INIMITABLE STYLE

Kim has become closely connected with designer Marc Jacobs. Before she went to prison, Kim and Jacobs collaborated on a T-shirt emblazoned with Kim's image and the words "I love Lil' Kim" on the back. The shirt was sold to benefit a Brooklyn youth organization called the Door. Kim has of late been accompanying Jacobs to events and has restyled herself as his muse. In Jacobs's styles, Kim has found a more sophisticated, demure, less garish way to set herself apart from the baggy-clothes-wearing, sneaker-sporting, iced-out thugs who have defined the look of the hip hop nation.

Whether a sign of maturity or a transformation that has occurred since her conviction, Kim no longer seems to choose clothing that will create as much media attention as possible. In one outfit from the late nineties, Kim stepped out in hot pink hair extensions, a skin-tight, white off-the-shoulder dress tied closed on one side with multicolored ribbons, fishnet stockings, and knee-high boots with matching hot pink tassels. Emblazoned across the front of the dress were the words "look at me." It would be impossible not to. Outfits such as these epitomize Kim's disregard for the distinction between good and bad press. Still, in spite of her recent turn to haute couture, she doesn't seem to place too much stock in evaluations of her clothing.

Kim's most notorious style choice was undoubtedly the purple one (er, two?) piece jump suit that she wore to the 1999 MTV Video Music Awards. The spandex outfit left one of her breasts completely exposed, save for a strategic pasty. It made for a remarkable television moment when Diana Ross playfully fondled Kim's breast in incredulous amusement, while a positively dowdy-looking (by comparison) Mary J. Blige looked on. That was a significant year for Kim's style. Coming in the four-year interim between her debut and sophomore albums (a long stretch by anyone's count), the onus for Kim was to garner as much attention as possible. Worse than being judged a fashion disaster was being forgotten altogether. That same year, she stepped out to the VH1-Vogue fashion awards in a diamond-studded bodice, sheer skirt, and elaborate tiara/superhero mask with the letters QB studded out in diamonds over her forehead. These wardrobe choices reflect the ongoing trajectory of the inimitable style that Kim boasted even in her childhood in Brooklyn. "She was wearing Gucci before anybody knew what Gucci was," recalls her childhood friend Mo for VH1's *Driven* ("Lil' Kim").

The conservative morality that characterizes the disparaging appraisals of Kim's racy and outlandish fashion sense reveals the radical potential of Kim's fashion choices. Kim's fashion sense is another point of proof of the distance she maintains between her public identity and any type of collective or group. Her outfits are always left of center, always unexpected. Like the feminism that she styles to suit her own personal gains, fashion too is subjected to Kim's individualism. Not wishing to look like anyone else, Kim's style challenges the notion of solidarity through style.

Clothes often establish group memberships and identify the wearer with a specific set of ideas, politics, and projections. To refuse to look like the black collective (unlike Latifah, Erykah Badu, and Lauryn Hill, who take up the aesthetic of African solidarity) is to resist the myth of the essential unity of all people who share a particular skin color. Kim will never adopt an Afrocentric style or view of the world. The popular critical view is that her provocative clothes undermine the empowerment that black women are trying to achieve. It is also possible to read her style as a critique of race-based solidarities. Rather than find power in the sheer numbers contained in the black American collective, Kim's movement away from that style and its attendant politics inadvertently critiques the African American discourse of black unity.

Kim's experience of the ghetto was that it was full of black people, and all of them were poor and struggling. Here was a solidarity of black people in large numbers, but their numbers were irrelevant. As a group, they were barred from accessing the great capitalist American dream. Afrocentrism tends to try to step back from capitalism and the patriotism of the American nation-state. It is possible to interpret Afrocentrism as a discourse that continues to criticize Americans of a certain skin tone who cash in and check out of the projects. Kim defends that choice to make money and get out of the ghetto by any means necessary by stylistically separating herself from her critics.

THE ARTIST WHO FORMERLY LOOKED LIKE LIL' KIM

Unsurprisingly, women tend not to be as enthralled by Kim's silicone breasts, or may be enthralled by them for different reasons. In a 2000 article in *Essence* magazine, written in the form of a letter to Lil' Kim, Akissi Britton calls out Kim's central contradiction: She refers to Kim as a "self proclaimed feminist who is a poster girl for plastic surgery" and a "Black sex symbol who re-created herself to look like a blond Barbie doll" (112). Kim has tried to maintain the image of an ultraconfident woman with a "fuck you" attitude, but the plastic surgery suggests otherwise. Britton argues that there is a frightened and vulnerable woman beneath the altered exterior and that Kim has a responsibility to that woman. Being responsible to herself, to the realization that "money doesn't change the feeling of exploitation" would, Britton assumes, result in Kim taking into account every black woman who has had to bear the real-life consequences of the way that race and gender are represented in the rap industry. Kim claims to care about real women. The track "Hold On" (*Notorious K.I.M.*) reveals a woman in grief. She raps "to my ladies" that she knows what they are going through. Nonetheless, on another album she rhymes about broke bitches, raggedy-ass bitches, and so on, separating herself by virtue of her money from the poverty that affects the lives of many of her listeners.

Kim responds to the pressure to live up to the hype with which she is marketed. Her appearance has undeniably changed over the last few years. Her nose has shrunk as her breasts have gotten bigger. Her lips have grown plumper, her eyes are often hidden behind blue contacts, and her hair is as likely to be green as it is to be blonde. Beginning with Biggie encouraging her to play up her sexiness, the pressure escalated in the years between her first and second albums when the hip hop world waited to see if she could produce an album without Biggie's input. The success of the image that accompanied her first album, the loss of Biggie, the impact of being portrayed as Biggie's bitch, and the fear of failing on her second album, all led to the troubling equation, sex = money = power. It's evident that on *Notorious K.I.M.* and *La Bella Mafia* she stretched that equation to its breaking point. "How Many Licks" on the former album is one of the raunchiest singles to receive airplay, while "The Jump Off" on the latter album mentions fourteen separate product brands. The sex and money are certainly present, but where is Kim's power?

Kim's skin in recent photos is considerably lighter than earlier in her career; her hair is blonde, her eyes blue, her nose thinner and her lips fuller. Because she has undergone so much plastic surgery, some fans and critics have compared Kim to Michael Jackson. Jackson is criticized because he has used plastic surgery to lighten his skin and feminize his features, thereby morphing himself out of the prescribed categories of gender and race. Although Kim's appearance did not become masculine in the same way that Jackson's became feminine, her most outlandish styles mimicked the fashion style of drag queens. This look tries to overemphasize feminine qualities. The breasts become huge, the eyebrows overarched, the waist cinched. The drag queen tries to look more than female in his attempt to hide his masculinity and convince the world of her feminine beauty. Kim isn't trying to look like a transvestite, but she overemphasizes her femininity in the same way, making it appear that her own sense of femininity is not secure. Further, the thinning of her nose, the lightening of her skin, and the bleaching of her hair have all led to criticisms that Kim is trying to look like a white woman or play up to concepts of beauty that are rooted in white culture instead of black culture.

THE AUTHENTIC RAPPER

The loudest accusations that Kim was becoming white accompanied her recent alignment with such Hollywood society names as Donatella Versace, Marc Jacobs, and Victoria Gotti. The timing indicates that perhaps the critiques were equal parts discomfort with a woman who doesn't fit into rigid gender or racial categories and a discomfort with the shift in Kim's class position. It is easy to hate someone who used to be poor and then ostentatiously flaunts wealth. Any deviation on Kim's part from what observers determine is her most real subject position—poor, black, and female—is read as a betrayal or an instance of dishonesty. Kim has tried to counter these criticisms in her music and in interviews over the years. In "This Is Who I Am," a track on *La Bella Mafia*, Kim rapped unapologetically about having big breasts, about how you can't take the hood out of her, about how she'll never change. This song, as well as "Shut Up Bitch" from *The Naked Truth*, are explicit attempts to recoup her credibility within the hip hop community. On these tracks, Kim projects an attitude that aggressively defends her deviations from what others have decided was her most authentic self, which was the identity or persona she projected on her first recordings.

In a 2005 article in *Popular Music and Society*, Mickey Hess makes the point that rappers adopt a performative persona in order to deal with the contradictions between the identity that the ghetto demands from the performer and the identity that the market demands. He argues that if the rapper cannot satisfy the standards of authenticity and street credibility that the ghetto requires, then the marketing strategy falls apart. The question becomes how closely the persona, Lil Kim, represents the identity of the person, Kimberly Jones. Lil' Kim exists in the public as an iconic, imaginative construction of a set of carefully staged performances, outfits, press releases, albums, and photographs. This woman can kick back on a yacht in a video and be brash, unemotional, hard, and confident to the last. Kimberly Jones, however, exists in a world that is governed by the rules of economics, citizenship, time, and space. This latter world has consequences, is messy, unpredictable, full of joys and sorrows. This is the world where a woman feels the actual pain of recovering from plastic surgery, where she falls apart upon her lover's death, where her looks make her insecure.

Gangsta rap in particular depends on the rapper telling (and to some extent living out) a story that the listener believes to be true. In other words, 50 Cent is respected because he has been shot. Incarceration, shoot-outs, growing up in the projects—all of these are staples of the authentic gangsta rapper. Remember Vanilla Ice? Remember how hard he tried to *be* hard? Remember his downfall when everyone discovered that he was from a nice middle-class suburb of Dallas? The equation then would appear to be that in order to achieve respect, and album sales, the rapper and the individual must be one and the same. It is, in fact, far more complex than this. The distinction between persona and person begins with a name. Eminem is not Marshal Mathers, Snoop Dogg is not Calvin Brodis, Puffy is not Sean Combs, and Lil' Kim, the Queen Bitch, is not Kimberly Jones. Every rapper's government identity, or given name, refers to a personality that is apart from the moniker under which they rap. This personality tends to be more somber, subdued, less theatrical. He or she is the named defendant in a trial, some mother's child, the name on the tombstone that brackets the hip hop name; Christopher "Biggie Smalls" Wallace, Eric "Eazy-E" Wright, Lisa "Left Eye" Lopes. In adopting a moniker, or a persona to sell to the public, the performer protects this government identity from becoming a commodity. More sacred than the persona, the performer's government name is the wizard behind the curtain, the intelligent design that orchestrates the selling of the persona. Like the rest of us, such persons have insecurities, strengths, traumas, desires, joys, and so on, that they grapple with outside of and occasionally, when they are being honest, inside their music.

With her 2005 album, *The Naked Truth*, some unification is happening between Kim's persona and Kimberly Jones. She enacts the tough bitch persona in front of the judge, saying on "Slippin'" that "the Bee don't budge." This is the Queen Bee performing the thug loyalty which stipulates that you don't rat out the members of your posse. This performance had dire consequences for Ms. Jones, who was imprisoned as a result of this act. She associates her choice to perjure herself with having grown up in the projects and suggests that that history is worth more than anything else. In this track, Lil' Kim finds a point of unity between her ghetto childhood, the performer that she inhabits, and the woman that she has become as a result of the intersection of those two personalities.

LIL' KIM AND FOXY BROWN

The competition that is fostered between hip hop acts was most famously and tragically played out in the East Coast–West Coast "war" that the popular media blamed for the deaths of Tupac Shakur and Biggie Smalls. On smaller and less deadly scales, feuds often take place in hip hop between individual rappers and are played out in lyrical jabs. Lil' Kim got involved in a verbal war with Foxy Brown, a rapper who has been styled in a manner similar to Lil' Kim. The two women released debut albums at the same time, and both spit raunchy, sexually aggressive rhymes. Though the two were formerly friends, their record companies set them up as competitors (and they do compete for a similar slice of the rap audience) and a feud has continued between them ever since. Their conflict is fueled by the fact that Foxy is under contract with Def Jam, while Lil' Kim belongs to Atlantic (Puffy's Bad Boy Records' parent company). They represent each company cashing in on a gangsta bitch who will spit fire, wear next to nothing, and have male fans drooling over her while admiring the men with whom they appear on tracks, in videos, and on stage.

In 2000, Foxy appeared on a track for Capone-N-Noreaga's album and spit a verse calling Lil' Kim out for milking her Biggie connection for profit and fame. Foxy rapped that Kim was a whore and called her Junior M.A.F.I.A. family her "faggots" who "act more bitch than" she does. Kim responded on "I Came Back for You" (*La Bella Mafia*), calling Foxy "this Doo Doo Brown bitch." Kim did not take kindly to Foxy's accusations and the conflict came to an inevitable head in September 2001 outside of New York hip hop radio station Hot 97 (see sidebar: Hot 97, Where Hip Hop Lives and Dies). It is

---

Hot 97, Where Hip Hop Lives and Dies
Aine McGlynn

Hot 97, WQHT, is a New York–based radio station that claims to be the "Home of Hip Hop." With such iconic DJs as Angie Martinez and Funkmaster Flex at the station, their claim is not that far off. In the halcyon days of the early nineties, before the airwaves were controlled by Clear Channel Communication and playlists were entirely determined by corporate interests, DJs had far more control over what they could put on the air. As a result, Flex brought several underground acts to major success, such as De La Soul and Tribe Called Quest. He was the first DJ to play Jay-Z's debut, "Reasonable Doubt," in 1996. Angie has clout in the industry as well, having released her own album with big-name guest stars and having appeared on such tracks as the Grammy-nominated "Ladies Night" with Lil' Kim and Missy Elliott. Every up-and-coming rapper wants to get an on-air interview with either Angie or Flex. Their approval often translates into significant album sales.

Hot 97 is an impromptu second home for many rappers. During the blackout in New York City in the summer of 2003, basketball star LeBron James and a group of rappers reportedly spent the night in the lobby of the Hot 97 building. The station has seen its share of controversies, many of which involved publicity stunts that pushed the level of decency a little too far. Among the many tricky on-air moments, Smackfest was probably the worst. Pairs of women were invited into the studio to exchange blows on air. A winner was chosen each morning based on her style and enthusiasm. Paired with tasteless joking about Aaliyah's death and the 2004 Asian tsunami, the shock tactics of the DJs have garnered all sorts of negative press for the station.

As hip hop's unofficial mecca, there is no shortage of high-powered rappers milling around the building that houses Hot 97. They are often accompanied by their posses, which are sometimes twenty people strong. Because feuds between rappers are characteristic in hip hop, encounters between two rappers' posses often lead to trouble. It was outside Hot 97 that a member of 50 Cent's entourage was reportedly shot after tensions between 50 and a former member of G-Unit, the Game, escalated. 50 dissed the Game on the air in an interview with Flex, and the beef turned into gun violence shortly after. The sidewalk outside Hot 97 was also the scene of the gun battle between Lil' Kim's posse and Capone, Foxy Brown's recording partner, which landed one man in the hospital and two in prison, and resulted in Kim's incarceration as well.

Like many of the rappers it promotes, Hot 97 has been involved in legal battles, including one in response to attempts to evict the station from its building in Greenwich Village. In hip hop, there is no such thing as bad press, and the violence that occurred outside the station is a validation of Hot 97's position as center stage for the dramatic happenings in the rap world.

---

reported that Kim's entourage met rapper Capone's posse and words were exchanged, followed by gunfire. Foxy has called for a truce, as has Kim. At one time they were asked to record an album together, tentatively titled *Thelma and Louise*. The possibility of these two pairing up as a couple of vigilante women who intend to punish men for their piggishness is a provocative prospect. What is troubling of course about the comparison of Foxy and Kim to Thelma and Louise is the fact that in the end, all outlaw women are either reigned in by the law or choose death in order to escape it. Nonetheless, if Kim and Foxy were to unite on an album, the gesture, though it might alienate them, would be more powerful than each woman separately fading into obscurity as the public becomes tired of seeing their cleavage and pouty faces.

"WHO YOU CALLIN' A BITCH?" KIM'S IMPACT AND LEGACY

Kim refers to herself as "Queen Bitch," indicating a complex relationship between the B-word and the way that female and male rappers use it. Female rappers try to reappropriate the word in the same way that *nigger* has been appropriated by gangsta rappers. Unlike *nigger*, which had to be reclaimed from white racists, *bitch* had to be taken back from men who use it in a derogatory manner. For example on N.W.A.'s classic "A Bitch Is a Bitch" (*Straight Outta Compton*), or Dr. Dre's 1992 "Bitches Ain't Shit" (*The Chronic*) *bitch* is synonymous with *woman* and bitches are no more than whores. Kim turns that accusation around on "Suck My Dick" (*Notorious K.I.M.*), rapping that it's "niggas" who "ain't shit." For a woman, *nigga* stands in for *bitch* as a derogatory word when it is used aggressively.

Missy Elliott describes her use of the word *bitch* to identify herself. She suggests that in order to be successful in the rap industry, a woman has to be a bitch. In most industries this is the case. Women in power, such as Oprah Winfrey, Martha Stewart, or Condoleezza Rice, routinely have to deal with being called a bitch while their male counterparts, who are just as aggressive or even more so, are admired for knowing what they want and going to any lengths to get it. Missy feels that "she is a bitch in power," and that there is nothing wrong with having to "put your foot down." This is a definition of *bitch* that recoups the word from being associated with whorishness. It re-establishes it as a word that indicates power.

When Kim calls herself the Queen Bitch, it is a call to the rap world that she is on top of the pyramid of female rappers. While it also makes a troubling concession to male rappers who think of all women as bitches, her use of the word is preemptive and protective. Using the word to identify herself prevents it being used against her. If Kim uses the word first, then the power that it carries to insult and offend is neutralized. In an interlude on one of Missy's albums, Kim identifies herself and Missy as "rich motherfuckin' bitches, that's right" (Interlude "Checkin' for You," on *Da Real World*). Missy and Kim occupy the same position in terms of wealth and authority. They are peers, so the use of the term is playful and empowering. In the same way that *queer* and *nigger*, used among a group of people who can identify those words with reclaimed power, *bitch* can imply comfort and solidarity. Nonetheless at its root, whether it is used as a self-identification or in a derogatory sense, all three words carry a legacy of offense and violence. Proof of this lies in the fact that each word can still be used as a put-down.

Bitch is still thrown around as a means of demonstrating power and aggression. On *The Naked Truth*, the track "Shut Up Bitch" features a chorus of Kim's haters discussing various rumors about her plastic surgery, her relationship with Biggie, and her jail sentence. Each speculative sentence is answered with the refrain, "Shut up bitch!" It is clear that in this situation, the word is describing someone who is misinformed, jealous, and petty. In short, it becomes obvious that a bitch occupies two opposing categories: the woman with power, the "rich muthafuckin' bitch"; or the woman without power, the woman equated with whorishness, ignorance, and poverty. When a woman is called a bitch by someone more powerful than she is, and men can be included in this category, the implication is that what she has to say doesn't matter. When that same woman calls her equal a bitch, she is saying that she has authority over the word, and that what she has to say is important. Finally, when she calls herself a bitch, she does so with an authority that silences everybody, men and women alike.

See also: MC Lyte, Notorious B.I.G., Queen Latifah, Roxanne Shanté

WORKS CITED

Britton, Akissi. "To Kim with Love." *Essence* October 2000.

Gilroy, Paul. *Against Race: Imagining Political Culture Beyond the Color Line.* Cambridge, MA: Harvard University Press, 2001.

Guillory, Nichole Ann. "Schoolin' Women: Hip Hop Pedagogies of Black Women." Diss. Louisiana State University, 2005.

Hess, Mickey. "Metal Faces, Rap Masks: Identity and Resistance in Hip Hop's Persona Artist." *Popular Music and Society* 28.3 (2005): 297–313.

"Lil' Kim." Exec. Prod. Suzanne Ross. *Driven.* VH1. 2001.

"Lil' Kim: Countdown to Lockdown." Bet.com. 8 August 2006. http://www.bet.com/ Site+Management/Packages/LilKimCountdownToLockdown.htm??Referrer= {5538883B-DA39-4F14-8524-CA51A4742831}.

Rose, Tricia. *Black Noise: Rap Music and Black Culture in Contemporary America.* Hanover, NH: Wesleyan University Press, 1994.

FURTHER RESOURCES

Chang, Jeff. *Can't Stop Won't Stop: A History of the Hip Hop Generation.* New York: St. Martin's, 2005.

Levy, Ariel. *Female Chauvinist Pigs: Women and the Rise of Raunch Culture.* New York: Free Press, 2005.

Shapiro, Peter. *The Rough Guide to Hip Hop.* New York: Rough Guides, 1995.

SELECTED DISCOGRAPHY

Hard Core. Atlantic, 1996.
La Bella Mafia. Atlantic, 2003.
Notorious K.I.M. Atlantic, 1999.
The Naked Truth. Interscope, 2005.

Outkast

T. Hasan Johnson

ATLIENS IN ELEVATORS: PIMPS, GANGSTAS, AND SAGES RISEN FROM SOUTHERN STREETS

Andre Benjamin and Antwon Patton attended Tri-Cities High School in East Point, Georgia, and developed what would one day become one of the most influential groups in hip hop. Andre, born May 27, 1975, is also known as André (Ice Cold) 3000, Dookie, Dre, Johnny Vulture, Benjamin André, and finally Andre 3000. Patton, born February 1, 1975, has maintained his moniker Big Boi, alongside Lucius Leftfoot and Daddy Fat Sax. Outkast has become one of the most significant hip hop groups of all time, with Big Boi developing his patented rhyme style over the years while staying true to the sound of the Dirty South. Andre, on the other hand, has managed to develop a reputation for consistently changing his style of dress, performance (from rapping to singing and playing guitar), and overall rhyme flow. Their eclectic yet complementary styles work perfectly; Dre is perceived as the free-spirited artist, and Big Boi the anchor that keeps Outkast grounded in their cultural roots.

At the onset of their relationship, the two seemed to be at odds. Meeting in 1990, they developed a somewhat adversarial relationship by lyrically battling one another. It did not take very long for them to develop a respect for one another's lyrical skills. Benjamin was an only child and grew up with his mother until the age of fifteen, when he decided to moved in with his father. Patton, on the other hand, grew up in Savannah, Georgia, with his brothers and sisters and later moved to East Point as a teenager. It is said that they met at a party where Benjamin was supposedly standing in a corner holding a beer in one hand and a gun in the other. After that, they were said to have developed a close friendship, eventually forming their first group, called 2 Shades Deep.

2 Shades Deep was pursued by the Atlanta production group Organized Noize, and in 1992, Big Boi and Dre renamed themselves Outkast and officially signed with LaFace Records. As a southern group emerging into a hip hop world divided into categories of East Coast and West Coast, the name fit. Outkast became part of a larger hip hop collective called the Dungeon Family, which included Organized Noize and Outkast, as well Goodie Mob, and various other Atlanta MCs and singers. The Dungeon Family roster included Andre, Big Boi, Big Gipp, Cee-Lo, Debrah Killings, Konkrete, Kujo Goodie, Sleepy Brown, and T-Mo. Organized Noize producers Patrick "Sleepy" Brown, Ray "Yoda" Murray, and Rico Wade became well known for their signature combination of funk, G-funk, soul, and Dirty South (see sidebar: The Dirty South). They have produced award-winning material for TLC, Goodie Mob, Xscape, En Vogue, Ludacris, and, of course, Outkast.

The Dirty South
T. Hasan Johnson

Hip hop in the southern region of the United States has its own distinct history. Most of the country learned about hip hop through word of mouth, random floating mixtapes from New York, or select media venues. Eventually, in the early 1980s, a slew of movies started coming out that helped disseminate hip hop culture. Films like *Wild Style* (1982), *Flashdance* (1983), *Beat Street* (1984), and *Breakin'* (1984) delivered hip hop culture to the world in an unprecedented fashion. Television shows like *Yo! MTV Raps* (1988) and radio stations like Los Angeles's KDAY 93.5 FM further disseminated hip hop's burgeoning culture. Consequently, each area of the country (eventually the world) developed its own brand of rap, complete with its own sounds, techniques, and styles.

During the 1980s, the South yielded only a few artists. For the most part, the recording industry was still warming up to hip hop in the eighties (particularly after the success of Run-DMC, the Beastie Boys, and LL Cool J), but the South was not part of their agenda. As most companies and consumers fixated on New York and California, the South was mostly ignored until, eventually, several groups struck gold. 2 Live Crew (1985), the Geto Boys (1990), and Arrested Development (1992) introduced the South's first wave of successful artists to the hip hop world.

2 Live Crew's newly developed Miami sound was bass heavy and rooted in the Miami club scene. The group received national attention for their raunchy lyrics, forcing the group's lead rapper, Luther Campbell, to fight a series of court battles against federally sanctioned censorship. Conversely, the Geto Boys, from Houston, Texas, was the first southern group to receive widespread mainstream attention. 2 Live Crew's issues with obscenity and censorship prevented them from securing mainstream accolades, but because of the Geto Boys' emphasis on storytelling and their use of slower tempo, bass-heavy beats, the group could help bring the South international acclaim. Their signature song, "Mind Playing Tricks on Me," not only brought attention to the group, it brought attention to southern hip hop. Arrested Development, a southern-based group with a positive message, introduced a southern form of Afrocentric consciousness while using both African and distinctly rural aesthetic elements, employing instrumentation specific to black southern soundscapes.

It was not long before other artists followed. Jermaine Dupri, Da Brat, and Kriss Kross were part of the second wave of significant artists to claim the South as a point of origin. Their sound was much more experimental, colorful, and club friendly. Compared to the Geto Boys' brutal realism and 2 Live Crew's rampant sexuality, these newer groups included a more youthful energy. The third wave, beginning in 1993, consisted of groups like Outkast, Goodie Mob, and the rest of the members of the Dungeon Family. These groups helped continue interest in southern hip hop, while openly engaging southern drawl and slang in a much more overt fashion than their predecessors. In fact, it was in the mid-1990s that mainstream audiences began to incorporate more southern slang into the popular consciousness. This wave, whose signature sound was defined by the production group Organized Noize, emphasized sampling, limited live instrumentation, and slower-tempo beats with intricately interwoven background sounds. They also merged pimp culture, gangsta rhetoric, and socially conscious themes in their music.

Toward the end of the 1990s, the fourth wave of southern hip hop artists began to attract wide-ranging attention. Led by artists like Ludacris and producers like Lil Jon, this era saw the advent of crunk music. Emphasizing alcohol consumption, deep-sounding vocal backgrounds, and heavy bass, the crunk music genre ignited southern rap. Followed by artists like T.I., Young Jeezy, David Banner, the Big Tymers, Juvenile, and Slim Thug (to name a few), southern rap has finally marked its own niche in hip hop's legacy.

Outkast was the first hip hop group signed to LaFace, and they made their debut on labelmate TLC's remix of their hit single "Ain't to Proud to Beg." A year later, in 1993, Outkast released the first song from their first album, *Southernplayalisticadillacmuzik*, "Player's Ball." Although they were not the first hip hop group to release popular songs out of Atlanta, Outkast put Atlanta on the map with "Player's Ball." The success of this song signified a southern hip hop movement when it went gold before Outkast's album was released. It should be noted, however, that it was somewhat risky to be so openly representative of their southern home. Because they openly identified key locations in Atlanta like College Park and East Point, these types of references could have easily alienated them from their national audience, then polarized by East and West Coast musical production camps. What is important about Outkast's first submission to the music industry is that they broke from the binary production options split by California and New York artists. Thus, groups like Bone Thugs-N-Harmony (from Cleveland, Ohio), MC Breed (from Flint, Michigan), or Sir Mix-A-Lot (from Seattle, Washington), were, for the most part, all considered West Coast—although it could be argued that they each had very distinct sounds that were influenced by their respective cities of origin. But each used production teams and styles (and sampled funk groups) that were generally considered part of the West Coast gangsta sound, while Outkast used up-and-coming Atlanta-based production crews. This signaled a break from the conventional split between East and West hip hop aesthetics and openly demonstrated that the South could produce street-certified, quality music.

After "Player's Ball," Outkast released "Git Up, Git Out," a collaborative effort with Goodie Mob, an intertextual track that mixed gangsta and consciousness themes. This soon came to be known as the dominant Outkast-Goodie Mob composition, mixing what many assumed to be East Coast elements (consciousness and political awareness) with West Coast elements (violence, drugs, sex, and gangsta culture); articulating them simultaneously with a distinctly southern cadence. The music on the first album, heavily influenced by R&B and funk musical traditions, provided a new vehicle for southern rap to claim its own place in the pantheon of artistic distinctness, but more importantly, it worked. *Southernplayalisticadillacmuzik* went platinum within a year of its release. Conversely, when receiving their award for Best New Rap Group at the Source Awards in 1995, they were booed when they took the stage. Although Big Boi managed to give his shout-outs, Dre was a bit nervous and only managed to squeak out a couple of choice words—but they were nonetheless prophetic: "The South got somethin' to say."

Their second album, *ATLiens*, was released in 1996, selling 1.5 million units, eventually going double platinum, and reaching number two on the U.S. album charts. The title is partly a statement about being from Atlanta, while also signifying on the theme of the group's name (by using the term *aliens*), framing themselves as societal outcasts. The album garnered them critical acclaim because of their avant-garde subject matter and daring conceptual schemas that yielded them a wider audience with those listeners who believed hip hop music was stagnating in the wake of the East Coast–West Coast wars. Although Outkast still would suffer boos at concerts, their sales and overall support were rising exponentially. The title track, "ATLiens," went to the top forty, whereas their second release, the single "Elevators (Me and You)," went gold and reached the top twenty.

Starting with the *ATLiens* album, Outkast found new ways to infuse a wider and wider variety of styles and sounds into their music. They also subverted expectations by going in a new artistic direction (rather than sticking to what worked for them on the first album with Organized Noize). Contradicting audience expectations, in the tradition of artists like Parliament/Funkadelic and Prince, are risky in the entertainment industry. In one sense, you have to find new and more daring ways to impress your audience while at the same time you avoid deviating from what people want to hear. Outkast boldly decided to push the boundaries of their audience's palette and expand their fan base. On *ATLiens*, they decided to slightly reduce Organized Noize's influence on their work by doing more of their own production through their production group Earthtone Ideas. Hence, although Organized Noize produced the majority of the album (ten out of fifteen tracks), the remaining Outkast-produced tracks were the ones to receive critical acclaim —namely "ATLiens" and "Elevators (Me and You)."

ATLiens also marked the moment when Outkast began to address more complex and eccentric subject matter. Ranging from pimps and hustlers to spaceships and higher consciousness, they amazed (and lost) some of their *Southernplayalisticadillacmuzik* audience, while garnering a larger following inside and outside of hip hop's core group. Songs like "Babylon," "Millennium," and "E.T. (Extraterrestrial)," albeit less known than "Elevators (Me and You)," nevertheless pushed the boundaries of creative production and acceptable hip hop subject matter. Even their brilliant take on overused subjects in hip hop, like sex, was approached in a wholly different manner. In the song "Babylon," Andre talks about a sexual attraction to a woman while describing his upbringing, religious attitudes toward sex, and most intriguingly, his reflections on how such influences may have been problematic. He argues for a more humanistic approach to the matter.

The sounds they used were eerie, spacey, abstract, and at times incomprehensible, and saw the album break convention (consider the Organized

Noize–produced introduction, "You May Die," a strange mixture of anti-weed-smoking messages and an indeterminate, exotic-sounding language). Other songs, like "E.T. (Extraterrestrial)," offer much-appreciated breaks from the predictable by containing no drumbeat.

In 1998, the group released its third album, *Aquemini*. The title was a mixture of both Andre and Big Boi's astrological signs (Gemini and Aquarius, respectively), and the album reached platinum sales three weeks after its release, receiving five mics from *The Source* magazine. Needless to say, this creative collaboration broke from hip hop conventionality more than *ATLiens*, and like its predecessor, *Aquemini* also sold double platinum. They even spoofed their own work during some of the skits featured on the album. These skits featured gangstas who avoid buying an Outkast album because of their frequent change in personality (i.e., gangstas to aliens), but later return, unsatisfied with the typical gangsta album.

Nevertheless, *Aquemini* marked the degree to which Outkast would further march into unpredictable, uncharted aesthetic territory. In television appearances such as their 1998 performance on the *Chris Rock Show*, they visually challenged their audience by wearing more and more outlandish outfits, using live funk artists, and employing instruments that do not usually play a large role in hip hop. In the song "Rosa Parks," the harmonica is fitting but exotic because it is rarely used in hip hop. It also illustrates their appreciation for their southern roots, but somewhat contradicts their appropriation of more rock-themed elements, like the guitar riffs on "Chonkyfire," or the more laid-back guitar pickings in the title track, "Aquemini." But the subject matter of this album, much like *ATLiens*, extends the boundaries of hip hop conventionality. On "Da Art of Storytellin' (Part 1)," Andre tells the story of Sasha Thumper, an old friend that gets hooked into a self-destructive lifestyle and ends up dead from a drug overdose. It should be stated, however, that no description of the song's story could convey the emotionalism of the song. This is significant, considering that hip hop has predominantly articulated itself as an androcentric, masculinist art form with few avenues for emotional expression outside of bemoaning dead homies or lost fathers. Andre, here, manages to walk the fine line between emotionalism and masculinity by articulating this highly emotional narrative with an almost emotionless tone. This strange contradiction in styles maintains his status as a man but allows the listener to experience the tragedy of the character's outcome.

The most highly publicized issue with *Aquemini* was the litigation against Outkast by Rosa Parks. In 1999, Parks sued the group for the use of her name in the song "Rosa Parks." Parks sued for defamation of character and trademark infringement (on her name), and opposed Outkast's use of obscene language in the song. Dre and Big Boi insisted that the song was a tribute, and the initial suit was dismissed and then denied in 2001 on First Amendment grounds after Parks hired Johnnie Cochran to appeal. Eventually, in 2003, the Supreme Court allowed Parks's lawsuit and in 2004, the Parks family, after doubting the ethics of their legal representatives, asked the court to appoint some new, impartial representatives. Later, Outkast was dropped as codefendants while Parks's camp pursued LaFace Records and parent company BMG. The case was settled in 2005 and Outkast agreed to work with the Rosa and Raymond Parks Institute to promote Parks's legacy, with no one having to admit any wrongdoing. But this incident provoked more than just concerns about disrespecting historical figures. This incident helped to highlight the generational differences between the civil rights and hip hop eras.

Partly due to the changing concerns of the times, especially in relation to African Americans who did not benefit from the advances of the black middle class's integrationist political agenda, the civil rights movement focused on the burgeoning black middle class at the expense of the poor black communities they championed. As the black middle class improved its standing in society, the gap between the black affluent and the black poor only widened, and the later exploitation of the poor by state, federal, political, and corporate entities (on a then-unprecedented level) plagued the black community like never before. The dismantling of black labor unions, the lack of access to suitable job training, the reduction of job opportunities, the development of project housing in predominantly black neighborhoods, the displacement of low-income black communities in the interests of the more affluent, the heightened sentencing for crimes committed (statistically) by African Americans more than other racial groups (e.g., crack cocaine sales versus cocaine), the heavy reliance on nearly free black labor in the newly corporatized prison system, the widening technological gap between the black poor and societal elites, the depoliticization of the black church, the gentrification of urban black communities and disproportionate rates for real estate purchases by blacks versus other racial groups, the expansion of black entry into the military industry due to lack of career opportunities, and the use of misinformation to deny blacks access to voting polls all characterized post–civil rights America in the last thirty years of the twentieth century. These issues framed the sociopolitical context of many African Americans born in the 1960s and 1970s, and Parks's misunderstanding of Outkast's aesthetic expression only highlighted the differences between the generations.

Dre and Big Boi themselves were not the authors of many of the arguments ascribed to them; their lawyers wrote many of the statements issued in their defense. Nevertheless, the two members of Outkast became symbols for the frustrations that people felt across the black class generational divide. Parks represented the more conservative black Christian middle class, who looked at the black poor with disdain. Outkast, on the other hand, championed the poor, mainly from their lyrical identification with poverty, begrudging involvement in illegal activities, and ties with southern black culture—all common hip hop representations of African American cultural authenticity. This dichotomy not only polarized the poor and the middle class but also the old and the young, and highlighted the degree to which the elder community misunderstood their progeny's social plight (while the youth viewed their progenitors with disgust at their socioeconomic schizophrenia—ignoring the poor when they themselves had often grown up in such circumstances). Clearly, such generalizations oversimplify the issue, but they do nonetheless encapsulate how many perceived the lawsuit.

Therefore, predictably, many middle-aged listeners perceived Outkast's tribute to Parks the same way they perceived Cedric the Entertainer's statements about Parks in the 2002 film *Barbershop*. Cedric, playing the character Eddie, says that Parks "ain't do nuthin' but sit her black ass down; there was a whole lotta other people that sat down on the bus, and they did it way before Rosa did!" Soon, Al Sharpton and Jesse Jackson caught wind of the performance and pressured MGM to remove the scenes before the DVD was released in January 2003, but the film was released with the controversial scenes.

Strangely enough, Cedric's statements were partially factual; some did try to protest Montgomery, Alabama's, racist transportation policies before Parks. People like Claudette Colvin, the fifteen-year-old girl who refused to give up her seat and was arrested, or Irene Morgan, the twenty-seven-year-old who did it eleven years before Parks; or Jackie Robinson, the baseball legend. However, none of them had the symbolic capitol necessary to rally the black community. Colvin was pregnant and unwed, and thus a potential symbol for black immorality. Morgan fought the police when arrested, which could have been used to argue that black people were inherently violent and quick-tempered, while Robinson was a wealthy star athlete and thus not seen as representative of African American laypeople. It was Parks who best personified the civil rights agenda: she was a woman, playing on patriarchal notions of female vulnerability, highlighting the viciousness of institutional racism by publicizing the arrest of an innocent, delicate woman (also suggesting that people would be less sympathetic to a black male protester). She was pretty and light-skinned, further garnering attention; she held a respectable position as a seamstress and was married to a barber, and was an active participant in the African Methodist Episcopal Church. These things helped cement her as a respectable member of black society, and further secured her position as a civil rights icon. Yet, most important, Parks was an activist who was quite active long before her publicized arrest.

Nevertheless, Outkast and later Cedric were ostracized for seemingly chastising such sacred cows as Parks, Jackson, and Sharpton. They were publicly protested by elite members of the civil rights generation but applauded by those in the hip hop generation. Although much more for Outkast than Cedric, hip hoppers argued that the older generation lacked an understanding of their generation's concerns. This would not be the end of Outkast's accusations of non–political correctness.

In 2000, Outkast released their fourth album, *Stankonia*, to rave reviews, and it sold quadruple platinum. The album launched the group more into the mainstream than any other project to date, and the group's wildly diverse style started to get people's attention. Their influences ranged from funk, G-funk, rhythm and blues, and jazz, to electronica, jungle, and gospel-influenced choir traditions. Their new sound reminded people of the diversity of Jimi Hendrix, Bootsy Collins, and Prince, and they now found that they could do little, musically, that would not meet with fan praise.

The first song they released from the album was the highly energetic "B.O.B. (Bombs over Baghdad)," which ran like a freight train at 155 beats per minute and used the Morris Brown College Gospel Choir during its hook. The song shifts direction at several junctures, and its lyrical theme is somewhat easy to forget, but its aesthetic drive is irresistible (the group decided to use the Gulf War as an analogy for how mainstream artists function). Despite its title, the song was not a critique of the war in Iraq, but rather an analysis of mainstream music and the extent to which they felt that most artists do not complete their work. However, the song was banned from most urban Top 40 radio stations because of its title and assumed subject matter.

Andre, who developed a propensity for monikers (brandishing the name Andre 3000), began a relationship with Erykah Badu, and they eventually had a child they named Seven. When their relationship soured, Dre and Big Boi produced their next hit, "Ms. Jackson," a timely production that coincided with Dre's breakup with Badu. This led many fans to assume that the song was directed at Badu's mother. However, both MCs seemed to be talking directly to their mothers-in-law. Big Boi told a story of an angry mother-in-law that sided with her daughter, despite the daughter's unfair treatment of Boi at the disolution of their relationship. Dre's story focused on lamenting the end of the relationship and contended that what they shared was not "puppy love" as Ms. Jackson seems to imply, but that it was "grown." The interesting thing about the song is the title, "Ms. Jackson." It could have easily been "Mrs.," but it seems that Outkast wanted to emphasize that the primary figure who won't give them their due respect, the ex-girlfriend's mother, despite her judgment of their relationship, has not seemed to maintain a relationship herself. Did her husband die? Was she never married? Is she currently in a relationship? Although they never clarify what may have happened to her, it is clear that she casts judgment on both of them despite her own solitary relationship status. Nevertheless, the song has become a sort of anthem for black men that have tried to maintain relationships with their kids after divorce.

The final single released from the album was the Organized Noize–produced release "So Fresh, So Clean" with Sleepy Brown. The song helped lead Outkast to two 2001 Grammy Awards, one for Best Rap Performance by a Duo or Group (for "Ms. Jackson"), and another for Best Rap Album for *Stankonia*. In 2001, the group released a CD of their greatest hits, *Big Boi and Dre Present ... Outkast*. Alongside a list of their most accomplished creations, they added three new songs, one of which, "The Whole World," led to a 2002 Grammy Award for Best Rap Performance by a Duo or Group.

In 2003, the group would experience success on an unparalleled scale. Upon the release of their album *Speakerboxxx/The Love Below*, Outkast claimed a mainstream audience and sold an astonishing ten times platinum standing (10,000,000 units sold); going diamond and winning the Grammy Award for Album of the Year in 2004. This put the group on par with other diamond-selling artists like Prince, Lionel Richie, Boyz II Men, TLC, Phil Collins, 'N Sync, and Whitney Houston. MC Hammer and Notorious B.I.G. are the only other hip hop artists to claim such an achievement. This accomplishment was partly due to the brilliance of releasing a two-CD set (because each unit counted as two sales), thus meaning that 5 million actually sold, but they were credited with 10 million sales. Moreover, they were able to maintain much of their southern fan base as well, something not guaranteed when succeeding in the mainstream. Between Andre's eclectic expression and Big Boi's southern gangstaism, the group managed to keep one foot in the underground and one in the mainstream. Despite the duplicitous and problematic nature of underground and mainstream binaries in the music entertainment industry (a subject addressed in the introduction of this book), Outkast's navigation of both terrains has been exemplary.

Speakerboxxx/The Love Below, like much of Outkast's work, has continued to break conventional standards. The album was released as a double CD, one by Big Boi (*Speakerboxxx*) and one by Dre (*The Love Below*). *Speakerboxxx*, albeit bearing no creative surprises, was nonetheless a productive success. Reportedly, Big Boi made the album in about a month. He included Dre in much of the production but also included Jazze Pha, Jay-Z, Killer Mike, Goodie Mob, Ludacris, and Sleepy Brown. Dre, on the other hand, only included a select few others like Farnsworth Bentley, Rosario Dawson, Norah Jones, and Kelis, and only had Big Boi on one track, "Roses." Also, the album took considerably longer than Big Boi's, taking approximately two years to finish, and was only completed two weeks before the release date. Having very little rapping on the CD, Dre's *The Love Below* represented a break with hip hop standards (like rhyming, rapping, and the use of DJs) and included more of Dre singing, something prequeled by Dre's performance on the Grammy Award-winning "The Whole World" from their greatest hits album.

The album covers were also quite telling, as Big Boi's was somewhat of a tribute to Huey Newton's classic Black Panther picture, with Big Boi sitting in a wicker chair in a fur coat. Although not brandishing a rifle and looking menacing, he nonetheless made a general reference, while Dre wears sunglasses and a hat while holding a purple gun with purple smoke trailing out of the muzzle. Not surprisingly, Dre's use of purple, and his album's use of funk, inspired comparisons between him and Prince. Moreover, Dre's fearlessness and schizophrenic style of creative production also reminded audiences of Prince.

Dre's release "Hey Ya!" charted in twenty-eight countries and was eventually replaced on the U.S. charts by "The Way You Move," Big Boi's first single, which charted in seventeen countries (one song replacing another song from the same group on the charts had not occurred since the Beatles did it in 1964). "Roses" was the third single released from the album, followed by "Prototype" and "Ghetto Musick," securing their standing as the new kings of hip hop. They not only set a new standard for hip hop artists in mainstream circles (Nelly would release a double album in 2004 titled *Sweat/Suit* in an effort to capitalize on Outkast's success), but they did so with an unapologetic appreciation for their southern roots—a feat replicated by few other artists. Despite jeers that they were soon to separate, something addressed by Big Boi on *Speakerboxxx*, they managed to stay together despite their success, something not accomplished by hip hop duos and trios like EPMD, A Tribe Called Quest, and Eric B. & Rakim.

The success of Dre and Big Boi's music careers has also allowed for an unsurprising venture into acting, with both producing interesting performances, albeit in completely separate vehicles. Big Boi appeared on *Chappelle's Show* in 2004 (he performed and acted in a comedy sketch), egging on Dave Chappelle when he attempted to get Big Boi to hang out with him. He also played a neighborhood drug dealer in the 2006 film *ATL* with the rapper T.I. Dre appeared in the 2003 movie *Hollywood Homicide* with Harrison Ford and Josh Hartnett, playing an old friend of Hartnett's from high school. He later starred in the 2005 film *Four Brothers* with Mark Wahlberg, Tyrese Gibson, and Garrett Hedlund. Impressing many with their performances, both artists have already made Outkast's next performance, the 2006 period piece *Idlewild*, a potential success. *Idlewild* is an HBO-financed movie with Outkast's soundtrack of the same name released in August 2006.

THE *AQUEMINI* MILLENNIUM: (RE)MAKING SOUTHERN HIP HOP

Hip hop developed out of New York and spread throughout the country in the late 1970s and early 1980s. Songs from Afrika Bambaataa, Grandmaster Flash, Melle Mel, and Run-DMC helped extend hip hop's reach outside of New York. Films like *Flashdance, Beat Street*, and *Breakin'* helped illustrate how break dancing, rapping, and even graffiti art were connected (even if they initially weren't). This provided a sort of generic, loose-fitting blueprint for practicing hip hop that others could take and embellish to suit their tastes and interests. As with most parts of the country, and eventually outside of it, the South was no different. The South hit the national scene in the late 1980s and early 1990s with groups like the Geto Boys (from Houston, Texas), UGK (from Port Arthur, Texas), 8 Ball and MJG (from Memphis, Tennessee), and Raheem the Dream (from Houston, Texas).

Aesthetically, the East Coast was characterized by reliance on scratching, sampling, and the drum machine, while the South (and the West Coast) became more known for synthesizer melodies, replaying familiar sounds (as opposed to sampling), limited live instrumentation, and eventually gangsta subject matter. Outkast took it one step further. They managed to become the preeminent sound of the South in many mainstream circles, helping the rest of the hip hop world appreciate the experiences and issues pertinent to the southern experience. Also, they also gave listeners a framework for appreciating southern hip hop outside of underground hip hop circles. For other groups interested in getting into the entertainment industry, Outkast made being southern a benefit rather than a handicap, and therefore laid the groundwork for southern drawl, southern terminology, dances, and culture in general. Dances like the bankhead bounce, drinks like sizzurp (a drink that mixes prescription promethazine cough syrup with vodka or rum, and either Now and Later or Jolly Rancher candy), Freaknik (a popular Atlanta-based annual event that promoted partying, drinking, and dancing during the college spring break schedule), bling (expensive jewelry popularized by Louisiana-based rappers Birdman, B.G. [Baby Gangsta's], Lil Wayne, and Juvenile in 1999), and getting crunk (a term that many suggest means to be both crazy and drunk, or high on marijuana and alcohol simultaneously; although not invented by Outkast, the term was used on their 1993 album *Southernplayalisticadillacmuzik*) have all become part of the southern mythos. People have come to perceive the South through these terms, and for many, Outkast has been one of the major groups responsible for the South's acceptance in hip hop (see sidebars: Bling-Bling and Crunk).

Bling-bling
Nicole Hodges Persley

The hip hop vernacular expression *bling-bling* was originally used in the early 1990s to refer to expensive jewelry encrusted with diamonds in gold or platinum settings. Something encrusted with diamonds may be described as "blingy" or "blingin'." To have bling is to own either jewelry or something that is high priced. To be blingin' is to possess something such as a Bentley Mabach or a Rolex Presidential watch. The saying was later extended to include anything from twenty-inch car rims to a forty-foot yacht in St. Tropez. Bling-bling has its origins in the rap culture of Louisiana with the Cash Money Millionaire family, specifically with Baby Gangsta's song "Bling-Bling."

When pronounced, the phrase is supposed to imitate the sound of the gleam coming from high-quality diamonds when the light hits them. The sound effect, like a small bell ringing, is often used in cartoons when diamonds are shown in treasure chests. In songs such as Will Smith's "Everything That Glitters (Ain't Always Gold)" and Lil' Kim's "Chinatown," bling-bling is presented as a status symbol. In the UK, British performance artist Ali G has used satire to mock the bling-bling culture of hip hop by creating a white hip hop character who uses it to construct his gangsta persona. Today, the term translates around the globe in hip hop settings as indicating a lavish and expensive lifestyle that spares no expense.

The term is currently out of fashion in the hip hop community, but may return to popular rotation like earlier old-school hip hop terms of the 1980s such as dope and def. Bling-bling is now used as everyday vocabulary in mainstream pop culture by mainstream news anchors desperately trying to link to hip hop youth culture as well as suburban soccer moms and grand-mothers. The term was officially retired like a basketball jersey by MTV in 2004. The MTV network created a cartoon lampooning the usage of the term as out of date because of its overuse. The term has been used in children's films such as *Shark Tale* and television shows like MTV's *Wild 'N Out* and is usually used in relation to a character attempting to present himself as hip or urban cool. The term was added to the *Oxford English Dictionary* in 2003. In 2005, two books were published on the bling-bling phenomenon: *Bling-Bling: Hip-Hop's Crown Jewels* by Minya Oh and *The Life and Death of Bling-Bling: A Story of Innovation, Proliferation, Regurgitation, Commercialization and Bastar-dization* by Matthew Vescovo.

Although the South introduced the bling-bling phenomenon and partici-pated in rap's overemphasis on materialism and street culture, Outkast and other southern rappers helped introduce a sort of down-to-earth, pragmatic wisdom reminiscent of black southern culture. In their earlier albums (at least up to *ATLiens*), the group often talked about how little money they had, rather than celebrating how many cars and necklaces they could buy. This theme is characterized best by one of Dre's verses on the song "Elevators" on the *ATLiens* album, where he states, "I live by the beat like you live check to check," and suggests that even with Outkast's growing number of fans, he feels continuing pressure to produce music that sells so that he can survive. At the time of the song's release, Dre's statement ran counter to what rappers like B.G. rhymed about, and counter to the "Mo Money Mo Problems" mentality promoted by Bad Boy Records in New York. Even in the midst of the positive hip hop era of the late 1980s and early 1990s, rappers still bragged about their success and material fortune. Gangsta rappers even rhymed about their material wealth, mostly due to illegal activity, and at most mentioned poverty in terms of what they had pulled themselves out of. But Outkast openly talked about how much money they did not have. They also brought the issue of how artists are treated by the entertainment industry to light by voicing their financial woes. Big Boi, in the song "Ms. Jackson" on the *Stankonia* album, reveals "Private school, daycare, shit med-ical bills, I pay that." Although he does not state that these payments are a burden to him, to mention them in such detail, especially when outlining his dedication to caring for his kids, when other rappers talk about Bentleys and bling, is telling. It suggests that finances are not as abundant as most think, and that financial obligations such as these require effort, something that bling and gangsta rappers overlook when talking about their wealth.

Crunk
Katherine V. Tsiopos-Wills

Crunk is a hip hop slang term and subgenre that arose in the early 1990s in the Dirty South. The invention of the word *crunk* has been credited to at least two sources. In 1993, NBC's *Late Night with Conan O'Brien* urged its guests to replace profanities with "krunk," a new dirty word to confuse the network censors. That same year, Dirty South rappers Outkast used the term in their single "Player's Ball." The term itself means frenetic or excited, with MCs often urging the crowd to "get crunk"; Lil Jon and the Eastside Boyz and Lil Flip both have songs called "Get Crunk." In this popular usage, *crunk* is thought to be a combination of the words *crazy* and *drunk*. However, another Dirty South artist, DJ Paul of Three 6 Mafia, reports that crunk originated as a Memphis slang term that meant crowded (Cobb).

While crunk originated in Memphis, Atlanta's Lil Jon (aka the King of Crunk) popularized crunk as a slang term, a sound, and a brand. He marketed his own energy drink, Crunk Juice, and produced hit songs like Usher's "Yeah" and Ciara's "Goodies," which extended crunk to the worlds of R&B and pop music. Lil Jon is known for pioneering the sound known as crunk, which is built from the Roland TR-808 drum machine and synthesized sound effects and designed for dance clubs. Lil Jon's vocal style of shouting his rhymes as well as the words "yeah" and "okay" throughout his songs was parodied by Dave Chappelle on Comedy Central's *Chappelle's Show*.

Works Cited

Cobb, LaDessa "Willow." "Three 6 Mafia: The Ill Community Interview." All Hip-Hop.com. http://www.allhiphop.com/features/?ID=1237.

FUNKIN' AROUND THE WHOLE WORLD: AFROFUTURISM AND THE SIGNIFICANCE OF OUTKAST

Having reached diamond-level album sales, it is clear that Outkast has achieved mainstream success. Even though they are quite eclectic, Outkast's production quality, lyricism, charisma, and thematic style of dress (which changes with each album) has remained consistent. Outkast has grown in each of these areas with each album, reaching more and more toward a type of eclecticism rare for a hip hop duo; but each addition to their portfolio has remained a top-tier production. Although *ATLiens* was groundbreaking in its scope and content in relation to their first album, the group's creative ingenuity did not reach epic proportions, or at least international attention, until their 2003 album *Speakerboxxx/The Love Below*. Nevertheless, their third album, *Aquemini,* was a dramatic break from *ATLiens*, and *Stankonia* a break from *Aquemini*. Even their greatest hits album, *Big Boi and Dre Present*

... *Outkast*, broke from convention and provided new songs and new thematic elements to their mystique.

As Big Boi and Dre consistently reinvent their music, they have demonstrated a capacity to push beyond the boundaries of their own genres. On their first album, they talked about Southern California gangsta rap themes such as driving Cadillacs, smoking marijuana, and being players, as heard in the music of Outkast's contemporaries Dr. Dre and Snoop Doggy Dogg. However, if Outkast ever were part of gangsta rap, they quickly expanded out of that genre. Whether it is their approach to social issues like systemic black male underdevelopment (e.g., "Git Up, Git Out"), or the outright break from convention with *ATLiens* (the former being more subtle and the latter being an undisputedly different approach), Outkast has managed to do what only a few other artists have been able to: shed their audience.

Jimi Hendrix, Parliament/Funkadelic, and Prince are all artists that have made music that threatened to lose their audience base. Although it may seem an easy strategy, each artistic break with fan expectation, something the music industry usually frowns on, was a major risk. Hence, there was no guarantee that Prince's *Paisley Park* album would be accepted after having a smash hit with *Purple Rain*. Similarly, Outkast's shift from *Southernplayalisticadillacmuzik*'s aesthetic to the unsure ground of *ATLiens*' out-of-this-world point of view was a huge risk. However, as with Prince, they managed to develop an audience that followed them through each artistic change. More important, they have created an aesthetic space that allows them to do whatever they want and still have music and film executives clamoring for them. Few artists manage to find this kind of artistic power. Many artists who have the courage to break from fan expectations have failed to stimulate interest in their new endeavor. For many, shifting styles is career suicide. Yet for those that continue to sell albums, their newfound artistic freedom is a hard-earned badge of honor. Outkast has, without question, achieved this status.

Outkast has managed to keep their music ahead of the curve, anticipating the industry's shifting interests. Although it should be stated that they do not seem to follow the dominant trends, they do, however, manage to consistently shift their aesthetic focus, making it difficult to label their music. Clearly they are generally considered a hip hop group, despite that many are having an increasingly difficult time categorizing their sound. Dre only rapped in two instances on *The Love Below*, spending most of his time singing and verbalizing poetry. Yet this development could have been predicted if one listened to Dre in the song "Funkin' Around" on *Big Boi and Dre Present ... Outkast* (2001): "I'm out here knowin' hip hop is dead." Dre was becoming more and more disillusioned by the boundaries of what hip hop artists were supposed to produce as artists.

This leads to the fourth reason for Outkast's success—artistic fearlessness. Considering that Outkast has been critical of the extent to which hip hop has been hijacked by corporate interests, their desire to remain hip hop artists is exemplary. More to the point, they have been unswerving in their desire to expand, artistically, as hip hop artists. Thus, they have mixed Dirty South, Miami bass, electronica, soul, funk, P-Funk, G-funk, and rock to fuse together the Outkast portfolio.

The fifth reason for their success has been their approach to blackness. As southern rappers, their upbringing and point of origin refers, in many people's imagination, to a long-standing tradition of African American blackness. This blackness stems from the experience of enslavement, lynching, sharecropping, voting rights activism, civil rights, and state-sanctioned terrorism (e.g., Klan activity, lynching, police brutality, and antivoting violence against black people). Hence, the blackness and black southern culture that Benjamin and Patton grew up in is generally considered as the standard type of blackness within African Americana. However, although they represent such blackness, they have also come to symbolize a kind of intraracial diversity. In other words, they have championed a less rigid approach to blackness, one that embraces the more subtle and diverse trends of blackness.

Although much of this is articulated through Benjamin's eccentric persona, one can extrapolate that Benjamin's listeners often embody some of the characteristics of black America that the civil rights generation has been most uncomfortable with. Black homosexuals, nontraditional spiritualists, science fiction buffs, comic book readers, and those interested in a more self-reflexive type of hip hop tend to appreciate Outkast's work. Yet it is this dichotomy between Big Boi and Andre that leads us to the sixth, and probably most important, reason for their success.

Outkast's two personas, embodied by Big Boi and Andre, are the hustler and the visionary respectively. Superficially, Big Boi has become synonymous with hustling and maintaining multiple relationships with women. Andre, on the other hand, is perceived as more abstract and artistically driven. He experiments with mixing alternative musical styles, fashion, and subject matter in a manner that is inconsistent with other MCs in hip hop. Although they have both delved into each other's socially perceived personas, they are more consistently referred to in this manner.

The duo's dichotomous style is the group's most alluring and signature characteristic. Big Boi's persona grounds the group in southern hip hop culture. It could be argued that he is the primary reason that the group's early following, mostly underground hip hoppers in the southern (especially Atlanta) hip hop scene (see sidebar: The Dirty South), still salute Outkast as a southern group, even after Andre's expansive artistic growth since the *ATLiens* album. To be succinct, Big Boi grounds Andre's eclectic eccentricity, while Andre prevents the group from becoming a stereotype of southern-born, gangsta-oriented rappers, complete with gold teeth, southern drawls, and Cadillacs. The combination of the two creates a new blend of the old and the new, the contemporary and the alternative, the homegrown and the far away.

Also, most notably on *Speakerboxxx/The Love Below*, the group success-fully cross-pollinates different audience groups. Since that album, the group has expanded the listening palette of their initial fan base. They've expanded what their hip hop audience listens to and what they might consider hip hop, as now the hardest listener can enjoy Dre's "Pink and Blue" or "Roses." The group has also garnered new fans not normally considered hip hop listeners. For these listeners, having to purchase a double CD of Outkast's music was a brilliant move on the group's part. Many of them who never would have listened to southern hip hop (or any hip hop at all) are now being introduced to it (raising the interest in other southern MCs). For example, mainstreamers that only purchased *Speakerboxxx/The Love Below* for songs like "Hey Ya" or "Prototype" are formally introduced to Big Boi's "The Way You Move," "Tomb of the Boom," or "Flip Flop Rock" (all of which were critically acclaimed, but due to radio programming were not considered to have as much crossover appeal as most of Andre's *The Love Below*). Nevertheless, the brilliance of the group's dynamic is in their collaborative, highly creative approach to redefining hip hop's aesthetic boundaries, expanding their fan base, and, no doubt, their Soundscan sales ratings.

EXTRATERRESTRIALS AND CADILLACMUZIK: CATEGORIZING A PHENOMENON

Aside from their dichotomous structure, another quality Outkast possesses is what one might call an Afrofuturist impulse or aesthetic. Afrofuturism, albeit difficult to succinctly and wholly define, generally refers to an intersection between African diaspora culture, imagination, science fiction, technology, and notions of the future in an attempt to reevaluate harmful socially con-structed practices like white supremacy, patriarchy, heteronormativity, and highly exploitive forms of capitalism (i.e., economic policy). Groups and individuals that follow this logic are generally difficult to categorize, as they usually have an aversion to socially constructed categorizations.

Musicians such as Sun Ra, George Clinton, and Parliament/Funkadelic (who now tour as the P-Funk All Stars), Bootsy Collins, Prince, Afrika Bam-baataa, Digital Underground, Digable Planets, Me'shell NdegeOcello, Tricky, MF DOOM, and Outkast fall within this category. One of the preeminent characteristics of people in this category is the need for artistic freedom. Whether in business or artistic production, Afrofuturist artists usually help to create new and interesting ways to negotiate the boundaries of business and art. Sun Ra was one of the first jazz musicians to set up an independent label in the 1950s, while also employing electric keyboards, polyrhythms, and group im-provisational free-form styles of music (see sidebar: Hip Hop and Funk).

Clinton, among other things, blazed a trail from doo-wop to funk, influen-cing several generations of artists and discovering a wide variety of black

Hip Hop and Funk

T. Hasan Johnson

Many of the most popular musicians in hip hop cite funk as one of their primary inspirations. Funk music originates from West African musical traditions, African American spirituals, blues, work chants, and praise songs. Throughout its development, funk has been further influenced by jazz, R&B, and soul. Groups like James Brown, the Meters, the Isley Brothers, Bootsy Collins, and Sly and the Family Stone helped define the scope of funk music, serving to influence generations of musicians.

Some artists chose to embellish on funk's jazz influences and develop a more big band sound while others chose to mix funk with the contemporary R&B of the late 1970s and 1980s. Relying on live instrumentation and large horn and percussion sections, artists like George Clinton (and his groups Parliament/Funkadelic), Bootsy and his Rubber Band, the Commodores, Tower of Power, the Ohio Players, Confunkshun, Earth, Wind and Fire, War, and Lakeside helped redefine funk and take it in a more aggressive direction. Developing a more driving, experimental sound, groups like Jimi Hendrix and the Experience and George Clinton found new ways to experiment, often being cited as the originators of otherworldly-sounding guitar riffs and technologically driven synthesizers.

In the early 1980s, artists like Prince, Kool and the Gang, and Zapp took the use of computerized instrumentation even further, especially Roger Troutman and Zapp (popularizing the use of the vocoder talkbox), intersecting Jimi Hendrix, James Brown, and other funk musicians in the process. Starting in the late 1980s and 1990s, hip hop artists in the West and the South (and even the East Coast) developed the early stages of G-funk. Influenced by Clinton and Troutman, superproducers like Dr. Dre and Easy Moe Bee (producer of Notorious B.I.G.'s first album, *Ready to Die*) and groups like N.W.A., Tha Dogg Pound, Funkdoobiest, and DJ Quik developed the sample-based style of music that paid tribute to the funkateers of the 1970s. Eventually, after several landmark lawsuits against hip hop producers in the early 1990s, many G-funk artists moved to a more simplistic, minimalist approach to funk that strayed from sampling to limited live instrumentation. Currently, funk, as it is already an amalgamation, has been further mixed with newer and most diverse styles, becoming more and more a part of today's musical landscape. However, the legacy of funk music lives on through those that are attentive to its lineage and interested in carrying it on within new and emerging genres.

musicians that might not ever have had a chance to demonstrate their musical proficiency outside of the confines of conventional R&B frameworks, particularly in rock music (e.g., Eddie Hazel and Michael Hampton). Clinton, appearing on *Aquemini*'s "Synthesizer," was also adept at changing his band names in an effort to secure an almost independent status as an artist. Prince and MF DOOM, two artists that both had very difficult times maintaining some semblance of independence from the recording industry (although Prince's experience was far more public and dramatic), may have taken their cues from Clinton.

Afrika Bambaataa was one of hip hop's earliest visionaries, creating the preeminent hip hop organization, the Zulu Nation, to help frame hip hop as an international, interracial, and intercultural phenomenon. "Bam," as many affectionately call him, helped transform hip hop into a social force for the uplifting of poor, destitute communities. His influence helped youth in various communities to perceive connections between their socioeconomic status and that of other communities in similar conditions around the world. He has also led a series of discourses with other artists about how to pressure the entertainment industry into better supporting its artists.

Last, Me'shell NdegeOcello has been an ardent spokesperson for racial, gender, and sexual antidiscrimination practices in society, while challenging the music industry's approach to musical classification. Arguing against the racial categorization of music, especially her own, she has vehemently argued against the practice of classifying black music as either hip hop or R&B, while white musicians are generally termed rock artists.

Each of these artists has fought categorization in one form or another, and their approach to business, politics, and music has transcended similar boundaries. Interestingly enough, Outkast has benefited from the work of many such artists, especially those listed above. They have developed a reputation for the same type of originality that Sun Ra, George Clinton, and Bootsy Collins exude (and incorporated soul, funk, electronica, jazz, and rock music aesthetics into their brand of hip hop). Like Bambaataa and Clinton, Outkast supports new artists, particularly through Big Boi's record company the Purple Ribbon All Stars (formerly Aquemini Records). They have signed Bubba Sparxxx, Killer Mike, and Sleepy Brown to date, but will no doubt expand their repertoire. Also, they have fought not to be characterized as typical rappers, but as artists —a moniker that many MCs are not given by mainstream artists.

Last, Outkast has sought to maintain a sense of artistic freedom, reminiscent of the artists previously mentioned, which helps pave the way for other artists interested in breaking from convention. Hence, aside from Outkast's musical creativity, they have also been quite innovative in how they have conceptualized album infrastructure and coherence. In the age of digital music, one of the most significant changes has been how artists have had to conceptualize what an album means, what it does, and how it functions. Is it a cohesive collage? Is it a collection of freestanding individual songs? Although it can be argued that this development began more abstractly with CDs, it wasn't until MP3 technology that the ease of transferring music began to notably impact people's attitudes toward thematically integrated albums. Thus, Outkast's albums have been thematic, integrated, and yet wholly comprehensible to those who have only downloaded a few of their songs. Structuring their albums thusly has helped with their ability to cross over into more mainstream media networks. Although few artists seem to acknowledge the importance of structuring their albums to suit new means of file transfer (in fact, many oppose the use of it in such ways), Outkast has engaged it head-on, bolstering their sales and fan notoriety at the same time (and securing their status as Afrofuturists in that they acknowledge the importance of intersecting issues of blackness, southernness, technology, science fiction, and the imagination).

Another way they have managed to advance to the mainstream has been to do what older hip hop groups like Run-DMC, the Beastie Boys, and LL Cool J have done, using rock aesthetics and alternative instrumentation in their production repertoire. Songs like "Chonkyfire" on the *Aquemini* album and "Bombs over Baghdad (B.O.B.)" on their *Stankonia* album illustrate the band's artistic fluidity and reaffirm their standing as one of hip hop's greatest duos.

TWO DOPE BOYZ IN A CADILLAC: DEFINING OUTKAST'S INFLUENCES

The July 2006 issue of *Vibe* magazine asks this question on the cover: "Outkast: Are They Hip-Hop's Greatest Group?" Partly due to popularity and partly due to longevity, the group has been touted by media moguls, music video shows, critics, and listeners as potentially the best group ever. Outkast is an underground group that has managed to maintain its creative sensibilities in a highly visible mainstream context. Big Boi and Dre have managed not to change their style in relation to what is considered mainstream, but rather they seem to adjust their style in accordance with their own artistic voice. When compared to their hip hop forerunners, Outkast become part of a tradition and at the same time create a distinct style within this lineage.

For hip hop groups that have at least two lead rappers that share rhyming responsibilities, there are at least four categories: foundational groups, rapper-producer groups, unbalanced groups, and balanced groups. Foundational groups are those that laid the foundation for how hip hop groups are defined. These groups, although not easily classified, set a standard for all hip hop groups that came after them. In many ways, each of the categories used here apply to the foundational groups. Groups like Grandmaster Flash and the Furious Five, Afrika Bambaataa and the Soul Sonic Force, and the Treacherous Three fall into this category. They are generally flamboyant, lyrically experimental, and musically groundbreaking (often mixing styles of music in new ways). Bambaataa, as with Grandmaster Flash and the Furious Five, began with the DJ. Both groups were initially created to highlight the DJ and explain to the audience what the DJ does. They were flashy and usually wore loud colors and the kind of outlandish outfits consistent with the end of the disco era. Although there was a front man on lead vocals (usually the most charismatic in the group), these groups sang and rapped in four- or five-part harmonies. They sang short hooks for songs, had dance routines, and often rhymed in a syncopated fashion. It was only later that rappers like Melle Mel transitioned more to the front of the stage and became headliners—as opposed to the DJ.

Outkast may have inherited some of their outlandish styles of dress from these earlier groups. The group's occasional use of music to brandish their self-styled social, moral, and spiritual commentary (e.g., "Git Up, Git Out") might owe its origins to Melle Mel more than anyone else. Mel was one of the first hip hop artists to create a popularly known song that provided a socio-political critique and a moral lesson, "The Message." Although Kurtis Blow's "The Breaks" came out a few years earlier, Mel's onstage persona came out of a group context, while Blow was always a solo artist. Later groups like Run-DMC and Boogie Down Productions no doubt further influenced Dre and Big Boi's perceptions of what rap groups could do with a record, moving beyond regional materialism to international morality.

The second category, the rapper-producer dynamic, refers to artists that were technically members of a group but were the sole rappers to represent the group on the mic. Groups like Boogie Down Productions, Eric B. & Rakim, Gang Starr, and Pete Rock & CL Smooth provided burgeoning MCs with a strong appreciation for the producer. Taking the former role of the early 1980s DJ, the producers of the 1990s became central to hip hop (especially considering that since the late 1970s and early 1980s the DJ was the producer). Producers like Eric B., DJ Premier, Pete Rock, Dr. Dre, P. Diddy, and DJ Muggs became prominent albeit silent figures that earned respect due to their producing savvy (although Pete Rock would later release songs in which he rapped, and P. Diddy was seldom silent). Clearly, Outkast does not fit into this category, but their seamless relationship with Organized Noize may illustrate their appreciation for this legacy in hip hop.

The third category, unbalanced groups, refers to groups that had a front man and a less noticed lyrical partner. Groups like X-Clan (with lead rapper Brother J and partner Professor X), Public Enemy (with Chuck D and Flavor Flav), Cypress Hill (with lead rapper Be Real and partner Sen Dog), Funk-doobiest (with lead rapper Son Doobie and partner Tomahawk Funk), and the Group Home (with L'il Dap and partner Melachi the Nutcracker) defined these types of groups.

Brother J of X-Clan introduced a new Afrocentric consciousness in hip hop, while his partner Professor X ad-libbed with his distinct brand of esoteric observation. Chuck D provided scathing political and cultural critiques of society, while his partner Flavor Flav served as the hype man and comic relief to woo listeners who were not drawn to Chuck's political perspective. One of the Gang Starr Foundation's groups, the Group Home, was a duo started by superproducer DJ Premier and the Guru. L'il Dap, the lead rapper, was a breakout success with a cohesive rhyme style and a signature lisp, but Melachi was still in development, and probably started his professional career before he was ready. Cypress Hill, with superproducer DJ Muggs, featured the high-pitched, nasal stylings of Be Real, while Sen Dog's lyrics usually punctuated the themes of the songs—albeit far less intricate than Be Real's. Similar to Cypress Hill, the lyrical ability of Funkdoobiest's lead rapper Son Doobie far outshone his band mates. These groups, therefore, offer an unbalanced partnership that left the majority of the creative responsibility on the lead performer, while the other provided thematic support. Unfortunately, this arrangement often led fans to describe the group as a solo act, forgetting the other members.

However, Outkast is most specifically centered in the final category, balanced groups. These groups, as opposed to the last category, are more evenly keeled. Groups like A Tribe Called Quest, Brand Nubian, the Jungle Brothers, the Fugees (although fan appreciation for Pras and Wyclef took some time at the onset of their careers), EPMD, Binary Star, De La Soul, Das EFX, and Black Star all had at least a pair of MCs whose skills both rivaled and complimented one another. Q-Tip and Phife of Tribe, Erick and Parrish of EPMD, OneManArmy and Senim Silla of Binary Star, Posdnous and Trugoy the Dove of De La Soul, Mos Def and Talib Kweli of Black Star, and Books and Krazy Drazy of Das EFX all exemplify duos that have managed to equally balance each other. It should be noted that duos whose rhyme styles are similar to each other, like Das EFX or Binary Star, make it difficult to distinguish one artist from the other; but their styles usually produce a harmonious blend that their audiences don't mind. Adversely, groups with two artists with distinctly different rhyme styles, cadences, and signature voices tend to attract a lot of attention as well. Groups like A Tribe Called Quest, De La Soul, EPMD, Wu-Tang Clan, or Black Star all have members that have different styles; hence, each of these rappers tend to amass their own cult followings who like them for very specific reasons.

Outkast falls into this last category. Both Dre and Big Boi have noticeably different styles, but manage to consistently complement one another, much to the pleasure of their fan base. Their subject interests and musical references differ, and yet instead of conflicting, one provides the creative vision while the other provides the anchor. However, when asking who the best hip hop group in the world may be, taking past groups into account complicates the question to such a degree that the question may not be answerable. Recently, questions have begun to arise as to whether Dre and Big Boi's differences have finally pushed them too far apart to continue to work together.

AN END TO THE PLAYER'S BALL? OUTKAST'S IMPACT, LEGACY, AND RUMORS OF AN IMPENDING BREAKUP

Outkast's influence and impact on hip hop, and on music in general, has been tremendous. Yet, despite their film and album *Idlewild* (2006), rumors have begun to surface about their interaction. Although there is little evidence that the duo argues, they have, according to rumor, not been in the studio at the same time when producing tracks. It has been suggested that they did not tour after the *Speakerboxxx/The Love Below* album's release because Dre decided the stress of performing material that he had outgrown was too great. Big Boi, on the other hand, was more concerned about how much money they would lose if they did not tour. So, Big Boi went on tour without Dre, and the two have not discussed it since. However, in the recording of *Idlewild* and a new Outkast album tentatively titled *The Hard 10*, the two are seldom in the studio at the same time. In 2006 television appearances to promote *Idlewild*, Big Boi and Dre agreed not to perform onstage together. Dre sits out the performances but does participate in interviews.

One question that many Outkast fans have is whether or not the group will follow the Wu-Tang Clan model or completely break from one another altogether. This model refers to the practice of some groups who continue to function as a group while fostering solo careers. Unlike groups who break up, go solo, and come back together again later (like EPMD), these groups function as individual artists and groups simultaneously from the onset of their professional careers. Wu-Tang Clan artists Method Man, U-God, Ghostface Killah, Ol' Dirty Bastard, Raekwon, Masta Killa, Inspectah Deck, RZA, and GZA all remained part of the group while simultaneously developing their solo careers, independent merchandising, and publishing rights; more important, acclimating their audiences to their onstage personas so that when they released solo projects they would be recognized.

Currently, both Dre and Big Boi have engaged in solo projects while claiming to remain a group. Dre's film career has taken off, while Big Boi's film career is just getting started. Although Dre is active musically, it is Big Boi's new project, the Purple Ribbon All Stars, that has recently released an album with the hit song "Kryptonite." Yet, amid further rumors, it seems that the question of a conclusive split might be worth pondering. Nevertheless, the group insists that it is not splitting up, and both artists have commented on their frustration with such rumors.

Discussions about Outkast's potential breakup tend to obscure all their achievements and accomplishments by focusing on what looks like two different agendas within the group. Yet Outkast was founded on such independence. Aside from raising the bar on what hip hop artists can achieve in musical, business, and artistic freedom, the group has established a new standard for remaining creatively independent. Today's highly corporatized entertainment industry tends to look past individual expression to seek those artists who best fit into current trends, and many artists have not figured out how to (or do not have the power to) determine their own creative direction. This has never been a problem for Outkast, and their latest strategy seems to be to allow each other that same kind of room for self-expression.

Earlier artists like George Clinton and Parliament/Funkadelic may have laid the groundwork for artistic freedom, but many of today's artists tend to view them as a product of a different age—and to some extent they're right. But what most people overlook is that when these artists were paying their dues, there was no guarantee that their careers would survive the ordeal. In other words, their wisdom is a product of hard-earned experience and should not be dismissed. Outkast has already gone through similar experiences, setting new standards for artistic independence for today's artists in hip hop and alternative music. Outkast's intersection of southern rap, funk, and alternative musical genres is as groundbreaking today as George Clinton's experimentations with funk in the 1970s, or Prince's approach to combining Minneapolis-based, black alternative rock with R&B and soul music in the 1980s. In this light, Outkast should be perceived as a groundbreaking pioneer group that reinvented the South in many people's minds, dared to take hip hop to new creative levels, and reminded people that the outlandish and absurd can still be funky thirty-six years after the landing of the Parliament/Funkadelic mother ship.

See also: The Geto Boys, Native Tongues

WORKS CITED

Good, Karen R. "Back to the Future." *Vibe* July 2006: 98–105.
Outkast-Web.de. http://www.outkast-web.de/.

FURTHER READINGS

Chang, Jeff. *Can't Stop Won't Stop: A History of the Hip-Hop Generation.* New York: St. Martin's, 2005.
Dee, Kool Moe. *There's a God on the Mic: The True 50 Greatest MCs.* New York: Thunder's Mouth Press, 2003.
Kitwana, Bakari. *Why White Kids Love Hip Hop: Wangstas, Wiggers, Wannabes, and the New Reality of Race in America.* New York: BasicCivitas Books, 2005.
The MC: Why We Do It. Dir. Peter Spirer. Perf. 50 Cent, Common, Ghostface. Q3 Productions, 2005.
The Original Hip-Hop Lyrics Archive. http://www.ohhla.com.
Outkast official Web site. http://www.outkast.com.

Courtesy of Photofest.

Eminem

Katherine V. Tsiopos-Wills

Born October 17, 1972, Eminem rhymed his way onto the hip hop scene in the 1990s with lyrical innovations and multiplatinum sales, securing his place as an icon of hip hop. As hip hop's first new white superstar since Vanilla Ice was exposed for lying about his upbringing and criminal background, Eminem regained respect for white rappers by showing an understanding of hip hop traditions and keeping his lyrics true to his own experiences.

Eminem was born in rural Missouri. Throughout his childhood, he and his tattered family moved back and forth between Kansas City and Detroit, cities known for their rich heritage of jazz, blues, soul, and rhythm and blues. Detroit, where Eminem spent most of his teenage years, was the birthplace of Motown Records, Berry Gordy's black music powerhouse that signed the Jackson Five, the Temptations, and the Supremes in the 1960s (see sidebar: Detroit). It was three white artists, however, who would bring the most attention to Detroit's hip hop scene. Along with Eminem, Kid Rock and Insane Clown Posse broke into the mainstream in the 1990s, these two other artists fusing hip hop with hard rock, metal, classic rock, and country, while Eminem's music remained truer to hip hop itself. Eminem spent his teenage years in Detroit, where he derived his street credibility from his lower class experience and geographic proximity to hip hop culture. Eminem performed and recorded with black artists, including Proof, D-12, and Royce da 5´9˝, and after his records went platinum, he would seek record deals for these friends back in Detroit. Eminem got his musical start by memorizing and rapping songs to neighborhood kids who would listen. He emulated rap artists such as LL Cool J., Run-DMC, Big Daddy Kane, and the Beastie Boys by standing in front of a mirror practicing songs and moves. With his

---

Detroit
Katherine V. Tsiopos-Wills

Detroit, Michigan (aka Motown or Motor City) at one time was one of America's strongest cities for music production and nightlife. According to *Billboard* and *Pollstar* magazines, the Detroit metro area was the number one U.S. summer concert destination in box office gross and attendance, often surpassing Madison Square Garden. In the sixties and seventies, Berry Gordy's Motown Records promoted such artists as James Brown, Diana Ross and the Supremes, and the Jackson Five. Motown remained at the center of funk, R&B, and soul music, and this brought national attention to Detroit as a musical powerhouse.

The grassroots energy and prolific talent of Detroit's hip hop scene, both underground and commercial, contributed to the 1990s Detroit music renaissance, with Eminem, D-12, Obie Trice, Proof, Royce da 5´9˝, Insane Clown Posse, Kid Rock, J-Dilla, and Slum Village, to name a few who built on the legacy of Berry Gordy's Motown Records. Detroit was regarded as the birthplace of eponymous Detroit techno electronic dance music, which was eagerly appropriated by European markets. Detroit metro also drew strong rock and roll audiences for groups such as the White Stripes.

Nationally, hip hop venues diversified though the mid-1980s, spearheaded by chocolate cities such as Detroit, Atlanta, Washington, DC, Baltimore, St. Louis, and Memphis. Concurrently, Boston, Chicago, Seattle, Houston, Miami, and locales in New Jersey developed hybrid hip hop artists and styles.

---

whiplike rhymes, storytelling skills, and blistering lyrical anger, Eminem had the makings of hip hop's next superstar.

Eminem makes clear in his lyrics and in interviews that he wants to be seen as a rapper, not as a white rapper (see sidebar: Wiggers). After a decade in the music business and multiple platinum albums, Eminem has in many ways

---

Wiggers
Katherine V. Tsiopos-Wills

As black urban underclass markers flooded the cultural scene in the 1980s in the form of hip hop culture, droves of white North American and European youth latched onto hip hop slang, fashion, and music. "Wigger," a derogatory term for a white usurper of hip hop culture, is a combination of the words "white" and "nigger." Wiggers (aka wiggas, whiggers, wiggas, Wafrican Americans) suffer from "ghettoitis," or a denial of their white upbringing and craving for hip hop credentials. The terms received wide media coverage when Senator Robert Byrd in a Fox News interview commented on "White Niggers." On "The Way I Am," Eminem steadfastly refuted that he was a "wigger who just tries to be black."

Today's wigger parallels the 1950s white hipster or "white negro," as scrutinized in Norman Mailer's *The White Negro: Superficial Reflections on the Hipster*. Mailer posited that following World War II, some white men began to appropriate the manners, language, and values of the black underclass. These hipster traits included living with a constant awareness of physical danger; seeing oneself as antagonistic to the "squares" or "lames" (mainstream people), communicating in a coded language that emphasized personal energy over class or social strength; staying composed or cool under stress; freeing repressed sexual desires and a primitive, pleasure-seeking nature within each person; and placing a premium on masculinity while repressing any appearance of femininity, which could be perceived as weakness.

Mailer's white Negro pervaded the beatnik culture of the 1950s, with Jack Kerouac's white, jazz-obsessed characters in books such as *On the Road*. Although Mailer was critical of the trend of white men adopting black mannerisms, slang, and attitude, Beat culture served to connect the counterculture of smoky jazz clubs with the ivory tower of poetry. Kerouac, along with Amiri Baraka (formerly LeRoi Jones), Allen Ginsberg, Herbert Huncke, Gregory Corso, and other poets, sought to bring their writing out of the universities and to the people. They created a literary performance culture modeled, in part, after jazz performances.

Despite this lineage, however, the wigger holds a much lower cultural position than the 1950s hipster did. The appropriation by whites of jazz, blues, and rock and roll culture has created a mistrust of white people who become too fully immersed in black culture. The 1991 scandal of Vanilla Ice's fake biography reinforced this mistrust in the hip hop community.

Because wiggers cross racial boundaries, they are criticized by the ethnic group from which they come, as well as the ethnic group to whose culture they aspire. The effects of the wigger's place both as a race traitor and a cultural leech is parodied in the Jamie Kennedy film *Malibu's Most Wanted*. In 2003, Snoop Dogg's MTV comedy show, *Doggy Fizzle Televizzle*, aired a sketch in which distressed white parents called a hotline to help their teen sons who suffered from being wiggers. Parodying TV docudramas such as *Intervention*, Snoop Dogg and company kidnapped and deprogrammed the wiggers, turning them back into stereotypically white teens.

Works Cited

Byrd, Robert. Interview. *Fox News* March 4, 2001.

Mailer, Norman. *The White Negro: Superficial Reflections on the Hipster*. San Francisco: City Lights Books, 1957.

Further Readings

hooks, bell. "Representations of Whiteness in the Black Imagination." In *Black Looks: Race and Representation*. Boston: South End, 1992. 165–179.

Kitwana, Bakari. *Why White Kids Love Hip-hop*. New York: Basic Civitas, 2006.

achieved his goal. Worldwide, he is the biggest-selling rap artist of all time. His sales, his rhyme skills, his acceptance by black rap stars, and the way he reopened hip hop to new white stars such as Paul Wall and Bubba Sparxxx now outweigh reservations about whether a white rapper belongs in hip hop. At the beginning of his career, however, Eminem found his white skin a detriment to his success. After Vanilla Ice, it was difficult for record labels to promote new white rappers. In 1990, Vanilla Ice entered the hip hop scene with his *To the Extreme* LP, featuring the hit single "Ice Ice Baby," which depicted Miami street life as Ice cruised in his car and witnessed gunfights. The song became a pop hit with nationwide airplay. Casey Kasem on his Top 40 radio show heralded "Ice Ice Baby" as the number one rap single in history. Vanilla Ice's success was stopped in its tracks, however, when a journalist exposed several lies in the official biography released by his record label (see sidebar: Vanilla Ice, under Beastie Boys). Soon after Vanilla Ice's biography was called into question, he was subjected to a long succession of criticisms that he stole his hit song's chorus from a black fraternity. This accusation was especially pertinent because Ice's bio had attempted to present his background in lower-class neighborhoods, where he impressed his black peers with his rhyme skills. Combined, these infractions made Ice look like a white kid with no hip hop credentials making unprecedented money from hip hop music. Eminem, in contrast, writes intensely personal music about growing up poor and being criticized as a white kid trying to make it in hip hop.

Along with Vanilla Ice, the Beastie Boys, 3rd Bass, and House of Pain were Eminem's primary white forerunners in hip hop. The Beastie Boys, whom Eminem named as an early and key musical inspiration, were born into affluent upper-middle-class Jewish families in the New York area. They began their career as a punk band in the early 1980s. Their school of hard knocks was in underground New York punk clubs, and later playing for hip hop crowds opening for Schoolly D, Run-DMC, and other rap pioneers. Affluent background aside, Ad-Rock, the youngest of the Beastie Boys, and an accomplished lyricist and MC, left his imprint on Eminem and the direction of hip hop and rock music through his lyrical innovations and decidedly high-pitched vocal style.

Eminem made one of his most significant contributions to hip hop early in his career. He reframed hip hop's racial narratives in terms of lived authentic class experience instead of only color (Hess 372), thereby rescuing the future of white rap and rappers from Vanilla Ice's legacy of co-optation by whites and assimilation into the mainstream. Eminem's rap career was established through his close association with gangsta rap legend Dr. Dre, his intimately autobiographical lyrics, and the rhyme skills that helped him shine in MC battles. Further, Em didn't try to hide his whiteness, but instead brought his race into lyrics, arguing that his whiteness encumbered his acceptance as a rapper, even as his "conspicuously white" (Armstrong 342) persona enhanced his marketability to broader and whiter audiences and smoothed the way for upcoming white rappers. He did not appropriate blackness per se; rather he reiterated his roots in poor white trash culture, with his living in trailer parks and growing up in a broken, dysfunctional family. He did not try to be black by imitation, but projected his lived experiences in poverty and the way he had paid his dues within hip hop culture, rhyming in Detroit clubs where the audience was less than accepting of the new white MC. Learning from the successes of the Beastie Boys and the failures of Vanilla Ice, Em learned how to better market himself as a crossover act by studying his white hip hop predecessors.

Eminem personified hip hop values: An MC must maintain composure while rhyming, whether on stage or in the street; an MC should draw source material from his own hardships; an MC should keep meter and rhythm. In gangsta rap, the subgenre from which Eminem develops much of his subject matter, artists present themselves as members of an oppressed group who take matters into their own hands to survive through crime. In the culture gangsta rap claims to represent, oppression and its resultant self-loathing create animosity toward those perceived as weaker or threatening. Gangsta rap, then, has been criticized for homophobic and misogynist lyrics. Eminem's music is not gangsta rap per se, yet Eminem validated his position in hip hop by writing and performing, at times, a gangsta litany of homophobic and misogynist lyrics. Although Eminem emerged after the heyday of gangsta rap, his association with Dr. Dre, a founding member of N.W.A., places him in a gangsta rap lineage that is reflected in his lyrics. Dre is featured prominently in Eminem's lyrics and videos, and on the songs "My Name Is" and "Guilty Conscience," he reminds his listeners of his link to N.W.A.

At the beginning of his career, Eminem was renowned for witty, often humorous freestyling that charmed audiences and won him MC battles. As recreated in his partly autobiographical film *8 Mile*, Eminem bested his opponents by revealing intimate and embarrassing details of his personal life. This public vulnerability disarmed the MCs he battled and ultimately proved to be another of Eminem's signature traits that strengthened his hip hop cachet. Trash-talking lyrics aside, these tortured rants and confessions endeared him to audiences and colleagues. Eminem's lyrics tell complex stories in songs like "Stan," "Toy Soldiers," and "Mockingbird," yet he could improvise lyrics in a battle, spewing verbal riffs in the same way that jazz musicians improvised with their instruments. Audiences could see Eminem was accomplished musically and had created a unique vocal style and a tactical approach to the MC battles where he would make his name.

WELFARE, BABIES, AND BASEMENT RAP BANDS: THE MAKING OF A RAPPER

Eminem's first twenty years would serve as the emotional well from which he dipped to produce his art and provoke listeners. Eminem was born Marshall Bruce Mathers III in 1972, in St. Joseph, Missouri, near Kansas City. Eminem's mother, Deborah Briggs-Mathers, was fifteen years of age when she gave birth to her son. He was under a year old when his father, Marshall Bruce Mathers II, abandoned his family. Eminem's itinerant life oscillated between Kansas City and metro Detroit as Debbie moved in and out of trailer parks, relatives' homes, and public housing. She proved unable to provide an economically and socially stable home life for her family. This unstable lifestyle contributed to Eminem's skill in connecting with his audience. A significant portion of childhood was spent in an almost all-black public housing project in Detroit, where he developed quick-witted wordplay and salty rhymes to defuse violent bullies and gangs. For a few years, the family lived near Eight Mile Road, which serves as a dividing line between Detroit's poorer black and white communities. Eminem eventually dropped out of Lincoln High School in Warren, a suburb of Detroit, at the age of seventeen. Nonetheless, he established key friends and professional connections at high school, in his Detroit neighborhoods, and in the underground Detroit club scene, which would serve him well as he became a full-time musician. Eminem would also meet his future wife Kimberly Ann Scott at his Detroit metro high school. He and Kim had their first child on December 25, 1995, Haile Jade Scott. Haile would serve as a topic in several albums along with Eminem's themes of unrequited maternal and paternal attention that he was denied as a child.

Eminem was nine years old when his uncle, Ronald (Ronnie) Dean Polk-ingharn, introduced him to his first rap song. Eminem and Ronnie were less than three months apart in age. Ronnie played Ice-T's "Reckless" from the 1984 *Breakin'* soundtrack. From then on, the two best friends listened to rap tapes and recorded their own whenever they could. Ronnie committed suicide on December 14, 1991, at the age of nineteen, leaving Eminem to deal with the loss of his uncle, close friend, and rap partner. The impact of this loss is evident in Eminem's life and career: he tattooed his arm in tribute to his uncle, and he commemorated him in the song "Cleaning Out My Closet." Prior to Ronnie's death, Eminem had begun working toward a career in rap, and Ronnie's suicide gave him even more motivation toward making his music.

In 1990, Eminem and Proof (DeShaun Holton) formed D-12. Proof, who also performed with the group 5 Elementz, had the idea to form the band as they continued to practice and perform their music in Detroit basements. The band name D-12 is derived from Dirty Dozen: there are six MCs in the band but each MC has an alter ego. With Proof's vision, Eminem progressed from performing in basements with the rap band Sole Intent (with Proof and DJ Butterfingers), which eventually led to his first independent album, *Infinite*. It sold about about 500 copies, most of which were sold out of car trunks. It was with Proof that Mathers decided to call himself M&M. Then Mathers changed his self-chosen name to Eminem or, more affectionately, Em. Emi-nem toyed with naming as a process of self-recreation. His alter egos, Slim Shady, Marshall Mathers, and Eminem, would appear in the eponymous albums *The Slim Shady LP* and the *The Marshall Mathers LP*.

Eminem credits much of his success to the close and savvy inner circle of friends, Proof in particular, who compensated for years of familial instability. With Proof and the other four members of D-12, there was no separation between work and life. Eminem recalled a time when Proof, tired of seeing Eminem wear the same dirty old shoes, bought him a new pair. The early appeal of Eminem could be better understood if one were to look at his and his crew's effect on the Detroit club scene. Even before Eminem had signed a deal with Dr. Dre's label Aftermath Records, his presence onstage was un-deniable. Eminem began to gain notoriety in freestyle battles in local clubs. One key element of his success was the element of surprise. When the pale and relatively geeky-looking Eminem closed in on the mic, the audiences often booed; after all, he was not black. Yet Eminem turned both black urban and white suburban scowls of distrust into smiles and hip-swinging affirmation. He could woo multiracial urbanites at Manhattan's Sound Factory or sub-urban teens from Michigan's Upper Peninsula.

Like the Beastie Boys in the 1980s, Em found acceptance among his black hip hop peers. The B-Boys were one of the first acts signed to the Def Jam label, and they recorded and toured with hip hop artists such as Run-DMC, Schoolly D, Public Enemy, Biz Markie, De La Soul, and A Tribe Called Quest. The Beastie Boys built a bridge between black and white audiences that

Eminem later utilized. Certainly, the fact that the Beasties were managed by African American Russell Simmons did not hurt the band's access to black venues and audiences, just as Dr. Dre's vouching for Eminem's skills helped him gain a wider audience. Dre provided a link between newcomer Eminem and a tradition of hip hop culture. Furthermore, Eminem was quick to credit the early musical influences on his musical heritage, including both East and West Coast rappers.

Upon accepting his 2003 Grammy for Best Rap Album (*The Eminem Show*), Em gave props to those rappers whose influence helped him make it: Run-DMC, the Beastie Boys, LL Cool J, Kool G. Rap, Masta Ace, Rakim, Big Daddy Kane, Dr. Dre and N.W.A., Treach from Naughty by Nature, Nas, Tupac, Biggie, Jay-Z, and the Notorius B.I.G. This list proved Eminem's knowledge of hip hop history, as well as emphasized his desire to pay homage to the MCs who influenced his own unique style. Eminem also paid homage to Tupac Shakur for his enormous contributions to hip hop. Eminem would later produce the track "Runnin'" for the film *Tupac: Resurrection*. Eminem used existing vocal tracks from the late rappers Tupac and Notorious B.I.G. to create a new song in which the two rival MCs posthumously reunite.

As a fan of hip hop from an early age, Eminem understood the importance of tradition and of giving proper credit to the old-school innovators who influenced his own style, and Eminem certainly created his own style, with vocals drawing from the cadence of Masta Ace, the subject material of N.W.A., and often the speed raps of Big Daddy Kane as well as Em's southern contemporaries, Outkast. Before deciding to go solo, Eminem performed with groups such as Basement Productions, the New Jacks, and Sole Intent. In 1997, his *Infinite* CD received a less than lukewarm reception from the local hip hop community, who believed that his work was derivative of New York rappers Nas or Jay-Z. Not to be deterred, Em pursued with renewed vigor appearances at local radio stations and national MC battles through the late 1990s. Eventually, a promotional tape reached Dr. Dre, who signed Eminem to his label. The collaboration of Dre and Eminem led to the crossover triple platinum success of *The Slim Shady LP*.

DR. DRE: PRODUCING A NEW TALENT

Eminem's hard work in the Detroit hip hop underground paid off when he won second place in the 1997 Rap Olympics MC Battle in Los Angeles. This battle credential, along with Dr. Dre's sophisticated production and marketing, brought Eminem to MTV audiences and crossover status. Although Eminem's rhyme skills are evident, his commercial appeal may have also been built from the fact that he was white. Some evidence suggests that Eminem was selected by Dre as a white artist to appeal to what has been called rap's largest market: white teen suburbanites (Armstrong 336). Dre provided some guest vocals and appeared in the music video for Eminem's first single, "My Name Is," in which Emimem parodies contemporary pop icons such as Marilyn Manson. The song's title and chorus, as well as the personal revelations of the song's lyrics, reflect Dre's and Eminem's strategy for introducing this new white rapper to the world.

Though thousands of miles apart, Eminem and Dre shared similar passions and childhood experiences. Both grew up poor with a passion for music. At a young age, Dre was playing turntables in his Compton, California, home to entertain the adults of his extended family. Dre's mother surrounded him with the sentiments and sounds of Detroit Motown, Aretha Franklin, Diana Ross, Smokey Robinson, and James Brown. Any funky sound was a good sound. Music was an emotional release. Dre, like Eminem, quit school to focus on his music; he formed the proto–hip hop band World Class Wreckin' Cru. Both Eminem and Dre started locally at the bottom of their neighborhoods with music as a survival tool. In 1986, Dre, Ice Cube, and Eazy-E cofounded the controversial gangsta rap group N.W.A., whose 1988 song "Fuck tha Police" catapulted them into the national limelight, if not onto the airwaves. In 1992, Dre's Death Row Records, cofounded with ex-football star Suge Knight, released *The Chronic*, the epitome of West Coast hip hop sound that flooded the airwaves across the nation. *Spin* magazine named the Grammy-winning album, with its $50 million in retail sales, one of the most influential albums of the 1990s.

The not-so-obvious complexity of Eminem and his rise to hip hop stardom is that while he lived and exploited his outsider, bad boy lifestyle, he was also willing to play by the rules to study the hip hop business and understand his tenuous place in the culture. While Eminem's lyrics often seemed to indulge his emotions, he exhibited the discipline, humility, and foresight to build his name in underground Detroit rap battles and to design a business model to promote his self-financed recordings. Like his hip hop contemporaries Master P and Wu-Tang Clan, he was simultaneously an underground rap artist, an ambitious businessman selling albums out of his car trunk, a visionary, and a musician. Eminem had the street cred, the ambition, and the talent. More important, he was willing to subordinate his personal ego and trust his career to Dr. Dre, who would enhance each of these features. His production skills would take Eminem's rhymes to a new level, and his label, Aftermath Records, would provide the worldwide promotion and distribution that Eminem could not have achieved on his own. Beyond these more obvious advantages of signing to Dre's record label, Eminem also benefited from Dre's hip hop lineage. His work in N.W.A. aside, Dre introduced rap listeners to Snoop Doggy Dogg and the D.O.C., and was known for discovering exciting new talents and helping to shape their sound.

Dre produced Eminem's *Slim Shady LP*, which sold over 3 million copies in the first eighteen months of release. Raw to the point of being mean spirited and embarrassingly naked, the personal nature of *Slim Shady* impressed those in the music business. One of the contributions Eminem made to hip hop was to use lyrics and topics that explored his own interior landscape. Hip hop culture in the 1990s had focused heavily on a handful of embedded values premised on authenticity, or being real. In gangsta rap, a hip hop subgenre, rappers often demonstrated their realness through masculine posturing, misogyny, violence, and homophobia. Gangsta rap's exemplars had to have street credibility that most often came with documented criminality and underclass status. Disrespecting people who were called hos, sluts, bitches, and fags was standard fare on gangsta rap tracks; Eminem, however, took the material one step further. Eminem not only disrespected women; he dared to disrespect his mother and his wife in detail and repeatedly as part of his performances. While gangsta rappers lauded guns, money, and bitches as status symbols, Eminem turned these symbols inward to vocalize the psychological costs of being a member of an underclass that spawns self-hatred, crime, and cycles of violence and poverty. His violent songs played out as revenge fantasies born from a wounded psyche more than they stood as gangsta posturing or testaments to his aggressive nature. In fact, the songs were clearly fantasies, and on "Stan," Eminem describes the use of violent fantasy in his music. Eminem brought to the light that family and friends in similar circumstances of poverty do not support each other; rather, they claw at each other's emotional independence and economic success. In his raps, Eminem attacked not only women but the matriarchy that invisibly scaffolds the masculine posturing in gangsta rap.

Eminem became famous selling songs that aired his grievances against the women that molded his life. With fame and fortune often come legal complications, and it was no different for Eminem. However, Eminem turned a classic ghetto trope by remixing the legal entanglements of his life into his art. Eminem's stories of childhood poverty, drugs, and family turbulence with his wife and mother had nurtured his art. Now his lyrics provided fodder for personal and legal retaliation. In 1999, Eminem's mother filed suit for defamation of character after hearing her son's lyrics that reported her drug use. On "My Name Is," for example, Eminem rhymes, "I just found out my mom does more dope than I do." Laying bare such personal trauma is part of Eminem's appeal. When his mother sued him, he incorporated this new development into his lyrics for "Marshall Mathers."

Eminem remixes the events of his life and exposes not only his anger but his emotional vulnerability, leaving no separation between his art and his life. In his lyrics, there is no suburban propriety and no urbane distance. Eminem develops his authenticity through being real with his audience and telling true stories about his life. Bringing a tradition from the blues into gangsta rap (as Ice Cube and the Geto Boys did before him), Eminem writes about his woman troubles. His mother, wife, and daughter make frequent appearances in his lyrics. Not to be left out of the public humiliation of family dysfunction, Kim Mathers openly took offense at Eminem's graphic lyrics in the songs

"'97 Bonnie & Clyde"and "Kim." Eminem would also rehash his and Kim's marriage problems into the song "Soldier."

BEEF

Eminem's lyrics chronicle his anger and frustration, and these emotions don't stop with his family. Like many other hip hop artists such as Tupac and Biggie or Jay-Z and Nas, Eminem has been entrenched in conflicts with other artists, known in hip hop lyrics as beef. Beef promotes hip hop music in three ways: It provides ample topic material for tracks as rappers dis each other; it stimulates discussion about who is the better rhymer or lyricist, and therefore challenges each rapper involved to showcase his or her ultimate skills; and beef turns hip hop recordings into a competition that recalls the battles of hip hop's earlier days, when MCs went head to head at parties or in the parks, in rhyme circles known as ciphers. Hip hop's lyrical rivalries could be compared to verbal professional wrestling: They entail airing of animosity in songs, and public banter and dissing in magazine interviews and on radio shows. Beef functions as a way to secure a place in the hip hop hierarchy, gain publicity, and air one's discontents. These conflicts require quick responses to one's opponent, utilizing the verbal practices of African griots or storytellers who prized verbal quickness. This keen control of language could disarm opponents. In African American culture, the tradition translated to the practice of the mostly good-natured but important game called the Dozens. This verbal exchange exemplified a code of conduct and control expected among members of an underclass. The ability to stay composed while arguing one's case with wit and poise remains a coveted form of street power. These sophisticated verbal exchanges were essential to establishing a sense of hip hop community.

In the 1970s, DJs tried to outdo each other by using competition as a way to heighten excitement among people at block parties. The goal of Kool Herc, the father of hip hop, was to build a stronger sound system than his competitors, DJs like Afrika Bambaataa and Pete DJ Jones. When MCs started rhyming over these DJ routines, their vocal crowd incitement soon led to verbal challenges from other MCs about who was better on the mic. On one hand, beef can be a marketing strategy that promotes a feud between two artists as a way to connect their records. When one MC answers another's challenge, the new record is geared toward a waiting audience that expects a response. In the 1980s, the beef between Roxanne Shante and U.T. F.O. spawned close to 100 answer records from various rap artists. These artists attacked each other's personas, fashion style, gender, and sexuality, along with rhyme skill, but the animosity was limited to their songs. In the 1990s, beef infamously spilled over to physical violence with the murders of Tupac Shakur and Notorious B.I.G. While neither murder has been solved, the long-term beef between these artists is believed to have set in motion the events that led to their killings. Eminem, through his association with Dre, falls into the lineage of the Tupac-Biggie beef. Their rivalry created a rhyme war for ascendancy between West and East Coast rap artists, specifically Death Row Records on the West Coast and Bad Boy Records on the East. The East Coast was the undisputed birthplace and world center of hip hop until 1992, with the phenomenally successful release of Dre's *The Chronic*. *The Chronic* heralded the breakout of a West Coast flourishing of artists and labels: Tupac Shakur, Snoop Dogg, and Death Row Records. Bad Boy's stars, to name a few, were Notorious B.I.G., Mase, Junior M.A.F.I.A., Lil' Kim, and Puff Daddy. The deaths of Tupac and Biggie forever removed beef from the merely discursive and local plane. Yet their deaths did not stop beef from happening. Rather, the rivalry seemed to spark new beefs. With two of the biggest selling hip hop artists murdered, a battle for supremacy took place. Jay-Z challenged Nas for the title of King of New York, and a series of new beefs were initiated by artists associated with Eminem: Proof and D-12 versus Royce da 5′9″; 50 Cent versus Ja Rule; 50 Cent versus the Game; 50 Cent versus DJ Green Lantern; G-Unit versus Fat Joe; and 50 Cent versus Lil' Kim.

The most significant beef for Eminem himself has been his ongoing and contentious rivalry with Ray Benzino (Raymond Scott), co-owner and editor of *The Source,* at one time hip hop's premier magazine. Benzino did little to hide his animosity toward Eminem as he argued that Eminem's success as a white man hindered Latino and black recognition and financial growth. If Eminem got too large a cut of the rap album profits, no profits would be left for rappers of color. Curiously, Benzino is himself biracial and Dave Mays, co-owner of *The Source,* is white. Even so, Benzino and company saw Eminem, Jimmy Iovine, and Interscope Records as barriers to recognition for authentic black hip hop culture. Benzino recorded a track disrespecting Eminem. When Eminem heard about the upcoming dis, he recorded two dis tracks against Benzino. Escalating the vitriolic rhetoric, Benzino attacked Eminem personally, calling him the "2003 Vanilla Ice" on his song "Pull Your Skirt Up." He obliquely threatened Em's daughter Haile and threatened physical violence to Eminem if they ever met face to face. The verbal wrestling match spread to the radio when on-air personality Angie Martinez invited Eminem to air his views. Benzino called the radio station, challenging Eminem to a physical fight.

Benzino consistently rated Em low in the *The Source* magazine's one- to five-mic rating system, while Benzino rated his own groups consistently in the four- to five-mic range. In 2000, *The Source* gave the nine-time-platinum *Marshall Mathers LP* only a two-mic rating. This was later upped to four mics on the heels of vehement protest from readers and the hip hop community. In a press conference, Benzino stated that Em was ruining hip hop and provided an early freestyle tape by Em in which he disrespected black women by calling them money hungry gold-diggers (a topic used by black rappers such as Big Daddy Kane in the eighties, and one that Kanye West turned into a hit record with "Gold Digger" in 2005). Benzino, with *The Source* as his weapon, pounded away at Em because he used the word *nigger* in a song. In both cases mentioned above, Em apologized publicly and blamed his lapse in judgment on youthful indiscretion and ignorance, thereby quickly deflating public disapproval. Em replied to Benzino in two underground dis tracks, "Nail in the Coffin," and "The Sauce," and extended the beef in the track "Yellow Brick Road" (*Encore*).

Arguments for black purity in hip hop notwithstanding, *The Source* featured Em in its pages. Ultimately, Eminem profited from the beef when he was awarded a large sum of money for defamation and copyright infringement. In the end, Benzino's credibility, his lagging album sales, and his legal entanglements brought him under scrutiny at *The Source*. He ignored a legal injunction and published some of Eminem's lyrics. As a result, *The Source* was found in contempt of court and forced to pay compensation to Eminem and his label, Shady Records. Benzino was fired and in 2006 shareholders of *The Source* ousted Benzino, though his legal troubles did not end there. Benzino's bias hurt the magazine itself, which lost credibility as the top hip hop magazine, making way for newcomers such as *XXL*. Many fans still believe that the high-profile public battle between Benzino and Eminem was an elaborate publicity stunt.

In other beefs, Everlast, the former front man of the white, Irish, hip hop group House of Pain, insulted Eminem in retaliation for a perceived insult. The beef went back and forth on rap tracks with disses including jabs at family members. On "Quitter," Eminem ridiculed Everlast for his religious conversion to Islam, his failure with House of Pain, and his move to a rock music format with his solo album *Whitey Ford Sings the Blues*. The beef between Eminem and Insane Clown Posse (ICP) started in 1995 when Em was handing out flyers for one of his performances. The flyer mentioned that ICP might make an appearance. Violent J and Shaggy 2 Dope took offense at the assumption that ICP would play with Eminem. They scorned the thought of playing at Em's party, which prompted a series of dis tracks such as "Get You Mad" and "Drastic Measures." The Eminem and ICP beef was turned up a notch when Eminem dissed ICP on Howard Stern's radio talk show.

In response, ICP with rap crew Twizted returned to the Howard Stern show with a dis track called "Slim Anus," ridiculing Eminem with samples from his own song "My Name Is." "Slim Anus" alluded to Eminem's homosexual tendencies with Dr. Dre, and borrowed from prison slang to depict Eminem as Dre's bitch, a tactic Dre himself had used in earlier beefs with Eazy-E and Ice Cube. ICP continued to deride Eminem's mother and his wife, Kim. Eminem would shame ICP by calling them merely Detroit suburbanites without real hip hop roots. His beef with ICP would eventually lead Em to his arrest for pulling an unloaded gun on Dougie Doug, a friend of Insane Clown Posse. Em was charged with brandishing a firearm in public, assault with a dangerous weapon, and two counts of concealed weapons possession. He pleaded no contest and received one year of probation concurrent with another sentence. Currently, ICP and Eminem are known to have declared a truce.

In another Detroit beef, Em had an on-again off-again conflict with Royce da 5´9˝. Em's beef with Royce is likely his most personal beef, because Royce was Em's close friend and hype man during the Detroit underground years. Together they rapped "Scary Movies," "Nuttin' to Do," and "Bad Meets Evil"—Royce being the former and Em being the latter. "Bad Meets Evil" is considered by many to be their best collaborative track (*The Slim Shady LP*). True to hip hop form, nonetheless, the two maintained a testy relationship that exemplified how beef could benefit and destroy rappers within the hip hop promotion industry.

Eminem opened the doors for Royce in 1999 to Dr. Dre and a successful collaboration, until Royce's manager leaked in a radio interview that Royce was ghostwriting Dre's lyrics, the implication being that Royce was better than Dre at writing lyrics, and that Dre was hiding something. Dre summarily shut the door on Royce's opportunity by cutting off any of his material and imminent record deals. Royce harbored a belief that Eminem never gave him a chance at Shady Records because of Em's ties to Dre and ongoing problems between Eminem and Proof's D-12 crew and Royce's D-Elite crew. In 2002, Eminem refused to allow Royce to sign on with Shady Records but signed 50 Cent. Royce and D-Elite still agreed to join Em's Anger Management Tour. The partnership soon soured and turned into a beef between D-12 and D-Elite over Royce's dis lyrics complaining about the Anger Management Tour. Detroit radio stations sizzled with dis tracks from each band, playing retribution tracks "Smack Down" and "Back Down" against "Malcolm X" and "Bang Bang." Em and Royce hovered above the fracas, never confronting each other. The beef between Royce and Proof of D-12 simmered for two years until it boiled over when the crews flaunted guns at each other. Both crews were hauled off by police to cool down in a Detroit jail cell. Since that time, Em, Royce, and their respective crews have cooled their animosities. Royce bounced among many different recording labels, but did release the *Independent's Day LP* in 2005. Like Em, Royce began to reflect on personal and professional blunders in his tracks. He mourned friends who lost their lives to violence and friendships lost and squandered in music career aspirations ("Regardless" and "Death Is Certain").

Outside of hip hop circles, Eminem has been targeted by critic and author Heshem Samy Abdel-Alim, who pursued more esoteric and less visceral beefs by scorning Eminem's hip hop pedigree. Abdel-Alim implied that Em was a latecomer to the hip hop scene in the 1990s, which was already on the streets in the very early 1970s, before Em's birth. Further scorn came from critics who labeled Em's use of street vernacular as infantile and sophomoric and his poetics of hard end rhymes as doggerel; these critics missed Eminem's complex rhythms and complicated internal rhymes (see sidebar: Hip Hop

Hip Hop and Poetry
Katherine V. Tsiopos-Wills

Content aside, the primacy of the word in hip hop music has linked hip hop lyrics to slam poetry, jazz poetry, the talking blues, bad man legends, toasts, and other oral poetic traditions. Even though lyrics, nuance, and stylistics were subordinated to the beat, early hip hop's acute sense of wordplay opened discussions among scholars, musicians, critics, and fans about a poetry renaissance. University instructors in the United States and United Kingdom added curricula to English language and literature classes examining hip hop lyrics generally and Eminem specifically.

With his complex rhythms, bridge rhymes, and visual imagery, Eminem brings a poet's skills to his lyrics. However, he is not as involved in connecting hip hop and poetry as other artists have been. In 2002, Russell Simmons, founder of Def Jam Records, developed an HBO series, *Def Poetry Jam,* to showcase readings and performances by poets. On *Def Poetry Jam* and in spoken-word venues like the Nuyorican Poetry Café and the Bowery Poetry Club, spoken word often crosses boundaries with hip hop performances. The artists Saul Williams, Jill Scott, and Sage Francis each incorporate hip hop styles into their poetry readings, and hip hop culture itself is often a topic for spoken-word poets. Williams's "Telegram" finds hip hop lying in a ditch, "dead to itself." The poet proceeds to offer hip hop culture a litany of advice on how to revive itself by abandoning consumer-driven rhymes about cars and jewelry and returning to its roots.

Further Resources

Alim, H. Samy. "On Some Serious Next Millennium Rap Ishhh: Pharoahe Monch, Hip-hop Poetics, and the Internal Rhymes of *Internal Affairs.*" *Journal of English Linguistics* 31 (2003): 60–84.

Def Poetry Jam Season 1 DVD. HBO, 2004.

Heaney, Seamus. *BBC News* 30 June 2003.

Rose, Tricia. *Black Noise: Rap Music and Black Culture in Contemporary America.* Middletown, CT: Wesleyan University Press, 1994.

Simmons, Russell, et al. *Russell Simmons Def Poetry Jam . . . and More.* New York: Atria, 2005.

Wood, Brent. "Understanding Rap as Rhetorical Folk Poetry." *Mosaic: A Journal for the Interdisciplinary Study of Literature* 32.4 (1999): 129–146.

and Poetry). Another attack on his lyrics came from pop star Christina Aguilera, who feuded with Eminem over his references to her in lyrics. Eminem alluded to both Britney Spears and Aguilera's sex lives in the track "The Real Slim Shady" (2000). While not strictly a hip hop beef, Em's clash with gay coalitions, religious fundamentalists, and parents captured worldwide attention—and publicity that eventually secured more publicity and sales. The Gay and Lesbian Alliance Against Defamation (GLAAD) and other gay activists declared his lyrics "hate speech." Em captured the ire of conservative Lynne Cheney, wife of the sitting vice president of the United States, mother of Mary Cheney, a lesbian, and author of *Sisters,* a novel with some lesbian themes. She castigated Em as a "violent misogynist" to the Senate committee hearing on violence in the entertainment industry, saying that his words posed a danger to children and the nation. Parents fumed as *Teen* magazine reported that 74 percent of its readers surveyed would like to date Em.

Contrary to ghetto form, Em chose not to enter into a global beef with these detractors from outside of the hip hop community. Rather, Em embraced gay white Anglo icon Elton John and let his actions speak louder than his words as he performed a duet with Elton at the 2001 Grammy Awards and hugged him at the end of the song. He would later deny any knowledge of or problem with Elton's homosexuality. The message to detractors was that they should focus on his art instead of lobbing ad hominem attacks. Like other great artists, Em played to all sides of the sexuality spectrum by contradicting his homophobic lyrics with his tolerant words in interviews. Where the real Slim Shady, or Eminem, or Marshall Mathers stood on homosexuality was ambiguous. Dance clubs with both straight and gay audiences continued to play his rap songs. Another unqualified indication of support came when Academy Award-winning actor Jodie Foster closed her speech at the 2006 University of Pennsylvania commencement ceremonies with a standing ovation to lyrics from Eminem's Oscar-winning "Lose Yourself."

Eminem's beefs often had little to do with his own conflicts with other rap artists; he was involved by association in his friends' beefs. The beef between 50 Cent and Ja Rule entangled Emimem, although it existed from the old days of 50 and Ja hanging around South Jamaica in Queens, New York. 50 Cent volleyed the first recorded dis on "Life's on the Line," rejecting friendships and partnerships from the streets: "We ain't partners and we damn sure ain't friends." Eminem catalogued his take on the beef on the track "Like Toy Soldiers": "We just inherited 50's beef with Murder Inc [Ja's record label]" With 50 Cent securely ensconced with Dre and Eminem, rappers Busta Rhymes, Obie Trice, and G-Unit joined the East Coast entourage. Ja Rule fueled the beef by dissing Eminem's wife, calling her a slut and crackhead while also targeting Eminem's daughter Haile.

EMINEM'S POLITICS: THE EVOLUTION OF AN "I DON'T GIVE A FUCK" RAPPER

Except for a few instances, Eminem's early lyrics did not highlight sociopolitical themes as consistently as those of artists like Tupac Shakur or Kanye

West. While Tupac challenged police brutality and government corruption (on "Point the Finga"), and Kanye took on the global diamond trade (on "Diamonds (From Sierra Leone)") and conspiracy theories that the U.S. government created AIDS and the crack epidemic (on "Crack Music"), Eminem for the most part raged at the personal exploitation he felt at the hands of his family and friends. His lyrics bubbled with anger at women and beef with his colleagues. He rapped class rage as a cultural spectacle lacking political protest or outrage. It was only after increasing criticism and ridicule was heaped on him by gay activists, women's rights groups, and political conservatives such as vice presidential wives Lynne Cheney and Tipper Gore that he responded with lyrical vitriol about censorship and participated in more strategic interviews.

His most overt sociopolitical consciousness-raising songs include "White America" and "Mosh." In "White America," he reintroduced black modes of expression into white suburban homes. He spoke to "suburban kids" who without him would not have to face certain truths about their own culture. He was the poster boy for the low-class, urban hip hop gangtas rubbing fear into the faces of white suburban parents. Eminem's antiwar/pro-voting video "Mosh" was released just before the November 2004 election as an indictment of George W. Bush and the Iraq war. Within twenty-four hours of the "Mosh" premiere on MTV's *Total Request Live*, it hit number one. The protagonist in the video resembles Eminem as he begins to mobilize police forces, soldiers in fatigues, and black-hooded masses to storm the White House, but then winds up calling for social action through voting. The term *mosh* goes through several iterations in the song. Em envisions mosh pits outside the Oval Office. He calls for everyone "to mosh through this desert storm." Finally, he castigates Bush for trying to impress his father and calls for the end of blood for oil. At the end of the video, no violence occurs. Instead, the screen fades out to the words "Vote Tuesday, November 2." The message of "Mosh" was powerful because it rekindled public discussion among Eminem's generation about the U.S.-Iraq war.

EMINEM AND THE NEW BREED OF WHITE SOUTHERN RAPPERS

A burgeoning movement of southern rappers and rap groups both black and white began incrementally infiltrating the hip hop music scene in the mid-1990s. Many of these artists were less well known than Eminem but were performing at the sime time as Eminem developed his musical oeuvre. White rappers Bubba Sparxxx and Haystak heralded the "new South" movement. In the context of rap music, the new South music reflected southern ethnic diversity and urbanization. Bubba Sparxxx, born in LaGrange, Georgia, blended rapping with banjos, fiddles, and harmonicas while claiming country authenticity of poverty, violence, drugs, and dysfunctional families. Sparxxx did not escape the eye of Jimmy Iovine of Interscope records, who signed Sparxxx with the New Beat Club label of southern record producer Timbaland, who had also produced for LL Cool J, Xzibit, Jay-Z, Tweet, and the Game. Timbaland produced both Sparxxx's debut album *Dark Days, Bright Night* (2002) and *Deliverance* (2003). Sparxxx's hit singles "Ugly" (2001) and "Ms. New Booty" (2006) brought him name recognition and created a buzz about white southern rappers and new subgenres of southern hip hop out of locales like Houston.

Haystak, of Nashville, Tennessee, pressed three albums (1998's *Mak Million*, 2000's *Car Fulla White Boys,* and 2002's *The Natural*) that sold hundreds of thousands of copies with almost no marketing, radio, or financial support. Haystak, a white country boy, grabbed the attention of Scarface of the Geto Boys, who signed him to the Def Jam South record label. Unlike Eminem, Haystak refused to contextualize rap as a fundamentally African American musical form necessarily growing out of hip hop urban culture. To Haystak, rap is a genre without racial categories. There are white rappers and there are black rappers. Haystak sought to dispel the social myth that white equates with wealth and black equates with poverty. Hip hop is a culture of the poverty class, not race or region, and for these reasons lower and lower-middle-class white Americans embrace rapping.

Another white rap artist from Detroit, Kid Rock, played on white southern identity through his connections to country music in his fashion style and his lyrics in songs like "Cowboy." Kid Rock has maintained an ongoing relationship with Eminem since they were reputed to have gotten into an argument at a Kid Rock autograph signing when Eminem was seventeen years old. The two would eventually form a professional bond when Eminem provided a guest verse on Kid Rock's *Devil Without a Cause* album. Kid Rock was from the Detroit suburbs. He escaped boredom and familial angst by going to the Mount Clemens, Michigan, housing project to spin records at basement parties. Kid Rock is purported to have earned his nickname as he spun records and rapped in lounges and parking lots when listeners exclaimed, "Look at that white kid rock." Kid Rock's high-energy stage presence was undeniable, as was his musical breadth and virtuosity. He rapped, vocalized, and played guitar, bass, percussion, keyboard, banjo, and turntables.

He released his first album, *Grits Sandwiches for Breakfast* (1989) with producer Too $hort on the Jive label. Joining Atlantic Records in 1998, Kid Rock released the eleven-times-platinum *Devil Without a Cause* in 1998. Sustained mainstream success eluded Kid Rock as he experimented with country hip hop crossover riffs, provoking confusion and a loss of his listener base. Idiosyncratic and multitalented, Kid Rock captured media attention when he dated and announced his engagement to actress Pamela Anderson in 2003 (they late split in 2006). Though Kid Rock politically leaned to the conservative right as a supporter of George W. Bush, his explicit sexual lyrics, profanity, and rumors of an orgy sex tape surfacing from his past prevented

Eminem   **499**

him from being taken seriously as a supporter by the political right. Furthermore, the Federal Communications Commission levied the largest government fine to date on college radio station WSUC-FM at the State University of New York for indecency: $23,750 for airing the track "Yodeling in the Valley" with its graphic and metaphoric riffs on oral sex. The FCC fine was eventually decreased. Though Eminem and Kid Rock were blond, disenfranchised, musically talented and ambitious whites from the Detroit environs, their audiences differed, with Em capturing primarily the hip hop listeners and Kid capturing the rock market. Unlike Eminem, Kid Rock did not solidify his core constituency within the tight Detroit hip hop community.

RUMORS OF A THIRTY-SOMETHING EARLY RETIREMENT FOR EMINEM

Rumors of Eminem's early retirement in his thirties started surfacing in 2004 with the release of the *Encore* album. Eminem was quick to dispel rumors of his retirement in an MTV interview, affirming that he would never stop making music and being involved in the music business. In fact, he said he was using his time to explore other music avenues such as promoting other musicians' careers and finding new artists for his record label. Fans' concern and his comments about retirement came on the heels of three disturbing events between December 2005 and April 2006 that made Eminem more reclusive, thus less visible on the club and music scene.

First, there were the Detroit-based shootings of his inner circle: Obie Trice and Proof. Obie Trice was shot in the head by a highway drive-by shooter on New Year's Eve, 2005. Obie survived the assault but could not have the bullet removed from his skull. And Proof, one of Eminem's best friends, was fatally shot at an 8 Mile club on April 11, 2006. More than just a friend, Proof was Em's hype man and coperformer during almost all of his performances, and was best man at his wedding. Proof's absence would have significant effects on both Em's personal well-being and his artistic production. The track "Like Toy Soldiers" (*Encore*, 2004) could easily be interpreted as a swan song. The album cover pictures Em giving a bow, and the set closes with the track "Curtains Down." The "Like Toy Soldiers" track blends marching band sounds with a powerful lyrical message about Em's exhaustion with the ongoing strife in the hip hop community.

Em provocatively said "Like Toy Soldiers" was about walking away. The track's meaning was ambiguous as to whether it meant walking away from his music career or just putting past bad business dealings behind and moving on. In the track, he specifically referred to going "toe to toe with Benzino" and *The Source*, losing his composure when his daughter Haile's name was mentioned by another rapper, and being sickened by the 50 Cent and Ja feud. He mourned the ongoing feuds in the rap community. He reiterated personal and professional problems with *The Source* magazine and its editor Benzino. The greatest hits album *Curtain Call* (2005) suggested that Em was considering retreating from the hip hop limelight. In closing, Em called for a peaceful resolution to the hip hop strife. Like an omen, the music video for "Like Toy Soldiers" depicted Proof being killed in a shooting. Perhaps as Eminem entered his thirties, he was thinking it was time to ease out of the hip hop scene and into something less hazardous before the ghetto struck again, as it had with his closest friends.

Em would find both musical and acting opportunities in filmmaking venues premised on his success with *8 Mile,* his quasi-biographical film about a poor white rapper (B. Rabbit) seeking to transcend the limitations of his family, class, and environment by rapping his way to acceptance and recognition from his urban hip hop community. The film was notable for its naturalistic camera style that captured in stark verisimilitude the Detroit streets on the poor side of town by highlighting smoky blue backgrounds, gray skies and factories, and squeaky, rusty beater cars. Shot on location in Detroit, the film contained all the classic dramatic elements found in Aristotle's *Poetics:* protagonists, antagonists, a simple plot with rising action, climax, and denouement—plus the elements of music and humor for periodic catharsis. Some critics discredit *8 Mile* for its rock-pop-rap movie genre clichés and sly referential narrative; yet the film struck an emotional chord with a significant viewer base that approved of the emotionally raw scenes and characters. The film earned a box office take of $51 million on opening day (November 8, 2002) and worldwide gross of $243 million by spring of 2003. Solid performances by Eminem, Mekhi Phifer, Britanny Murphy, and Kim Basinger, and direction by Curtis Hanson complemented the filmmakers' apparent goal to pull back the veil on race and class turmoil in the gritty hip hop underclass.

Eminem's trajectory seems headed toward public and professional contributions in the areas of politics and music production and personal attention to his daughter, Haile. As Em entered his thirties, he joined a cohort of thirty fellow hip hop artists and Detroit Mayor Kwame Kilpatrick at the Detroit Hip-Hop Summit 2004, encouraging listeners to vote and broach pressing sociopolitical issues. After initially being bankrolled by Interscope Records, Eminem's Shady Records company is succeeding at developing hip hop talent as a Detroit-based label, albeit headquartered in New York. He continued to grubstake and nurture new talent through Shady Records by producing albums and tracks for D-12, Obie Trice, Status Quo, 50 Cent, and G-Unit. Moving into Dre's role as impresario, Eminem seeks and develops new talent. Eminem nominated 50 Cent as his most inspirational rapper, and Dre followed suit by signing 50 Cent, including him in more CDs and the *8 Mile* film soundtrack with the hit "Wanksta."

If Eminem does retire from the hip hip community, he will do so at the top of his game with four solo studio albums: 1999's *The Slim Shady LP,* 2000's

The Marshall Mathers LP, 2002's *The Eminem Show*, *Encore*, nine Grammies, and a Best Song Oscar for the *8 Mile* track "Lose Yourself." He will be the best-selling hip hop artist up to 2006, having sold more than 25 million albums in the United States and generating more than $1 billion in global album sales by attracting a larger and more diverse hip hop audience worldwide.

See also: Beastie Boys, Dr. Dre and Snoop Dogg, Tupac Shakur

WORKS CITED

Armstrong, Edward G. "Eminem's Construction of Authenticity." *Popular Music and Society* 27.3 (2004): 335-355.

Hess, Mickey. "Hip-Hop Realness and the White Performer." *Critical Studies in Media Communication* 22.5 (2005): 372–389.

FURTHER RESOURCES

Aaron, Charles. "Chocolate on the Inside." *Spin* May 1999.

Bozza, Anthony. *Whatever You Say I Am: The Life and Times of Eminem*. New York: Crown, 2003.

8 Mile. Dir. Curtis Hanson. Perf. Eminem, Kim Basinger. Universal, 2002.

Eminem. *Angry Blonde*. New York: ReganBooks, 2000.

Eminem: All Access Europe. Documentary. Interscope Records, 2002.

Eminem: The History of Eminem. Documentary. Locomotive Music DVD, 2005.

Eminem Official Web Site. http://www.eminem.com.

Kenyatta, Kelly. *You Forgot About Dre! The Unauthorized Biography of Dr. Dre and Eminem*. Los Angeles: Busta Books, 2001.

Perry, Imani. *Prophets of the Hood: Politics and Poetics in Hip-Hop*. Durham, NC: Duke University Press, 2004.

Rize. Dir. David Chapelle. Documentary. Eminem as himself, uncredited. 2005.

Rose, Tricia. *Black Noise: Rap Music and Black Culture in Contemporary America*. Middletown, CT: Wesleyan University Press, 1994.

Shady Fiction Quotations. May 20, 2006. http://www.shadyfiction.com/article14.htm.

Shady Records Web Site. http://www.shadybase.com.

Smitherman, Geneva. "The Chain Remains the Same: Communicative Practices in the Hip-Hop Nation." *Journal of Black Studies* 28.1 (1997): 3–25.

The Wash. Dir. D. J. Pooh. Perf. Snoop Dogg, Dr. Dre, and Eminem uncredited. Lion's Gate, 2001.

Watts, Eric King. "Border Patrolling and Passing in Eminem's *8 Mile*." *Critical Studies in Media Communication* 22.3 (2005): 187–206.

SELECTED DISCOGRAPHY

Soul Intent. Duck Records, 1992.

Infinite. Web Entertainment, 1996.

The Slim Shady EP. Web Entertainment, 1997

The Slim Shady LP. Aftermath/Interscope, 1999.

The Marshall Mathers LP. Aftermath/Interscope, 2000.

The Eminem Show. Aftermath/Interscope, 2002.
8 Mile Soundtrack. Produced by Eminem. Shady/Interscope, 2002.
Encore. Aftermath/Interscope, 2004.
Curtain Call: The Hits. Aftermath/Interscope, 2005.

Courtesy of Photofest.

Missy Elliott

Joi Carr

Missy Elliott, a five-time Grammy Award winner, has carved out a hip hop niche all her own. Beyond being the best-selling female hip hop artist to date, and often referred to as the queen of hip hop, what separates Missy Elliott is her ability to allow her aesthetic to speak for itself. She uses her artistry to transcend cultural norms in hip hop and in the music industry. In hip hop, women have had to be hard (excessively masculine) or rely on overt sexuality. Missy, on the other hand, showcases a quirky, edgy, unconventional, and progressive aesthetic that pushes the boundaries of hip hop, transcending prescribed genre norms. In addition, Elliott has created a powerful digital identity that allows her to transcend the normative gaze foisted upon female artists. Just as Michael Jackson transcended being labeled another "black artist" in the 1980s, Missy has overcome the trappings of the usual feminine images of women in hip hop.

Melissa Arnette Elliott, who would single-handedly redefine the notion of a female hip hop artist, was born in Portsmouth, Virginia, on July 1, 1971. She credits her mother, Patricia Elliott, a survivor of domestic violence, with fostering in her a sense of strength and courage that helped define her career path. As an only child, Missy, nicknamed by her mother, spent countless hours listening to music to escape the abuse her mother suffered at the hands of her father. As early as age four, Missy sang and wrote songs to express her feelings and escape the harsh realities of her home. She would isolate herself in her room and sing to her dolls.

The family lived for a brief time in Jacksonville, North Carolina, while Missy's father, Ronnie Elliott, was an enlisted Marine. The family then returned to Virginia, where their poor quality of life reflected the reality of many African Americans during that time. Her mother was a woman of faith and quite protective of her daughter, rarely letting her out of her sight. Elliott also stayed close to home in fear that her mother would be beaten or even killed in her absence. The daily atmosphere in the home was unpredictable. In moments of desperation, Elliott even wrote numerous letters to pop stars with dreams of being rescued from her difficult life of abuse and poverty, among them Diana Ross and Michael and Janet Jackson. She made up stories about being handicapped, hoping to attract someone's attention. As she became increasingly isolated, music became her refuge.

For Elliott, this time alone forged a deep connection with music and with her imagination. For most of her childhood she found hope in music, listening to the radio, playing records, and watching music videos and TV shows like *American Bandstand* and *Soul Train*. Although she was identified scholastically as a gifted child, a school official insisted she be tested twice, doubting the initial IQ score was accurate. Still, her grades suffered. She would often neglect homework to spend most of her time practicing dance moves and singing along with her favorite artists' records. Elliott knew every dance move from Michael Jackson's "Thriller" video. She performed for her family members at picnics; she was placed on a table and would dance and sing for her family and friends. At home, she opted to stand on trash cans outside, using a hairbrush as a microphone. Eventually her relationship with music provided an important aspect of her aesthetic: her desire to create music that offered an entrée for others into her playful world of escape, hope, and joy.

Her early interest in music developed into a passion and a vocation that she acknowledged as a gift from God. Even so, the turning point in her life occurred when her mother mustered the strength to leave her father.

For Elliott, her mother's strength as a single parent changed her life. The now "fearless" thirteen-year-old, though still deeply impoverished, felt at home with her dream of becoming an artist. Imbued with her mother's iron will and her own active imagination, Elliott embarked on a musical journey that led to the top of the charts, redefining the boundaries of hip hop.

Although Elliott had dreamed of becoming an entertainer, she was not convinced there was a place for her in the industry. As a young woman, she felt alienated, especially since she rarely saw images that reflected her body type in the media. She was also rejected by record executives who viewed her as overweight and outside of market standards. Among other things, the rap and hip hop industry was still in its nascent form, featuring prominent male artists like Run-DMC, Big Daddy Kane, Kool Moe Dee, Doug E. Fresh, LL Cool J, and the Beastie Boys. In the late 1980s, however, Missy began to envision a place for herself in the industry. She was inspired by Salt-N-Pepa, a hot female rap group from New York. Their longevity as female artists in a male-dominated genre encouraged Missy to pursue her dream with more fervor.

Salt-N-Pepa also helped Elliott realize the importance of relying on her talent rather than copying others. They reinforced what she sensed from childhood. From childhood she viewed herself as distinctive, an original. She believed her talent was second to none and capable of opening industry doors. Other female MCs like Queen Latifah, MC Lyte, Monie Love, and Roxanne Shanté began to make inroads, building Elliott's confidence. She honed her vocal talent by singing in the church choir with her mother and started entering and winning talent shows, enlisting friends to help her. Her public persona as an artist began to emerge.

THE ROAD TO MISSY "MISDEMEANOR" ELLIOTT

Believing female artists now had an opportunity to stand out in the male-dominated landscape, Elliott formed an R&B girl group called Sista after graduating from high school in 1990. She wanted to create a genuinely talented group with longevity, eschewing the music industry's notion that one's body type should be a primary factor when scouting talent. Elliott, after a series of auditions, found Chonita Coleman, LaShawn Shellman, and Radiah Scott, and the four began developing a unique sound by performing as a group in local talent shows. She partnered with Timothy "DJ Timmy Tim" Mosley, a neighborhood friend and local track master. She used this collaboration to create a new sound for her dream girl group. Mosley, serving as producer, and Elliott, as singer-songwriter, created original material for demo tracks.

Elliott's first big break came in 1991 via Donald "Devante Swing" De-Grate, a singer-songwriter and primary producer of Jodeci (the hot R&B

act with Uptown Records, Elektra), whose debut album went double platinum. In a backstage impromptu audition, Sista performed a cappella for DeGrate and within a few days Elliott and Sista moved to New York City and signed with Elektra Records on DeGrate's Swing Mod label. Sista became the opening act for Jodeci and released "Brand New," a single slated for their upcoming project. The quartet was originally called Fay-Z but changed their name after landing their contract. Elliott, who was fiercely loyal, took along with her Mosley, later nicknamed Timbaland by DeGrate, and their friend, rapper Melvin "Magoo" Barcliff. Elliott and Mosley's partnership would soon prove to be a musical partnership for hip hop history.

Elliott's first project was a dream come true but more demanding than she could anticipate. It was the point of departure for demonstrating her extroadinary productivity and work ethic. While working and writing material for Sista's first album, *4 All the Sistas Around the World,* Elliott also contributed songwriting duties, both credited and uncredited, to Jodeci's next two albums: *Diary of a Mad Band* (1993) and *The Show, the After Party, the Hotel* (1995). In the midst of these endeavors, Elliott's dream was temporarily interuppted when Sista's LP, finally completed in 1994, was shelved and never released due to a financial upheaval at Uptown Records. Sista soon was defunct. Though disappointed by the abrupt end to a multiyear labor of love, Elliott remained hopeful.

For the next few years, Elliott lived as a starving artist in a two-story house in Hackensack, New Jersey, with a large cohort of other artists from Swing Mob all hoping to develop their own projects under DeGrate's tutelage. Included among them were future R&B stars Ginuwine and Charlene "Tweet" Keys. Ginuwine signed with Elektra the same day Sista did and Elliott contributed two songs to his platinum-selling debut album. Tweet, formerly a member of the R&B quintet Sugah, later signed with Elliott's label, and Playa, an R&B trio from Kentucky.

By 1995, Swing Mob had folded and many of its members dispersed. Elliott and several Swing Mob members remained creative partners and continued to live togerther, collaborating on each other's projects. The group referred to themselves collectively as "Supafriends" or "Da Bassment" while under DeGrate's label. Elliott and Mosley, however, began to acquire an impressive roster of hits, and music executives in R&B and hip hop circles began to take notice. Before long, Elliott had a burgeoning career behind the scenes as a songwriter-producer. Her first professional credit as a songwriter was for the 1993 hit, "That's What Little Girls Are Made Of," for *The Cosby Show*'s child star Raven-Symoné.

Despite all this, the music industry did not significantly respond until Elliott and Mosley wrote and produced a string of hit tracks for Jodeci ("Sweaty," "Want Some More," and "Won't Waste Your Time") and, most notably, tracks for Aaliyah's double-platinum sophomore album, *One in a Million* (1996). This album consisted of several hit singles, including "If Your Girl

Only Knew," "One in a Million," "Hot Like Fire," and "4 Page Letter." The work on Aaliyah's LP made the Elliott-Mosley songwriting-production team stars. They crafted hit after hit in a concentrated period of time for several artists, among them SWV ("Can We?") and 702 ("Steelo"). Mosley (Timbaland) gained individual attention after producing 702's "Steelo" remix.

During this time, Elliott gained street credibility as a performer after her breakthrough guest performances on MC Lyte's 1996 single "Cold Rock a Party (Remix)," and on Gina Thompson's "The Things You Do," both of which were produced by Sean "Diddy" Combs. Her characteristically distinct and witty rhyme, featured on Thompson's track and video, garnered her the moniker Hee Haw Girl. Though she remained relatively unknown, people began to stop her in the streets and ask her if she was the Hee Haw Girl, requesting her to laugh and dance in the same manner she performed in Thompson's video. Elliott's trademark laugh and playful rhymes created an audience that openly embraced her. Industry heavyweights soon began courting her to write, produce, and perform on their tracks.

After her performance on Thompson's track, Elliott's talent as an artist finally convinced music execs that her unconventional style and image had a place in mainstream music. Elliott was finally rewarded after a decade of unrelenting perseverance and multiple behind-the-scenes successes. She was able to enter the image-centric music industry on her own terms: a talented, dark-skinned, fingerwave-wearing, overweight, and—by industry standards —over-the-hill twenty-four-year-old. Her now-svelte five-foot frame has graced the cover of several prestigious magazines. In 2000, Elliott shed more than seventy pounds in less than a year to reduce her high blood pressure after her mother suffered a near-fatal heart attack. Elliott had received a doctor's warning about her significantly reduced life expectancy if she did not lose weight and take better care of herself. Elliott, who is notorious for being a workaholic, responded.

Elliott soon had multiple opportunities and several impressive offers. At twenty-two years of age, she accepted and signed a production/label deal with Elektra Entertainment Group in 1996. Under Goldmind, Inc., she was given complete creative control, but she was initially reluctant about entering the market as a solo artist; she desired to spend most of her time in the studio writing. Elliott and Timbaland returned to Virginia and continued producing tracks for other artists such as Total ("What About Us," 1997) and scouting for new talent to help launch her new label. Even with peer pressure and a great deal of encouragement from her newly aqcuired fans, Elliott did not record her own work until she felt prepared.

After about a year in her new venture, Elliott enlisted Mosley to collaborate with her on her long-awaited solo project. With this record she became Goldmind's first act and it became the first solo collaboration with Timbaland, who has subsequently partnered with Elliott on all her projects to date. The production duo reportedly completed the LP in one week, releasing her groundbreaking debut *Supa Dupa Fly* in June 1997 to critical acclaim, which entered the genre-defying singer-lyricist Missy "Misdemeanor" Elliott into contemporary American music history. The album debuted on Billboard's R&B Hip-Hop Albums chart at number three, the highest debut for a female hip hop artist. By September, *Supa Dupa Fly* was certified platinum. Elliott also became the first female hip hop artist to perform on the renowned Lilith Fair Tour (1998) and later with the Jay-Z/50 Cent "Rock the Mic" Tour.

The first single, "The Rain (Supa Dupa Fly)," helped establish Elliott as an iconic figure. The video was directed by Hype Williams and touted as one of the most innovative videos of the year. The short was nominated for three MTV awards and won two Billboard Video Music Awards. *Rolling Stone* named Elliott the Best Rap Artist of the Year and "The Rain (Supa Dupa Fly)" the Best Video of the Year. In December 1999, MTV ranked "The Rain (Supa Dupa Fly)" as the fifteenth greatest video of all time; it has been featured on MTV's *100 Greatest Videos Ever Made*.

Shortly after the release of her debut, Elliott, who is often characterized as shy and unassuming, began speaking out about her childhood, astonishing her mother. Becoming the spokesperson for Break the Cycle (a nonprofit organization whose mission is to end domestic violence by working proactively with youth) was the beginning of her long-standing commitment to important humanitarian efforts, especially for women. Teaming up with model Iman in 1999, she created a line of lipstick called Misdemeanor, donating more than $1 million of the proceeds to Break the Cycle. During this time, Elliott began to share vivid memories of the abuse she and her mother experienced. Although her mother never intended to speak publicly about that chapter of their lives, she supported Elliott in her endeavors. She also began speaking publicly about the sexual molestation she suffered when she was eight years old. A teenage cousin raped her repeatedly for about a year until another relative caught him. Regarding her father, Elliott reportedly is in intermittent contact with him, and although she is still haunted by the memories, she believes she has moved beyond the pain toward healing.

She continues to avidly support work designed to help important contemporary issues. In 2002, she was a featured act in *Vanity Fair's* In Concert series ("Where My Girls At"), a benefit concert in partnership with the Step Up Women's Network, a nonprofit organization dedicated to strengthening community resources for women and girls. The organization raises awareness and funding for breast cancer research and other women's causes. The concert event was also a musical celebration honoring Elliott's longtime friend Aaliyah, who died in the Bahamas in a plane crash in August 2001. Elliott also performed at MTV's World AIDS Day concert, raising awareness about the growing crisis in South Africa and around the world.

The little girl who used to tell her mother she was going to be a star is now known as the first African American female, Grammy Award-winning, multiplatinum artist-producer and music executive. Though often described as a consummate professional, she discusses the perils of being a business-woman in the corporate arena on her second solo release, *Da Real World*. Beyond her success as an executive, her ability to continue to break new ground with each of her subsequent solo recordings makes her one of the most original artists in the last decade, a pioneer and visionary. Like Bessie Smith, Sarah Vaughan, Ella Fitzgerald, Mahalia Jackson, Miles Davis, Jimi Hendrix, Chaka Khan, Michael Jackson, and Prince, among others, who created new borders in their respective genres, Elliott has provided new space for contemporary hip hop artists to explore. By fusing R&B, hip hop, rock, soul, and funk elements, Elliott and Mosley's revolutionary work expanded the borders of the once-fledgling genre. Their individual production discographies are quite expansive.

Elliott and Mosley, in the midst of both of their own solo careers, continue to produce hit singles and albums for other artists, such as Janet Jackson, Mariah Carey, Whitney Houston, Destiny's Child, Christina Aguilera, Justin Timberlake, Mel B, Monica, Lil' Kim, Eminem, Nelly Furtado, Fantasia, Ciara, and protégés Nicole Wray and Tweet, to name a few. Mosley now manages his own label with Interscope Records called Mosley Music Group. In 2004, Elliott moved Goldmind from Elektra Entertainment Group to Atlanta Records, where she continues to develop her artist roster. Broadening her production efforts, she coscored the Disney/Touchstone Pictures film *Stick It*, and released "We Run This," a single from the soundtrack.

Elliott is now a bankable commodity, and she has been featured in numerous multimillion-dollar ad campaigns from soft drinks to diamond jewelry. She is the first female hip hop artist ever to appear in a Gap commercial (2003), in which she was featured together with Madonna. In 2004 she appeared with Madonna, Britney Spears, and Christina Aguilera in the controversial opener of the MTV Video Music Awards at New York's Radio City Music Hall. She was nominated for eight awards. Elliott also appeared in ads for Vanilla Coke, MAC Cosmetics, Chrysler/Jeep, and Garrard & Co. jewelers.

Some of her latest ventures include an Adidas-sponsored clothing line with shoes and accessories called Respect M.E. and a reality series with UPN called *The Road to Stardom with Missy Elliott*. She enters the reality show market with other pop stars, including Blink 182's Travis Barker, INXS, Tommy Lee, and TLC (see sidebar: Hip Hop and Reality Television). *The Road to Stardom* premiered January 5, 2005 and followed thirteen aspiring R&B and hip hop artists ranging from nineteen to twenty-nine years old. Elliott served as co-executive producer and judge. Jessica Betts, who won a cash prize and a record deal with Elliott's label, released her album in 2006. Following Eminem's and 50 Cent's lead, the story of Elliott's life will be featured in a biopic being developed by Universal Pictures. Robert De Niro and Jane Rosenthal have signed on as producers for the motion picture, and Diane Houston will serve as writer-director for the film.

Hip Hop and Reality Television
Mickey Hess

Hip hop stars have parlayed their personalities into roles on several reality television shows. The debut season of MTV's long-running reality series *The Real World* featured Heather B, a rapper associated with KRS-One's Boogie Down Productions. The first episode of *The Real World*'s first season was marked with racial tension in an interchange between Heather B and Julie, a young, white, cast member from Alabama. When Heather's beeper went off, Julie naively asked her if she were a drug dealer. After *The Real World*, Heather would go on to release a single, "All Glocks Down," that was promoted on the strength of her reality show appearance. In a later season of *The Real World*, Slim Kid Tre from the Pharcyde became involved with one of the cast members.

Outside the aspiring rappers featured on *The Real World*, VH1's *The Surreal Life*, in which celebrities live as roommates, regularly includes a rapper among the cast, and has featured MC Hammer, Vanilla Ice, Da Brat, Pepa from Salt-N-Pepa, and Public Enemy's Flavor Flav. Flav's escapades on the show, including an on-screen romance with Brigitte Nielsen, led to two spin-off series: *Strange Love*, which chronicled Flav's relationship with Nielsen, and *Flavor of Love*, in which women compete to be Flav's new love interest. VH1's "Celebreality" lineup also features *Celebrity Fit Club*, which brings together overweight celebrities in a competition to develop a healthier lifestyle. The series has featured overweight rappers Biz Markie, Bizarre from D-12, and Bonecrusher.

In other reality shows, rap artists have become talent scouts, developing shows like Diddy's *Making the Band* and Missy Elliott's *The Road to Stardom*, in which contestants work to establish a career in music. The R&B group TLC created a UPN series, *R U the Girl*, as part of a search to replace Lisa "Left Eye" Lopes, a singer and MC from the group who died in a car crash in Honduras in 2002.

MISSY'S UNIQUE CONTRIBUTIONS TO HIP HOP

Missy Elliott is an important songwriter, perhaps the most innovative and prolific African American female songwriter in contemporary American music. Her unique ability to capture and communicate complex relationships in everyday parlance, while at the same time including subtleties that are difficult to articulate, especially in song, is uncanny. While most rap and hip hop artists discussed the perils of street life, as in gangsta rap, Elliott entered the conversation with a palpable truth that resonated with her audience. Her innovation is exhibited in her cadence, lyrical content and structure, mixture of singing and rapping, and willingness to discuss taboo subjects. She is characterized as a risk taker, sonically and visually. She pushes the envelope without apology and is able to produce evocative critical work.

During her time with Swing Mob, Elliott honed her talents and acquired a keen personal voice. As a songwriter and producer, she formulated a dual role: to create music that provides a temporary escape from personal issues (i.e. dance music) and to raise valuable questions about life and artistry without moralizing. This dialectic allows for a type of critical space that allows one to face problems without becoming immobilized by them. Her personal experiences have sharpened two important developmental skills: critical self-reflection and her ability to learn from observing others. She channels her personal knowledge of social problems into humorous dance tracks and melodic airy ballads. Her quirky and somewhat self-conscious conversation about sexuality also makes her material seem less threatening. Her sexually provocative and politically charged material invites her listeners into a dialogue while at the same time disarming them.

Like a blues woman singing in a juke joint hidden in the middle of a Louisiana bayou in the early twentieth century, Elliott airs her woes of love and loss, sexual desire, personal conflict, and feelings of female empowerment. She speaks the once private and forbidden thoughts of women. The tragicomic nature of her songs lifts once-unthinkable topics to speakable space. Though at times she blushes at her own candor and use of expletives, she cites her relationship with God as a point of inner conflict. She still feels comfortable with her subject matter and in her honesty, though she has admittedly tried to eliminate the use of profanity in her lyrics. She appears conflicted about her inability to do so. Still, her honesty lends itself to an open dialogue about common issues in life, primarily personal relationships. Rather than creating a false representation about a life she does not know for the sake of commercialism, Elliott broaches subjects that ring true for her. She gives her audience the opportunity to scrutinize her credibility. Her exploration of loss and dispossession and concomitant survival sets a cathartic feminine space, communicating her personal message of strength and empowerment.

In addition to the subtle and profound themes, Elliott's style has distinct and identifiable characteristics. Like a jazz musician, Elliott first introduces a motif, riffing and improvising around it. The structure and language of her rhymes are tight pithy clusters of thought that relate various scenarios. She then uses short statements and simple concrete language to construct the bulk of her storytelling. Her sparse use of definite articles creates short staccato lines, which complement Mosley's rhythm tracks. She even plays with the balance between connotation and denotation, using allusions to give depth to her tight diction. She also plays with patterns of sound and perception of sound and pauses. The use of internal rhyme adds weight or airiness to a given line, often repeating phrases. Known for her rich sensory detail that evokes sounds more than pictures, she onomatopoeically imitates sounds associated with experiences (vroom, beep, blat). This thematic approach to her work gives each of her albums unity and a unique voice. It also allows for that characteristic playfulness of the one formerly known as the Hee Haw Girl.

As a rapper and singer, Elliott experiments with tone and delivery, emphasizing the unique aspect of each song. She communicates through rhythm, pitch, tone, and inflection. She uses her speaking voice like an instrument, varying between a smooth relaxed delivery and a squeezed higher timbre. She also incorporates slurred intonation, like a jazz trombone player, bending and sliding tones in a given line. At times, she operates below conventional linguistic structures to convey her feelings (grunts, moans, and hums). Rhythm in her work plays with patterns of sounds, rhyming phrases, alliterated consonants, and vowel sounds. She uses pauses and variations in pitch and intonation to add meaning and drama to her delivery. The movement of her tracks creates a unique and distinguishable style and composition. Her sultry, soulful alto voice also reinforces the uncomplicated melodic hooks, frequently layered in harmony. Rather than sampling vocals, she sings her vocal hooks live all the way down each track to add new texture to each refrain.

Elliott has managed to stay ahead of trends. She credits her partnership with Mosley and now, ironically, her self-imposed distance from listening to the radio. Though deeply influenced by old-school hip hop pioneers, Elliott and Mosley's music dictum is to "make it new." She also often credits Mosley for providing the necessary diversity and creative fodder she needs to make each project new and innovative. Their extensive body of work marks a noticeable shift in R&B and hip hop, making the two genres less distinguishable. The duo also marks a turning point in the ubiquitous use of sample-driven tracks. Mosley's staccato beats and eclectic use of ambient sounds from world music help define a new direction in American popular music. His sound, initially reserved for Elliott and close collaborators, is now sampled and copied by many in the industry.

THE ALBUMS

Supa Dupa Fly (1997)

Elliott released her debut LP, *Supa Dupa Fly*, in July 1997, which included the hit single "The Rain (Supa Dupa Fly)" that introduced Elliott to radio and television airwaves. The genre-blurring material was received with mostly high praise for its innovation. The disc is still ranked as the highest debut for a female hip hop artist on the Billboard charts, peaking at number three in its first week of release. The follow-up single was "Sock It to Me," a moderate success charting in the pop Top 20 and Top 40, which was certified gold, featuring Lil' Kim and Da Brat. The subsequent singles were "Beep Me 911," featuring Timbaland, Magoo, and 702; and "Hit 'Em wit da Hee," featuring Timbaland, Lil' Kim, and Mocha. The album also featured other hip hop and

R&B artists such as Busta Rhymes, Aaliyah, and Ginuwine. The debut was certified platinum and nominated for two Grammy Awards for Best Rap Album and Best Rap Solo performance, "The Rain (Supa Dupa Fly)." Among the several accolades the album received, *Spin* magazine ranked *Supa Dupa Fly* number nine in their Top 20 Albums of the Year and *Rolling Stone* named Elliott Best Rap Artist of the Year.

The lyrical content of the album reveals Elliott's complex, creative, and challenging discussion about womanhood; her demand for respect, respect for her personal voice and her desire for fulfilling intimacy with lovers and friends. The album alternates between these two primary subjects. The production features Mosley's signature rhythms, similar to dance hall beats, and midtempo funky bass-heavy grooves. *Supa Dupa Fly* opens up with an interlude featuring Busta Rhmyes as a town crier admonishing everyone to be attentive so they will not miss the historical event about to unfold. Through storytelling Elliott presents her discourse.

The first track, "Hit 'Em wit da Hee," featuring Lil' Kim, discloses the genesis of Elliott's distinctive laugh. Songs like "I'm Talkin" and "Gettaway" declare that Elliott is prolific and the dynamic production duo will remain eminent in the hip hop food chain. The refrain in each song repeatedly reminds any potential competition of her stylistic originality and confident voice. "Beep Me 911" reveals a woman frustrated with her boyfriend, who refuses to level with her about his lack of commitment in the relationship. Though she changed her life to become the object of his affection, her intuition tells her she is being exploited sexually. Magoo, featured on the track, replies that her intuition is right. In "Best Friends," a woman encourages another female friend to stop complaining about her unfulfilling relationship and simply move on with her life. Elliott, the voice of the supportive friend, refuses to listen to the complaints of her companion, viewing the act of listening as enabling. The same sentiment is echoed in "Don't Be Commin' (In My Face)." Elliott also critiques women who use their bodies for material gain in "Why You Hurt Me." She views this action as self-hatred and likens that lifestyle to a bad song she no longer wants to hear.

In 1998 under Goldmind/Elektra, Elliott released protégé Nicole Wray's debut, *Make It Hot*. Elliott and Mosley produced the album, releasing two singles, "Make It Hot" and "Eyes Better Not Wander." The album was certified gold, reaching number nineteen on the R&B charts and forty-two on the U.S. charts. The same year, Elliott penned and produced for several other artists, including Spice Girl Mel B's "I Want You Back" and songs for Whitney Houston's *My Love Is Your Love*.

Da Real World (1999)

Missy released her sophomore effort in July 1999; *Da Real World* was produced by Mosley. The success of her debut and the multiple hit collaborations with other artists—in such a short period of time—made creating a new project with a fresh sound challenging for Elliott. She reportedly spent two months in the studio writing and recording for the follow-up disc. The much-anticipated recording was certified platinum by February 2000 and nominated for a Grammy for Best Rap Album, among other honors. *Da Real World* showcases a range of style influences from reggae to underground hip hop.

Da Real World also features several top hip hop and R&B artists: Outkast's Big Boi and Nicole Wray ("All N My Grill"), Aaliyah and Da Brat ("Sticking Chickens"), Beyoncé of Destiny's Child ("Crazy Feelings"), Eminem ("Busa Rhyme"), Redman ("Dangerous Mouths"), Juvenile and B.G. ("U Can't Resist"), Lady Saw ("Mr. DJ"). and Lil Mo ("You Don't Know") and interludes featuring Lil' Kim. With so many guest appearances, the album could be considered a duets project. However, Elliott is able to make her presence the center of the production.

On this album, a more assertive and politically charged Elliott raises questions about power, race, and gender. She invites her critics and nay-saying competitors to a verbal joust. The first single, "She's a Bitch," sets the tone for the rest of the album. This song takes issue with the notion that for a man aggressive behavior is positive, but for a woman the same behavior is the object of criticism. The song suggests that strong, articulate, and assertive women should be accepted as normative. The chorus hurls the insult. The rest of the song replies that if success requires "masculine" behavior, she will perform the forbidden behavior and gladly accept the accompanying derision and label. The provocative song reclaims and reinvests the word *bitch*. She inverts its meaning, redefining it for self-confident women. Elliott says, "I am a bitch."

Other singles included "All N My Grill" and "Hot Boyz," which spent six weeks on the Billboard R&B/Hip-Hop chart. "Hot Boyz," certified platinum, remained on the Billboard Rap Singles chart for almost an entire year, retaining the number one spot for eighteen consecutive weeks, breaking the previous eleven-week record (held by Da Brat, Coolio, and Puff Daddy aka Diddy). The single also hit number one on Billboard's R&B Singles chart for six consecutive weeks.

Miss E . . . So Addictive (2001)

Elliott's *Miss E . . . So Addictive*, released in May 2001, was hailed by critics as one of the best albums of the year, debuting at number two on the Billboard charts. Elliott was nominated for numerous prestigious awards, including a BET Award for Best Female Hip-Hop Artist. Inspired by Marvin Gaye's *Sexual Healing*, Elliott delivers a contemporary conversation about female sexuality. She presents a realistic range of female sexuality by juxtaposing conventional and progressive ideas about intimacy and female sexual desire.

She upends the notion that frank sexual talk is reserved only for socially marginalized women. In the opening interlude, Elliott invites her audience to get lost in the funky new beats and sound that she and Mosley deliver, a retro feel with an edgy contemporary flavor.

The album produced four singles that carried her third release well into 2002. The single "One Minute Man," featuring Ludacris and Jay-Z on the remix, produced the megahit for the album, entering the Billboard Top 20. The song was nominated for six MTV Video Awards for Best Hip-Hop Video, Best Direction (Dave Myers), Best Cinematography (Karsten Gopinath), Best Art Direction (Mike Martella), Best Editing (Jay Robinson), and Best Special Effects (Marc Varisco and Nathan McGuinness). The recording and the video engage both male and female perspectives on this taboo subject. The Indian-influenced "Get Ur Freak On" and the remix featuring Nelly Furtado were equally successful, earning Elliott her first Grammy Award for Best Rap Solo Performance. The remix was featured on the *Lara Croft: Tomb Raider* soundtrack and was heard in the motion picture. "4 My People" became the club anthem from the album, both domestically and internationally. "Scream a.k.a. Itchin'" earned Elliott her second Grammy Award for Best Rap Solo Performance.

"Take Away" was a moderate success, which featured Ginuwine and introduced Elliott's new protégé and label mate, Tweet. Tweet released her debut, *Southern Hummingbird*, in April 2002 to rave reviews. In 1999, after leaving the Swing Mob and Sugah's failed attempts at musical success, Tweet became despondent and contemplated suicide. Tweet credits Elliott with saving her life, calling her a guardian angel. Elliott called Tweet to invite her to work on *So Addictive* the day before Tweet planned to end her life.

Elliott includes a religious presence on the album that continues to point to her spiritual sensitivity; she does not separate her faith from her artistry. On a hidden track, her smooth mellow vocals accompany Yolanda Adams, Mary Mary, and the legendary members of the Clark Sisters on "Movin' On." The preceding spoken interlude and song illustrate Elliott's belief in God's forgiveness and her need to look forward rather than dwelling on the past. She acknowledges her humanity and reliance on God's presence in her life despite the criticism from others; she declares that though some misunderstand her work, her faith is a constant source of strength and presence in her artistry. Busta Rhymes, Da Brat, Eve, Ginuwine, Method Man, Redman, Lil Mo, and Mosley aka Timbaland are other *So Addictive* contributors.

The same year, Elliott was featured on Janet Jackson's "Son of a Gun" remix with Carly Simon and served as producer on a cover of Patti LaBelle's 1975 hit "Lady Marmalade" featuring Christina Aguilera, Mya, Pink and Lil' Kim. The song and video became the biggest single of 2001 (domestic and international), selling 5.2 million units and winning a Grammy Award for Best Pop Collaboration with Vocal.

Under Construction (2002)

Elliott's fourth album, *Under Construction,* is her best-selling album to date, moving nearly 3.5 million units worldwide and being certified platinum within a month of its November 2002 release. "Work It" spent ten consecutive weeks at number two on the Hot 100 and VH1 ranked the single number seventy-seven on *VH1: 100 Best Songs of the Past 25 Years.* On this disc, Elliott and Mosley continue their "make it new" production philosophy by borrowing elements from early hip hop. Critics recognized that the album offers a new palette for hip hop and deemed the duo successful. Elliott utilizes her lower vocal register, layering harmony beds with rich dark octaves, adding to the soulful nostalgic sound of the album. She teamed up with Method Man ("Bring the Pain), Ludacris ("Gossip Folks"), Jay-Z ("Back in the Day"), Ms. Jade ("Funky Fresh Dressed"), Beyoncé Knowles ("Nothing Out There for Me"), and TLC ("Can You Hear Me"). The celebratory nature of the album was well received by fans and critics alike. Elliott's honors included an American Music Award for Favorite Rap/Hip-Hop Female Artist, a BET Award for Best Hip-Hop Artist, and her third Grammy Award for Best Female Rap Solo Performance for "Work It." The album was nominated for Album of the Year, Best Rap Album, and Best Rap Performance by a Duo or Group for "Gossip Folks" at the 2004 Grammys.

Elliott was deeply affected by personal losses, the death of her close friends Aaliyah and Lisa "Left Eye" Lopes, and the tragedy of September 11, 2001. These events caused her to become more reflective about her own life and her position in the industry. *Under Construction* is her attempt to bridge gaps in the hip hop community. The album literally fuses the old with the new by utilizing retro beats, electro-stylization, allusions, and direct quotes from iconic old-school recordings, making the old progressive and new. It is a veritable homage to hip hop. She encourages her peers to take back hip hop, and love it and nurture it rather than exploiting it. The title is symbolic of her life, her artistry, and the world itself as a work in progress.

Elliott still considers music a refuge. "Can You Hear Me," a duet with TLC, transports the listener back to moments and days right after Aaliyah's death when her family began making arrangements for the funeral. Elliott paints a vivid picture of the pain and desire to make sense of her friend's death. Her grief and concern for Aaliyah's family are representative of her same concern for the loss of Lisa "Left Eye" Lopes of TLC, who died in a car crash in 2002. This cathartic space is extended to the families still grieving, as a lasting memoriam and celebration of their artistry (see sidebar: TLC).

Under Construction was nominated for Album of the Year for the 2004 Grammy Awards and for Best Rap Album. The song "Gossip Folks" was nominated for Best Rap Performance by a Duo or Group. "Work It" was nominated for Best Rap Song and won for Best Female Rap Solo Performance. Elliott also won two Lady of Soul Awards, for Best Song of the Year

TLC

Jennifer R. Young

TLC, an R&B trio composed of Tionne "T-Boz" Watkins, rapper Lisa "Left Eye" Lopes, and Rozanda "Chilli" Thomas, formed in 1991 and joined LaFace Records that same year. Their debut album, *Ooooooooh . . . On the TLC Tip* was released a year later, going gold and platinum within months. Their three other albums, *CrazySexyCool* (1994), *Fanmail* (1999), and *3D* (2002) also sold well. The Grammy Award-winning albums *Crazy* and *Fanmail* have gone megaplatinum numerous times over; *3D* has gone platinum. Left Eye also released a solo album, *Supernova* (2001). TLC is one of the first groups that regularly combined singing, dancing, and rapping.

Other R&B groups in the early 1990s like Jodeci, Mary J. Blige, and Total had guest appearances from rappers on their singles. However, TLC raised the stakes by being a multigenre group; their songs are a combination of rap, R&B, funk, blues, and rock and roll. Their choreography, song harmony, and thematic appearance give the trio a unique identity that audiences with different tastes favor. TLC is also one of the groups that should be credited for their influence on the music industry overall. Noticing the success of TLC's albums going platinum and receiving critical acclaim, producers and artists began incorporating more rap into the remix versions of R&B songs. This trend changed the nature of music in both popular culture and hip hop culture.

Their first album had three songs that set a new precedent: "Ain't 2 Proud 2 Beg," "Baby, Baby, Baby," and "What About Your Friends." Instead of being an R&B group that only sang standard love songs, TLC rhymed about sex, romance, womanhood, and sisterhood. Their debut single, "Ain't 2 Proud 2 Beg," was an upbeat song about sexual liberation. The music video also promoted safer sex as Left Eye wore a wrapped condom packet on her left eye and T-Boz and Chilli wore condom packets on their clothes. In a time when the lyrical content of music was becoming more graphic, TLC was noticed for their female perspective on sexual desire and conquest.

Similar to something blueswoman Bessie Smith might have sung, "Ain't 2 Proud 2 Beg" positions women as the gazers and men as their objects. TLC continues this trend with songs like "Creep," "Red Light Special," and "Scrubs." TLC celebrates women and encourages them to love men and to demand respect from their men and from themselves. Songs like "Waterfalls," "Unpretty," and "Damaged" discuss physical, mental, and emotional health. The song "Waterfalls" contains uncommon subjects such as promiscuity, incarceration, family crisis, and HIV/AIDS. "Unpretty" challenges societal notions of beauty. The music video has its characters contemplating face lifts, breast augmentation, drastic diets, and other types of body alterations. "Damaged" gets into the psychological effects that physical and emotional abuse can have on a woman's life. TLC is popular not only for their party anthem songs, but also songs that address profound issues. The group has endured numerous personal troubles, having to file for bankruptcy in the late 1990s, enduring public scrutiny during their interpersonal struggles as a trio, and withstanding the loss of Left Eye, who died in a car accident in Honduras in August 2002.

---

and Best Video, and won two of eight MTV Video Music Awards nominations for Best Hip-Hop Video and the coveted Video of the Year.

This Is Not a Test! (2003)

Debuting in November 2003 at number thirteen on the Billboard 200 chart, *This Is Not a Test!* earned Elliott her fifth consecutive platinum album, selling 144,000 copies in its first week of release. The album incorporates a range of genres, integrating early rap ("Wake Up" featuring Jay-Z), dance hall ("Keep It Movin'" featuring Elephant Man), and R&B ("I'm Not Perfect," featuring the Clark Sisters). The album declares that this recording is an authentic representation of hip hop and encourages other artists to move away from commercialism (gimmicks) and return to true artistry.

Elliott's singles were "Pass That Dutch" and "I'm Really Hot," which was nominated for two MTV Video Awards for Best Dance Video and Best Choreography (see sidebar: B-Boys and Break Dancers). On this recording she officially drops "Misdemeanor," the nickname she received from a childhood disc jockey who claimed that Elliott's style was unlawful. She earned a Radio Music Award nomination for Artist of the Year Hip-Hop Radio, among other accolades.

The same year, she appeared on the cover of *Rolling Stone*'s October issue with Alicia Keys and Eva Pigford (Tyra Banks's America's Next Top Model winner) and performed on the venerable *Saturday Night Live* broadcast. She was also featured on two singles, Wyclef Jean's "Party to Damascus" and Ghostface Killah's "Tush." In 2004, Elliott collaborated with Christina Aguilera on the remake of "Car Wash" featured on the *Shark Tale* motion picture soundtrack and *The Fighting Temptations* soundtrack featuring Beyoncé Knowles, MC Lyte, and Free. In addition to making her acting debut as a costar in the motion picture *Honey*, starring Jessica Alba, she joined the Ladies First Tour alongside Alicia Keys and Beyoncé Knowles. Elliott ended the year on top with her appearance on Ciara's Billboard Top 10 single "1, 2 Step."

The Cookbook (2005)

Elliott released her sixth album, *The Cookbook*, in July 2005, which debuted at number two on the Billboard 200, selling 176,000 copies in the first

B-Boys and Break Dancers
Mickey Hess

Dance, as one of hip hop's vital four elements of MCing, DJing, graffiti writing, and b-boying, has always been central to the culture. When hip hop music began with Kool Herc's creation of the breakbeat, the b-boys and b-girls took to the dance floor. In fact, before MCs began to say rhymes over the beat, they worked as hype men to help the DJ draw people onto the dance floor. The term b-boy, still used to designate a hip hop dancer, derives from "break boy," and the term break dancer also derives from the "break," Kool Herc's isolation and repetition of key instrumental breaks in funk, jazz, R&B, and soul records. Early New York City b-boy crews like the Rocksteady Crew, Floor Masters, Dynasty Rockers, and the Disco Kids faced off in dance competitions much like MCs would come to do with rhymes. Legendary breakers like Ken Swift, Crazy Legs, and Frosty Freeze propelled b-boying into worldwide fame as breakdancing.

Because the dance moves and fashion styles of these b-boy crews added a dynamic visual element to hip hop music, b-boying was featured prominently in films, from the documentary *Style Wars* to the movies *Wild Style, Beat Street,* and *Flashdance.* While New York City had its b-boys and b-girls, Los Angeles had poppers and lockers. LA dancers were given their own coverage in the films *Breakin'* and *Breakin' 2: Electric Boogaloo.* Break dancing became a popular umbrella term for New York and LA dance styles, including flashy moves like head spins and back spins that drew attention to hip hop dance in the 1980s. Break dancers were featured in films and on television talk shows. They performed for Queen Elizabeth and were showcased at the 1984 Summer Olympics in Los Angeles. The sudden and overwhelming popularity of break dancing made b-boying seem like a symptom of hip hop culture's entrance into mainstream culture. As break dancing's popularity grew in the mainstream, hip hop artists began to turn their backs on the flashy spectacle seen in Hollywood versions of hip hop culture, and break dancing lost its centrality to hip hop, making a return in the late 1990s within a burgeoning underground hip hop culture that sought to return to hip hop's old school roots.

Dance, however, did not leave the hip hop scene with break dancing's overexposure. Artists like Big Daddy Kane, Salt-N-Pepa, MC Hammer, Redhead Kingpin, 3rd Bass, and Heavy D and the Boys made dance central to their performances. Biz Markie, Public Enemy's Flavor Flav, and Ed Lover of *Yo! MTV Raps* created their own signature comic dances. Several hip hop dancers from this era went on to become MCs and hip hop singers: Tupac Shakur began his career as a dancer for the group Digital Underground, and the Fly Girls and Fly Guys who danced on the Fox comedy series *In Living Color* featured Jennifer Lopez and future members of the Pharcyde.

When pop rappers MC Hammer and Vanilla Ice scored multiplatinum album sales in the early 1990s using flashy costumes and dance moves, hip hop began to experience a backlash against dance. With the popularity of West Coast gangsta rap throughout the mid to late 1990s, dance was relatively absent from hip hop videos. Dr. Dre, who did not dance in his videos, parodied the dance styles of his rivals Eazy-E and 2 Live Crew's Luther Campbell in the music video for "Dre Day." Dance returned to rap videos with releases from Bad Boy Records that featured Puff Daddy's dance moves, and with Missy Elliott, whose videos featured innovative choreography and special effects.

Further Resources

The Freshest Kids: A History of the B-Boy. Dir: Israel, Perf: Afrika Bambaataa, Mos Def, Crazy Legs. Los Angeles: Image, 2002.

Lhamon, W. T. *Raising Cain: Blackface Performance from Jim Crow to Hip-Hop.* Cambridge: Harvard University Press, 2000.

Veran, Cristina. "Breakin' It All Down: The Rise and Fall and Rise of the B-Boy Kingdom." *The Vibe History of Hip-Hop.* Ed. Alan Light. New York: Three Rivers Press, 1999: 53–59.

week of release. By January 2006 the single "Lose Control" was certified triple platinum and had won two MTV Video awards for Best Dance Video and Best Hip-hop Video. The video was also was nominated for Breakthrough Video, Best Direction (Dave Meyer and Missy Elliott), Best Choreography, and Best Special Effects. The album was nominated for four Grammy Awards: Best Rap Album, Best Rap Song, Best Rap/Sung Collaboration, and Best Short Form Video for "Lose Control."

Although considered an industry veteran and one of the most powerful and influential artists in contemporary music, Elliott, competing now with herself, found an innovative balance between her edgy experimental nature and respect for old-school hip hop. Each producer, performance, and guest appearance on the album helps develop the notion that *The Cookbook* is a recipe for hip hop success. After almost exclusively working with Mosley, the concept album features a variety of producers including the Neptunes, Warren Campbell, Craig X. Brockman, Rhemario Webber, and Elliott on "Lose Control," featuring Ciara and Fat Man Scoop. Each track offers a distinct hip hop voice. While Mosley only produced two tracks on the album, "Partytime" and "Joy," Elliott remained in contact with her longtime collaborator during the project's development.

Elliott varies her rap lyrical delivery from track to track. For example, "On and On," produced by Pharell of the Neptunes (one of the most sought-after contemporary producers and a childhood friend of Mosley's), showcases a straightforward lyrical style absent Elliott's characteristic ornamentation. The track earned the Neptunes a Grammy Award nomination for "Producer of the Year." Rap pioneer Slick Rick joins Elliott on "Irresistible Delicious." Elliott's rap delivery on this track is a tribute to Rick, slurring over a breakbeat track with lush harmonic vocals lacing the refrain. With Elliott as the *Cookbook*'s chef, she enlisted Mike Jones, Fantasia, M.I.A., Vybez Cartel, Mary J. Blige, and Grand Puba. Blige and Puba are on Elliott's most personal track to date, "My Struggles," produced by Qur'an H. Goodman. Elliott rhymes about how she witnessed her father's abuse of her mother. The same year, Elliott participated in the Donate a Phone, Save a Life campaign sponsored by the Body Shop and the National Coalition Against Domestic Violence.

In addition, her commercial stock rose considerably. She was selected to launch Chrysler/Jeep's Commander, a new luxury sports utility vehicle, which would include an unprecedented multimedia campaign (television, Internet, and in-dealership). She also launched Yahoo!'s new music subscription service, was featured on the cover of *Dub* magazine, and appears in *Vanity Fair's* coveted music issue.

THE VIDEOS

For a solo artist in any genre, visual imagery is an important aspect of marketing. Unfortunately, artists have to rely on music executives to approve their visual representation of their artistry. This tradition is especially detrimental for female artists. Women's bodies are sexualized and become the primary prisms through which their art is visually represented and experienced by spectators. In hop hop, this representative situation is even more notorious for victimizing female artists and ubiquitous video vixens. Despite this practice, Elliott was able to break through and become arguably the most important video icon of the decade. As her own music executive, she trusted her intuition and remained open to experimentation. Her body, already an aberration in the industry (overweight and with distinctly African American features), is consequently considered "not marketable," meaning not typically accepted as sexually alluring. Ironically, these differences provided an opportunity for her to transcend accepted norms.

As a result, Elliott was able to create a digital identity more in line with her artistic power and imagination. Her futuristic musical sensibilities are seamlessly translated visually without regard to stereotypical female representation in music videos. Just as her music is ahead of trends, her visual representation is revolutionary as well. Her consistent originality helped usher in a new visual era in music videos. Her fresh approach has made her a multimedia star and a new norm of beauty. Her solo videography, for instance, has merited video awards and honors from Billboard to the Grammy's including twenty-five MTV Video Award nominations, being rivaled only by Madonna.

Elliott's videography initially constructed a larger-than-life digital identity where she seemingly defied nature. The otherworldly and futuristic space Elliott inhabited helped her transcend industry stereotyping by helping her to create powerful iconography. This cyberworld created a space absent a patriarchal system. The surreal imagery presented her as a powerful agent who commands the camera's attention. In her video, she used her body to display power and sexuality on her own terms. By doing this, she portrayed superhuman characteristics—acting as a powerful lord who inhabits space disrupted normative discourse about her body and gender.

To illustrate, her first short film introduces her as a cartoon character. Her groundbreaking "The Rain (Supa Dupa Fly)" video, directed by Hype Williams, hit the airwaves in May 1997, featuring cameos by Sean "Diddy" Combs, Total, and Lil' Kim. The video catapulted Elliott into pop consciousness. Williams used a fish eye lens and wide angles to construct the exaggerated imagery. Elliott's character has bulbous eyes, a black balloon suit, and full black lips, engaging spectators in her artistry rather than objectifying her sexuality.

Akin to a cartoon sequence, humorous images draw the spectator into her playful world. The video opens with her back to the audience in her black bubble suit. The first shot of her face reveals a beautiful smile as she laughs. This opening sequence introduces a woman who does not take herself too seriously, a woman willing to risk her reputation on her artistry. Most of the close-ups of the guest artists are playful, but Elliott's face cannot be easily read. She is playful but coy. Her lips and eyes pop out like a Looney Tunes character to the rhythm of her track. Her body ticks and jerks to the same pulsating rhythms, bending and contorting. The setting is vibrant; the color palette consists of bright primary colors, which add to the playful tone. But throughout the entire video, a sexualized female body is not the focal point of the imagery.

In the video as a character she becomes a living cartoon, but more important, as an artist she transcends narrowly prescribed female representation. "The Rain (Supa Dupa Fly)" is still considered one of the most important videos ever made. Elliott was rewarded with several coveted video honors for her efforts: Billboard Video Music Awards, Best New Artist Clip, Billboard Video Music Awards, Best Clip (Rap), *Rolling Stone*'s Best Music Video of the Year, and three MTV nominations for Breakthrough Video, Best Rap Video, and Best Direction. The awards attest to the importance of the groundbreaking video in the life of hip hop videography. The comparable follow-up "Sock It 2 Me," also directed by Hype Williams, continued the animation theme. "Sock It 2 Me" is inspired by Mega Man, a video game published by Capcom in 1987 for the Nintendo Entertainment System.

In her next few videos, Elliott continued building her videography around this potent imagery. In the fantasy fairy-tale video "Beep Me 911," directed by Earle Sebastian, Elliott is a doll that comes to life. This video continues the powerful imagery set up by the first two videos by creating an anti–fairy tale. Elliott plays several different dolls, including the most powerful doll, who dons a gold gown reminiscent of the flowing blue and white gown worn by

Disney's Snow White. The video features Timbaland and Magoo, male dolls who cheat on their girlfriends by engaging in male sexual fantasy. 702, the R&B female trio also featured on the track, are also dolls that come to life. Throughout the video, the women use their sexuality to lure the men into close proximity in order to punish them for betrayal. The women are scantily dressed and wear fantasy clothes and hairstyles. Though the women are sexualized, they all use jerky doll movements emphasizing their fantasy existence, blinking their eyes without purpose. Elliott upends the typical fairy-tale ending. Instead of the prince and princess living together happily ever after, she destroys him because of his deception and willingness to live a double life (a reference to the song). Elliott, the giant gold princess doll, stomps on the diminutive men in their miniature car just as they try to make their getaway.

In addition to fairy tales, she also uses historic time periods to disrupt gendered ideology. "Hit 'Em wit da Hee," directed by Paul Hunter, transports her back in time. The medieval set design provides the backdrop for Elliott to showcase her dance choreography. Elliott is presented in a gender-bending pin-striped suit and hat. The brim covers her face for most of her dance sequences. She is endowed with special powers that allow her and her companions to float through the air. Again, she is clearly the most powerful and central figure in this world. Her primary visual representation is male and evokes classic imagery generally associated with Michael Jackson. The tone and mood are mysterious, signifying that her style resists demystification.

Her classic example of this period in her videography is "She's a Bitch," directed by Hype Williams. This provocative video is considered the apex of her introductory period as an artist. In this futuristic video, Elliott's androgyny personifies a conscious resistance against gender power relations. Elliott dons a black leather Grace Jones-like persona that is both male and female. Her charcoal-black body (painted), bald head, and warrior breastplate signify a powerful black she-male presence; a new representation for a female artist absent an intrusive sexualized male lens. The video introduces Elliott as the central figure in her surreal apocalyptic world. The camera lingers on her every move. She struts powerfully toward the camera as her long black leather coat flows in the wind behind her.

The opening sequence conjures up images of Shaft's powerful strut down the dangerous New York streets as a fearless private detective. Elliott, however, wears her bullets on her vest and rhinestones around her eyes, making her look more feline. The close-up shots focus on her face as she speaks directly into the camera, boasting about her position of power, rubbing her bald head. In her insolence, each time she is called a bitch her arms rest around her head. The jerky movements call attention to the chorus. One of the most powerful images comes near the end of the video when she and her imps emerge from a black sea as dark clouds attest to her powerful presence in nature.

After this early period from 1997 through mid-1999, there is a noticeable shift in the imagery in her next few videos. The change reveals Elliott as a more mature artist. Now firmly established as a visionary and a trendsetter, her visual imagery becomes more accessible—featuring more realistic settings and her signature throwback stylization, with dance choreography in the forefront of most video treatments. The spectator can easily compare his or her own existence to the images on the screen. Elliott is presented as a real person in a real world with real problems. "All N My Grill," "Gossip Folks," and "Take Away" present relatable worlds. In "All N My Grill," she is a woman scorned but walks down the street and discusses her problem with her boyfriend in a car. She returns to high school and relives her fantasy of being the most popular girl on campus in "Gossip Folks." In her most personal video, "Take Away," she mourns the loss of her friend and collaborator Aaliyah.

However, Elliott still incorporates supernatural and otherworldly elements in her visual representation. She uses a combination of these two elements depending on the nature of the song. Some videos are completely realistic while others are not. For example, in "Hot Boyz," Elliott is still self-possessed, but presented in an easygoing fashion; her sassy attitude and sensuality are displayed through the way she tilts her head and speaks out of the side of her mouth. This video is one of Elliott's first straight performance videos. In this short, an industrial warehouse sets the backdrop for Elliott's introduction as a female rap artist. Beauty shots are intercut between her performance shots. The set is a semicircle with three or four levels of metal scaffolding with partygoers peering through the beams. She stands on a high pedestal in the center of the crowd and performs directly for the camera. Here, Elliott exudes a quiet confidence. "Hot Boyz," released in November 1999, features Nas, Eve, and Lil Mo. The video was well received and won a Soul Train Lady of Soul Award for Best R&B/Hi-/Hop Soul or Rap Music Video.

On the other hand, "Get Ur Freak On," "One Minute Man," and "Work It" are concept videos that incorporate both realistic and surreal elements. Elliott does not, however, abandon her larger-than-life digital persona. Rather, she integrates the powerful persona into the real world. For most of "Get Ur Freak On," Elliott inhabits a seething underworld where batlike creatures dwell, and she is able to stretch her neck out like a snake. She is comfortable and in charge. Above the earth she is a military commander holed up at a dilapidated mansion. Her troops dance behind her in military garb and combat boots as she hangs from a chandelier. She was rewarded again for her efforts with three MTV Video Music Award nominations for Video of the Year, Hip-Hop Video of the Year, and Best Female Video. She also won the Soul Train Lady of Soul Award for Best R&B/Soul or Rap Music Video.

Again in "One Minute Man," one of her most sexually provocative videos to date, Elliott is still able to defy gravity and contort her body. Though most of the action takes place in the real world (a hotel), she is able to take her head off while her dismembered body dances. The video features Ludacris and Trina, and was soon nominated for a Grammy Award for Best Music Video/Short Film. "One Minute Man" also garnered Elliott another MTV Video Music Award for Best Hip-Hop Video and Soul Train Lady of Soul Award for Best R&B/Soul or Rap Music Video. In "Work It," she defies gravity, eats a car, spins on her head, and raps with bees on her face without being harmed.

Her latest videos are even subtler in her attempt to integrate her self-understanding with realistic imagery. The power and self-will exhibited in her early videos have been reduced to special effects, making them almost undetectable. For instance, in "Lose Control" and "We Run This," Elliott uses special effects to present herself doing tasks that require professional training. In "We Run This," released in February 2006, Elliott's head is digitally placed on Dominique Dawes's body. Elliott uses the Olympic gymnast's body to perform extremely difficult balance beam and floor routines. In "Lose Control," the first video released from the *Cookbook* album, Elliott uses a professional dancer's body to perform advanced high-energy dance moves. "Lose Control" is primarily a dance video, which features a contemporary stylized rendition of the Lindy Hop, a dance made popular at Harlem's Savoy Ballroom from the early 1930s through the mid-1940s. Elliott won her fifth Grammy Award for Short Form Music Video and two MTV Video Awards for Best Hip-Hop Video and Best Dance Video for "Lose Control."

Since Total's 1996 "What About Us," Elliott has been featured in over forty-five videos. She continues to work with longtime video collaborators, directors Hype Williams and Dave Myers. Elliott, moreover, has helped create an identity for female rappers beyond hackneyed objectification. In addition to her musical contributions, her visual imagery makes her, arguably, the most important artist of the decade. She has created new space for male and female artists who take risks to be successful.

A HIP HOP PIONEER

Patricia Elliott wanted her daughter to pursue a career in gospel music. Though seemingly far from the pulpit of a church, Elliott has found a way to make a deep connection with her gospel roots by creating art that transcends hip hop and industry norms. She taps into the rich black vernacular tradition. Hip hop has always been a way for black youth culture to speak out about marginalization. However, Elliott goes beyond speaking about disempowerment; she constructs a world, a hopeful place where she finds refuge and freedom to express her individuality. Like slaves who, in the face of dehumanization, sang and hummed their lives into existence through spirituals, Elliott too declares her self-knowledge through her music. Her hermetic musical world helps her transcend her personal history and oppressive music industry norms.

This notion is visually represented in her "Work It" video when she declares that Kunta Kinte will never be a slave again. In one scene, a black slave refuses to say yes to his master and then slaps him in anger. When the slave slaps his white master's face, he becomes black. The once-white man is now black but still dressed in his regal attire. The slave master begins to scream in dismay as he examines his new ebony hands. In this scene, Elliott explicitly declares that there has been a reversal of power and her art will never be held captive by anyone. She argues that if she embraces gimmicks and stereotypical hip hop lore about women, that action would be akin to a contemporary black slave obeying a white master.

Elliott has sustained a successful career that spans a range of artistic platforms. As a solo artist, her peers and critics respect her; from her frenetic stage presence to her retro-futuristic recordings, she innovates. She is, in fact, the only female singer-rapper, songwriter-producer, and music executive in contemporary American music. She is successful in each category. Moreover, in less than one decade, she has managed to become one of the most sought-after songwriters in the music industry. As a songwriter-producer, her song catalogue currently includes over 200 songs. Elliott's vocal arrangements, rap performance, vocal performance, songwriting, and production are featured on hundreds of published recordings. In addition, Elliott is the only African American female record executive in history to produce hits for both herself and other artists she has collaborated with.

For Elliott, her reality is her artistry and as such she will continue to maintain a critical position in hip hop. Her primary contribution is her ongoing innovation. Elliott has been able to develop an aesthetic that transcends industry norms and hip hop conventions while at the same time remaining commercially relevant. Each of her albums moves in a new direction, challenging artists to create work that has its own originality and integrity. She is often quoted as saying music is her true love, and she is most herself in the studio. There she feels at peace. If that is the case, her consistent quality of work and enviable work ethic will indeed make her a legend.

FURTHER RESOURCES

Bialek, Anna. "This Is Not a Test!: Missy Elliott Tells Teens to Break the Cycle of Violence." Sex, Etc. 10 July 2006. http://www.sexetc.org/story/2200.

Chambers, Veronica. "Be Like Mike? No, Missy." *Newsweek* 6 October 1997: 77.

Chappell, Kevin. "Eve and Missy Elliott: Taking Rap to a New Level." *Ebony* August 2001: 68–74.

Collis, Clark. "33 Things You Should Know About Missy Elliott." *Blender: The Ultimate Guide to Music and More.* 22 March 2006. http://www.blender.com/guide/articles.aspx?id=33.

Diehl, Matt. "Missy Elliott." *Interview* 1 September 2005: 152.

Ehrlich, Dimitri. "Missy Elliott." *Interview* 1 May 2001: 114–117+.

Elliott, Missy. Atlantic Records. http://www.atlanticrecords.com/missyelliott.

Elliott, Missy. MTV. http://www.mtv.com/bands/az/elliottmissy/artist.jhtml.

Elliott, Missy. Official Web Site. http://www.missy-elliott.com.

Emery, A. "Supa Dupa Fly." *Muzik* December 2002: 46–49.

Hoffman, Melody K. "Hip-Hop Innovator Missy Elliott." *Jet* 12 January 2004: 58–63.

Lee, Elyssa. "Schoolhouse Rap." *In Style* March 2003: 294.

Mitchell, Gail. "Missy Elliott's on Top of Her World." *Billboard* 19 June 1999: 11.

Morgan, Joan. "The Making of Miss Thang! Rap Singer Missy Elliott Interview." 1 March 2000: 92–94.

Mulvey, Laura. "Visual Pleasure and Narrative Cinema." *Feminist Film Theory*. Ed. Sue Thornham. New York: New York University Press, 1999.

Ogunnaike, Lola. "Hip-Hop's Missy Elliott: So Addicted to Her Music." *Milwaukee Journal Sentinel* (Wisconsin) 21 May 2001: 1E.

Sheffield, Rob. "The Sure Thing." *Rolling Stone* 25 December 2004: 121.

Silberger, K. "Supa Fly Girl: Missy Elliott Bugs Out." *Rolling Stone* 2 October 1997: 22.

SELECTED DISCOGRAPHY

Supa Dupa Fly. Elektra, 1997.
Da Real World. Elektra, 1999.
Miss E ... So Addictive. Elektra, 2001.
Under Construction. Elektra, 2002.
This Is Not a Test! Elektra, 2003.
The Cookbook. Atlantic, 2005.

Courtesy of Photofest.

Jay-Z

T. Hasan Johnson

Icons are people whose abilities and talents are molded by the times, fashioned by the moment, and shaped by the past. Jay-Z, one of today's most notable hip hop moguls, exemplifies these iconic virtues. Born on December 4, 1969, in Brooklyn, New York, Shawn Corey Carter (also known as Jigga, Hov—short for the Jewish name of God—Jehovah, Jay-Hova, Hova, and Young Hov) experienced one of the most significant and meteoric rises to success ever recorded in hip hop, having sold over 32 million albums.

Carter was the last of four children raised in a single-parent household by his mother, Gloria Carter. Carter grew up with little financial security, no father (his father, Adnis Reeves, left when he was twelve), and complete access to the streets he later became famous for rhyming about. Crime, drug dealing, and violence in the Bedford-Stuyvesant section of New York in the 1980s was hardly unusual, nor were Carter's experiences in Marcy Housing Projects, but how he articulated his experiences and perceptions to millions across the world was has made him an icon.

He attended high school for a brief period in New Jersey, and then dropped out. He also stopped drug dealing after several close brushes with death, helping him determine which vehicle to pour his creative energies into—his music or the streets. Carter's early nickname, "Jazzy," has been suggested to be an homage to the J-Z subway lines that travel from Manhattan to Brooklyn, poetically suggesting a link between uptown and downtown, a link of opposing cultures that one might see later in his life when he bridged underground and mainstream cultures in hip hop. All the same, his name is also said to be an homage to his early hip hop partner, the Jaz, remembered in hip hop circles for the song "Hawaiian Sophie," a comical yet somewhat typical braggadocio song about a man in Hawaii who fights off his woman's ex-boyfriend and wins her. If one watches the video closely, a young Jay-Z made his first media appearance. Carter was not only in some of the Jaz's early videos but recorded verses on some of his records. Such early performances, and some well-chosen underground battles, helped get his name to the right music labels, officially launching his career.

Although his work with the Jaz and another group, Original Flavor, seemed preliminary to the recording career of Jay-Z, it may have proven to be quite instructive. It could be argued that these early commercial failures taught Carter more about the music business than one might presume. If nothing else, to a young MC starting out in the late 1980s and early 1990s, the entertainment industry could be quite heartless. Unlike today's record industry, record labels in the past were unsure about hip hop's potential to make money. Although there were a number of successful bids by breakout groups like Run-DMC and the Beastie Boys, this period was a vicious time for rappers, DJs, and producers alike. Several groups experienced problems with record labels. The Cold Crush Brothers had disputes over distribution with Tuff City and Profile Records. Grandmaster Flash and the Furious Five disputed royalties with Sugar Hill Records. Even in the early 1990s, the GZA, who would go on to form Wu-Tang Clan, felt that Cold Chillin' Records could not envision how to market his 1991 solo release *Words from the Genius*. These problems reflect the constant struggle artists had with labels about how hip hop should look and sound.

Record labels were unsure what to do with hip hop and had some difficulty trying to market it. For the most part, their early ambivalence toward hip hop existed partly because many MCs were not formally trained in recognized musical traditions. Often they only came with a pad of paper, a pencil, and countless hours of experience rhyming in back rooms and on the streets with friends and rivals. So although hip hop offered opportunities for poor, uneducated youth with a talent for wordplay and onstage charisma, record labels left many of them destitute. Yet by the late 1980s, record companies had long figured out that it was more lucrative, easier to sell to specific audiences, and cheaper for them to find individual MCs rather than DJs to headline shows and appear on album covers. Thus, ironically, corporate media moguls influenced this underground culture more than many would anticipate by helping to replace DJs with MCs (who, in the past, were only onstage to help hype up the crowds and draw attention to the DJ by translating for the crowd what the DJ was doing, how difficult it was, and when they should applaud).

Carter witnessed these trends early on and managed to avoid many of the dangers of the entertainment business. In fact, in his song "Izzo (H.O.V.A.)," Jay-Z talks about how he planned to exploit the very industry that exploited his early hip hop predecessors. In the example he gives in "Izzo," he describes how record labels Tuff City Records and Profile Records underpaid the Cold Crush Brothers, and suggests that current rappers will rectify the exploitation of past artists and stabilize the entertainment business for future recording artists. Jay-Z never identified, however, what today's artists would do to put money into the pockets of their predecessors.

No doubt, some of hip hop's greatest rhyme pioneers influenced Jay-Z's appreciation for lyricism. Artists like Run-DMC, Kurtis Blow, Melle Mel, and LL Cool J showed that hip hop was marketable. These people were some of the first to make money and sustain careers as hip hop artists. For young people growing up in the projects of Brooklyn, such lifestyles were attractive, but more important, far less dangerous than the some of the illegal alternatives. Rappers like Grandmaster Caz of the Cold Crush Brothers, Kool Moe Dee of the Treacherous Three, Rakim of Eric B. & Rakim, and Run-DMC helped develop Jay-Z's understanding of what one could do in hip hop. Caz and Kool Moe Dee helped introduce more complicated lyrical flows in the early 1980s, and these flows were later enhanced by the likes of Big Daddy Kane, Kool G Rap, and Rakim. Known for lyrical flows that seemed reminiscent of jazz riffs, Rakim alone would develop a reputation for innovating how rappers conceptualized the notion of the verse, what could be done with it, and how much information and content one could convey while manipulating the tempo and measure of a beat. In fact, he helped redefine what it meant to rap by rhyming at a syncopated pace unheard of before. Without question, Jay-Z's comfort with such lyrical complexity owes its origin to these predecessors.

After having difficulty securing a worthy record deal, Carter and partners Damion "Dame" Dash and Kareem "Biggs" Burke decided to venture on their own and create Roc-A-Fella Records (see sidebar: Roc-A-Fella Records).

Roc-A-Fella Records
T. Hasan Johnson

Roc-A-Fella Records was started in 1995 because Jay-Z could not find a suitable record deal. In 1994 he, Damion "Dame" Dash, and Kareem "Biggs" Burke formed Roc-A-Fella Records. They pressed their own albums and sold them locally, without a major distributor. Eventually, Priority Records noticed them and signed them to release Jay-Z's first album, *Reasonable Doubt*, as a joint-release venture. Later, Roc-A-Fella became a limited liability company that shared its assets, especially sales, with its parent company Def Jam, which proved to be a lucrative venture for all parties involved. After the first major hit from *Reasonable Doubt*, "Ain't No Nigga" with Def Jam's then-unknown Foxy Brown, Jay-Z introduced Roc-A-Fella to the world.

Roc-A-Fella is part of the Island Def Jam Music Group, a record label produced by Universal Music Group when it merged its two subsidiary companies, Island Records and Def Jam Records. They have an impressive list of artists, including Beanie Segal, Kanye West, Cam'Ron, and the late Ol' Dirty Bastard. They have recently ventured into filmmaking, apparel, and liquor. However, in January 2005, Island Def Jam announced that it purchased Roc-A-Fella and that Jay-Z would preside over Def Jam, but Dash and Burke were released as cofounders. This motivated them to start Damon Dash Music Group and split artists between Dash and Jay-Z. During Roc-A-Fella's award-winning ten-year run, they launched a sizeable number of careers and would eventually make history by being the vehicle for Jay-Z's rise to the top.

The name Signified on the wealthy New York–based Rockefeller family. Like the rags-to-riches stories of some notable hip hop figures like Too $hort, Master P, the Wu-Tang Clan, and even MC Hammer, Carter sold albums out of the trunk of his car. He shopped his own albums and hustled interviews wherever he could. The advantage for Carter was that he had a marketable product, unlike many others trying to get their careers going (many artists had demos with underground credibility, but Carter's had well-known producers, subject matter that was accessible to new audiences, and dance-friendly beats and samples). Tracks on his 1996 debut album, *Reasonable Doubt*, were produced by the likes of DJ Clark Kent, Irv Gotti, and arguably one of the most credible and talented hip hop producers of all time, DJ Premier. It is said that this entrepreneurial drive impressed Priority Records; albeit far more likely they saw something that could actually sell (since hip hop's entrepreneurial drive was already abundant in New York, especially in the mid-1990s). Nevertheless, Priority Records opted to go in on the album and help release it in a joint arrangement with the newly devised Roc-A-Fella Records.

The album did well, reaching number twenty-three on the Billboard album chart. Tracks like "Dead Presidents" and "Can I Live" helped sketch out a new era in the gangsta rap subgenre of hip hop—the advent of what I call the reflective thug. Although technically this trend could be traced to artists like Afrika "Bam" Bambaataa, Rakim, or Ice-T, the new era of Jay-Z, Biggie Smalls, and Tupac had its own distinct approach. Despite what critics argued, these artists did not solely glamorize violence; they often questioned violence, or rather they helped create a language that framed violence in alignment with consequences (an approach that was more common in early gangsta rap than some critics acknowledged). At the same time, Jay-Z did not seek to repeat the preachy, high-browed approach of conscious hip hop artists in the late 1980s (see sidebar: Conscious Hip Hop). Instead, Jay and his contemporaries

Conscious Hip Hop
T. Hasan Johnson

The conscious hip hop movement began with Kool Herc, Grandmaster Flash and the Furious Five, and Afrika Bambaataa and the Soulsonic Force. Although such statements are subjective, there is one clear division between these groups and others—subject matter. Mostly, conscious artists address issues like spiritual uplift (instead of materialism), community (instead of individualism), mobilization (instead of apathy), universal familyhood (instead of racial divisiveness), and at times, the use of a party as a momentary release rather than the primary goal of musical production. Considering when hip hop emerged, it is not surprising that the Reagan era inspired conscious artists to respond to the destitute conditions of urban America. Government-imposed poverty, the CIA-embedded crack cocaine epidemic, and wealth-for-the-wealthy government policies helped ensure that poor people of color found few avenues for economic uplift.

Hip hop helped frame a national and international critique of societal inequities. These artists, pulling from the remains of disco and R&B to craft their new sound, found new ways to articulate the nature of post–civil rights, post–Black Power oppression. This was most clearly articulated in Melle Mel's song "The Message" (1982), which defined the potential of a rap record. Yet before this, there were many artists that contributed to the foundation of conscious hip hop.

For the sake of clarity, one could argue that there have been at least four generations of conscious rappers. Although this list is not exhaustive, it does outline the range of artists that frame conscious hip hop's development over time. The first generation, roughly traced from 1975 to 1983, consisted of artists like Kool Herc, Africa Bambaataa, Melle Mel, the Cold Crush Brothers, Kurtis Blow, Treacherous Three, Run-DMC, the Beastie Boys, and Ice-T. The second generation, from 1983 to 1989, consisted of KRS-One and Boogie Down Productions, Eric B. & Rakim, MC Lyte, Public Enemy, Gang Starr, Queen Latifah and the Flavor Unit, Naughty by Nature, Monie Love, Salt-N-Pepa, the Native Tongues (De La Soul, A Tribe Called Quest, and the Jungle

Brothers), and Stetsasonic. The third generation, 1989 to 1996, consisted of N.W.A., X-Clan, Paris, Leaders of the New School, Tupac, Nas, Brand Nubian, Jeru the Damaja, Outkast, Scarface, the Roots, the Fugees, and Goodie Mob. The current generation dates from approximately 1997 to the present, including artists like Lauryn Hill, Common, Mos Def, Talib Kweli, dead prez, Immortal Technique, Kanye West, Asheru, and J-Live.

In the aftermath of the September 11 attacks, the U.S. war with Iraq, and Hurricane Katrina, MCs that were not normally considered conscious have started to bemoan the state of things, radically breaking with audience expectations. Hence, a number of artists like MF DOOM, Trick Daddy, David Banner, Jay-Z, and, most legendarily, Tupac Shakur have been notorious for complicating these supposed boundaries. Each of these, and numerous others, have developed reputations for their musical content but have also made some very soul-stirring, deeply emotive records that warrant a close examination of the categories and standards of conscious hip hop, and, more important, who gets to determine how it is defined.

---

sought to use storytelling as a medium for outlining the kinds of repercussions associated with violence and criminal behavior. After Biggie and Tupac's deaths, Jay-Z kept this tradition alive while trying to keep from being labeled a mere purveyor of violence for material gain.

Along with controversies about the overemphasis on money and violence on *Reasonable Doubt*, Jay-Z introduced Def Jam's Foxy Brown to the mainstream on the track "Ain't No Nigga," also released on the *Nutty Professor* soundtrack, receiving underground kudos for its original sound. Symbolically, the song also introduced a sexy, intelligent female counterpart to Jay-Z that added to the artistic integrity of the track and challenged Jay-Z lyrically (despite rumors that he wrote her lyrics). Nevertheless, the album did have problems, and it raised concerns. The album was released amid the East Coast versus West Coast drama that centered on Bad Boy Records versus Death Row Records or, more specifically, the feud between Tupac and Biggie Smalls. Jay-Z ended up in the feud when Tupac singled him out because of his affiliation with Biggie. This led to a number of rivalries that included the aforementioned artists as well as Mobb Deep, Snoop Dogg, Ice Cube, Suge Knight, Dr. Dre, and others. Although this rivalry between coasts eventually led to the deaths of Tupac Shakur and Christopher Wallace (the Notorious B.I.G.), it also had more subtle ramifications. Namely, it stifled Jay-Z's early sales, especially on the West Coast. This made his rise a bit difficult for a time, but his difficulties soon yielded to his lyrical and musical creativity.

In 1997, Jay-Z released *In My Lifetime, Volume 1*, with Bad Boy Entertainment's Sean Combs at the production helm. Although he sold more albums than before because of his appeal to pop audiences, and garnered far more radio play than his previous effort due to less violent songs (the album went platinum and reached number three on the Billboard charts), Jay-Z simultaneously received critical praise and underground criticism. Almost as if it were scripted, it seemed the more praise he received from mainstream sources, the more criticism he received from the underground (although the lines between both were as nebulous as ever). Jay-Z responded by releasing an onslaught of creative productions. In 1998 he released *Volume 2: Hard Knock Life*, his highest selling album to date, going platinum five times over. *Volume 3: Life and Times of S. Carter* followed in 1999 (marking his most widespread collaboration with other artists yet), preceding 2000's *The Dynasty: Roc La Familia* (three times platinum), and 2001's *The Blueprint* (including the reissued 2002 *The Blueprint 2: The Gift and the Curse*).

However, his most noteworthy album may have been his 2003 retirement album, *The Black Album*. Coupled with his film, *Fade to Black* (a documentary and large-scale concert at Madison Square Garden in New York that featured Jay-Z, Ghostface Killah, Foxy Brown, Mary J. Blige, and R. Kelly, among others), Carter's *Black Album* spawned an underground renaissance of epic proportions—the producer's remix. After the release of various unauthorized remixes, Jay-Z released an a capella version of the album for both established and up-and-coming artists to experiment with. This helped create over 100 remixes of Jay-Z's final album, advertising Jay-Z on an unprecedented level (see sidebar: The *Black Album* Remix Phenomenon). Although

---

The *Black Album* Remix Phenomenon
T. Hasan Johnson

Jay-Z released *The Black Album* in 2003, and later released an a cappella version specifically for DJs and producers. Although a definitive number is still in question, there are over a hundred remixes, with the top albums being *The Brown Album* (by Kev Brown, former A Touch of Jazz producer), *The White Albulum* (from Kno of the Atlanta-based group Cunninlynguists), DJ Cheap Cologne's *The Double Black Album*, and Danger Mouse's *The Grey Album*.

Kev Brown was the first to do a remix; his rendition offers a laid-back, jazzy interpretation. However, before he could claim credit, he was soon overshadowed by DJ Danger Mouse. Mouse received attention because of his use of samples from the classic *White Album* by the Beatles. After releasing 3,000 promotional copies, he was served with a cease-and-desist order from EMI, who owns the rights to *The White Album* master. After threatening others who tried to release the album, the company finally backed down and the album can still be found online.

What is most significant about DJ Danger Mouse was the Grey Tuesday protest. Despite cease-and-desist orders from EMI, over 170 Web sites posted his album, in its entirety, for free download. On February 24, 2004, over 1 million computer users downloaded the album. This protest argued that such creations, and the Internet itself, should remain a free zone for artists and fans to enjoy and exchange artistic productions. This propelled Mouse's popularity to an unparalleled degree for several reasons; aside from the obvious gesture by fans to support free music and their desire to support creative license, they were also launching a preemptive strike against what many perceived as a looming threat to such creative exchange—corporate and government regulation of Internet practices. In other words, since corporate crackdowns on Napster (and the rise of P2P file-sharing communities like BitTorrents, Fast-Track, Gnutella, KaZaA, Limewire, Morpheus, OpenNap, and WinMX), corporations and the politicians they are rumored to be funding have been trying to find new ways to inhibit how people use the Internet. In light of this, online activists wanted to make a statement about creative freedom and overarching corporate control. Nevertheless, such protests prompted the remix phenomenon to even greater levels.

Kno of the group Cunninlynguists released *Kno vs. Hov: The White Albulum*, a well-produced challenge to the original, from the track order to the overall feel of the album. Cheap Cologne gained attention because he opened the door to rock listeners by sampling from Metallica's *The Black Album* (hence the *Double Black* in the title). He later received a cease-and-desist order from the Recording Industry Association of America (RIAA), a group that represents the five major record labels. The letter threatened jail time and a $250,000 fine if he didn't stop distribution of the album. Nevertheless, although these remixes are mostly made for fun rather than money, they illustrate the recording industry's need to develop new ways to keep up with consumers' interests, especially when consumers start creatively remixing their favorite artist's albums themselves.

Works Cited

"Grey Tuesday: Free the Grey Album." 24 February 2004. http://www.greytuesday .org.

Jay-Z was hardly the first hip hop artist to promote remixes, he did capitalize on it in a whole new way.

In 2005, Jay-Z became the president and CEO of Def Jam Recordings. This followed a widely publicized split with Damon Dash and Kareem "Biggs" Burke, who, after the falling-out, started a new company, Damon Dash Music Group. Jay-Z went on to redevelop Def Jam's image, and in 2005, at a New York radio station's (Power 105.1) annual concert, showed up onstage with Nas, ending the much-publicized feud between the two (see Nas essay). He has also made plans to firmly legitimate his relationship with the West Coast by starting Roc-A-Fella West and signing a Bay Area artist named Immense. However, despite his success and his supposed retirement (which many consider as unrealistic as the retirement of Too $hort, who released several works after he announced he was calling it quits), Jay-Z managed to escape his most dogged followers—his critics. But what do critics see in Jay-Z? What bothers them? What scares them? What makes some of them love him, and most important, what does Jay-Z's success say about what he means to people?

DEFINING THE FORMULA FOR SUCCESS

Jay-Z has complained about having to dumb down his lyrics for mainstream consumption (in *The Black Album*'s "Moment of Clarity"), pointing out that it's only when he does such things that he goes triple or quintuple platinum. However, several factors contribute to Jay's success and simultaneously reflect the state of hip hop. Jay-Z's flow has developed and changed over the years. Early on, he was known for his fast-paced flow and dizzying lyrical performances. This and the fact that he performed these songs live in concert made him a well-respected figure in underground circles. He could rhyme the material performed in the studio onstage without losing a beat. Also, he is rumored to have never written a song down; he claims to have memorized his lyrics from freestyle performances in the studio. It is said that Jay-Z could go to a studio, listen to the track, and then drive around in his car for a while until he had freestyled a new hit. This way, his topics and materials could stem from whatever was on his mind at the time he got to the studio. Ironically, this would prove difficult for some of his producers (namely Kanye West who, on his 2004 debut album *The College Dropout*, on the song "Last Call," mentioned how he made a beat for Jay-Z and hoped he would not get the "introspective, meditative" Jay-Z, but instead the "light-hearted" Jay-Z). Nevertheless, which Jay-Z a producer might get was hard to anticipate as he would not write anything until he meditated on a beat). Unfortunately, by the mid-1990s, such talent was becoming more and more infrequent. Few artists mastered the balance between lyrical complexity, metaphorical delivery, and storytelling, as many could only do one (or maybe two) at one time. For Jay-Z, although his earlier work emphasized fast wordplays, he developed a solid reputation for achieving this balance. After *Reasonable Doubt*, most notably on tracks like "Izzo (H.O.V.A.)" and "Hard Knock Life," Jay-Z illustrated his ability to use metaphor (and tell stories) as opposed to just quick flows. More important, Jay-Z learned to package his gritty life story into a narrative that made him a bootstrap success story. In other words, he learned that creating a rise-from-the-ghetto narrative made him more palatable to mainstream audiences (most were used to hard-luck stories in hip hop, but were new to MCs that could create a persona they could not only understand, but one they could identify with even if they did not regularly listen to hip hop). Essentially, he learned a hidden golden rule in entertainment: Make it as easy as possible for your audience to remember you.

Along with creating a persona in the entertainment industry, the use of a marketable narrative can help with album sales. As KRS-One said on his 1995 self-titled album in the song "Health, Wealth, Self," "Sell your image, never sell a record." Understanding this principle helped Jay-Z achieve another goal —increased marketability. Jay-Z now sold albums, represented himself on the radio, and marketed himself more easily because people outside of New York, the underground scene, and most notably, outside of hip hop could relate to what he was saying. This meant that suburbanites, rock listeners, and alternative music fans alike could not only understand Jay-Z but could understand how to understand him. Additionally, at this point, they could also become more acclimated to hip hop music in general—especially artists affiliated with Jay-Z's Roc-A-Fella label. Clearly, production played a strong role in his marketability, and Jay-Z had a reputation for working with the likes of DJ Premier, Puff Daddy, the Neptunes (Pharell in particular), Timbaland, Just Blaze, and most notably, the up-and-coming Kanye West.

More important than production, though, are Jay-Z's lyrics. For the most part, Jay-Z's choice of subject matter is more easily accessible to those as yet uninitiated into the hip hop aesthetic. This may have been part of what he complained about regarding "dumb[ing] down" his lyrics on "Moment of Clarity," but it nonetheless helped make his music more popular on MTV and other more mainstream media outlets. Possibly due to his rhyme writing style, Jay-Z was criticized for years for not addressing more complicated subjects, engaging political issues, or explicating how MCs could be more responsible for the impact of their work on the youth community. Seldom acknowledging these critiques openly, he eventually argued that the fact that he spoke out about the ghetto was a form of political activism in itself. Albeit a clichéd remark by MCs by the mid-1990s, Jay-Z seemed adamant about his stance and argued that as long as he rhymed about such things, he was helping to address social ills by bringing the harsh conditions of the ghetto to national and international scrutiny.

Despite the desire to speak out on social issues, Jay-Z understood the difficulty that came with being a social critic in hip hop. As a student of the history of hip hop, Jay-Z was quite familiar with the dangers of being pigeonholed by his audience, a record label, or any other institution invested in his album sales. Artists like Public Enemy, X-Clan, and Paris demonstrated how restrictive both the record industry and audiences could be toward what artists may want to produce, and what record executives and fans want to hear. Alternatively, rappers who were labeled as gangstas or criminals had difficulty making any other kind of music than what people expected from them. Whether it is due to intelligence, creativity, or just luck, Jay-Z managed to somewhat avoid inhibiting categories (at least compared to other artists), despite his complaints about the limitations in subject matter available to him.

Tangentially, Jay-Z's approach to spirituality also caught a lot of people's attention. He is abstract, vague, and yet inspiring for many hip hoppers navigating the difficult spaces of nondenominational forms of spiritual inquiry. Jay speaks with the boldness of a member of the Nation of Gods and Earths, the casual practicality of a Sunni Muslim (almost lackadaisically so), and the popular appeal of a Catholic pope. His spiritual message, albeit unclear, has used short statements and occasional references to provide his listeners with a nontraditional approach to spirituality that may be more reflective of today's postreligiosity than anything else. While it is nonreligious, nondenominational, and yet open to the possibility of a spiritual force in the universe, many of Jay-Z's fans identify with his approach to spirituality (often articulated through hard and gritty stories about life, death, violence, and survival). Speaking as a sympathetic (and almost apologetic) ex-drug dealer and criminal, Jay has acknowledged the difficulties of following a spiritual path while addressing the practicality of making a daily living. In many ways, this approach resonated with many of his fans, and quite possibly, it may have also taught some of them about why they should be remorseful about what they do.

Another reason for Jay-Z's success was that he understood the notion of symbolic representation. In essence, he knew that to represent himself as the preeminent rags-to-riches paragon, he could attract those that were living in the same conditions he grew up in, while supplying them with the hope that they could also get out of a life of poverty, criminality, and violence. He also understood that he could attract youth from black, white, Latino, and Asian middle-class (and suburban) communities through his descriptive lyrics on style, taste, and material acquisition. Although some of them may not be able to identify with his hard-knock origins, they could identify with the desire to be able to purchase nice clothes, buy expensive cars, and drink trendy alcoholic beverages (most preferably with your name endorsed on the bottle). In other words, they could identify with the relationship between possessing the means for increasing their material ownership and the idea that material items are signifiers for status in American society. This phenomenon should be understood as more complex and challenging than it may appear. For the generation of youth born after the 1970s, the civil rights movement, the Black Power movement, and COINTELPRO's war against the black activist community, the turbulent 1960s do not generally resonate as real. Instead, much of the legacy of these historical movements are somewhat amalgamated, assumed to be part of the milieu of daily reality for today's youth. Hence, class can be constructed and understood in slightly different ways by today's youth, who are hopelessly mixed and blended (racially, politically, and socioeconomically) in ways almost unheard-of forty years ago. Therefore for Jay-Z's audience, instead of what job, academic degree, or type of house they owned, questions of class and status could be attributed to more fluid approaches to material wealth, like how much money they have access to (not how they got it), how well they could acquire wealth without working a conventional job, and how well they could find new ways to bring the street experience to the boardroom. Although to some these divisions may not be any better than the last set of standards for class stratification, they do allow for larger groups of younger people to participate in society on their own terms.

The fourth reason for Jay-Z's success is his approach to black masculinity. Although not entirely original, his casual approach to pimpin', money making, style, material wealth, and business acumen made him a new type of hip hop icon, a sort of laid-back pimp in control. Arguably taking the New York MC crown in the wake of Biggie Smalls's death, Jay-Z claimed (repeatedly) to be the "best rapper alive" (e.g., "Dirt Off Your Shoulder," *The Black Album*). He also articulated his disapproval of his rivals (Nas, Prodigy of Mobb Deep, Tupac, etc.) by retaliating against them in his music, suggesting that he would attack anyone who challenged him, and more important, be more masculine than them. This resonated with many of his fans, mainly young men who want to identify with Jay-Z's pimp-in-control image. Also, his approach to women, mainly framed as a player who controls and manipulates them, suggests a form of masculinity that may complicate black male-female relationships. In the song "Girls, Girls, Girls" on his 2001 *Blueprint* album, he describes how many girls he has and how well he controls each of them, despite that he portrays most of them as characteristically flawed.

On the surface, the problem is that the type of masculinity Jay-Z exemplifies is often destructive, clichéd, and confrontational. Although this has become the norm for many rappers in hip hop, such behavior still raises questions about whether or not there can be a new, more productive form of masculinity that artists could espouse other than stereotypical pimps and gangsters. For example, in the song "Friend or Foe '98" on *In My Lifetime, Volume 1* (1997), he tells a story about surprising an assassin who has been planning to kill him. He then proceeds to kill the assassin, but only after taking the time to explain to him how much more of a man he is—suggesting that whoever gets to kill first is more the man. Despite such lyrics, more recently, Jay-Z has redefined his machismo persona. In a feud with Nas, both artists demonstrated the capacity for maturity in hip hop by publicly reconciling (discussed later). Nevertheless, Jay-Z's popularity is closely related to his approach to black male masculinity, and after the deaths of his predecessors Biggie and Tupac, he had to reevaluate the value of the macho approach to manhood.

A fifth reason for Jay-Z's success is how his music lends itself to "virtual blackness." Virtual blackness refers to the idea that the socially constructed notion of blackness, rooted in a history of racism, negativity, and depravity, can be experienced vicariously through a medium that separates the listener from the experience, leaving them free to experience stereotypical forms of blackness without the societal repercussions that come with criminal behavior (e.g., jail, violent retaliation, death, etc.). In the past, black entertainers and athletes were often used by white (and other) elite audiences in this manner.

However, intrinsic to the rise of entertainment-based technology, people of all class stations, races, colors, genders, and sexual orientations can experience virtual blackness. This might just be partially what draws mainstream audiences to rap music—the desire to experience blackness. Such blackness, usually perceived as a form of otherness, is also projected on nonblack MCs who participate in hip hop culture. Yet it is not surprising that the types of blackness mainstream audiences are exposed to in hip hop are limited, or as bell hooks said in her 1992 book *Black Looks*, "we are most likely to see images of black people that reinforce and reinscribe white supremacy, [not challenge it]."

In Jay-Z's case, virtual blackness relates to the popular idea that the violence in black ghettos across America is highly adventurous and entertaining. Because Jay-Z's music has always been associated with such violence, and his lyrics are often quite explicit and detailed, people of all backgrounds and orientations can safely experience blackness, violence, and ghetto life without enduring the repercussions that come with it. However, in a positive sense, people can also imagine what it may be like to be a black multimillionaire who drives a Bentley, scoffs at the police, dates Beyoncé Knowles, and can command a stadium full of people when performing. Essentially, blackness can now be associated with wealth and success as well as violence and chaos. Yet the overly indulgent imaginings of black success can also be perceived in unrealistic ways, often to belie the harsh economic conditions that many African Americans experience daily. This, in turn, can create problematic ideas about how black people expend wealth. Thus, if one learns about wealth through hip hop, and by extension Jay-Z, one only learns about the most superficial and materialistic aspects of it, not its less obvious components (investing, real estate acquisition, and saving for life after retirement).

But what is the definition of success? For Jay-Z, the question has already been answered—wealth and fame. However, even he has admitted that if he had his way, he would like to create music more like those that don't sell half of what he does. MCs like Common, Mos Def, and Talib Kweli represent the next phase of an underground segment of hip hop usually referred to as conscious. Although they have made great strides to distance themselves from this term (arguing that it has limited the types of audiences they can attract, the wealth they can accumulate, and the types of music they can make), they are still able to make music that reaches people and addresses a wider range of issues and topics than other hip hop artists, even issues of spirituality. Jay-Z criticized Common on *The Black Album* by pointing out how many albums he's sold in comparison, but the line seemed to express a degree of sincerity in his wish to create music not limited to materialism and gangsta bravado. On another track, Jay bemoans having to dumb down his lyrics, but then quickly states that when he does he sells more albums, sort of admonishing his audience for forcing him into his musical style. Nevertheless, this conflicted and complicated assessment of his self-styled persona begs the question, what is success? True, to be worth $320 million is clearly a success for most people, but how successful is it when you cannot make the kind of music you want to for fear of losing your audience? Jay-Z himself followed this line of questioning in his film *Fade to Black* (2004) when, in conversation with another MC in a studio, they discussed how rappers have to make music that stays within a static, formulaic framework of violence and misogyny. Although using another artist to make his point, one might easily assume that he was also talking about himself.

It would seem, nonetheless, that Jay-Z did finally answer the riddle of how to be yourself in the entertainment industry: do it behind the scenes, not onstage. Do it by bringing the street hustle to the corporate boardroom. Jay-Z's decision to preside over Def Jam in 2005 might be the opportunity for him to create his brand of music, albeit more indirectly than he might wish. Jay-Z has helped spawn the careers of a number of artists like Memphis Bleek, Beanie Sigel, Amil, Kanye West, Freeway, Cam'Ron, Young Gunz, Immense, and Samantha Ronson. However, as CEO of Def Jam, he might be able to write policy that determines funding and supports the development of new artists with vastly different styles and skills than his own.

UNDERGROUND VERSUS MAINSTREAM: MANUFACTURING MARKET APPEAL

When analyzing Jay-Z's success, one factor that consistently comes up is the question of mainstream market interest versus underground hip hop aesthetic. In many ways, Jay-Z is the perfect figure to examine this dynamic, as he was perceived as an underground MC (like many other artists) early in his career. In fact, even Nas was amazed at the degree of underground respect Jay-Z achieved back in 1992. Prior to the release of his first album, Jay-Z had achieved a degree of notoriety that other, more experienced MCs could not match for a good period of time. However, by the time his 1997 album *In My Lifetime, Volume 1* was released, Jay-Z was a superstar whose fans complained that he was pandering to mainstream audiences too much. Although Jay-Z did not see the problem with collaborations with producers like Puff Daddy and Rick Rubin, his reputation for maintaining his underground grit began to suffer. In response, Jay-Z released the straight-to-video film *The Streets Is Watching* in 1997. His goal was to remind his underground fans that he was still an artist to be reckoned with, and he was still as hard as ever.

Nevertheless, the quest for a wide-ranging audience has its costs, and after the release of his 1998 album, *Volume 2: Hard Knock Life*, Jay-Z seemed solidified in his position as a commercial artist. He has managed to maintain his core audience in the long run, which is a difficult feat not easily accomplished once accusations of selling out set in. But Jay-Z walked the line between both for a long time. Eventually, his fans overlooked his overproduced, uber-mixed sound. Albums like *Volume 3: Life and Times of S. Carter*

(1999) and *The Blueprint* (2001), considered in many circles to be classics (most notably the latter), seemed to acclimate Jay-Z's audience to albums that were a hodgepodge of mainstream and underground tracks alike. This worked to Jay-Z's advantage as a means of making music that maintained his street credentials and appealed to his expanding fan base (mostly due to MTV and BET's all-day video format).

Although mainstream appeal is not an issue that started with Jay-Z, it has plagued hip hop artists since its inception. Whether talking about the Sugarhill Gang, Will Smith, MC Hammer, Vanilla Ice, or Eminem, questions of mainstream appeal have been a long-standing point of contention in the hip hop community. Many artists argued that they were merely trying to help hip hop by expanding its audience base, raising the issue about the degree to which hip hop might find itself oversaturated with fans who do not appreciate its history, even posing a threat to the culture.

Currently, the difficulty is that hip hop has become a global phenomenon. Five-year-old kids in Ghana, England, South Africa, Japan, Jamaica, India, and Brazil can quote Jay-Z's lyrics as well as he, and more to the point, have crafted their own forms of hip hop. It has reached across the world from the streets of Brooklyn and the Bronx and has sparked a worldwide response. However, to the extent that it has reached the world, the recording industry and corporate media institutions have also grown due to the marketing of hip hop culture. If anything, hiphop has become synonymous with youth culture, and for many youth it has become a necessary part of their self-identity. Jay-Z, Nas, Biggie Smalls, Tupac, Ice Cube, and many more have become part of the lexicon of hip hop lingo and comprise a hip hop pantheon of sorts. Although their representations have become synonymous with hip hop, and by extension American hip hop culture, they have also become symbolic of something else—or rather a series of other issues. Corporate media (via television, radio, and Internet), corporate production, the marketing of consumer commodities, and the culture of Western consumerism have used MCs as vehicles for the sale of their products. Therefore, CDs and music videos pave the way for the production and sale of sneakers, liquor, cars, clothes, jewelry, and other consumer items, but more important, they become the vehicle for the unilateral and unidirectional imposition of Western cultural values on non-Western people. Since the United States primarily establishes trade from its borders to other borders unilaterally (especially with third world countries), ideas about gender, color, class, and sexuality have all become standards for "civilized" behavior. Moreover, attitudes about violence, rape, and aggression—and their ties to black masculinity—have become part of the social memory of "American-ness," "hip hop-ness," and "blackness" around the world. Although this is not accepted without challenge from global consumers, it is nonetheless part of what they must contend with once received. Therefore, consumers who support underground hip hop often understand that their local culture is intricately tied to the global experience, and contradict corporate attempts to use hip hop culture as a marketing vehicle by advocating a global culture of nonmaterialism and artistic proficiency.

It is from this vantage point that questions about Jay-Z's marketability, crossover appeal, and mainstream success become more poignant. What does his success, and those who strive to duplicate it, mean in the larger view? Jay remarked on the song "Moment of Clarity" (*The Black Album*) that he decided that the only way he could help the poor was to become rich and give back, but having spent so much of his time describing his material wealth—or at least his aspirations for acquiring more of it—can a promaterialist hip hop aesthetic be used to help people less fortunate? Although it may be difficult to measure, some hip hop artists have attempted to developed philanthropic practices. In 2002 Jay-Z and his mother founded the S. Carter Scholarship Fund, a nonprofit organization that provides financial assistance to those interested in furthering their education. Other artists have developed philan-thropic practices as well, as the Game and Chingy were said to have given funds for victims of the 2004 Asian tsunami and Sri Lanka earthquake. 50 Cent and the Game, as a symbolic gesture of peace to end their feud, decided (at the behest of Russell Simmons) to each give donations to the Boys Choir of Harlem. Such acts may seem sparse and underwhelming when compared to the kinds of riches these artists flaunt in their music and in videos (and it is difficult to determine how much these artists actually do give back to the communities they hail from), but it is still worth mention. However, whether or not these artists understand the connection between their on-wax materialism and the impact it may have on young listeners has yet to be determined.

For Jay-Z, his music communicates a series of values and ideas that he himself may only be partly aware of. Jay-Z sees his wealth as a testament to his hard work, effort, and talent, and, to be sure, this is true. But his wealth is only possible because of the sacrifices of the economically impoverished com-munities that helped mold his cultural aesthetic. It is hoped that hip hop artists like Jay-Z have reflected on the weight of their cultural influence on society, as the poor communities that manufacture consumer items sold by rappers (com-munities whose members often strive to own these consumer items themselves) have internalized the values espoused in these albums. It is this level of respon-sibility and analysis that many of Jay-Z's critics and fans would like to see him address. How does an MC from humble beginnings reach the pinnacle of stardom and wealth, albeit on the backs of other poor people, and not come to grips with this intrinsic irony? What does an MC who realizes this do? Moreover, how much can any one artist be expected to do about it?

THE ROLE OF BEEF IN JAY-Z'S FORMULA FOR SUCCESS

One of the staples of hip hop culture has been the battle, and Jay-Z is no stranger to it. Having had issues with Tupac, Mobb Deep, the Terror Squad,

Cam'Ron, R. Kelly, and Nas in particular, Jay-Z has helped reinstitute the significance of the battle in hip hop after the deaths of the Notorious B.I.G. and Tupac.

For the most part, the battle in hip hop has always been about competition and proving one's lyrical skills to be superior to another's. Hip hop has helped refine the art of the battle to encapsulate the concerns, issues, attitudes, and perspectives of fans, thus making many battles iconic in the memories of hip hop fans. Also, battling has helped frame the development and trajectory of hip hop's aesthetic. Battles between Busy Bee and Kool Moe Dee, Big Daddy Kane and Kool G Rap, Kool Moe Dee and LL Cool J, X-Clan and KRS-One, Tupac and Biggie, LL Cool J and Canibus, Eminem and Benzino, and Jay-Z and Nas each represent turning points in hip hop culture. Busy Bee and Kool Moe Dee almost single-handedly shifted the aesthetic value of battle rapping above party pleasing, with Bee representing the old tradition of sparking the party, and Dee representing the newer tradition of battling and demonstrating one's superior skill. Big Daddy Kane and Kool G Rap redefined the craft of lyrical precision and complicated syncopation, much like Rakim, but in adversarial conversation with one another. Kool Moe Dee and LL Cool J battled on wax, extending their feud for years by trading song for song on sequential albums. X-Clan and KRS-One set a standard for the first significant battle in hip hop over Pan-African/Black Power ideology, while Eminem and Benzino raised issues of race, whiteness, and privilege in hip hop culture (and among hip hop consumers). However, the battle between Tupac and Biggie might be the most widely known. Theirs may represent the first public battle in hip hop to not only end in bloodshed, but with each of their eventual deaths.

Tupac and Biggie's battle terrified rappers from the East and West Coasts (with many refusing to go to the opposite's coast, even when not affiliated with either Biggie or Tupac). After their deaths, people from within and outside of hip hop began to question the efficacy of the battle. Instead of criticizing the extent of that particular battle, they began to question the concept of the battle, suggesting that if it can go this far at this moment, what might happen in the future? However, battle rapping is unavoidable in hip hop, and according to Jay-Z, one needs an incredible ego just to handle the pressure that comes with being an MC. Inevitably, these mammoth-sized egos collide, and battles begin. Yet it seems that through such contention, hip hop culture flourishes, develops, and advances.

Jay-Z and Nas's beef actually extended, somewhat, out of Biggie and Tupac's. After Biggie's death, questions about who would be the King of New York began to surface. For most, it did not take long before the fans' gaze focused on Nas and Jay-Z. Jay-Z is actually rumored to have started the feud by dissing Nas at a concert. Nas responded, and between several radio freestyles, released songs, and recorded interviews, they split New York (and the hip hop world) in half. Many sided with Nas because they saw him as the more sincere MC, representing the tradition of hip hop, void of the excessive pandering for mainstream appeal that many associate with Jay-Z. But Jay-Z's undeniable appeal, tight production, and creative off-the-cuff style was, and always has been, more accessible to the casual listener than Nas's. Although Nas could enjoy creating more esoteric lyrics and concepts, Jay-Z's style seemed simple enough for anyone to grasp, and yet his metaphors, similes, and flow patterns captured people's attention more readily than Nas's. Nevertheless, people debate to this day as to who won the battle, which may be, quite possibly, the sign of success for both of them over the industry. The battle heightened both of their album sales and it would not take long before they both could do no wrong, creatively speaking. Surprisingly, the most significant part of their battle was how they chose to resolve it. Until then, hip hop could not claim to have had a great number of reconciliations (X-Clan/KRS-One and Common/Ice Cube aside), but Jay-Z and Nas had the most widely known hip hop battle to end in a resolution.

In a 2006 interview on an MTV show called *Beyond Beef*, Nas and Jay-Z discussed their battle, its reconciliation, and the potential for the future. Wisely, Jay-Z described how this monumental decision to end the beef may reverberate throughout hip hop, offering an alternative to Biggie and Tupac's disastrous end. For some, it reminded artists that they are just that, artists, and not necessarily the figures they paint themselves to be (and even if they ever were, after that, many chose different ways to represent themselves). In the interview, Nas questioned some of the newer MCs that do not seem to have a connection to the history of hip hop and its culture, challenging them to take their craft more seriously; and more important, to use this reconciliation as an example of how not to allow violence to be the inevitable consequence of beef.

This represented a critical juncture for hip hop because it was the first such statement since the period of the mid-1980s to the early 1990s. The conscious hip hop movement, curtailed by the collusion of dwindling record sales and preachy lyrics, was more impactful than many gave it credit for. Aside from influencing hip hop artists directly, it also demonstrated the potential for hip hop to influence the social reality that many poor African Americans, Puerto Ricans, Chicano-Latinos, Asians, and others lived in. However, the industry was more concerned with less politically aware artists who were more marketable to mainstream audiences, staggering the growing consciousness movement in the early 1990s. Thus, it was primarily interested in mainstream record sales, and although positive hip hop albums sold well in predominantly black communities, they did not necessarily sell well in white communities. Simply put, positive albums about African American social uplift was not necessarily an unappealing concept for white (and other) communities, but it was not a particularly lucrative one. More important, it did not mesh with the dominant narratives about blackness that many were accustomed to. Despite portrayals of African Americans as upright, well-to-do citizens by such figures as Bill Cosby, most were more familiar with myths of black criminality, depravity, and materialism. The legacy of postenlightenment Jim Crow ethnic caricature is so deeply embedded in Western culture that it is no accident that mainstream consumers would most strongly gravitate toward its most base impulses. This shift by the recording industry to redefine what types of artists should be touted as MCs for public consumption marked the decline of the conscious hip hop movement. Seemingly, Jay-Z represented the type of commercial MC the industry wanted—stylish, apolitical, trendy, and seemingly obsessed with material wealth. However, Jay-Z and Nas's public acknowledgment of the correlation between hip hop and social awareness was important because it suggested that hip hop can still deal with more pressing social issues than materialism, especially at a time when America is more politically conservative than it has been in decades, and the ghetto may have more black men in prison than in the hood. But along with challenging materialism in hip hop, can artists with clout, like Jay-Z, challenge hip hop's most dogged problem—sexism? Can they challenge the negative and oppressive representations of women in hip hop? And can such a challenge help address why consumers support the production of hyperexotic notions of femininity?

THE PROBLEM WITH "99 PROBLEMS"

For the most part, celebrity relationships have become a public institution. Much like other celebrity couples, Jay-Z and Beyoncé Knowles (of Destiny's Child fame) have become the ideal hip hop couple. The two have become the topic of much conversation in the hip hop world. Mainly because hip hop has been known for its composition of young, adolescent males, the idea of Jay-Z with one of the most desirable women in the industry reaffirmed his persona to his fans. Although no one could say whether or not their relationship is genuine, its benefit as a marketing tool cannot be denied. However, such iconic status begs the question: Can hip hop overcome the difficulty it has always had with portraying women and overarching notions of domineering patriarchy? Can this new image of Jay-Z help mend fences with women who have argued for decades about misogyny in hip hop?

Despite the ways mainstream hip hop has portrayed women in music videos, songs, and other marketing paraphernalia, one of its most dangerous impacts has been the normalization of patriarchal attitudes. Accordingly, both men and women participate in the subjugation of womanhood and femininity. Jay-Z is hardly innocent. From the beginning of his career to his retirement album, he has seldom addressed women in a positive way. "99 Problems," one of his more popular songs, represents the same kind of repetitive misogyny that has been a trademark in hip hop, even if the "bitch" in the song is not the primary topic of conversation.

One of Jay-Z's landmark songs in relation to women was the duet with Foxy Brown, "Ain't No Nigga." In it, the hip hop world is introduced to a new development—the mafiosa figure. The mafiosa, as played by Brown, is a materialistic woman crime boss who only answers to her previously incarcerated boyfriend (there is no information as to whether the two were ever married). She also exerts her power by pointing out that she is responsible for his financial success, style, and wealth because she has "cultivated" his talents and in her words, "made [him] a don." She also does not care if he sees other women, as long as he treats her right by making sure that she continues to drive new cars and wear expensive furs. Brown's caricature would make her famous in her own right (rivaled only by Lil' Kim and Adina Howard); she soon embodied the female caricature articulated by Tupac in his song "Me and My Girlfriend" (1996). This song, about a man and his gun, is not a far stretch from Brown's representation, as guns and women are still symbolic representations of objects owned by men. In fact, both guns and women are only useful when providing pleasure or exacting revenge for men. They are both, by nature (or so some MCs would have you believe), objects for men's imagination. Love for both is solely contingent upon male fantasy, and neither has an independent voice. Interestingly enough, the character Brown portrays is as palpable as Jay-Z's, as both are consistent with the stereotypes about black men and women: criminal, violent, sexually promiscuous, and manipulative. Both characters represent caricatures that seem quite consistent with stereotypical notions of blackness, at least in the mainstream imagination.

However, what Jay-Z may not do in his music to challenge stereotypes, he may accomplish in his private life. In one sense, Beyoncé is seen as the embodiment of postmillennium women's pride, at least as far as pop music celebrities who address women's issues are concerned. Songs like "Independent Woman Part I" (2001) and "Survivor" (2001) helped mold public perceptions of Beyoncé as one of the most exotically beautiful and outspoken R&B singers. For Jay-Z to perform with her in the song "Bonnie and Clyde" (2003) shows the continuation of the narrative that he, Tupac, and Biggie used before, albeit with a slight twist. Beyoncé, considered by some to be a more reputable feminist than Brown, offers a new type of mafiosa that appears far less materialistic and violent, but nonetheless supportive of her man. Beyoncé's persona is confident and intelligent, with extensive experience with men who have tried to manipulate her. She outsmarts them and has sought to tell other women to do the same. In her music, acting career, and advertising roles, she has (to one degree or another) stayed true to this representation. Her relationship to Jay-Z, however, communicates a specific narrative in itself, considering that Jay-Z has always described himself as a pimp who manipulates women to suit his interests. In this regard, she has become an addition to his harem (a compliment to Jay-Z's prowess), and rather than finding the type of man she has been looking for, she has instead found the type of man she has admonished others for falling for. No doubt, both public personas are pop culture fabrications that do not accurately reflect who they are as people, but such personas can be read in a narrative, textual fashion that communicates complex (and problematic) thematic codes on black male-female relationships.

Despite the apparent contradiction in the relationship between the public personas of both figures, the Jay-Z/Beyoncé union may offer a new idea about what type of woman, and by extension what type of masculinity, men in hip hop should consider valuable. As Beyoncé does not represent the typical woman articulated by male MCs, especially considering that she has a voice of her own (this refers to criticisms of Foxy Brown and Lil' Kim as being mere "puppets" for male rappers Jay-Z and the Notorious B.I.G., respectively, who wrote their lyrics), she may provide a foil to many MCs' perceptions of women. Even conscious MCs have trouble here, as artists like Jeru the Damaja on his *The Sun Rises in the East* (1994) and *Wrath of the Math* (1996) albums tried to delineate between "bitches" and "women," arguing that the difference had to do with self-respect. Yet he was nonetheless criticized for making "bitches" the subject of the song, and not the respectable women he applauded. Where even conscious rappers have failed, Jay-Z may succeed and shift the standards for male-female relationships simply by publicly (and quite possibly strategically) associating with Beyoncé.

JAY-Z, GLOBALIZATION, AND THE FUTURE OF THE NEW RECORDING INDUSTRY

The record industry is undergoing a dramatic shift in both its infrastructure and its approach to musical production. Although this change is slow and plodding—brought on more by rogue artists and independent labels than its own decision to change—there is need for new blood (and new direction) at the decision-making level of many entertainment corporations, especially in regard to artistic production and management. There is a need for new parameters, new approaches, and a new overall scope of vision for the production of music in general. It is more plausible than people may think that Jay-Z could help spearhead, at least as far as public perception is concerned, this new infrastructural corporate movement. But what are some of the indicators of this need? Are the impending changes in the entertainment industry this deep and sweeping?

As far as the industry is concerned, downloading, or file sharing, in post-2000 cyberspace cost the recording industry millions. Record stores, labels, and artists themselves lost revenue because the industry could not determine how exactly to keep up with its clientele. Listeners no longer waited for industry-determined release dates for new albums. They could no longer be forced to purchase whole albums when they only wanted to buy their favorite songs (a phenomenon exacerbated by the recording industry's decision not to sell singles in an effort to make more money from CD sales). In fact, even older albums that were difficult to find, or were unreleased, were now only a few clicks away from online consumers. However, not only did pirated copies of unreleased albums find their way into people's computers, but people used file-sharing programs like Napster, Morpheus, and Limewire to share remixes and revisions that were as prevalent as the original albums. Hence, listeners were no longer satisfied with the gulf between artists and consumers. They also wanted to be artists but did not want to go through the initiatory process of paying for studio time, shopping demos, or finding a label to sign them. Instead, they downloaded needed sound-editing software to portable laptops, sampled and edited sound bites from the Internet, self-published albums, and marketed their creations globally over cheap (and easily made) Web sites. This new, more interactive approach to music production has made it difficult for the record industry to sustain itself comfortably and may still pose a serious threat to the security of the entertainment industry (as has also been the case with other forms of media, like film), unless they figure out a way to control the new and ever-expanding market. In alignment with this new mode of creation and distribution, artists like MF DOOM, Danger Mouse, Pharoah Monch, and Third Sight have also begun to create music that radically breaks from traditional norms and threatens to redefine hip hop's aesthetic framework.

It should be stated here that this new framework also expands aesthetic standards beyond geographic and national boundaries. Such a process is usually confined to limited geographic areas (and heavily dependent on local radio stations, now locally franchised national corporations that control local and national news, music, trends, and styles), but as the Internet becomes more and more useful in the dissemination of music, new aesthetic standards are now starting to branch out and disturb conventional standards and traditional radio formats. What may be even more shocking to the industry is that some of these artists may make more money than the artists we see on MTV, despite the notably lower album sales and name recognition. Because they manage to keep a larger percentage of the profit from their album sales than the more widely known artists, they don't need to sell as many albums to make a profit (especially if their albums were made on "indie" equipment—meaning far less money spent on production and sound editing—and especially if sold and distributed online, or rather, without major label involvement). This will be just one of the challenges Jay-Z will face in his position as CEO of Def Jam.

In order to address some of these concerns, Jay-Z has been quite ambitious about releasing new artists, groups, and record labels in order to both diversify Def Jam and keep up with the dizzying pace of consumer interest. Potentially, one of his most notable projects has been Def Jam Left, a subsidiary label under Def Jam designed with a specific purpose. Described by Jay-Z as a way for Def Jam to nurture new artists without pressuring them to produce an immediate gold record, Def Jam Left may prove to be more innovative than meets the eye. It coincides with the responses that many artists have begun to voice toward the Iraq war, post-9/11 society, the Patriot Act, exploitive (international) globalization practices, pharmaceutical monopolies, police brutality, electoral cover-ups, and legislative fraud at the federal government level. Artists that would not have been concerned with these issues five years before, alongside artists considered politically active, are now becoming more and more outspoken about political issues, both local and far-ranging. Artists like Kanye West, Jadakiss, and Ludacris are now listed along with Common, Talib Kweli, Mos Def, and Black Thought from the Roots (who were, by the way, the first group signed to Jay-Z's new Def Jam Left label) as being part of a new configuration of consciousness that did not exist before. Between the late 1980s and the mid-1990s, hip hop was somewhat polarized as far as conscious (alternative) and mainstream music is concerned. There was little room for an artist that tried to do both, but now MCs are desperately trying to transcend such classifications, although many of them are still interested in speaking out when they deem it necessary. It seems that Jay-Z may have just given them the means to do so. In fact, he may have developed the means for hip hop to reevaluate its own standards for political activism, gender, masculinity, and class by creating the corporate vehicles best suited to support artists with new approaches. Also, he may have done the impossible and found a way to do the impossible—make the entertainment industry serve the interests of the artist.

WHICH WAY FOR JAY-Z NOW?

Jay-Z has carefully crafted his rags-to-riches story about his rise from Marcy Projects to the heights of the industry. Yet there are other narratives that Jay-Z espouses that offer more complex, potentially damaging sentiments. Different from other artists at the time of his first album, Jay-Z represented a new type of gangsta: one who was slightly remorseful about his activities, reflective about his life in the streets, and almost apologetic about his past. However, his bravado, confrontational attitude, and reliance on violence pose problematic and yet understandable narratives that many black men face. These problematic tropes in how black masculinity is articulated in hip hop come out of real, lived experiences. The systemic racial profiling of black men by city, state, and federal law enforcement institutions; the incredible rates at which they are imprisoned; and the extent to which they are used as free labor in the prison system (reinstituting slavery in ways that seem to disassociate it from past formations) all point to an extremely hostile context. Hence, the bravado in hip hop music, albeit repetitive and somewhat predictable, may also be a response to the difficulty of negotiating an impossible situation. On the other hand, there may be a point where hypermasculine rhetoric can become a hindrance to saving black maleness from the onslaught of society, in effect becoming toxic and self-destructive. Regardless, Jay-Z's legacy may require further study, along with the extent to which his persona has influenced (for better or worse) how black males are perceived.

The critical question for Jay-Z and his legacy is whether or not his work falls into a new age of minstrelsy or a planned, strategic approach to redefining the potential for artistic success. If the former is the case, then Jay-Z has merely fulfilled the legacy of many that have come before him and played to the fantasies that many already have regarding black males. He has advocated stereotypes about black males and violence, sex, misogyny, drug selling, trafficking women as prostitutes, and material ownership over speaking out on societal issues.

However, if Jay-Z's actions were the product of a planned assault on the record industry, then he has succeeded. His current worth is rumored to be roughly around $320 million, a staggering amount that few artists (in any genre) have managed to achieve. His position as CEO of Def Jam puts him into a key position to generate new artistic careers, while manipulating the direction of hip hop culture. His creation of Def Jam Left has essentially developed the means to bring the underground to the mainstream, and instead of trying to revamp his image into that of a conscious rapper, he has instead used his superstar status to help rappers of many styles into the business. Accordingly, Def Jam Left also seeks to help artists release their work through low-finance deals that minimize the stress of meeting record label expectations. Such a vehicle could be crucial to the restructuring of hip hop and the inclusion of the underground into the mainstream. However, on a more negative note, it could be used to keep underground artists consigned to his label, much like African American sharecroppers in post–Civil War society, by keeping them indebted, indefinitely, for minor accrued expenses. Unfortunately, only time will tell which direction Jay-Z takes this new label.

When raising the question about whether or not Jay-Z embodies negative black stereotypes in his music or has crafted a strategy for success that used such stereotypes to gain wealth and position to help others, it is more likely that the real motivations behind Jay-Z's rise to prominence are somewhere in between, with the leadership of Def Jam as a welcome capstone to a stellar sales career. Although Jay-Z was probably quite aware that certain types of music, and the subsequent messages therein, were more appealing to mainstream audiences than others, it is unlikely that as a teen he was knowledgeable about the history behind the images and characteristics that mainstream audiences were interested in. The legacy of the brute, Zip Coon, and Sambo (three stereotypical caricatures that helped mold white attitudes and legislation about African Americans in post–Civil War America) have helped to influence how many consumers interpret black masculinity in hip hop culture. This is the terrain that the MC has to contend with if she or he is interested in selling to a large audience. In essence, Jay-Z may have developed a new way to define success, and achieve it, through a careful climb up the recording industry's ladder. Most important, regardless of Jay-Z's perception of his own impact on society, he is helping to bring underappreciated MCs to the fore-front. If properly executed, Jay-Z may also redefine consciousness in hip hop by creating new standards for success by making the industry more supportive of artists with alternative approaches to music and business.

See also: Tupac Shakur, Notorious B.I.G., Nas, Kanye West

WORKS CITED

hooks, bell. *Black Looks: Race and Representation.* Cambridge: South End Press, 1992.

FURTHER READINGS

African American Registry. "Rap, a Music, an Industry, and a Culture." 3 April 2005. http://www.aaregistry.com/africanamericanhistory/789/RAPamusicanindus-tryandaculture.

Beyond Beef: Jay-Z and Nas. Host Toure. Perf. Jay-Z and Nas. BET, 2006.

Chang, Jeff. *Can't Stop Won't Stop: A History of the Hip-Hop Generation.* New York: St. Martin's Press, 2005.

Ethnic Notions. Dir. Marlon Riggs. 1987. Videocassette. California Newsreel, 2005.

Fade to Black. Dir. Patrick Paulson and Michael John Warren. Perf. Jay-Z, Sean "P. Diddy" Combs, Damon Dash, Rick Rubin, Kanye West, Common, Afeni Shakur, Voletta Wallace, and Pharrell Williams. DVD. Paramount, 2005.

Kitwana, Bakari. *Why White Kids Love Hip Hop: Wangstas, Wiggers, Wannabes, and the New Reality of Race in America.* New York: Basic Civitas Books, 2005.

Kool Moe Dee. *There's a God on the Mic: The True 50 Greatest MCs.* New York: Thunder's Mouth Press, 2003.

Letter to the President. Dir. Thomas Gibson. Perf. Common, David Banner, Chuck D, Snoop Dogg, and Wyclef Jean. 2005. DVD. Image Entertainment, 2005.

The MC: Why We Do It. Dir. Peter Spirer. Perf. 50 Cent, Common, Ghostface Killah, Talib Kweli, Method Man, Mekhi Phifer, Raekwon, Rakim, Twista, and Kanye West. 2005. DVD. Image Entertainment, 2005.

Rashbaum, Alyssa. "Online Exclusive: 50 Cent and the Game Squash Rap Beef." Vibe.com, 24 April 2006. http://www.vibe.com/news/onlineexclusives/2005/03/onlineexclusive50centgamesquashrapbeef/.

Roc-A-Fella Records. Jay-Z: Hova da God. 19 March 2005. http://www.rocafella.com/Artist.aspx?id=1&avid=121&idj=352.

Rose, Tricia. *Black Noise: Rap Music and Black Culture in Contemporary America.* Middletown, CT: Wesleyan University Press, 1994.

© AP Photo/Kevork Djansezian.

Kanye West

Todd Dills

Though Kanye West's icon status in the annals of hip hop history is largely still a work in progress, by mid-2006 he seemed well on his way. Though neither of his two albums was awarded the coveted five-mic rating from *The Source* magazine, he came close with both records. Both 2004's *The College Dropout* and 2005's *Late Registration* were Billboard chart toppers with successful singles. The former's "Jesus Walks" won the Best Rap Song Grammy for 2004, and the latter gave us "Gold Digger," featuring celebrity titan

Jamie Foxx, "Diamonds (From Sierra Leone)," "Heard 'Em Say," and "Drive Slow." The singles represented a variety of sounds and were widely played in various corporate radio formats and on free and college radio as well. West was making guest appearances and producing on an ever-expanding number of high-profile records, including, in 2005, Common's four-and-a-half-mic-rated *Be* (released by West's own G.O.O.D. Music label). In addition to the Grammy for "Jesus Walks," he had won a series of others for his own work, plus more for production and writing he had done for others. West had been included in *Time*'s 2005 year-end "People Who Mattered" issue and graced that magazine's cover on August 29, 2005. Finally, and arguably most importantly, West's solid entrenchment in various political skirmishes in wider debates over issues like censorship and minority and gay rights, in which he didn't so much choose a side as emerge from the melee unscathed by the right or left, marked him as a singular, accessible voice not only to the so-called hip-hop generation, or the under-thirty crowd, but to a wide swath of the American public.

He's a different sort of rapper, for sure. Counting flamboyant pink shirts and Gucci loafers among his eclectic wardrobe, he never played the hustler's game—not traditionally, anyway. He cites Roc-A-Fella Records' initial reluctance to take him on as a rapper, in spite of his obvious skills, as a product of this slick image, a direct opposite of the rough-hewn gangsta character of many of that label's rappers and the outgrowth of West's childhood, a relatively placid American life outside the black market economy of guns and drugs. What they didn't understand at first, West told *Time*, was that he "had to hustle his own way." He contends that life itself is a hustle—we all do what we have to do to get by. And somewhere therein lies his appeal. West emerged in a myopic age, when the number of bullets a man had taken seemed to represent the gauge of his possible success as a rapper. In the wake of the seemingly endless mythologizing surrounding the bullet-riddled corpses of Tupac and Biggie Smalls, West's contemporary 50 Cent, despite debatable skills as an MC, has ridden thug appeal to its apotheosis in his success. West redefined boundaries, bringing millions of fans with him in the process. WestABut his valuable critique of hip hop's contradictory cultural identity—his stance in opposition to homophobia, his antithug persona, his portraits of the women in his life as characters with more than a single dimension, and so on—was not only a critique. West managed via a complex strategy to at once deliver the contradictions in all their splendor. Rather than occupy a pulpit, he seemed to prefer the populist's strategy: He walks among his fellow travelers in the game, including his fans. His lyrics, though often quite personal, just as regularly proceeded from a point of view as theatrical as that of Andre 3000 of fellow genre-benders Outkast, in which he spoke from the heart, undercutting hip hop convention, and at once played the part of the MC as it has been traditionally known—as in the work of a genre-defying novelist, there's just enough separation between the two stances to render his message in the minds of listeners as simultaneously authentic, told from a singular perspective, and the product of a brilliant artist with an important agenda. He is unique in this light, in addition to being among the select company of Dr. Dre and Wu-Tang's RZA as an MC-producer to see success in both arenas simultaneously.

With two albums in the bag, by mid-2006 Kanye had played a prominent performative role in the hip hop feature film *Dave Chappelle's Block Party* and was working on his own film, a grouping of short stories linked by a central theme and backed by his music, with multiple directors overseen by George C. Wolfe (director of the erstwhile TV miniseries *Lackawanna Blues*). He was likewise working on a third in what he'd planned as a sort of tetralogy of records connected by an overarching scholastic theme. The first sees the protagonist dropping out of school to do things his own way. On the second he's back in; the planned third album sees his triumphant *Graduation*, to be followed hopefully by *A Good Ass Job*. The jury was out on whether West could sustain the wild success of the first two, *The College Dropout* and *Late Registration*, but he showed little sign of becoming complacent. His extreme self-confidence—many of his detractors called it arrogance and predicted it would be his tragic flaw—led him down a path toward either greatness or hubristic dissolution. But meanwhile his legacy with regard to the genre on the whole, still far from certain, was beginning to solidify.

EARLY YEARS

"My mama told me go to school, get your doctorate."
Kanye West, "Hey Mama"

Kanye Omari West was born June 8, 1977, to Donda and Ray West, then living in Atlanta, Georgia, the latter a former Black Panther and prize-winning photographer, the former an English professor who would find work at Chicago State University when Kanye was three. Ray and Donda, who had separated when he was eleven months old, would likewise split for good around that time, an event to have significance in their son's later musical output. Still, Donda describes Kanye's childhood as relatively serene and middle class, and says that from early on her son had an artistic temperament. He lived during his early years in the area of 79th Street and Lake Michigan on Chicago's south side but attended Polaris High School in an inner-ring suburb. Through it all, though, he remained connected to the city's vibrant hip hop scene, in which he met the producer-DJ No I.D., with whom he became fast friends, learning to sample and program beats after he got his first sampler at age fifteen.

No I.D. was working at the time with young rapper Lonnie Rashid Lynn, then known as Common Sense, who would go on to drop the "Sense" (after a dispute with a West Coast reggae group using the same name) and inject a fresh spoken-word-style poetic consciousness into rap music, a style and approach to hip hop lyricism that would come to be associated with Chicago. This style eschewed the growing gangsterism of the scenes on the East and West coasts and in the South in favor of style and content reflective of the lives of common people, also infusing traditional hip hop's repetitive beats and simplistic song structures with complicated rhythmic cadences and hooks worthy of pop songs, often sampled directly from them. But Common at the time was still a relatively unknown artist outside of the Chicago scene. Over the years, as Common's career began to take off, West worked out his production chops and became enamored of rising coastal rap stars of the mid-1990s, groups like Wu-Tang Clan and the Queensbridge, New York, rapper Nas, "people that sold records," he told *Vibe*'s Noah Callahan-Bever in a 2005 cover story. But Common's influence on West was clear as well. As No I.D. tells it, West was always on Common's case to let West produce beats for him, but the latter's headstrong nature prevented it from happening. West's youth and imitation of New York rhyme styles conspired with Common's arrogance to prevent the union from happening, but the two did enjoy a budding friendship, and on the part of Common a grudging admittance of the younger West's budding skills—the two even battled in 1996, at a time when Common was at the apex of his popularity. As Kanye says, "He knew that I had a spark lyrically, otherwise he wouldn't have let me battle him."

West got a scholarship to attend Chicago's American Academy of Art to study painting but shortly thereafter transferred to Chicago State University, where his mother taught, as an English major. But he also began to get a few breaks as a producer. Around this time, among his first major beats sold were to Chicago rapper Gravity and Bad Boy Records' Mase. His class schedule wouldn't allow him to devote the time to his production work he felt he needed, so against his mother's wishes he dropped out. This move would define the young man's future work. His first album as an MC, *The College Dropout* (2004), would be devoted to self-affirmation, the rapper-producer's life presented as a grand metaphor for trusting your instincts and living life your own way. His mother, Donda, told Kot, "It was drummed into my head that college is the ticket to a good life . . . but some career goals don't require college. For Kanye to make an album called *College Dropout*, it was more about having the guts to embrace who you are, rather than following the path society has carved out for you."

FROM BEATS TO BILLBOARDS

> "To all the hustlers, killers, murderers, drug dealers even the strippers."
> Kanye West, "Jesus Walks"

West stayed in the Chicago scene, coming together with locals GLC, Really Doe, Timmy G, and Arrowstar to form the Go Getters (working with local promoter John Monopoly), whose shows for a time electrified the Chicago club scene and eventually landed them airplay—of the single "Oh, Oh, Oh"—on local black music FM giant WGCI and other stations. The group also put West in touch with Craig Bauer's Hinge Studios, where most of the Go Getters' output was produced, and it would be from this base that West began to really extend feelers into the national scene. But it wasn't until he moved to Hoboken, New Jersey in 2001, across the Hudson River from New York City, that his career as a producer took off. In 2000 he'd done work from the Hinge base for both Lil' Kim and Jay-Z (a track on, respectively, *Notorious K.I.M.* and *The Dynasty: Roc la Familia*), but now his popularity soared with his work for Jay's record *The Blueprint*, whose release happened to coincide with the 9/11 terrorist attacks. Despite all, the album was something of an instant classic, particularly with the ubiquity of track three, "Izzo (H.O.V.A.)" (the single was a Billboard Top 10), which prominently included a sped-up sample from the Jackson Five's "I Want You Back." This technique of speeding up samples, which West adapted from Wu-Tang Clan's RZA, quickly became the young producer's signature. It marked a shift that followed trends in other genres away from electronics-heavy production and back to the earthy feel of 1970s music, in this case the soul that West and countless other up-and-coming producers knew as children. After the violence that marked 1990s hip hop and the subsequent oftentimes sharp-edged nature of the music, this approach to music making was bound to catch on. In a certain sense it harked back to the birth of the genre, as it relied on direct, earthy samples of vinyl records, imparting a soft-edged feel to the backing track, a fine contrast to Jay-Z's microscopic flow. Also, it introduced a significant crossover appeal with its use of easily recognizable samples on an album from a protoypical gangsta rap artist, cementing the gangsta subgenre fully in the mainstream—this can at least partly be attributed to West. Shawn Carter (aka Jay-Z) called the boy a genius around this time, and *The Blueprint* featured a host of tracks produced by West in addition to "Izzo (H.O.V.A.)," six in total and among them the seminal "The Takeover," the track that flamed the fires of Jay-Z's then-budding war of words with Nas and others among his competition. The track West worked up for "The Takeover," channeling hip hop's early giants Run-DMC and Grandmaster Flash, borrowed from a rock song, the Doors' "Five to One," an audacious move in and of itself that would inspire a mostly innocuous but clearly homagelike 2004 parody by Mos Def.

But all the while West's ambitions were to MC himself. At first, anyway, he was getting nothing but the cold shoulder from his pals at Roc-A-Fella Records, Jay-Z and Damon "Dame" Dash, who initially looked at the kid and saw a flashy joker without the authenticity required of marketable MCs in the then gangsta-dominated hip hop scene. But content or credibility wouldn't be long in coming. On October 23, 2002, it met him head-on in a car crash in LA that put West in the same hospital where Biggie Smalls died and nearly ended his life. This event spurred him on to make his own music no matter who said yea or nay, even if he had to quite literally rap through his teeth—his jaw was wired shut as it healed. A few days into the ordeal, still laid up in a hospital bed, he got to work, calling Dash at Roc-A-Fella and asking for a drum machine. A few weeks later, out of the hospital and back in the studio but with his jaw still wired shut, he cut "Through the Wire," utilizing the classic Chaka Khan hit "Through the Fire" on the backing track and rapping through the cage in his mouth about the entire ordeal, doubling the vocal track at times to compensate for his compromised flow. Still, the results employed what would become his trademark singsong style, with lyrics that spelled a narrative about the crash and convalescence at once harrowing, moving, and hilarious.

In the months following he worked out other tunes for what would become his debut, and after a tentative deal with Capitol Records fell through, he presented the demo to Dash and Jay-Z—also performing at a sort of private unveiling of the new material at a New York club—and won the two over. It wasn't simply a one-way affair, though. West's lyrics pay tribute to his admiration for and the advice and mentorship provided by both Jay and Dash over the course of preparation for the debut. *The College Dropout* was released in mid-2004, and "Through the Wire" climbed the charts as its first official single—though the feel-good party hit of the year, "Slow Jamz" (with Twista and Jamie Foxx), had been released well in advance of the album to generate buzz and had already become a smash. It was a hit across the nation for its multivalent voicing, synthesizing the crooning of Foxx, Kanye's soul-bap flow, and Twista's rapid-fire delivery. A longtime rapper on the Chicago scene, Twista languished in obscurity for over a decade, despite his flow earning him the 1992 *Guinness Book of World Records* plug as the "world's fastest rapper," before this collaboration with West catapulted him into the mainstream with a platinum-selling album, *Kamikaze*, featuring West's production (see sidebar: Fast Rappers).

Kanye and *The College Dropout* would garner eight Grammy nominations and win two, Best Rap Album and Best Rap Song for "Jesus Walks," with

---

Fast Rappers
Mickey Hess

Twista, who scored a hit with the song "Overnight Celebrity" in 2004, worked for over a decade to achieve the celebrity status that he gained with this single and "Slow Jamz," a collaboration with Kanye West and Jamie Foxx, which catapulted his 2004 album *Kamikaze* to platinum sales. Twista, who originally recorded under the name Tung Twista, was named the "world's fastest rapper" in the 1992 *Guinness Book of World Records*, but while the careers of other high-speed rappers such as Das EFX, Bone Thugs-N-Harmony, and Fu-Schnickens took off, Twista's sophomore album, *Resurrection* (1994), was relegated to the Chicago underground scene rather than MTV airplay.

With his 1991 album, *Runnin' off at da Mouth*, Twista's rapid-fire delivery set the stage for a new era of hip hop vocal style that moved away from the smoothed-out jazzy delivery of Rakim and the laid-back drawls of Too $hort and the Geto Boys. Rather than "rappin' to the beat" as Sugarhill Gang put it on hip hop's breakout hit, "Rapper's Delight," Twista rapped over and around the beat, with the tempo of his vocals sped up beyond the music. Big Daddy Kane, a fast rapper who preceded Twista, created a rapid-fire delivery that took hip hop vocals to a new level and would influence the styles of Twista, Eminem, and Outkast. Outkast, known also for the slow southern drawl of their vocals on songs such as "Ms. Jackson" and "Elevators," brought speed rap to singles like "Bombs over Baghdad." While speed rappers Das EFX and Fu-Schnickens built their rhyme styles from frenetic Jamaican dance hall routines, Twista's is distinctive in that it is both faster and more controlled. Busta Rhymes, known for his gruff vocals and dance hall-influenced delivery on his work with the group Leaders of the New School, began moving toward speed rap in a 1992 guest appearance on A Tribe Called Quest's "Scenario." By 1999, Busta had developed a faster and smoother vocal style for "Gimme Some More." The Eazy-E protégés Bone Thugs-N-Harmony, hailing from Cleveland, Ohio, developed speed raps that they combined with singing and harmony on songs like "First of the Month."

West sharing the latter with then little-known MC Rhymefest, who cowrote the first verse. West also shared a songwriting Grammy for his production work for Best R&B Song with Alicia Keys and Harold Lilly for "You Don't Know My Name," from the West-produced *The Diary of Alicia Keys*. In short, it was a smash year for the young rapper, then only twenty-seven.

The College Dropout was a commendable first effort, and for it West drew on the credentials he'd built up and contacts he'd made during his relatively brief tenure as a big-name producer, drawing cameos from Jay-Z, Mos Def, Ludacris, Jamie Foxx, and other A-list rappers and R&B singers, to build the last rung of the bridge between early hip hop's party music sensibility, the late-eighties political and social consciousness of acts like Public Enemy and De La Soul, and the nineties gangsta reportorial style. Track two, "We Don't Care," after a goofball intro by Cedric the Entertainer, is a satirical sing-along featuring a chorus with backing vocals by kids extolling the virtues of drug dealing to achieve a middle-class life. It was a strategy he was to employ to great effect across the record, which had the effect of anticipating catcalls and accusations of inauthenticity by in effect employing the double-edged theatrical sword of the satirist. "We Don't Care" at once examines and embraces something that is commonly portrayed in our culture as the first resort of the lowlife, and in the gangsta subgenre as the exact opposite, the be-all and end-all of dog-eat-dog ghetto life, raising orphans to the height of kings—but West struck a new pitch with equal parts humor and bile by humorously portraying drug dealing as a means to just getting by, a simple requirement of existence, just another job, driving audiences to both tears and hilarity. And not only traditional hip hop audiences. *The College Dropout* was admired by hardcore aficionados and suburban mothers, by high school kids and hip hop legends like Darryl McDaniels (aka DMC), who told *Time* that Kanye's "Jesus Walks" had interested him in hip hop again.

Indeed, "Jesus Walks" marked West as an artist of the highest caliber and quickly became for 2004 what "Izzo (H.O.V.A.)" was for 2001. It secured for West a reputation as a man fully prepared to embrace the contradictions inherent in all of our lives, not just those of the young rapper-producer on the make. West, particularly since his accident, sees God at work in his life, and "Jesus Walks" is as much a testament to this fact as it is a spiritual celebration of humanity's imperfections. Cowritten with fellow Chicago area-bred rapper and close friend Rhymefest (aka Che Smith), the song engages the hip hop world's aversion to spirituality in favor of hard-nosed street themes, but also it celebrates religion as a balm for the wayward soul. Rhymefest's part in the writing of "Jesus Walks" was significant. He alerted West to the Arc Choir sample that dominates the track. He also wrote part of the first verse, and he receives half the royalties from the single's sale. West's detractors seized on this as proof of his lack of abilities as a writer-MC, but Rhymefest told *Time* that Kanye developed the central themes of the song (Tyrangiel).

MYTHOLOGY, BACKLASH

> "But is it cool to rap about gold?"
>
> Kanye West, "Breathe In Breathe Out"

If appealing to the everyman defined the young rapper's goals from the beginning, and he began voicing the sentiment time and again in interviews, he certainly threw obstacles in his path toward realizing them. While West was filming the video for "Jesus Walks" celebrity prankster Ashton Kutcher, for an episode of his MTV show *Punk'd*, pulled off a stunt with a posse posing as representatives of the Los Angeles Film Commission, shutting down the shoot and confiscating the tape already shot on account of an invented rule about filming on Sundays without a permit. Kanye stole the tape back and tried to get away in a van before Kutcher appeared and the gag was up. Later that year, in November, at the American Music Awards West had been nominated in three categories. When he didn't win, passed over in the Best New Artist category for country singer Gretchen Wilson, he delivered a postshow tirade. Speculation reigned in the tabloids, on the Web, and in the music press about what he would do at the Grammys, and during his acceptance speech for the

Best Rap Album award for *The College Dropout*, he said, holding up his trophy, "Everybody wanted to know what I would I do if I didn't win. I guess we'll never know." Fans wrote it all off as endearing hubris, while critics scoffed. Meanwhile, certain hip hop bloggers were calling him gay for his high-fashion sensibility, among a host of other insults, one particularly over-the-top trickster calling himself "Bol Guevara" even having gone so far as to launch an ill-fated campaign to ban West from the Grammys. In Chicago, West's hometown, the hard-core scene flourished in reaction to his popularity. On the Web site of Molemen Records, the label and production unit anchored by the duo of Panik and PNS, chat boards posts with titles like "Kanye West is a sensitive fag" took issue with West's perceived hypocrisy with regard to his upbringing. On *The College Dropout*, West frequently shouts out to Chicago's South Side, a term commonly reserved for anything in the city limits south of Madison and east of Ashland. Though West lived most of his childhood in the city, his attendance at a suburban high school garnered mockery and gave rise to the false impression that he'd grown up outside the city. Said one post on the Molemen board, "not that there's anything wrong w/being from the burbs, as long as you don't scream 'South Side!' on every song." While such a sentiment is uncharitable at best and simply erroneous, the fact remains that West wasn't above the mythologizing that so often sells hip hop acts, despite his claims to the contrary. The final track on *College Dropout* was "Last Call," in which West capped the overall heteroglossia of the record with an extended narrative about his career, essentially telling the story told above—from Roc-A-Fella's early dismissal of West as an MC to the broken deal with Capitol Records to finally seeing the album through production and distribution. The intent seems to be an airing of grievances—West letting fans know that he holds nothing against his cohorts for dismissing him for so long—combined with jubilation at impending success. But the effect is to build a mythology around West, clearly a multi-talented artist, to imbue his simple skills with a sort of rags-to-riches, Chicago ghetto to East Coast stardom narrative—or one marked by the ever-bankable pull-yourself-up-by-your-bootstraps motif. The story was, at its core, generally true, but its exaggeration, like the hard-core gangsta posing of N.W.A.'s Ice Cube, served to create something akin to myth more than the true story of a man making his way in the world, something listeners could view not as an empathetic so much as an archetypal American story.

At the same time, West was gunning for his place among the great rappers, and seemed to want to be remembered as the man who gave us America as it was, the authentic representation. He took reporters to task for misrepresentation, for overmythologizing him. When commentators singled him out as unique in music for writing, producing, and performing the majority of his own tracks—breaking what sometimes seemed like an impermeable barrier in the pop hip pop world, with the rare exceptions of Dr. Dre and Wu-Tang's RZA—he typically responded by placing himself in a long line of producer-performers, including one of the greatest, Stevie Wonder. If Kanye's dual producer-MC role didn't mark him as particularly unique, the authenticity of the final product certainly benefited from it. West the consummate artist proved to indeed know best. As with the lyrical content of "Jesus Walks," the true artist in West wholly embraced the contradictions inherent in the producer-performer relationship. The act of creation for West became an exercise in self-consciousness. This quality does make him unique to the hip hop genre. Like the work of certain postmodernist playwrights and novelists who take the genre in which they work and their own creative processes and make them the very subjects about which they write, West's rhymes often lay bare the structure that underlies them, or take up the mantle of a hip hop convention only to expose the pose for what it really is at the same time. This schizophrenic style—though previously utilized in lesser degrees by lesser artists—has never been grasped and laid bare with so much exuberance, an achievement that showcases not only West's performative and production skills but his knowledge of the genre's history and conventions, and a fine sense of what life in America really is.

A *College Dropout* track called "Breathe In Breathe Out," about what West calls "ice rap," featured none other than iceman par excellence Ludacris on an absolutely frigid chorus, Ludacris shouting above a slow crunk-esque track a sort of pseudo call-and-response to himself, the very picture of the tough-man rapper on the street. And West sets up a grand contradiction in his verse, apologizing at once to Mos Def and Talib Kweli, the Black Star duo known for their meaningful verse (and one of West's early tours was with none other than Kweli himself, whom he went out with unpaid just to learn the tricks of the trade), for rapping about the same old stuff—cash, women, and rims—when he really wanted to say something with some substance behind it, then playing the part of the ice rapper straight up. He undercuts it all with self-conscious lines that expose the lie. The blogger Bol called this track "one of the better songs on the album," perhaps missing half of its satirical message, that the posing machismo of the hip hop community is empty and useless, at best a cynical put-on crafted to sell records, at worst mean-spirited and bigoted.

In his less theatrical moments on *The College Dropout*, West brings across a simple message. On "All Falls Down," another single, West tells the story of life in an America obsessed with material gain by comparing himself to a prototypical character—a young student whose eyes are opened to the uselessness of her college major and who drops out to work full-time as a hairdresser. The ensuing economic hardship—including all the useless purchases made along the way—West casts as a quintessential American story, putting it up next to his own experience spending way too much on watches and cars while ignoring what he really needs.

And in the end the naysayers were far outnumbered by the admirers the nation over. With his Grammys in the bag, the man kept his course, preparing for his next offering even while picking up production work for ever-higher-profile acts. His mother retired from her chair position in the English department at Chicago State and went to work for her son as his general manager. She remained proud and dedicated. West devoted a song to her on the next record, the much-ballyhooed "Hey Mama," in which he assured her he was going back to school. It was a metaphorical school, of course, but nevertheless she continued to be an inspiration and a source of comfort and pride for the young man.

ETERNAL RETURN

> "Ahh … the sweet taste of victory."
>
> Kanye West on Common's "They Say"

West amped releases from his new record label, G.O.O.D. Music, an acronym for Getting Out Our Dreams, putting out in 2005 both John Legend's R&B debut *Get Lifted* and Common's much-anticipated comeback, *Be*. Both were platinum sellers, were produced by West, and would see accolades of their own.

Legend was a sort of child prodigy pianist whose work with Lauryn Hill, Alicia Keys, and West himself, among others, was marking him as a talent to be reckoned with as far back as 1998. Kanye's production on his first solo effort launched him into the popular consciousness as a veritable star. *Get Lifted* was nominated for eight Grammy Awards and ended up winning three. And Common, who by now needed no more convincing of West's skills, allowed Kanye free rein on the production work for *Be*, and West contributed rhymes to a number of the tracks. West is credited by many with fully reviving the elder rapper's career. Common's previous endeavor, 2002's *Electric Circus*, was the prototypical "ambitious" effort, an album that unabashedly attempted to combine hippie feel-good mysticism and rock and roll with hip hop, with its Beatlesque cover art (most closely resembling the cover of *Sgt. Pepper's Lonely Hearts Club Band*) and flower-child song titles like "Aquarius," "Jimi Was a Rock Star," and others. Common remained without a new release until May 24, 2005, when *Be* debuted. It promptly garnered accolades, standing up well against *Electric Circus*. Where the latter had traded in expansive pseudo rock-anthem styles, West's tracks put Common back in touch with his roots in R&B, hip hop, and earnest spoken word. "They Say," a track on which both West and John Legend appeared, represented a perfect synergy between these elements—with a vintage West track utilizing a sample from Miles Davis pianist Ahmad Jamal and Legend's vocals to provide an old-soul feel, over which Common spun his free-form spoken-word rhymes, responding to criticism of his past efforts directly and, generally, making a triumphant return. "They Say" garnered a Grammy nomination for Best Rap/Sung Collaboration, and *Be* got the nod for Best Rap Album.

West and Common both were jubilant over the record, on the whole. West was understandably proud, considering his and Common's relationship going back to their early days in Chicago. West told All Hip-Hop.com, "I'm telling you right now it's five mics, five stars across the board. ... Common's album will go down in history" (Williams and Hope). Later on in the same story, Common slapped West on the back for his work in bringing him back to the basics, and a good piece forward at the same time, but still spoke to a great deal of the speculation then reigning in the press that West was the main force behind the album, saying, "Only I truly can bring back me, however he is helping me to create music that the masses and people can enjoy and love. ... I have to give credit where it is due. Kanye has been a big plus to my album and this new part of my career and that is why we are riding together." "He's not going back, he's going forward," Kanye said. "There are songs on there that only me and Common could have done together."

And in the end, *Source* gave the album four and a half mics—West bickered about it in the press a bit, but at that point his label was at least fully off the ground. That wouldn't be the end of an already great year for the rapper-producer. Both of his label's artists would be eclipsed in 2005 by West himself. His second disc, *Late Registration*, broke on the airwaves in summer with the single "Diamonds (From Sierra Leone)," a track whose lyrics, in a manner similar to that of "All Falls Down," laid bare a personal story while self-consciously engaging the political-cultural issue of diamonds borne of violent African conflict. But though "Diamonds" made a bit of splash for West as a track with strong content, it didn't break the Top 40 on Billboard's Hot or Pop 100 lists. It would be another track entirely, which appeared shortly afterward with the release of the album, "Gold Digger" (about women who chase rich men, in which West urges women to stay with their broke-slob boyfriends—the punchline being that even if they stay true their men are likely to leave them for white girls) that made the biggest waves, propelled by a bouncy dance beat and a cameo from Jamie Foxx doing Ray Charles's "I Got a Woman," as well as the occasional sample of Ray himself. The song was a runaway hit and climbed the pop charts to number one—ending its tenure there only after a lengthy ten-week run—by which time West had made an even bigger mark on the U.S. public.

POLITICS

"Who gave Saddam anthrax? George Bush got the answers."
                                                      Kanye West, "Crack Music"

By the advent of *Late Registration*, West's perceived authenticity, combined with his obvious ability to lure a public outside hip hop's traditional audience, was further marking him as the genre's most important artist. The album's release, after being repeatedly pushed back, happened on August 30, 2005, one day after Hurricane Katrina made landfall just east of New Orleans on the Gulf Coast. It was a manic day that would undoubtedly be imprinted in the minds of Americans for years to come, as the airwaves rocked with pictures and reporting from New Orleans, a city by the end of the day nearly 80 percent underwater. But just as Jay-Z's *The Blueprint* rose from the ashes of the 9/11 attacks, the New Orleans tragedy would ultimately buoy West's profile.

Earlier that summer, he had already entered the realm of political exchange with his participation in the Philadelphia event in the Live 8 series of concerts held globally to pressure world leaders at a then-imminent G8 summit in Scotland to, among other things, relieve the world's poorest countries of their debts. West risked a lawsuit from promoters of a previously scheduled performance to take part, and among the media hype surrounding the show, West spoke out about the African AIDS epidemic, endorsing the view that AIDS is a manmade disease foisted upon the world's poorest by its richest. The inflammatory comments, delivered to MTV News, caused head-scratching for many, and others, including various media pundits, seized on them to deride West's and the rest of hip hop culture's tendency to believe in various "conspiracy theories." West, as he's done with many different issues, would invoke his past, citing his parents as having taught him about injustice in the world—this issue was simply one of many, he said, for which he would work on behalf of those less well off in the world.

Two weeks before *Late Registration*'s release, West walked out on a host at Toronto's Flow 93.5 FM in protest of the station's bleeping of the phrase "white girl" on "Gold Digger." Before storming out, he was attempting to make his ire known on-air to the program director, and when the host, Hollywood Rich, wouldn't quit interrupting him, he shoved the table and walked out. Flow later stopped censoring the phrase.

Then on August 22, a week prior to the album's official release, MTV aired "All Eyes on Kanye West," West's spot in the well-known interview series. In conversation with Sway Calloway, West dropped a bomb on the heads of haters and the hip hop community in general with a forceful outcry against homophobia in rap music. West came to the issue in response to a question Calloway proffered about his mother's influence on his life. As with the African AIDS issue, Kanye's response was typical only in that he once again defied his audience's expectations. After West's parents' divorce, the young man saw his father at "Christmas, spring break, and summer," he said. Consequently, the majority of the time his mother was the figure on which he modeled himself. He said, "It gets to the point that when you go to high school and you wasn't out in the streets like that, and you ain't have no father figure, or you wasn't around your father all the time, who you gonna act like? You gonna act like your mother. ... And then everybody in high school be like, 'Yo, you actin' like a fag. Dog, you gay?'" West's response to this sort of treatment, he said, was to become the opposite—an overt homophobe.

"Anybody that was gay I was like, 'Yo, get away from me,'" he told Calloway. "And like Tupac said, 'Started hangin' with the thugs,' and you look up
and all my friends were really thugged out." But then he learned that one of
his close relatives, his "favorite cousin," was gay, and he renounced his views.
During the interview, he urged fellow MCs to stop their continual bashing of
gays. "I wanna just come on TV and just tell my rappers, just tell my friends,
'Yo, stop it fam'" (see sidebar: Hip Hop Homophobia).

It was a courageous position to take, in a world in which even Mos Def—
among the more socially conscious of rappers—flings around antigay epithets

---

Hip Hop Homophobia
Mickey Hess

Homophobic lyrics have existed in hip hop at least since hip hop's first
commercial record, Sugarhill Gang's 1979 single "Rapper's Delight," in which
Sugarhill calls Superman a "fairy" and compares his superhero costume to
pantyhose. Homophobia is rampant in lyrics, where MCs often assert their
dominance over competitors by feminizing them and calling them homosexuals, using terms like "bitch," "fag," and "homo" to emasculate them.

On August 22, 2005, Kanye West called for an end to homophobic insults in
lyrics. He suggested on MTV's "All Eyes on Kanye West" that hip hop's
treatment of gays as second-class citizens mirrored the treatment endured
by African Americans over the past century in the United States. West's
statements regarding being raised by his mother and adopting feminine traits
from her recalled the 1965 publication *The Negro Family: The Case for National
Action,* also known as the Moynihan Report, in which Senator Daniel Patrick
Moynihan suggested that an increase in female-headed households in African
American communities would feminize the young black men who grew up
with no father present. Moynihan's report remains controversial because of its
stereotypical depiction of African American families as poor and uneducated,
and because it undermines the accomplishments of black women by suggesting that they are emasculating their sons.

In hip hop lyrics masculinity equals power, and in rap battles MCs seek to
emasculate their opponents. The lyrics generated in certain gangsta rap beefs
recall male prison culture, where dominance can be asserted in sexual terms.
To be claimed as another inmate's "bitch" means that a prisoner can be
sexually dominated by that inmate. Many gangsta rappers, who embrace
criminal culture, reflect prison culture in their lyrics as they threaten to
sodomize their enemies. After Ice Cube left N.W.A. over what he considered
an unfair contract, the remaining members of the group recorded "A Message
to Benedict Arnold," in which they called Cube a traitor and threatened to
shave his head and sodomize him with a broomstick. Cube responded with
the track "No Vaseline," in which he threatened to sodomize Eazy-E in
retaliation. These threats didn't stop within the group. On "Dre Day,"

Dr. Dre threatened to sodomize Luther Campbell, whose song "Cowards in Compton," disrespected Dr. Dre and the city he represents in his music.

"Dre Day" also displays homophobia when Dre's partner, Snoop Dogg, claims that Campbell's mother is "A Frisco dyke." This type of homophobic name calling is common in hip hop lyrics. In his first two albums, Eminem frequently used the terms *fag* and *faggot*, yet claims that he does not intend the terms to be homophobic or hateful, but only to designate weakness. Eminem's detractors argue that the origins of these terms as disparaging slang for homosexuals give his usage of them the connotation that being gay equals being weak. In response to his critics, Eminem invited the gay British singer Elton John to perform a duet at the 2001 Grammy Awards. At the end of their performance of Eminem's "Stan," Elton John hugged the young rapper. The performance was boycotted by GLAAD, the Gay and Lesbian Alliance Against Defamation.

Works Cited

Moynihan, Daniel Patrick. *The Negro Family: The Case for National Action*. Office of Policy Planning and Research United States Department of Labor. March 1965.

Further Readings

Constantine-Simms, Delroy, Ed. *The Greatest Taboo: Homosexuality in Black Communities*. New York: Alyson, 2001.
Harper, Phillip Brian. *Are We Not Men?: Masculine Anxiety and the Problem of African-American Identity*. New York: Oxford University Press, 1996.
hooks, bell. *We Real Cool: Black Men and Masculinity*. New York: Routledge, 2003.
Majors, Richard, and Janet Mancini Billson. *Cool Pose: The Dilemma of Black Manhood in America*. New York: Touchstone, 1993.

on his records, and the blowback was extreme from certain quarters: Rumors circulated, for instance, that West himself was gay. His ode to his mother, "Hey Mama," didn't help matters: Various critics pointed to it as further proof. In early 2006, West addressed the issue with *Rolling Stone*'s Lola Ogunnaike, "I knew there would be a backlash, but it didn't scare me, because I felt like God wanted me to say something about that."

A week after "All Eyes on Kanye West" aired, the *Time* cover story had West deliberating the use of the word *nigger* in his music (Tyrangiel). He described his attempt to negotiate its use in the chorus of the song "Crack Music," on *Late Registration*, by saying "homey" instead, which he felt didn't have the same effect on his listener. Another week later, after *Late Registration* had hit stores and Hurricane Katrina had done its work on the Gulf Coast, it was anger and frustration that moved West to make his most visible political pronouncement of the summer. He joined comedian Mike Myers for a spot on NBC's "Concert for Hurricane Relief" benefit on Friday, September 2. The comedian followed the teleprompter, but West, visibly nervous, deviated from the script, saying in a halting, near-breathless voice, "I hate the way they portray us in the media. You see a black family, it says, 'They're looting.' You see a white family, it says, 'They're looking for food.' And, you know, it's been five days [for many stranded families, waiting for help] because most of the people are black. And even for me to complain about it, I would be a hypocrite because I've tried to turn away from the TV because it's too hard to watch. I've even been shopping before even giving a donation, so now I'm calling my business manager right now to see what is the biggest amount I can give, and just to imagine if I was down there, and those are my people down there. So anybody out there that wants to do anything that we can help—with the way America is set up to help the poor, the black people, the less well-off, as slow as possible. I mean, the Red Cross is doing everything they can. We already realize a lot of people that could help are at war right now, fighting another way—and they've given them permission to go down and shoot us!" West referred to developments at the time—widespread reports of violent looting, snipers shooting at Coast Guard helicopters from New Orleans roof-tops, and other incidents—that were cause for National Guard soldiers to be issued a directive to shoot if fired upon. The reports later proved to be wildly exagerrated or simply wrong: In moving testimonial after testimonial on the radio program *This American Life* and in other venues, eyewitnesses debunked the tales of rape and murder at the convention center and other reports of lawlessness, largely validating West's indignation.

After West's deviation from the awards-show script—the comedian Myers now completely ruffled but determined to follow the teleprompter to the letter—West's eyes darted back and forth as he waited for Myers to wrap up. When he did, he passed back to West, who then delivered a line that would sit in the minds of Americans for weeks to come: "George Bush doesn't care about black people."

The network's monitors, who routinely watch the live feed (typically run-ning on a several-second delay before broadcast) for obscenities to bleep, didn't realize West had deviated from the script because he hadn't used an obscenity, but by the time he delivered this last line they'd been well in-formed, and Myers only got out "Please call" before the broadcast cut to comedian-actor Chris Tucker, who continued with another scripted message. In a half-triumph for free speech, NBC only cut West's comment about the president from the later West Coast feed, but the damage was done. As personal messages and media reports echoed around the land, it would be that line that resonated; and with it, the conscience of a nation reeled.

West joked about it, after a time. In a later conversation with All Hip-Hop. com, the rapper said, "Like honestly, right now I was eating some chicken and [if] I had choked on this chicken bone right now people would never hear the end of it. I can have no honest death now. I can't go out in the street, trip and bump my head [because] people would be saying 'They put special government grease on the floor!' If anything, [the government] would want to try and keep me as safe as possible" (Williams). But at the time he was dead serious, and as if in response, the next week "Gold Digger" began its reign on the pop charts, followed by Kanye's third single, "Drive Slow" (see sidebar: Drive Slow: Hip Hop and Car Culture), and *Late Registration* sales skyrocketed.

Reactions to all these developments were widely varied. The usual suspects among his detractors accused West of simply being provocative in order to boost the profile of his new record. Some seized on "Diamonds (From Sierra Leone)" and its two versions on the record in an attempt to neutralize the

---

Drive Slow: Hip Hop and Car Culture
Mickey Hess

Kanye West's 2006 single "Drive Slow," featuring Chicago's GLC and Houston's Paul Wall, fits into a long tradition of hip hop songs about cars, cruising, and sound systems. In 1988, Seattle's Sir Mix-A-Lot released "Posse on Broadway," a song about cruising down the strip in Mix-A-Lot's "home away from home," his Mercedes Benz limo. Sir Mix-A-Lot parodied his own use of cars as a status symbol one year later, with the 1989 single "My Hooptie," which described his backup vehicle, a car with mismatched tires, a broken stereo, a dragging tailpipe, and a broken bumper. Mix-A-Lot explains in the song that his hooptie is reserved for when his Benz is at the mechanic. Like "Posse on Broadway," LL Cool J's 1990 single "The Boomin' System" is devoted to exalting the pleasures of driving around, bumping his music. Masta Ace's "Jeep Ass Nigga" (1992) defiantly calls out police for harassing black teenagers for playing their car stereos at high volume. LL and Masta Ace focus more on describing their sound systems than their cars, but the act of cruising is what links these hip hop songs together. From New York's Jeeps and Land Cruisers to LA's lowriders and 1964 Impalas to the Dirty South's Cadillacs, hip hop music is made for the cars as well as the clubs.

Releases such as Masta Ace's *Sittin' on Chrome*, Three 6 Mafia's "Riding Spinners" and "Swervin'," and Mike Jones and Paul Wall's "Still Tippin'" all speak about wheels, rims, and customized cars. In 2004, West Coast rapper Xzibit became the host of an MTV series, *Pimp My Ride*, in which he takes old, broken-down cars and has them customized for their owners. The technicians at West Coast Customs, the car shop featured on the series, often add televisions, video game consoles, and other electronics to the vehicles. In-car televisions are a status symbol for Paul Wall, who mentions them on Kanye's "Drive Slow" as well as on his guest verse on Three 6 Mafia's "Swervin'," another song devoted to cars and cruising.

The link between hip hop, cruising, and car culture has led to problems at events like Atlanta's Freaknik festival, which took place each April during Black

College Weekend (also called Black Spring Break), and drew upward of 250,000 people. Freaknik ended in 2000, after the city of Atlanta experienced gridlock and increased criminal activity during the event. Cruising is also an issue for Louisville's Kentucky Derby and has overworked that city's police department in an attempt to control traffic, drug use, and assaults. In Louisville's West End, Derby cruising can involve an estimated 200,000 people, and in 2000 led to 158 arrests. Cruising became such a draw on the city's resources that year that city alderman promoted a free hip hop concert at the Louisville waterfront, intended to draw fans out of their cars and away from their West End neighborhoods. The concert plans fell through because of security concerns, and the tradition of Derby cruising continued through 2006, when Louisville imposed a formal ban on cruising.

---

force of Kanye's ascendant political engagement. The more politically inspired of the two versions, the first on the album and featuring a guest spot from Jay-Z, was not the single that was released. The single's lyrics, while clever in spots, showed West simply responding to the various criticisms that had arisen in the wake of *The College Dropout* and the various awards show fiascos. The first version on the album, though, was a direct engagement of Americans' (and West's in particular) fetishizing of the gemstone and the subsequent violent conflict the fetish has fueled in African countries. The verses are peopled with children missing limbs and Kanye agonizing over his Roc-A-Fella chain. It was a prototypical display of West's double-edged approach to hip hop lyricism. Critics accused him of acquiescing to the music —or, worse, the diamond—industry and, worse still, theft: Chicago MC Lupe Fiasco freestyled over the track during a session with West, resulting in a mixtape track called "Conflict Diamonds," and certain critics questioned West's authorship of his own take.

But as a testament to the prevailing opinion, in *Slate* Hua Hsu called him "Hip-hop's Hamlet" and lauded him for his injection of conscience into the spirit of pop music. Hsu also noted West's many flaws, pointing out that *Late Registration* worked for much the same reason *The College Dropout* did, thus making it something of a repetitive endeavor, its most powerful songs soliloquies about moral contradictions, the central one being the same materialism versus authenticity theme addressed in "All Falls Down" and other tracks on *Dropout*. But Hsu left no doubt that West's record was the best-sounding thing to come across the pop transom in a long time, though he attributed that to the rapper's sharing production credits with Jon Brion, renowned for his work with Fiona Apple and other rock acts, whom West admired for his ability to sweeten up tracks as a producer with real instrumentation. On "Diamonds (From Sierra Leone)" Brion added a haunting chorus of strings to darken the mood of the track. He made possible Maroon 5 crooner Adam Levine's vocal on "Heard 'Em Say" and overall he lent years of experience to young West's bombastic studio energy. Seemingly following his albums' educational motif, with *Late Registration* West was indeed back in school.

As on *The College Dropout*, there was something for everyone on the record. As evidenced above, West's winking, self-conscious swagger was in full effect on tracks like "Gold Digger" and "Diamonds," but he'd taken it all to a significantly higher level of intensity. Where *Dropout* had been slightly giddy in its youthful exuberance, *Late Registration* was more sober, downbeat, dark, and morally focused if eclectic. On "Heard 'Em Say," the opening track, the rapper riffs further on the notion that AIDS was invented to oppress communities of color and engages the hypocrisy of America and the first world's elite. The pose struck is of an embattled yet proud American telling his story to an unreceptive audience. The overall mood of the song, with Levine's melancholy guest vocals, is soulful and almost mournfully contemplative. Then there's the searing "Crack Music," with its dark strings, propulsive beat, symphonic backing vocals, and tough message. The lyrics riff on an archetypal hip hop trope, as of course the "crack" of the title is the eponymous narcotic and the extended metaphor depicts hip hop music as both borne of and a remedy for addiction and the trials of life in general. On this song, West waxes overtly political as well, again picking up an old notion, or conspiracy theory, that crack cocaine was introduced in black communities by the American government as a way to temper the inroads the militant Black Panther Party had made there—along with certain more contemporary topics, such as the hypocrisy of American foreign policy ("Who gave Saddam anthrax?"). "Crack Music" rose above the kind of reportorial gangsta chronicles of pushing rocks of the days of yore—the song's overall approach is to exist through engagement of Jay-Z's "bricks to billboards" metaphor for West's rise to stardom as a monument, or a memorial of sorts, a look back at the truth of the history of hip hop as a genre. West's aggressive tone and cadence are sufficiently exaggerated to create a kind of presentational or narrative distance from the material at hand.

Finally the symphonic, uplifting "We Major"—featuring a guest spot from another of West's idols, and one of Jay-Z's enemies, Nas—though equally rich production-wise, turned lyrically on a sort of spiritual exultation at generational and personal success. Anticipating Jay-Z's possible objections to Nas's inclusion on the record, as West told Sway Calloway, he went out of his way to make the song "Jay's favorite song on the album. ... When you hear the horns on 'We Major' and you hear the chorus come in and you hear Nas, that could like warm somebody's heart. Good music can break through anything and maybe start to break down the wall between two of the greatest MCs that we have." Indeed, at a New Jersey concert Thursday, October 27, that very year, Jay brought Nas onstage to bury the hatchet. "This is for hip hop," he told the crowd.

The whole of *Late Registration* had a greater continuity of sound than West's previous effort, and he capitalized on every opportunity to pack the lyrics with more serious stuff than that on *Dropout*. The end result is a record that communicates a fantastic range of American experience. The obligatory skits, too, made a more cohesive picture than the occasionally, some said, bizarre antieducation rants on *Dropout*. The idea behind them was a bunch of broke dudes banding together to form a fraternity—Broke Phi Broke—to celebrate life without money, a world outside of the material American culture. The men share a single pair of pants and take pride in giving up their girlfriends to the guys with cars—they can't afford to buy gas, anyway, much less a vehicle. Kanye, of course, is a charter member, but by the last of these skits he's begun cheating, making beats for cash on the side. He gets caught with a new pair of shoes and is then summarily admonished by the group's leader. Again, West brazenly embraces a contradiction at the core of contemporary American life: the need to belong, to fit in, with your fellow humans versus the Darwinistic mad grab at material things, success in the latter being the very definition of success in our culture.

But Hsu was right in saying that *Late Registration* operated on the whole in a manner very similar to *Dropout*, as the record is infused with this singular embrace of contradictory impulses and is very much about West himself. It remained on Billboard's best-seller charts for months; even as the Grammys approached, in late January 2006, it stood at number twenty-nine, having been out for over five months. The record had garnered nominations for Album, Record (for "Gold Digger"), and Rap Album of the Year, plus five others, including nods for a couple cowriting and collaborative credits on songs by Mariah Carey, Alicia Keys, and John Legend. Legend, whose debut was released by Kanye's own label, garnered eight nominations himself. West was in top form, telling *Rolling Stone*'s Lola Ogunnaike in that magazine's cover story one week prior to the event, "Don't ask me what I think the best song of last year was, because my opinion is the same as most of America's. . . . It was 'Gold Digger.'" Ogunnaike went on, "Just to be clear, he would also like the Album of the Year Grammy, thank you very much." In a moment of seeming humility in the piece, West disavowed his nomination for Best Rap/Sung Collaboration, for his work on Common's "They Say," only to then admit, "Not to sound arrogant, but how was 'They Say' nominated over 'Heard 'Em Say,' and how was that song nominated over 'Gold Digger'?" (The last featured Jamie Foxx in Ray Charles mode, be reminded.)

LEGACY

"I'm tryin to right my wrongs"

Kanye West, "Touch the Sky"

Meanwhile, back in Chicago, in West's wake the scene crawled with major-label scouts looking to scoop up the next talent. Molemen MC Vakill's *Worst*

Fears Confirmed (though an indie release on Molemen Records) was being highly touted in both the alternative and mainstream press. Rhymefest (who cowrote "Jesus Walks") had nabbed a major deal with J-Records, an Arista imprint, and his debut, *Blue Collar*, was scheduled for a 2006 release. Bump J and Lupe Fiasco (who guested on "Touch the Sky" on *Late Registration*) had both also been scooped up by major labels. The perception of Chicago's scene lived on, now even in the minds of its principal participants. Indeed, much of what little local resentment appeared with West's success had died down, and his hometown seemed proud. But though his presence was felt via his continuing production work with local MCs, West was long gone, renovating a loft in Manhattan and building a sort of dream headquarters in California. In Ogunnaike's *Rolling Stone* story, West introduces the journalist to his home-in-progress in the Hollywood Hills. But as Ogunnaike portrayed him, West is ever on the move, working till the wee hours in the studio on his next offering, even as the Grammys approached to recognize his endeavors of the past year.

The cover image of that issue of *Rolling Stone* ignited a firestorm of both criticism and glee, as it featured Kanye done up in caked-on fake blood and wearing a crown of thorns—tagged of course with the hackneyed headline "The Passion of Kanye West." Fundamentalist Christians, predictably, derided it as sacrilege—dedicated fans couldn't praise it enough. The *Village Voice*'s "RiffRaff" blogger Nick Sylvester struck a note between the extremes and took both Kanye and *Rolling Stone* down a peg for disingenuous marketeering. "Beyond the fact that ... there should be a moratorium on 'The Passion of X' headlines, ... can we talk about how *boring* this cover is?" Sylvester wrote. "How far a cry from the truly 'shocking' *Rolling Stone* covers, be it the naked Lennon/Ono, so tender beyond the thrill of glossy flesh, or the Chili Peppers cocksocks one, which was just sorta funny? Here the shock is so transparent, the board room meeting and aha! moment so needlessly vivid, so too the night they opened up the 'Kanye Jesus' issue boxes and saw the cover and started laughing, hee fucking haw, about what they were about to *do* to the American public." Kanye West's over-the-top self-image and the projection of said image onto the American public seemed to have lost a bit of its crucial authenticity in the hands of the national media. After his numerous political pronouncements of the previous summer—and the ubiquity of his tracks on mainstream radio—West was perhaps suffering from overexposure. In the article, he defended himself partly (likewise attempting to explain away his braggadocio) by saying, "In America, they want you to accomplish these great feats, to pull off these David Copperfield-type stunts. ... You want me to be great, but you don't ever want me to say I'm great?" The blogger Bol, meanwhile, had taken to calling him "The Fudge."

This appropriately contradictory climate followed him into the February 8 Grammy Awards show at the Staples Center in Los Angeles. West was scheduled to perform, plus he'd been nominated in eight different categories, including the coveted Album of the Year and Record of the Year (for "Gold

Digger") slots. The man arrived dressed in white from head to toe, and later gave a spirited performance of "Touch the Sky" and "Gold Digger," refraining from using the word *nigga*, as he has several times in the past on television. Injecting an element of theatricality into his performance, West dressed as a high school marching band drum major leading the procession. He was playing by the rules again, but perhaps it was too late. *Late Registration* lost out in the Album of the Year category to U2, and Record of the Year went to pop-punk outfit Green Day. West did garner three awards, in total—in various rap categories, including Rap Album of the Year—though many interpreted it as industry backlash to his rocking the boat just a little too forcefully over the previous year. Nonetheless, his after-party was purportedly the place to be, and he basked in the glow of youth and fame. And if he resented not winning in the big categories, he mostly held his tongue that year. As if anticipating young West's ire, Bono, U2's lead singer, when accepting the Album of the Year award, said, "This is our second 'album of the year,' but we've lost two, *Achtung Baby* and *All That You Can't Leave Behind*, so we know how it feels—Kanye, you're next" (Caro).

Critical prediction had indeed favored *Late Registration* to win in the Best Album category. The *Chicago Tribune*'s Greg Kot, writing just three days prior to the awards ceremony, pointed out the impossibility of a critic or an association sifting through this morass of material, but went on to describe a coherent convergence of opinion around *Late Registration*. The *Village Voice*'s well-respected Pazz & Jop poll, a nationwide critics' poll, had West at the top of the list for best album for the second year in a row. Kot's choices well reflected the nationwide sentiment, though he presented skepticism about West's actually winning.

Almost a week later in the same paper, Mark Caro looked back at the awards through the comfortable lens of a little bit of time, comparing Pazz & Jop Poll winners from years past to their Grammy counterparts and coming to similar conclusions—rarely do the two match up. Even so, Kanye West, with two Pazz & Jop top slots in a row, seemed to bear out another trend, that of critical lauding portending commercial and hence Grammy success. As Bono suggested in his shout-out to the rapper at the awards show, it was only a matter of time.

See also: Jay-Z, The Native Tongues, Dr. Dre and Snoop Dogg

WORKS CITED

Bol Guevara, "Ban Kanye West from the Grammys." 27 August 2005. byroncrawford.typepad.com/kanyegate/.

Callahan-Bever, Noah. "Kanye, Common, Legend: Too G.O.O.D. to Be True!" *Vibe* 14 June 2005.

Calloway, Sway. "All Eyes on Kanye West." MTV. 22 August 2005.

Caro, Mark. "The Pop Machine: U2 vs. Kanye revisited." ChicagoTribune.com. 13 February 2006.

Christian, Marqena A. "Why Everybody Is Talking About Producer-Turned-Rapper Kanye West." *Jet* 31 January 2005.

"Concert for Hurricane Relief." NBC. 2 September 2005.

Hsu, Hua. "Hip-Hop's Hamlet: The Fascinating Contradictions of Kanye West." *Slate* 8 September 2005.

Kot, Greg. "The Grammys Just Don't Get It." *Chicago Tribune* 5 February 2006.

Kot, Greg. "Rapper's Rise: From South Side to Top of Charts." *Chicago Tribune* 11 February 2004.

Mehr, Bob. "Who the Hell Is Vakill?" *Chicago Reader* 27 January 2006.

Ogunnaike, Lola. "The Passion of Kanye West." *Rolling Stone* 27 January 2006.

Reins, Dan. "Common: *Electric Circus*." *SF Weekly* 18 December 2002.

Sylvester, Nick. "Riff Raff: Kanye West on *Rolling Stone* Cover, Tasteless?" VillageVoice.com. 24 January 2006.

Tyrangiel, Josh. "Why You Can't Ignore Kanye." *Time* 29 August 2005.

Williams, Houston. "Kanye West: 'Ye Day: It's a Celebration'!" Allhiphop.com. September 2005.

Williams, Houston, and Clover Hope. "Common, Kanye Talk 'Be'." Allhiphop.com. 1 April 2005.

FURTHER RESOURCES

Allmusic.com. Kanye West Artist Page. http://www.allmusic.com/cg/amg.dll?p=amg&sql=11:3amsa9ugi23h, 7 July 2006.

Brown, Jake. *Kanye West in the Studio: Beats Down! Money Up! The Studio Years (2000–2006)*. Phoenix: Colossus Books, 2006.

Kanye West: College Dropout—Video Anthology. Roc-A-Fella, 2005.

Kanye West Official Site. www.kanyewest.com. 7 July 2006.

SELECTED DISCOGRAPHY

College Dropout. Roc-A-Fella, 2004.

Late Registration. Roc-A-Fella/Island Def Jam, 2005.

Late Orchestration: Live at Abbey Road Studios. Universal (UK), 2006.

Let 'Em in: An Interview with DJ Premier

Shamika Ann Mitchell

Formerly called Waxmaster C and born Christopher Martin, super-producer DJ Premier is often lauded as one of the top two hip hop producers of all time. There is very little that cannot be said about his achievements and milestones. For one, he has had the privilege of working with New York City's elite MCs: Rakim, Big Daddy Kane, Kool G Rap, KRS-One, Notorious B.I.G., Nas, and Jay-Z. He is also considered a remix king, having produced tracks for artists such as Mary J. Blige, Craig David, and the Black Eyed Peas. His love and passion for the culture keep him quite busy; he has a prolific career that spans over two decades and features over 500 album credits to date. Furthermore, he is one half of Gang Starr, one of hip hop's most innovative groups. As if this were not enough, in addition to establishing his own record label, Year Round Records, DJ Premier owns HeadQcourterz Studio (formerly D&D Studio), which is a landmark in New York City hip hop history. With new projects constantly on the horizon and more wrongs needing to be corrected in the hip hop world, DJ Premier often maintains a pace that would lead the seasoned ultramarathoner to collapse from exhaustion; yet he has no retirement plans in the works. Born March 21, 1966, the recently-turned-forty-year-old b-boy is still in love with hip hop and remains loyal to his muse. Always official in his b-boy stance, the world has proven to be DJ Premier's oyster. Here is what keeps him going.

You first put beats together in 1989, while using an SP12, but how did you learn about production?

Listening to the records that intently. I've always had a good ear for music. I took piano lessons when I was in the second grade and you know how boys are, "That's girlie stuff," so I quit and stopped doing recitals and all that. I played sax in the band when I was playing football in high school, but I couldn't march with the band because I was on the field. Even that, learning about notes and measures, it's crazy because I never cared but now I see how it applies. Working with Christina Aguilera, she's like, "Hey, I wanna do a B-section and a bridge." I knew what a bridge was, but what was a B-section? So she explained it to me, but at least I knew measures. She had asked me what key we were in and I told her G-sharp. I know keys and all that and even if I didn't learn all that, if I didn't have piano lessons, I still listened intently to what made all the stuff come together. I wanted to know what each sound was and who was playing it. When it came to a drum machine, when all the records were a hard drum sound, I tried to pick that apart. The 1200s didn't sound like the record. Since they sampled, I started to take those sounds off those records: the kick and the snare and the high hat and then, work around that. Once I started hearing other artists do it, like Marley Marl with the drums, that's when I got it. I catch on to things fast anyway. Once you show me a couple of times, it's in memory. Then I can take it to a greater level.

I read that you said hip hop is your Viagra. Do you still feel that way?

Yeah. It's all about representing us as black people. Making black music that represents us and the struggle. I saw hip hop start from day one, you know, I'm forty years old, so I have an understanding of the culture and where it's grown from. Being that it's growing from the streets of New York, I don't ever want to see that element die because it did a lot for me to make a career and make me a bigger person. Because of that I don't ever disrespect it. I have a respect for music that other people don't—they just listen to it and buy whatever's popular. Whereas me, I've always been a person who makes my own judgments on what I think is good through my upbringing and my family and again, being around the culture from day one. I'm from Texas and I used to stay with my grandfather in Brooklyn back in 1973, '74 when hip hop was just starting to grow, way before records were made. All those elements still go back to the streets of New York City and the ghetto, and most people in the ghetto are predominantly black and they're struggling hard to maintain. Even if you look at how Harlem is now slowly but surely starting to become less culturally oriented with our own kind, it comes to us having a hold on something we can call ours.

My accountant, God bless her, before she passed away, she always used to say, "Shop in the black neighborhoods," "Bank in the black neighborhoods," which I still do. When she died, I still followed that. Again, it takes nothing away from my white friends or my Asian friends or other people that I'm cool with, but I still make sure that I stay grounded on knowing who I am and what my people are going through.

Hip hop is definitely the same situation, you know, the right hip hop, not all the garbage out there that's got everybody confused. For the most part, all that is combined in the way I'm thinking. That's the reason why I don't ever, ever, think that I do it wrong. I always strive on doing it right based on how I was taught. I have a lot of heroes that made me want to do it. As a consumer and a fan—which I still am—and as a DJ it's my responsibility that I rep it right, so I stay in the mind state every time I go into the studio to bang out.

Let's stay on this race consciousness theme for a second. I read somewhere that you enjoy reading black literature and that you attended Prairie-View, a historically black college. How does your race consciousness have an impact in the music you create? How does it become black music for you?

With hip hop, it's automatic. The style of dress, the way we dance, all of that, even our slang, everything was created brand new from this culture and from the parties that was rocking during that era. When I was a child and didn't have hip hop, I had Stevie Wonder and Gladys Knight, Aretha Franklin, Grover Washington, Al Green, Curtis Mayfield, the Jackson Five, James Brown, Rufus, and Chaka Khan. I had all of that as a child, and again, this was pre–scratching and mixing and cutting, pop and locking and doing windmills. I used to do all that. I used to battle all the kids in my neighborhood. One of the bigger kids was Harvey Williams, who played for the Oakland Raiders. He used to come down to the parties in the black tux and the white gloves, and he used to do the moonwalk better than Michael Jackson. I recently ran into him after damn near twenty years, and I'm telling him about me starting up my record company now, and he is saying, "Yo man, I still got a little money. If you want me to throw some of my NFL money into the label, let me know." I told him he has to hear the music first and he's like, "Man, if you're doing it, I know it's great because you always kept it raw. The stuff we came up listening to, you still keep it like that. I already trust you." For somebody to say that, when I'm talking about borrowing a million dollars from somebody and they're not even wanting to check the product first to see they're not making a bad investment, that makes me feel good on the strength that he respects what I've done to keep this thing going. Again, respect is what makes the whole thing complete for me because [without it] then it's fake, and I just can't stand fake anything.

You talk a lot about your past. In looking back, how would you classify your career thus far?

I'd classify it as highly successful. That's minus the finances, just on the love I get from all the people I looked up to in the business that I wanted to like me, told me that I was great. From Rakim to Big Daddy Kane to even KRS-One.

The people who matter.

Yeah. EPMD, like when I was still buying their records and everything. When they told me that they were feeling everything I was doing and they wanted to get with me in the studio, I felt like I had made it. I didn't worry about the dough. I always knew in my early days, even when I was doing funny stuff in high school and my mother found out I was dealing—she never caught me—but word got around, I always knew that the financial part of it will kick in as long as you're busting your ass. That's something my father instilled in me, to always have a good reputation, make a name for yourself and always be responsible, which although I did not do it in the beginning—the responsibility part I was worst at—but as far as making my name known I was always a go-getter. I think it comes from my mother and my father combined because they're both in their late seventies now and they don't sit around. They still travel. My mother just had a major knee surgery—her second one—and she's already going on another trip. She came to my birthday party. She came to New York to see me and I took her to Jay-Z's place to eat. She's into, my whole family's into sports where my mother can tell you about the draft and really talk it like the way fellas chop it up. Not just the basics. She can talk everything from tennis to basketball to track so all that ran in our family, but music was definitely number one. I do consider myself one of the great ones. I consider myself a hall of famer. I got a nickname—instead of Mean Joe Green, I call myself Mean Joe Preem.

Well, since you consider yourself one of the great ones, one of the issues that I've seen with people is that once they get to that level, people start pushing them into retirement. What is left for you to accomplish?

I want to do films, in regard to directing. I've shot a couple of videos. I directed the "Full Clip" video for Gang Starr back when Big L passed away. That was the first one I ever shot. I'm into editing anyway because to me editing and doing pictures and putting music together—I want to do soundtrack work because all that to me is like music with just pictures. Being that I mix down all my records anyway, I can do it with visuals, getting the right actors, casting the right things, it all will turn into what I want it to be before I release it. I'm like that with my music at this point anyway. You know, if it's something I record in the studio, even if I got a lot of money from the artist, I don't let it leave the studio until we're both happy. If they're happy with it and I'm not, I'm not letting it go. I don't care if I have to write them a check back or whatever. It has to satisfy me before it leaves the studio.

Do you consider yourself a perfectionist?

Oh, without a doubt. Definitely.

Well, I guess it has to have your seal on it, right? "Reputation is the cornerstone of power" [quoting a tattoo on his forearm]; your reputation's on the line with every track you do. Is that how you see it?

Yeah. And I put my own self under that judgment. I know how to step outside of myself and listen to a record that I worked on. I know how to listen to it and judge it with an open mind instead of saying just because I did it, it's great. I don't sweat myself like that. I think I am great, but I don't think everything I do is incredible. So, I step outside [of myself] and with an open mind, I'll play a record two, three, sometimes even four or five times in a row just to be sure it's ready to go. If it's still got me like that, then it's a go. No matter what critics think or how they judge it, I know it's right because I know how to listen to hip hop music. I know how to listen to music period. I know how to judge the greatness of it and the wackness of it. That's just from my respect for it and my knowledge and the history. My knowledge of the history of music in general is very, very vast. I'm really good with these game shows . . . um . . .

Trivia shows?

Yeah. I'm real good with that.

Since we're talking about the qualities and characteristics of your music, I'm paraphrasing, but I've read that you have a passion for women, food, and watches. Of the qualities and characteristics that you find appealing in those things, what translates into your music?

All of them. The women-side thing is the feeling side. Because I aim to please in all aspects. I was very close with my sisters while growing up. They taught me about women, how to kiss. One is four years older and the other is two years older. We all used to do things together, until they went to high school and started dating. I'm still very, very close with my sisters. I'm real, real close with my oldest sister. She's the illest. Food . . .

Yeah. Your love of ice cream and cookies. I don't see anything sweet in the music you create. It's very aggressive.

I'm a dessert fanatic, so ice cream, cheesecake, cookies, warm brownies, all that stuff. All of that is something that you crave and I crave music just as much. So, I mean, I don't think about the desserts when I'm making the music, but the craving—I have to satisfy that.

And watches? What about watches manifests itself in your music? What do you go for? Breitling? Rolex?

I had a Rolex years ago because as a kid I always saw that logo over on Thirty-fourth Street over by the Tourneau store. From seeing that logo I said I wanted to get one. I started getting more into watches when some friends of mine—they owned the studio I worked at, which was D&D—they were best friends with this watch dealer from the Diamond District. He used to have all these nice watches, Bertolucci, Baume & Mercier, Tag Heuer, and so I started getting into the craftsmanship of it and the mechanics. I'm into cars and working on engines. Me and my brother-in-law are building a truck right now that I'm doing from scratch. All I have is a frame. I'm buying everything, all brand-new parts. My brother-in-law is an electrical engineer, but he builds transmissions and everything. So all of those things keep me going. All of that stuff.

Your music is supposed to be for everyone, it's supposed to be for the common person. So when I read about your affinity for these things, I'm thinking, watches like Seiko? Especially because, if you made music that was so exclusive and for a select population, it wouldn't be you. And I understand that you keep yourself very humble.

Without a doubt. Definitely. I've been with so many people in the business who have completely changed. On all types of levels. People I knew when they got their first jobs working at a record company, and I ran into them at Jay-Z's *Reasonable Doubt* after-party. I was cursing them out—I'm not a troublemaker, but they were not letting me holla at Jay. They said, "Only you, but your manager has to fall back." I'm like, "Yo, I produced on that album. I was part of that whole jump off." My manager went to junior high and high school with Jay. He knows who he is. Jay was cool, but the people handling the access to him were being weird. I see all these other people in there—Jadakiss had like ten people and he's my dude. But all these people in there who didn't work on the album. I did and I can't even bring one person. I know they'll be apologetic, but whatever. They think they're bigger than what they are and a lot of executives are the reason why the music is getting worse. Then they wonder why the sales are going down. They're the reason why the sales are going down because most of them want to be famous like us. Their position is to work to push the product and now they are all playing that "I wanna be a star" game with the shades in the club, who's got the biggest chain, the biggest watch, like crazy. It's just bugged out how all these people changed in the last couple of years. And these are the same people who are saying how the music should sound now. I'm like, "Damn, when's the last time you was even in the street?" I was hanging the other day with gangbangers and I didn't see you. You can't even walk down that same block. So it's outta control. I call these executives at these labels murderers. Straight up. The radio station people, all that. They're all murderers. They get no love and respect from me. I'm gonna continue to stay that way so I can keep away from all those negative energies.

In the same vein, regarding programming directors and industry executives, you've openly criticized radio DJs and commercial mixtape DJs for abandoning the tradition. What are some aspects that you feel are overlooked?

Being that hip hop originated in New York City, it should always be the capital of having the roots of it still exist on a big scale with the commercial stuff that's more popular. I have nothing against Lil Jon, Paul Wall, all that stuff. I won't make that type of music, because I am the traditional style. It's cutting and mixing. The DJ was the major part of the rhyme back then, because the MCs would talk about "my DJ Jam Master Jay," Mixmaster

Ice from U.T.F.O., and Roxanne came out with Howie Tee—the DJ was always the focal point.

It was DJ Jazzy Jeff *and* the Fresh Prince.

Yup. On top of all that, it has to exist in order for the culture . . . if you don't keep that part going, it's going to bow out eventually. So someone has to preserve that part of it. With Sirius Satellite Radio, they let me do it the way it's supposed to be done. If I never heard the mix shows with Marley Marl and Red Alert, they way I heard it back in the early eighties, maybe I wouldn't be doing what I do. But I heard it that way, so when I learned how to cut and scratch and mix, I was like, "All right, I got it." And they were breaking records. It wasn't about taking the check. I mean, if you pay for respect, you're fake anyway. Most of these people are paying for their respect of getting their record spun. You know, payola always existed but when it comes to hip hop, even if you do it, I guess do whatever you do. But when it comes to a mix show, every single DJ has to play whatever songs are on that list. It doesn't even sound authentic and the thing is, a mix show means that you mix your style for two or three hours, then the next person comes on and they do their style. The way it is now, it's two or three mixes back to back, they all have to play what's on that list, tacked on the wall. Even if they put two or three unheard-of songs, they still have to pick at least ten to fifteen songs out of that list. Their job is on the line. If we were bolder, if we grouped together and said, "Nah, it ain't going down like that. You ain't gonna do our culture like that," then we could lock it down and make them follow the rules of how it's supposed to be. But everybody's more worried about their check and their job and all the benefits of getting into the concert free. Their whole mind state basically is, "I gotta suck a dick." This is mainly aimed at the men. The women, you know, they suck whatever they gotta suck, but more so toward the men because they talk slicker on the radio, and their mouths are full of something they shouldn't be chewing on.

Now, you talk about preserving the culture. I attended a recent show of yours in Brooklyn and the crowd was predominantly Anglo and Asian. It was a huge turnout and a successful show, but who owns hip hop now? If it's about the need to preserve the culture, it seems that they are the population, or am I mistaken?

No doubt. The reason why they're the population now because once something blows up out of our culture, white folks are always going to embrace something that's fresh and new. We're that intriguing as black people anyway. So when it comes to the shift in the crowd, it is a little weird to see less black people involved in it. But we have short attention spans to where once it's out of our hands we either let it go or privately wish for things to be right again.

With me, one of the ways that you bring it back to being correct is that you gotta aim your music toward what's missing. Ghetto people are missing. I welcome all races to come into our world and to enjoy the music—that part isn't even a problem. I don't care if I'm the only black person in the room, that part is cool. In order for you to grab your own people back into it, you have to have stuff that they can relate to that makes them say, "You know what? I wanna get back into investing in this." Most of the stuff is so really, really watered down, you can't relate. I can't relate to a lot of the garbage that's out here now because it's like, every day ain't a party. I mean, there's nothing wrong with escaping and keeping your mind off the stresses of the day, but the music came out of hard times. You still have to address the matters at hand. We still have a lot of issues that's messed up with our people and someone's gotta speak on it to make sure it gets corrected. The hustlers and gangbangers on the street are more hardheaded, so I aim my music at them so they can get right. They are the future. Most of our black males are getting killed off, so I know in order to hit them, I have to speak their language. In order for them to really enjoy the stuff, what I do is keep it as raw as possible. It's gotta be so hard-core that they're like, "Yo. This is what I'm spending my money on." I'm trying to restore that and again, some artists should be preserving the history—they do it with rock and roll, they do it with jazz—hip hop's the only one that says once you hit your thirties, you can't rap no more because you're too old. Why are we letting this happen? I had to be on a mission so that once other people do it, it will change things around.

You call some pop-rap "garbage" and "watered down." What is real hip hop? Who determines the criteria?

Real hip hop is dedicated to those who know how to listen to it and for those who appreciate every aspect: the graffiti, the DJing, the rapping, the break dancing, and the fifth element, which is beatboxing. All those elements and the style that made it so good has to be appreciated. The guys appreciating it are my age from forty on down to late thirties, or the ones who got to see it develop from its early stages to where it is now. We're the ones that I aim it to. I don't care if it's only ten people that really liked "real hip hop." That's cool because we can all get together, start a whole movement from scratch and turn it into something. But I've seen more than ten people appreciate the artists that I appreciate, without having to be influenced by just me. Just on their own judgment, they know that Brand Nubian is great, A Tribe Called Quest and even Gang Starr, Cold Crush and Run-DMC, I'm not really concerned with the people that don't care about it. In order to build a foundation, you have to recruit small and then go big, so if we have to start from zero, then so be it. I never tried to push this culture on people who don't really care for it. Even if they listen to the stuff on the radio, being that it's getting less and less pure, that's why the sales are declining. People take it for granted that there aren't a lot of real people out there. There aren't a lot of real people left, so the percentage that exist, we don't want the stuff that we're hearing now. We want something else.

So you don't want the "tinkerbell" sound?

Never. It doesn't go with our format. You know, create another type of music.

In another interview, you've said that just because someone's rapping over it doesn't make it hip hop.

Exactly.

Okay. So the fact that someone contemporary, say Nelly Furtado, has teamed up with Timbaland. That's considered hip hop.

That's a good pop record.

What about Justin Timberlake and Pharrell?

Good pop record.

What about the boundaries determining what's hip hop and what's not? Does it box hip hop in and give it a limited definition?

In order to love hip hop, no matter where you come from, I don't care what generation, you have to have an appreciation for the people that opened the door for you. No one cares about the Rakims and the Big Daddy Kanes of the world, and they are so vital to the culture. If we don't include them as being appreciated, it's not gonna live long. Now that the money has been a bigger issue of keeping it going, no one cares about the history. If it doesn't generate money, no one's really concerned. Me, I'm always concerned because without the stuff that existed before, we wouldn't have what goes on now.

History and context are important for you. Is that what keeps you inspired to keep making music? Are you out to save hip hop from itself?

Without a doubt. I'm going to keep preserving, keep it going. I love what it did for my family, for my friends. I was able to get houses. It kept my boys off the block, outta jail. Keeping it raw kept them outta jail, so they can do what they do. Get money and feed their families. I know for fact, from experience, that this is what I'm going to continue to do in that aspect of keeping it true to the art form. So there's no other way I can do it but that way.

It sounds like you have a serious love-affair with hip hop.

Definitely.

This love affair that you have, it doesn't sound like it's going to be over anytime soon. Retirement's not on the horizon?

Not at all. I'm gonna do this forever. When I see all these artists like Prince, U2, and they're still touring. Shit, the same thing applies to hip hop. You just have to respect it and have knowledge of it. All that has to go into the mix in order for it to be authentic. That's why to this day, if Whodini never makes another record, their history is better than most of the artists who sold 10 million. They're the Rolling Stones, the Led Zeppelin of our culture.

Are there any past or present producers who you feel don't get enough recognition?

Rick Rubin.

Should these people have icon status? What producers do you feel deserve mention?

Definitely Marley Marl, definitely Rick Rubin, definitely Larry Smith, who worked with Orange Crush, Run-DMC, Whodini, and Kurtis Blow albums. Howie Tee ... these are people in the early stages, so you gotta give it up for them. They were doing it. Large Professor did a lot of work on the Rakim album but he didn't get his credit. Of course Dr. Dre is a hall of famer. Of course me, Pete Rock. Alchemist hasn't reached it yet. He and Havoc are great, great, great producers. I wouldn't put them in hall of fame status yet. I'm a big fan of theirs. When it comes to hall of famers, I gotta give it up to the old timers because they were doing it when it was still new and fresh and hard-core. With no money and hard-core. The money came and everybody got lazy and softened and sweetened up the music. It's like putting cream in the coffee. I don't drink coffee like that but when I do, always, me and my father, we always drink it black.

Are there any producers on the upswing? In the past, you've mentioned Kanye West, Havoc of Mobb Deep, Nottz, Marley Marl, Alchemist ...

Definitely Kanye, for bringing back sampling. I like Just Blaze, he's really dope. He's really good with the sampling. He's very unique and knows how to pick a sample and put it into a jillion pieces and make it just bananas. So I gotta put him in the rankings. I like 9th Wonder, Nottz from the Teamstaz ...

Of course, J. Dilla.

J. Dilla, man. Shit, I can't even explain how great he was. He's a chop master. Also Showbiz from Showbiz and AG. He's another great, great, great producer. He made "Sound of the Police" with KRS-One. He did "Party Groove." You know, people like that.

I notice of all the people you named, you didn't mention any women because there are none. Missy Elliott kind of qualifies as hip hop because she raps. Based on your criteria I'm not sure if ...

She's hip hop.

Okay. So then Missy is the only female hip hop producer right now. There are no other women at the boards now, are there?

Cocoa Shanelle is on the come-up with doing production. She's starting to do it more now. But Missy has more experience. I gotta definitely give Missy hers because there's no women producers that are on a big scale.

Well hip hop's always been a man's world, so I guess our time is coming.

Oh for sure. I'd never turn my back on it. I don't discriminate. It's an open-door policy. Let 'em in.

Word Up: An Interview with DJ Scratch

Shamika Ann Mitchell

Not all DJs and producers can say they were discovered by the hip hop music industry moguls Russell Simmons and Lyor Cohen, but for DJ Scratch, it was just one part of a story that is twenty-three years in the making. Born George Spivey, the thirty-eight-year-old Brooklyn native has experienced more in his career than most in the hip hop industry can dream of. Not only is he a renowned battle DJ, but he is an equally successful producer. The walls in his recording studio are so heavily laden with gold and platinum plaques that scores of others remain without a nail or proper hanging or are simply hidden from public view. His resume includes being the DJ for legendary rap duo EPMD, touring in 1988 with Run-DMC during the pinnacle of their career, being the tour DJ for Jay-Z, and having a rare opportunity for an extended set at each show. Scratch is also a resident DJ for a popular New York City nightclub and has a hit single, "New York Shit," with rapper Busta Rhymes. While talking about his career and his perspective on the hip hop industry, Scratch's realness as an artist becomes evident. As an advocate for innovation and originality, Scratch has no love for biters, the sucker DJs who strive for success on the backs of others' efforts. His style is authentic; often imitated but never duplicated, Scratch is in a league of his own. The following is a sampling of what makes him an iconic figure who has inspired countless others to get behind the turntables and mix things up.

Congrats on your current hit track, "New York Shit" with Busta Rhymes and Swizz Beatz. Other than being hip hop's birthplace, what makes New York City rap special?

What makes it special is the wordplay. New York always tries to find the slickest way to say anything. For example, a rapper from a different region, say the South or the Midwest, they're very simple with the wordplay. You know, New York is always slangy. We slick talk. We're city slickers. So, for example, a rapper from the West Coast might say, "My pockets stay fat." It's some slang, but New York always gotta say it the flyest. So instead of saying that, we might say, "My pockets stay nine months."

That's also Brooklyn though. That's very Brooklyn.

That's definitely Brooklyn. I'm a Brooklyn dude. But you know, New Yorkers are the slang cats.

Do you think that because New York is cosmopolitan, the lyrics should be more complicated?

It's just the way it always is. It's just common talk. We talk different from anyone else in the world. Once you go through any tunnel, or any bridge that leaves out of New York [City], the accent has a southern twang, even from Jersey on down.

Speaking of New York rap, I've read that Grandmaster Flash was your hero. Who is your hero right now? Who is your inspiration?

I am. I don't have anyone to look up to right now. I'm my inspiration now because, back when I used to look up to Flash, when I first met Flash, I told Flash that he was the reason I became a DJ. Through the years of being with EPMD and ten years after that, DJs come to me and say the same thing I said to Flash, and I never really paid attention to it. A few years ago I was like wow, I'm these kids' Grandmaster Flash, like how Flash was to me. So I'm my own inspiration. Now I inspire myself to still be in the game this long, because people don't be in the game this long and be consistent. Somebody might've had a record ten years ago, disappear and then resurface, but it's only three people, well really two, who have been consistent from day one until now: me and LL Cool J. We've been consistent and current and relevant to the game nonstop from then to now.

When did you start? When would you say your starting year was? When was "then"?

Man, my "then" was like three years after LL maybe, '87, '88. LL was '85.

That's a long time.

Even before '88 I was touring in '85 and '86. . . . I'd been around the country.

But not with . . .

Nah. Not with any groups. I went around the world before I even got with a group. . . . I traveled the world with Run-DMC. Before I got with EPMD,

I had traveled the world. My first major, major tour was overseas, so when I toured in the United States, it was nothing. I was roughing it overseas, taking showers at the venue and all that, so when I got here, the tour buses are different, there's bunks—it's like mini-mansions on wheels.

So by '88, '89, you were already seasoned. You had already earned your stripes.

I was seasoned, yeah.

Let's talk about EPMD. Now, Erick and Parrish did a lot of producing, but you produced for them as well. You didn't start seriously getting behind the boards until they split in 1992. Why the transition?

Because I had time to, actually. With EPMD, we were on tour like four, five months out of the year. Every year I was down with them. . . . So to be on tour for two months here, then go home for a week, then go on another tour— that's back when the touring business was really crazy, and good with hip hop —there would be tours all the time. Every season there was a tour and EPMD was on every one of them. So I didn't have time to do anything else. When I come home, I just want to be in my bed, be with my family . . . home-cooked food. That's it. I didn't think about beats or anything else. After the break I had time.

You said you weren't thinking about any beats. How did you learn to put beats together?

I'm just self-taught really. I was making beats before I had a beat machine or anything like that. It's this thing old-heads know. It's called pause-looping. The first beats I was making was pause-looping.

So you learned through trial and error?

Yes. Everything in this game you learn from trial and error. There's no school of hip hop. Well, now there's schools to learn how to DJ, but back then everything was trial and error. There's still no school to learn the business of it.

And the analog? Why do you prefer analog over digital?

Analog because of the sound. Digital is great too. I use digital, but digital is like a computer and computers crash. You might work all day and the computer just crashes. You don't have that problem with analog.

What about the quality of the sound?

The quality of analog is better. With hip hop, analog is the better sound. When you go digital, it strips down elements. Like, when you're going with a bass line, it strips it down. Analog is as pure as you record it.

What's the sound for you? I know it's heavy bass.

Yeah. My sound is like, damn near Jamaican yardie. You know, like reggae music. Bass lines hard like reggae music. Hard drums, smacking snares. Heavy bass and hard drums, that's my sound.

Do you consider yourself a hip hop producer or a music producer?

I'm a music producer.

What about sampling? Is that crucial for you? Do you have a particular formula?

My formula really is that I start with the drums. If I'm making a track, if it's R&B, or hip hop or whatever, my formula is the drums. Everything goes around the drums.

In a prior interview, you said that you still dig in the crates. In literature, Ahab had Moby Dick and Jason had the golden fleece. In hip hop, Bambaataa was looking for the perfect beat. What's your elusive record? Do you have one?

I just found my elusive record like two months ago. "I Can't Stop," the album version, it's a breakbeat. The John Davis Orchestra. The album version. I just found it. Two copies, fresh!

How does one even get an elusive record? Do you hear something and say, "I must have that"?

Yeah. It may be something you heard someone else play or you might've heard it on a movie or on a commercial. If I want it, I'm going to do everything to get it.

I've heard people say that the producer and DJ get no love compared to the front men. Fresh Prince got more love than Jeff; Rakim got more love than Eric B. Why is it harder for a hip hop producer or DJ to get recognition?

You just said it. Because they're the front men. The person with the mic is the one that's gonna get heard. If there's two people seen, the one that's getting heard is going to get the most recognition. We're behind the scenes. Like watching the TV show *Three's Company*—people know the stars but nobody's gonna know the producer for the show, the behind-the-scenes person. Even though he's getting more money than everybody, he's not making appearances on the show.

Is it a thankless job to be behind the scenes? Unless you want the shine ...

If you want the shine like that, you'll be the person on the mic, the person in the video, talking and performing. You usually never hear the DJ speaking unless you're at a concert, but you always hear the rapper speak.

Even though the DJ could've put the whole song together. So people love the song but don't necessarily love you.

Right. Some people want the shine.

Like Kanye.

Right. He wants the shine. But people who usually strive for that shine get in trouble for some reason. As long as my paperwork is correct, that's all I care about. I'd rather be behind the scenes. I have to show my face now, but if I shine now it's because of what I'm doing, not because I'm reaching.

You mentioned that most pay more attention to your DJ accomplishments than to your success as a producer. Flash inspired you to DJ, but who are some producers that inspired you?

Marley Marl, Premier, Pete Rock, Easy Mo Bee, King of Chill—another slept-on producer who was part of the group Brooklyn Alliance—Large Professor, J. Dilla, the Beatminerz. Those are my inspirations.

All hard-core hip hop for the most part.

Yeah. That's all it was. I respect and acknowledge the hands-on cats.

Earlier you said that you consider yourself a music producer as opposed to a hip hop producer. Why the distinction?

Well, people just put tags on everything. I say I'm a producer period. I can do different types of music. You have to show your versatility. I do that in every field. The same thing I approach with my DJing, I try to approach with my producing. With my DJing, I feel that every DJ should know how to scratch with both hands and most DJs don't. They can scratch really good with one hand and the other is just okay. If you're a DJ, you need to know how to do all sectors of DJing. If you're a battle DJ, you need to learn how to DJ in the club; you need to learn how to DJ in a concert. With producing, if you started out with hip hop, you need to branch out because it broadens your talents. If you're just a hip hop producer and, say, Celine Dion wants to hire you for a track, you gotta be able to know how to do that shit. Of course she's hiring you for the work that you do, but you still have to be familiar and broaden your shit out. You can still have some grit, but [have] some Celine Dion shit too.

What about radio DJs? Is that another component of DJing or is that something separate?

I don't really consider radio DJing as a different sector. Mix show DJs are just playing songs—you're not really pleasing the audience. You can play them any order you want but they're still gonna listen.

Even if there's scratching and cutting?

Yeah. It doesn't really require any certain skill when you DJ on the radio. You're not playing for an audience right in front of you where you have to please them and make them dance.

Because they'll leave or go to the bar.

Right. When you're DJing on the radio, you're relaxing. DJing on the radio is like you're on vacation. But when you're DJing for the actual consumer and they're right in front of you and you have to please them, or you're at the concert and you've gotta please 20,000 people or you're in a club and you've gotta please 1,000 people, that's when you're in the field, you're working.

Part of your career was that project the School of Turntable Arts. What's that about?

DJ tutoring. It's not like the Scratch Academy where you have a bunch of different DJs teaching people. These people are learning straight from me, not from my students, an apprentice, or colleagues. They're learning directly from me, the way I taught myself how to DJ.

Is it still running?

Yes. I think it's better. I think it's cool for business how the Scratch Academy runs because it makes a lot of money. I'm just doing it on the love of it. I know that shit sounds corny, but if I wanted to learn how to DJ, I'd want to learn from my favorite DJ or one of my favorite DJs. That is the shit right there. When you're taught something, you're not usually taught from one of the people that created the shit you wanna learn ...

Like taking basketball classes with Michael Jordan.

Exactly.

You mentioned the Scratch DJ Academy, which was cofounded by your late former mentor, Jam Master Jay. Also, the Berklee College of Music has a turntable technique course that has the longest waiting list on its campus. One can even take a class on break dancing and b-boying. What's your opinion about hip hop's official mainstream status and the interest it generates?

Everybody wants to do this hip hop. I just say, "See? I told y'all," because not too long ago corporate America wasn't messing with hip hop. Period. R&B wasn't even messing with hip hop. R&B was disrespecting hip hop, now R&B can't survive without hip hop. R&B hits have a hip hop beat with some strings on it and most of the time a rapper's featured on it. It's the only way it survives now. R&B is totally different, it's hip hopped out, it's diluted with hip hop. Corporate America, everything they market is hip hop, whether it's from break dancing or some type of DJ on a Burger King commercial. Even the Flintstones are dressed like Run-DMC. Everything is marketed around hip hop because they know this music is the biggest-selling music. It went past country, it went way past rock music, and this is the way that you reach the youth. For corporate America, it's about money.

After winning the New Music Seminar Battle for World Supremacy DJ Championship in 1988, you had the privilege of having Jam Master Jay as a mentor.

While on tour, we became cool and he would just give me advice about being a concert DJ. I was a raw battle DJ. I would show him tricks and routines and he basically converted me from a battle DJ to a concert show-man. He gave me advice all the time on tour, like what to do. I would just watch them, watch what he'd do. So when I got down with EPMD, I became Jam Master Jay because they weren't using vinyl. They used a half-inch reel —this was before DAT machines—I'm like, "Nah. Y'all gotta get rid of this tape machine. Y'all gotta get all the vinyl and whatever y'all don't have, you gotta get pressed up. We gotta do this shit like Run-DMC." That's what it was.

Who do you mentor?

I mentored a lot of DJs. We had a DJ camp and were just running a boot camp for DJs. Me and DJ Clark Kent. We would just snatch DJs from off the street, train them, and turn them into legends. We made legends. We created legends, like DJ Plastic Man, DJ Richie Rich. These were DJs we taught from the streets, brought them into Clark's basement and just showed them differ-ent routines. Now they're legends. We created legends. So those two. I was Spinderella's mentor, Cocoa Shanelle, DJ Mocha, DJ June currently. I was a mentor to a lot of cats. I've been in the game a long time so people always wanna pick my brain.

You began DJing when you were a boy of eight. Thirty years later, you're still making music. What's your motivation?

The longevity and just seeing the changes from day one to now. It's crazy. And businesswise, when people come into this hip hop music business, you don't come as a businessman. You learn how to become a businessman through trial and error.

Well, it wasn't much of a business when you started.

Yeah. It was a business, but we didn't know anything about it. Melle Mel, Grandmaster Flash and the Furious Five, the groups that made the first rap records, like Kurtis Blow ...

I'm talking about before then, when people just made tapes of house parties, copied and sold them.

Yeah. It wasn't much of a business then.

Now Sugar Hill Records ...

Right. That's what I'm talking about. The people who were recording on Sugar Hill Records and Enjoy! Records, they didn't get a dime. They didn't get the publishing. Artists right now still don't know their business. There's artists right now that don't get royalties. Don't get publishing. Don't know anything about it. So coming into this game, you have to learn the business. No one comes into this as a businessman—everybody that comes into this business gets jerked until you learn the business. If you don't learn the business, you're gonna be broke, basically.

So is the business aspect another part of your inspiration? Trying to help people to understand?

Yes, definitely. I hate to see people get taken advantage of.

If there were a DJ Scratch recipe, it'd be: one quarter battle DJ, one quarter concert DJ, one quarter producer, and one quarter party/club DJ. Is there one component you enjoy the most?

Concert DJ, because it's crazy when one person, not even a rapper, can make 20,000 people—male and female—scream from something he's doing with his hands and not with his mouth.

Since we're talking about hands, Grandwizard Theodore invented the scratch thirty years ago. Since then, a lot has developed in turntable arts. What are your contributions to the history of the craft?

My contributions are the best scratches ever recorded in the history of hip hop, recorded on songs like "So Whatcha Sayin'," "Rampage," "Funky Piano." The best scratches on record. Groundbreaking, like when I did the scratching on "So Whatcha Sayin'," no DJ was doing scratches like that on record. When I did that, it changed the whole game. Some of the illest, the best DJ tricks of all time, like "Friday the 13th I'ma Play Jason" ...

Did you ever do the handcuffs live?

Yeah, but that wasn't something that would make somebody never forget that forever. There's patented tricks that the whole world knows me for. Like the pulling my pants down routine, the "Your Pants Are Sagging" from "The Scenario." I have a video clip of it on my MySpace page. Um, taking off my shirt while I'm scratching at the same time, that trick. Picking up the turntable. Cutting with my private parts, that trick. A lot of body tricks that I came up with. A lot of my routines ... I've got so many routines that I'm known for. So my contributions are those routines that I just mentioned. I was doing innovative scratches, innovative routines.

Let's talk about the turntablism lexicon. We've already mentioned the scratch. There's also backspinning, cutting, the scribble, the blend, the uzi, and there's mixing. Has anyone been credited for those?

Backspinning is basically called clockwork. If the break is at twelve o'clock, and the record starts playing, you backspin it to twelve o'clock. I think Flash is the person who did that first. Everything else I don't know, but a lot of DJs do be putting their names on things they didn't create, which is a circus right now. There's a name for every little scratch and everything, which is crazy because if that was the case I would own a lot of it. . . . Everything else is just the basic fundamentals of DJing.

Other than you, the X-ecutioners, Q-Bert, and a few others, turntablists aren't given much popular exposure. In the past, you've mentioned Howie Tee, Mixmaster Ice, Barry B, and Grandmaster DXT, and you also mentioned Cutmaster DC earlier, as some of turntablism's unsung heroes. Are there other artists—past or present—that you feel deserve mention?

DJ Cash Money is one of the greatest DJs of all time. Everybody knows that but he doesn't get the shine that he deserves. DJ Cheese from Jersey. Grandmaster Dee from Whodini . . . damn . . . there's so many . . .

Well, the sung heroes we know about. But turntablism as a subculture makes it harder for artists to make the transition into a broader audience. What about LL Cool J's DJ?

Nah. He was never really a DJ like that.

Well, it was that one song, "Jack the Ripper" . . .

That wasn't him doing the scratches. That was DJ Bobcat, another unsung hero.

What?!

No disrespect, but everybody knows that. Cut Creator was never a DJ like that. He just spun the records. He couldn't scratch. Bobcat was the one doing it. Like the song "Go Cut Creator Go," that was Bobcat, because Cut Creator couldn't scratch like that. No disrespect, but the DJ world knows that. Cut Creator, he had the flyest name. . . . Um, DJ Joe Cooley from LA, DJ M.Walk who was Tone Loc's DJ, he's another dope DJ.

Of the battle DJs out right now, are there any who have potential icon status?

No. There are currently no DJs who inspire me. Now DJs are doing—everybody's doing the same thing. Nobody's doing anything original, so it's at a standstill. Everybody's just doing what they see on the DVDs. This term *turntablist* is like the term *rap*. I think Babu created that. It's all DJing to me, whether you're a battle DJ, a concert DJ, a club DJ, or a radio DJ. Battle DJs are turntablists. Nobody has stuck out to me. They're all good, but nobody's stuck out and has done something I haven't seen before. Just something different. I wanna see who's gonna take this shit to the next level.

With two turntables, two vinyl discs, and a cross-fader, how much more inventive could someone get?

The sky's the limit. Back when you was just backspinning and catching the record, which was considered turtle slow, back then, you was fast as lightning. Then the era with Flash and Theodore, they would catch a record every four bars, then DJs like me and DJ Cash Money and Mixmaster Ice, were catching every one second. So in Flash and them's era, they were fast as lightning, until we showed that we can be faster. Then, that whole eighties where the whole record doesn't play because we're going so fast. It's like, now, with the new kids, beat juggling got popular. Beat juggling's when you take two records and make a different beat out of it. We did that in the early eighties, we just never put a name on it. One person claimed that they created it and everybody ran with that. It's cool but that stuff had been a long time ago. In the eighties, we never put a name on anything. We never named scratches, we just did it. Anyway, the beat juggling thing got popular and that's all that's been going on since '94. Twelve years and it's still the same thing. Who's gonna take it to the next level from beat juggling?

Since we're talking about the craft of DJing, please share some details about your documentary project, *So Whatcha Sayin'.* **Is it all about you?**

Yes. Exactly. It's celebrating over twenty years in the game. Everybody knows my name, but everybody doesn't know my face. People rarely hear me speaking. You're gonna see things you've never seen before. There's rare footage from back during that EPMD reign. It features everybody I've worked with, artists that I produced for, artists that I DJed for.

When's your anniversary?

I don't have a particular date.

How long do you think it's been?

Definitely over twenty . . . about twenty-three [years]. I'm basically doing it because I've been in a lot of books about hip hop, a lot of DVDs and videos and all that. They ask questions but you can't tell my story in five minutes. You can't tell it in one paragraph. There's a whole lot and like I said before, there's only two people who've been in the industry this long and consistently, me and LL Cool J. So if someone wants to know about my story, it's gonna take a while to tell it, and I'd rather tell it than have somebody else tell my story.

And tell it honestly, right? You're not going to paint this picture of yourself . . .

I'm talking about good and bad. It's gonna be about me of course, but there's gonna be lessons in there also, and advice, and also paying homage to DJs that never get mentioned in these documentaries. A lot of these DJs, they're doing these DVDs and they don't even have common knowledge about certain DJs that put in the work in this game. A lot of people don't know where this comes from. When you ask them, "Do you know about the beginning of this shit? Do you know hip hop?" They say, "Yeah, I know Kool Herc. Kool Herc started it." Then they skip past the whole eighties, which was the most exciting era, the best in hip hop.

Yeah. You get left out. Red Alert gets left out. Mister Cee ...

Yeah. It's crazy. Cutmaster DC, I mean c'mon. He was cutting with basketballs and ten-speed bikes and shit. Like DJs don't know anything about that. They go from Herc, Flash, skip past everybody else, then go to the X-ecutioners, Q-Bert, to DJs of today. They skip past the whole eighties.

So you're trying to fill that gap?

I'm just doing my part. Cats get on camera and they tend to forget, or they don't wanna give up props. So I'm just doing my part.

What is in the future for you, other than *So Whatcha Sayin'*?

Just basically maintain. If something comes and it looks good, I'll try it. I'm seventeen years past the artist's life span in hip hop. Usually it's three years and you're out ... three albums and you're done. ... DJing is first. I'm a producer on the side. I didn't know that I would be as successful as a producer as I was as a DJ. I was doing the producer thing because I like to do it, but I never thought that I would have this much impact as a producer.

You call yourself "your favorite DJ's favorite DJ." Who is your favorite DJ?

My favorite DJ is Grandmaster Flash. I'll play you something from 1981 and you can't believe he was catching the record like that. It was crazy. Him and Theodore. And DJ Master Don. The one who made me wanna become a DJ when I heard him was solely Grandmaster Flash, but there were other DJs as nice as Flash and they were all my favorite DJs. It was Grandmaster Flash, Grandwizard Theodore, DJ Master Don, and DJ Whiz Kid. All from that era, the late seventies, early eighties.

Let's go back to the biters. Are you as possessive as Bambaataa was, taking the labels off your records?

Back then, I didn't let people videotape me because biting wasn't allowed. As far as DJing, back then, a DJ would sit there and videotape you, then go home and study your tricks, then go do a show and try to claim it. Back then, biting was enforced. Now, it's okay to copy somebody's whole routine. ... It's disgusting right now. There's no loyalty, there's no originality. Everybody's doing what they've seen someone else do instead of creating on their own, which leaves certain parts of DJing at a standstill. Everybody's biting and no one's creating ...

Taking labels off, that's what you did. I don't do that now. Everything was so exclusive back then, when you play a break and the other DJs are like,

"Oh shit. What's that?" And they're trying to look at the label, write it down, go to their party and are like, "I got the new hot shit that I discovered." For the sucker DJs, you would cover it up, or put the records in the tub to get the label lifted off. There's a guy who comes to the club I spin at now, who types my entire playlist into his Blackberry. He goes to his club and plays the same records—sloppy—but it's still my routine.

Well, that's like playing cards. The saying goes, "You can look in my hand . . ."
But you can't play them like me. Sucker DJs, they still exist.

Is that also part of your inspiration?
Yeah. Switch it up a little. You can play the same records, but you can't play them like me.

Afterword: The Twenty-Four Most Overlooked MCs in Hip Hop

Masta Ace

Those of us who consider ourselves to be true hip hop fans have at some point engaged in a spirited discussion with our friends about who might be the best rapper. The discussion inevitably escalates to a heated argument as we each try to make our point on why a certain artist deserves or doesn't deserve to be mentioned. Inevitably, there are some names that almost never get mentioned in these debates. For whatever reason, these artists get overlooked by the masses of hip hop fans despite their overwhelming talents and ability.

I have been asked to compile a list of the most overlooked MCs in the game, the cats that rarely get mentioned in discussions of who is the best. It seems appropriate that I was chosen to write this piece since in many people's minds, and my own I suppose, I myself fit into this category. It also is fitting that this section was chosen to be the afterword of this book since these MCs have gone through their careers being an afterthought in the minds of most hip hop fans.

Here are, in my opinion, twenty-four of the most overlooked MCs in hip hop history. The list is based on lyrical talent and not song making or record sales. The talent of these MCs is undeniable, but their lyrical significance has been overlooked.

1. CHILL ROB G
Chill Rob was killin'em with his lyrics in the early nineties with songs like "Court Is in Session" and "Let Me Show You" from his album produced by Mark the 45 King.

2. G DEP

Some may be surprised to see Dep on this list, but he's been consistently putting words together in unique ways since his appearance on Gang Starr's "At the Mall" from their *Moment of Truth* album.

3. GRAND PUBA

You cannot forget the impact that Puba had on the game with his colorful flow and one-of-a-kind style of bragging.

4. CHUBB ROCK

Most people write this guy off because of minimal record sales, but in terms of lyrics, Chubb really had a knack for connecting the dots and making words sound incredible.

5. COMMON

Com is not in most people's top twenty, but his lyrics speak for themselves. He has done it at the highest level lyrically and still remained true to his conscious message.

6. PHONTE (FROM LITTLE BROTHER)

Someone from the "now school" and reppin' Little Brother to the fullest, Phonte has really been raising eyebrows with his standout performances featured on several albums and LB mixtapes. His consistency gets him on this list easily.

7. LAURYN HILL

I am sure I'm not the only one who wishes L Boogie never discovered she could sing. Her lyrical prowess as a straight-up MC is missed by the many mainstream fans who bought her album.

8. GZA

How can you front on this Wu-Tang general who has been crushing us with the rhymes since his anchor leg on "Protect Ya Neck"?

9. JUICE

This cat has never released a commercially recognized album but yet deserves to be on this list for his ability to do it on the highest level with writtens and off the dome, which are both equally incredible.

10. LUDACRIS

I know you're thinking, "What is this guy doing on here?" With his overwhelming commercial success and his proven ability to make hits, Luda's talent as a lyricist gets lost in all the hype. Straight up, this guy is nice.

11. BLACK THOUGHT

Supertalented as an MC, Thought's lyrical ability sometimes gets overshadowed and often drowned out by the great Roots movement.

12. ROYCE DA 5′9″

Most don't mention Royce anywhere in their top twenty, but I have the freestyles of him and Eminem trading verses on several occasions. If it weren't Em on the other side of those exchanges, this guy would've made history already.

13. TALIB KWELI

Kweli has established himself as one of the most skilled from his early Black Star days to the present.

14. MOS DEF

For the casual fan, Mos Def's talent as an actor has overshadowed the fact that on the microphone he is incredibly talented.

15. ELZHI (FROM SLUM VILLAGE)

As in the case of Phonte, I hate to single out one member of a group because it's the contribution of each member that truly makes musical chemistry. With that being said, Elzhi has consistently delivered incredible lyrical performances on the Slum Village projects, yet most don't know his name.

16. CANIBUS

So many of us confuse song making with lyrical talent. Canibus is without a doubt one of the best MCs to ever spit a verse. His true talent can be heard on any number of fifty-plus bar freestyles floating around the Internet. His ability to put words together in unusual rhyme patterns is unparalleled.

17. LADY OF RAGE

Reppin' for the ladies, the Lady of Rage is one of those rare talents who writes all her own material and has always been able to hold her own against the best, male or female.

18. LORD FINESSE

With his crowd-pleasing punch lines and his affiliation with the DITC crew, Finesse has been one of the best and most entertaining MCs in the game.

19. BUCKSHOT

This original member of the Boot Camp Clik led the way with incredible flow and intense wordplay, first on the Black Moon album *Enta Da Stage* and then with his contributions on all the BCC releases thereafter.

20. TREACH

Somewhere in between all the success of Naughty by Nature and the long list of hit records that came with it, people forgot that Treach was pretty nice. Maybe we were too busy saying "haaay, hoooo" and "yeah, you know me" to recognize his talent, but he deserves to be on this list.

21. DAS EFX

These guys deserve to be on this list as a collective duo because in my opinion neither of them out performed the other. Their perfect balance of talent makes them one of the best groups ever, and their EFX on every MC from New York to New Zealand is well diggity documented.

22. KING TEE

I am not sure who his influences were, but it's clear that King Tee is a student of hip hop. His skill has transcended time and from his early days until his performance on Dr. Dre's *Chronic 2001*, Teela has been consistently nice on the mic.

23. KEITH MURRAY

You will rarely hear Keith Murray's name mentioned among the best. Some complain that they don't know what he is talking about. I suppose Keith is an acquired taste, but I guess I am used to his flavor because he makes my list.

24. SAUKRATES

Because he reps Toronto, Canada, there's no wonder why this young talent gets overlooked. The fact is Saukrates is supertalented, and maybe by virtue of this list, more people in the United States will recognize his ability.

HONORABLE MENTIONS

Madlib

Sean Price

Xzibit

Kurupt

Grand Daddy IU

Special Ed

Bahamadia

B Real (Cypress Hill)

Scarface (Geto Boys)

Andre 3000 (Outkast)

CL Smooth

Kwame
Young Z
Tha Alkaholiks
Large Professor
The D.O.C.
Rah Digga

Selected Bibliography

Adler, Jerry, and Jennifer Foote. "The Rap Attitude." *Newsweek* 19 March 1990: 56–59.

Allen Jr., Ernest. "Message Rap." *Droppin Science*: *Critical Essays on Rap Music and Hip-Hop Culture*. Ed. William Eric Perkins. Philadelphia: Temple University Press, 1996. 163–185.

Anderson, Elijah. *Code of the Street: Decency, Violence, and the Moral Life of the Inner City*. New York: Norton, 1999.

Armstrong, Edward G. "Eminem's Construction of Authenticity." *Popular Music and Society* 27.3 (2004): 335–355.

Baraka, Rhonda, and Mitchell, Gail. "Lady Rappers: Wider Acceptance, Big Ideas and an Expansive Entrepreneurial Spirit Animate Top Female MCs." *Billboard* 7 December 2002: 101.

Beastie Boys. "James Newton vs. Beastie Boys." 17 September 2002. http://www.beastieboys.com.

Beastie Boys. *Sounds of Science: The Beastie Boys Anthology*. Liner Notes. Grand Royal, 2003.

Caponi, Gena Dagel. *Signifyin(g), Sanctifyin', & Slam Dunking: A Reader in African American Expressive Culture*. Amherst: University of Massachusetts Press, 1999.

Cepeda, Raquel. *And It Don't Stop: The Best American Hip-Hop Journalism of the Last 25 Years*. New York: Faber and Faber, 2004.

Chang, Jeff. *Can't Stop Won't Stop: A History of the Hip-Hop Generation*. New York: St. Martin's Press, 2005.

Cheney, Charise. *Brothers Gonna Work It Out: Sexual Politics in the Golden Age of Rap Nationalism*. New York: New York University Press, 2005.

Coker, Cheo Hodari. *The Life, Death, and Afterlife of the Notorious B.I.G.* New York: Three Rivers Press, 2003.

Coleman, Brian. *Rakim Told Me: Hip-Hop Wax Facts, Straight from the Original Artists, the 80s*. Somersville, MA: Wax Facts Press, 2005.

Dennis, Reginald C. "Record Notes." *Street Jams: Hip-Hop from the Top, Part II*. Rhino Records, 1992.

Dyson, Michael E. *Holler if You Hear Me: Searching for Tupac Shakur*. New York: Basic Civitas Books, 2001.

50 Cent with Kris Ex. *From Pieces to Weight: Once Upon a Time in Southside Queens*. New York: Pocket Books, 2005.

Forman, Murray. "'Movin' Closer to an Independent Funk': Black Feminist Theory, Standpoint, and Women in Rap." *Women's Studies* 23 (1994): 35–55.

Forman, Murray, and Mark Anthony Neal, eds. *That's the Joint! The Hip-Hop Studies Reader*. New York: Routledge, 2004.

Frank, Thomas. *The Conquest of Cool: Business Culture, Counterculture, and the Rise of Hip Consumerism*. Chicago: University of Chicago Press, 1997.

Fricke, Jim, and Charlie Ahearn. *Yes, Yes Y'all: Oral History of Hip-Hop's First Decade*. Oxford: Perseus, 2002.

Gates, Henry Louis, Jr. *The Signifying Monkey: A Theory of Afro-American Literary Criticism*. New York: Oxford University Press, 1998.

George, Nelson. *Hip-Hop America*. New York: Penguin, 1999.

Gines, Kathryn T. "Queen Bees and Big Pimps: Sex and Sexuality in Hip Hop." *Hip Hop and Philosophy: Rhyme 2 Reason*. Eds. Derrick Darby and Tommie Shelby. Chicago: Open Court, 2005.

Goldman, Vivien. "Explorers." *The Black Chord. Visions of the Groove: Connections Between Afrobeats, Rhythm & Blues, Hip-Hop and More*. Photography by David Corio, text by Vivien Goldman. New York: Universe Publishing, 1999. 139–173.

Gonzales, Michael A. "The Labors of Hercules." *The Source* 100 (January 1998): 144–150.

Gonzales, Michael A. "Yo-Yo: Not For Play." *Vibe Hip-HopDivas*. New York: Three Rivers Press, 2001. 62–69.

Hess, Mickey. "Hip-Hop Realness and the White Performer." *Critical Studies in Media Communication* 22.5 (2005): 372–389.

Holt, Douglas B. *How Brands Become Icons: The Principles of Cultural Branding*. Boston: Harvard Business School Press, 2004.

Irving, Katrina. "'I Want Your Hands on Me': Building Equivalences Through Rap Music." *Popular Music* 12.2 (1993): 105–121.

Jackson, Kevin. "DJ Kool Herc: Hip-Hop Pioneer." *Jamaica Observer* 8 October 2004. http://www.jamaicaobserver.com/lifestyle/html/20041007T170000-0500_67281_OBS_DJ_KOOL_HERC__HIP_HOP_PIONEER_.asp.

Keyes, Cheryl. *Rap Music and Street Consciousness*. Urbana: University of Illinois Press, 2004.

Kool Moe Dee. *There's a God on the Mic: The True 50 Greatest MCs*. New York: Thunder's Mouth Press, 2003.

Kubrin, Charis E. "Gangstas, Thugs, and Hustlas: Identity and the Code of the Street in Rap Music." *Social Problems* 52.3 (2005): 360–378.

Kun, Josh. *Audiotopia: Music, Race, and America*. Berkeley: University of California Press, 2005.

Light, Alan. "The Story of Yo!" *Spin* September 1998.

Light, Alan, ed. *The Vibe History of Hip-Hop*. New York: Three Rivers Press, 1999.

Majors, Richard, and Billson, Janet. *Cool Pose: The Dilemmas of Black Manhood in America*. New York: Lexington, 1992.

Malone, Bonz. "Microphone Fiends: Eric B. and Rakim/Slick Rick." *The Vibe History of Hip-Hop*. Ed. Alan Light. New York: Three Rivers Press, 1999. 94–99.

Marriott, Robert. "Allah's on Me." *And It Don't Stop: The Best American Hip-Hop Journalism of the Last 25 Years*. Ed. Raquel Cepeda. New York: Faber and Faber. 187–201.

Martens, Todd. "Beastie Boys: Dolly Was Robbed at Oscars." 16 March 2006. http://www.redorbit.com/news/entertainment/432176/beastie_boys_dolly_was_robbed_at_oscars/index.html.

McDaniels, Darryl. *King of Rock: Respect, Responsibility and My Life with Run-DMC*. New York: St. Martin's Press, 2001.

McDaniels, Darryl "DMC," and Anita Kunz. "Beastie Boys." *Rolling Stone* 972, 21 April 2005: 84.

McIver, Joel. *Ice Cube: Attitude*. London: Sanctuary Publishing, 2003.

The MC: Why We Do It. Dir. Peter Spirer. Image Entertainment. 2005.

Mitchell, Tony, ed. *Global Noise: Rap and Hip-Hop Outside the USA*. Middletown, CT: Wesleyan University Press, 2002.

Morrison, Carlos. "Death Narratives from the Killing Fields: Narrative Criticism and the Case of Tupac Shakur." *Understanding African American Rhetoric: Classical Origins to Contemporary Innovations*. Eds. Ronald L. Jackson II and Elaine P. Richardson. New York: Routledge, 2003. 187–205.

Pough, Gwendolyn. "I Bring Wreck to Those Who Disrespect Me Like a Dame: Women, Rap, and the Rhetoric of Wreck." *Check It While I Wreck It: Black Womanhood, Hip-Hop Culture, and the Public Sphere*. Boston: Northeastern University Press, 2004. 75–102.

Quinn, Eithne. *Nuthin' but a "G" Thang: The Culture and Commerce of Gangsta Rap*. New York: Columbia University Press, 2005.

Quinn, Eithne. "Who's the Mack?: The Performativity and Politics of the Pimp Figure in Gangsta Rap." *Journal of American Studies* 34 (2000): 115–136.

Ramos, George. "30 Injured at Long Beach Concert; L.A. Show Off." *Los Angeles Times* 18 August 1986: 1.

Ramsey, Guthrie P. *Race Music: Black Cultures from Bebop to Hip-Hop*. Berkeley: University of California Press, 2003.

Ro, Ronin. "The Professional." *Rap Pages* January 1998: 64–68, 110.

Robbins, Ira A. *The Rolling Stone Review: 1985*. New York: Rolling Stone Press, 1985.

Rose, Tricia. *Black Noise: Rap Music and Black Culture in Contemporary America*. Middletown, CT: Wesleyan University Press, 1994.

RZA. *The Wu-Tang Manual*. New York: Penguin, 2004.

Shakur, Tupac A. *The Rose That Grew from Concrete*. New York: Pocket Books, 1999.

Shakur, Tupac A. *Tupac: Resurrection*. New York: Atria Books, 2003.

Strong, Nolan. "Roxanne Shanté: An Incredible Journey." *All Hiphop Features*. September 2004. http://www.allhiphop.com/features/?ID=914.

Strong, Nolan. "Roxanne Shanté Files Lawsuit Against Janet Jackson." *All Hiphop News*. October 2004. http://www.allhiphop.com/hiphopnews/?ID=3624.

Wallace, Voletta, and Tremell McKenzie. *Voletta Wallace Remembers Her Son, Biggie*. New York: Atria Books, 2005.

Williams, Saul. *The Dead Emcee Scrolls: The Lost Teachings of Hip-Hop*. New York: MTV Books, 2006.

Notes on Contributors

EDITOR

MICKEY HESS is Assistant Professor of English at Rider University and the author of *Is Hip Hop Dead? The Past, Present, and Future of America's Most Wanted Music* (Praeger Publishers). His scholarship on hip hop music has been published in *Critical Studies in Media Communication, Mosaic: A Journal for the Interdisciplinary Study of Literature, Popular Music and Society,* and *Computers & Composition.*

CONTRIBUTORS

JERU THE DAMAJA hails from Brooklyn, New York, where he was born and raised. Jeru was first introduced to hip hop in the local parks of his neighborhood at age seven, and started writing his own lyrics at age ten. Hip hop has been a part of his life for as long as he can remember. Jeru created and took on the persona of "The Damaja" (because he damages the mic) that is part conscious truth teller and part true to the streets' Brooklyn hard rock. He first showcased his hardcore Brooklyn style to audiences on "I'm the Man," a track from Gang Starr's 1992 album *Daily Operation*. In 1993 he released his first single, "Come Clean," which was produced by DJ Premier and became an instant underground hit. His first album, *The Sun Rises in the East*, released in 1994, and produced entirely by DJ Premier, is considered a classic, and was one of the most acclaimed hip hop albums of its time.

On wax or in the ride, MASTA ACE is a true hip-hop hall-of-famer and one of rap's greatest lyricists. The rhyme veteran found a renewed energy for making music in 2000 after a brief spell of industry disenchantment. The rapper/producer re-entered the scene, dropping acclaimed singles on a variety of independent labels, and a successful European tour in October of that year inspired him to connect with Yosumi and record *Disposable Arts*, his fourth masterfully crafted collection of clever, streetwise wordplay and bangin' beats.

Masta Ace was raised in the projects ("on the 7th floor") of Brownsville, Brooklyn. He made his rap world debut in 1988 on the classic posse cut "The Symphony," from legendary producer Marley Marl's *In Control ... Vol. 1* compilation, alongside Big Daddy Kane, Kool G Rap and Craig G. *In Control* also featured two Ace solo cuts, and a subsequent recording contract with Cold Chillin' Records led to his 1990 debut album, *Take A Look Around*, featuring hip-hop classics like "Music Man," "Letter to the Better," and "Me And The Biz." After Cold Chillin' failed to make Ace a priority, he bounced to LA-based label Delicious Vinyl, where he teamed up with the Brand New Heavies for a track on their *Heavy Rhyme Experience*, and dropped his own second album, 1993's *Slaughtahouse*. Grimy rhymes about stick-up kids, spraycan artists and wack emcees made *Slaughtahouse* an underground favorite, but it was "Born To Roll," a ride-ready remix of "Jeep Ass Niguh," that made the album a national success.

A custom car fanatic himself, Ace found a new audience in the world of shiny rims and boomin' sound systems, which drove him to create his third album, 1995's *Sittin' On Chrome*. Meanwhile, Ace kept his hardcore hip hop heads satisfied with joints like the 1994 title track from Spike Lee's *Crooklyn* soundtrack, rhyming over a Tribe Called Quest production with Special Ed and Buckshot as The Crooklyn Dodgers, along with elusive basement-bangers like "Top Ten List."

SHAWN BERNARDO was born and raised on the bassy, rubber-burned streets of Oakland, California, where he has been a lifelong participant in hip hop culture and an avid devotee of the urban vernacular arts. An art historian and a classicist by training—degrees from UC Berkeley and University of London flank his kitsch poster of T La Rock—he is a corporate liaison by profession who has spent the bulk of his professional career collecting break-beats and vintage tracksuits. Labeled a retro-purist (and a "hip hop snob"), he daily laments the passing of the golden era and frequently finds time to put fingers to keyboard as a freelance writer on all things subculturally old school, elevating underground hip hop and all of its former manifestations into the canons of high culture and greater academia.

JOI CARR is an assistant professor of English at Pepperdine University. Her research interests are interdisciplinary, including African American music and texts, literature and film, and African American literature and religion. She has written, directed, and produced several plays for the Multicultural Theatre Project, Seaver College, Pepperdine University. Her current work with this project is developing an interdisciplinary method for engaging students in critical reflection on difference: socioeconomic status, race and ethnicity, religion, gender, and disabilities. She is also an independent artist with several albums to her credit.

ROBIN CHAMBERLAIN is a doctoral candidate in the Department of English and Cultural Studies at McMaster University. Her research interests include the aesthetics of masochism in both contemporary popular music and Victorian literature.

GEORGE CICCARIELLO-MAHER studies radical political theory at the University of California, Berkeley. His interests include race, colonialism, and liberation, and his work has appeared in *Journal of Black Studies*, *The Commoner*, and *Radical Philosophy Review*. Additionally, he is interested in Latin American political praxis, and he currently lives in Caracas, Venezuela.

CELNISHA L. DANGERFIELD, MA (Pennsylvania State University) is a speech instructor at Chattahoochee Technical College in Marietta, Georgia. Her research interests include identity negotiation, intercultural communication, African American communication, and popular culture. Her related work includes "Lauryn Hill as Lyricist and Womanist" (2004), a piece that explores the intersection of hip hop music and spirituality.

DAVID DIALLO is a doctoral candidate at L'Université Michel de Montaigne, Bordeaux, France. His research interests focus on African American expressive forms, the sociology of art, and contemporary social theory. He has been a visiting research scholar in folklore at the University of Pennsylvania and at Memorial University of Newfoundland, and has contributed to the *Journal of American Folklore* and *Ethnologies*.

TODD DILLS is the editor and publisher of *The 2nd Hand*, the Chicago broadsheet and online magazine for new writing he founded in 2000. In 2004, he edited a best-of collection, *All Hands On: A The 2nd Hand Reader*. He is the author of a novel, *Sons of the Rapture*, and a collection of short stories, *For Weeks Above the Umbrella*, and his fiction and nonfiction have appeared in several publications, including *The Chicago Reader*. He holds an MFA from Columbia College Chicago's Fiction Writing department.

ATHENA ELAFROS is a doctoral student in sociology at McMaster University. Her master's thesis, "'Revolutionary but Gangsta': An Examination of Message Raps and Gangsta Raps in the Late 1980s," examined definitional debates in the music of four artists from the late 1980s North American rap scene. Her PhD dissertation, funded through the Social Sciences and Humanities Research Council of Canada (SHRCC), will continue to examine popular music from a sociological perspective.

JESSICA ELLIOTT is a freelance writer and a student at Indiana University Southeast, where she is editor of the *Undergraduate Research Journal* and associate editor of *The IUS Review*. She has presented her research at the Midwest MLA Convention, and her fiction has appeared in the literary magazine *The 2nd Hand*.

JASON D. HAUGEN is a postdoctoral research associate in the Department of Linguistics at the University of Arizona, where he earned his PhD in the Joint Program in Anthropology and Linguistics in 2004. He hails from Houston, Texas.

DANIELLE HESS is an administrator in Princeton University's Humanities Council.

FAIZA HIRJI is a doctoral candidate in the School of Journalism and Communication at Carleton University in Ottawa, Ontario, Canada. She is currently working on a dissertation about identity construction among Canadian youth of South Asian origin in relation to diasporic media such as Bollywood films. Her research interests include popular culture, ethnicity, and migration.

T. HASAN JOHNSON is a PhD candidate in the Cultural Studies Department at Claremont Graduate University in Claremont, California. A 2006–2007 academic year Ford Foundation Diversity Dissertation Fellow, he currently teaches at Pitzer College in the Intercollegiate Department of Black Studies and the International and Intercultural Studies Department. His research focuses on how Africana resistance cultures function in Africana communities. His work also emphasizes how political ideology, icon construction, identity formation, and the imagination have been used as tools for social agency, cultural development, and political mobilization.

DAVID J. LEONARD is an assistant professor in the Department of Comparative Ethnic Studies at Washington State University. He has written on sports, video games, film, and social movements, appearing in both popular and academic mediums. He has recently completed an edited volume on sports films, to be published by Peter Lang, with another examining race and the NBA scheduled for publication by SUNY Press. His work has appeared in *Journal of Sport and Social Issues*, *Cultural Studies: Critical Methodologies*, and *Game and Culture*, as well as several anthologies, including *Handbook of Sports and Media* and *Capitalizing on Sport: America, Democracy and Everyday Life*. He is a regular contributor to popmatters.com and *Colorlines Magazine*. His work explores the political economy of popular culture and globalized discourses of race, examining the dialectical interplay of movements of popular culture, white supremacy, and state violence through contextual, textual, and subtextual analysis.

ELIJAH LOSSNER is a journalism student at Indiana University Southeast. He has been involved in hip hop for twenty years.

WAYNE MARSHALL (PhD in Ethnomusicology, University of Wisconsin–Madison 2006) is teaching at the University of Chicago as a postdoctoral fellow during the 2006–2007 academic year. With an emphasis on migration, mass media, and music as cultural politics, his dissertation, "Routes, Rap, Reggae: Hearing the Histories of Hip-hop and Reggae Together," examines the long-standing and increasing interplay of American and Caribbean music. He has taught courses on popular and electronic music, hip hop and reggae, and ethnomusicological theory and method at Harvard Extension School, Brown University, and University of Wisconsin–Madison. He has published articles and reviews in *Popular Music, Interventions*, and *The World of Music* while also writing for public outlets such as *XLR8R* and the *Boston Phoenix* as well as on his blog, which has been featured in the *Village Voice* education supplement, and from which a post on reggaeton, "We Use So Many Snares," has been selected for the *DaCapo Best Music Writing 2006* anthology. He is also an active DJ and producer of hip hop, reggae, and related styles, embracing the ways his studies inform his performances and vice versa.

AINE MCGLYNN is a PhD candidate in English at the University of Toronto and has published articles on Kenyan novelist Ngugi Wa Thiongo. She researches contemporary South African and Irish literature as well as the literary historical context of transnationalism.

JEB ARAM MIDDLEBROOK is a doctoral student in the Program in American Studies and Ethnicity at the University of Southern California in Los Angeles. He is a hip hop MC, racial justice activist, and founder of the company AR-15 (AntiRacist Fifteen) Entertainment LLC (www.AR15entertainment.com). He is the author of "A Different Shade of White, Another Kind of Male: A Guide to Using Privilege Responsibly" (www.umn.edu, 2003) and is currently writing on gangsta rap and the prison system. Jeb has worked with national hip hop recording artists KRS-One, dead prez, and the Coup, and has been sought after by Def Jam Entertainment. Jeb is featured in the book *Other People's Property: A Shadow History of Hip-Hop in White America* (Bloomsbury Press, 2007) and the movie *Making Whiteness Visible* (World Trust, 2006).

SHAMIKA ANN MITCHELL is a doctoral student in the English Department at Temple University. Her research area of interest is ethnic American literature. She is an alumna of Seton Hall University and Syracuse University, where she completed her MA and BA in English (respectively). Currently, she is in the beginning stages of her dissertation, which will focus on constructions of identity in contemporary black and Latino fiction.

CARLOS D. MORRISON, PhD (Howard University), is Associate Professor of Public Relations at Alabama State University. Dr. Morrison's research focuses on black popular culture, rap music, and African American rhetoric. He is the author of "Death Narratives from the Killing Fields: Narrative Criticism and the Case of Tupac Shakur" (2003).

THEMBISA S. MSHAKA is senior copywriter for the world's premiere African American cable network, BET. She is the first creative services copywriter in their twenty-five-year history. A veteran of music advertising and urban music journalism, she contributed to the sale of over 120 million albums during her tenure at Sony Music, and was the first African American and female rap editor of *GAVIN*. An established authority on urban culture, the music industry, and radio, her opinions and insights have been featured in several print and television outlets including *VIBE*, *RapPages*, *Essence*, and NBC and FOX. She is also a board member for the Temple of Hip-Hop. Her writings have been published in Launch.com, Essence.com, *EMixshow Magazine*, and *Honey*. She is currently at work on her first book, *Handle Your [music] Business: Her Guide to Entering, Navigating, and Exiting the Record Industry*. Also a voice-over actor and music supervisor, she is a member of AFTRA.

NICOLE HODGES PERSLEY is a doctoral candidate in American Studies and Ethnicity at the University of Southern California. She is a professional actress, writer, director, and artist. Her solo performances have been featured at the World Stage, the Cali Hip-Hop Theater Festival, Harvard University, and the Arm & Hammer Museum as well as national and international academic conferences. Her writing has been published in academic journals such as *Theatre Journal* and pop culture publications such as *Chicken Soup for the African American Soul*. Her academic interests include race and performance, improvisation and identity, hip hop studies, critical theory, and African diaspora studies.

JAMES PETERSON is an assistant professor of English at Pennsylvania State University, Abington College. He was a visiting lecturer and preceptor in African American Studies at Princeton University and was the founding media coordinator for the Harvard University Hip-hop Archive. Dr. Peterson has assisted Dr. Cornel West and delivered the "Hip Hop Studies" lectures at Princeton University (2004). He has also assisted and guest lectured in courses taught by Dr. Michael Eric Dyson at the University of Pennsylvania (2004–2005). He has written numerous scholarly articles on hip hop culture, African

American literature, culture, and linguistics, as well as urban studies. He is currently working on a book that explores in detail the lyrics and life of Tupac Shakur (Praeger/Greenwood Press). Peterson has conducted interviews with Gil Scott Heron, Dr. Manny Marable, Sistah Souljah, Snoop Dogg, and DJ Jazzy Jeff and generally applies his journalistic skills and ethnographic training toward innovative academic inquiry. Dr. Peterson has been featured on BET and Bet.com (*The Jeff Johnson Chronicles*) and has published in *Callaloo, Black Arts Quarterly, XXL, Technitions*, and *Lexani* magazine. He has also been featured and/or quoted in *VIBE Magazine, Philadelphia Weekly, Southern Voices* and the *Wall Street Journal*.

KATHERINE V. TSIOPOS-WILLS is an assistant professor at Indiana University–Purdue University at Indianapolis. She has published original poetry and scholarly essays on rhetoric and cultural studies. She is the coeditor of two collections: *Politics of Information* (2004) and *Critical Power Tools: Technical Writing and Cultural Studies* (2006).

SUSAN WEINSTEIN is an assistant professor of English at Louisiana State University in Baton Rouge, where she directs the secondary English concentration. She became interested in hip hop through her ethnographic research with teenaged and young adult poets and lyricists in Chicago. Dr. Weinstein has published articles in *English Education* and the *Journal of Adolescent and Adult Literacy*, among others. She is currently working toward the publication of her book, *"That Ain't How I Write": What Urban Youths Know About Literacy and Learning*, and conducting research on the national youth poetry movement.

H. C. WILLIAMS is a graduate assistant at Florida State University, where she teaches Freshman Composition and Writing About Insanity. She has explored such topics as popular culture, postmodernism, literature and Eastern philosophy, literature and abnormal psychology, and poetry. Her poetry has appeared in several publications, such as *Mindfire Renew* and *Sage of Consciousness*.

JENNIFER R. YOUNG is assistant professor of English at Hope College in Holland, Michigan. She has written articles comparing hip hop culture and lyricism to traditional literature. One of her recent articles discusses the relationship between Roxanne Shanté, eighteenth-century poet Phillis Wheatley, and Niobe, a mythological character from Greco-Roman antiquity.

Index

2 Live Crew: hip hop timeline, xxvi; Miami sound, 459

2Pacalypse Now, Tupac Shakur, 396–97

2 Shades Deep, Andre Benjamin and Antwon Patton, 458

3MCs, Grandmaster Flash with, 43

3rd Bass, racial politics, 344–45

Acting career: Dre and Big Boi of Outkast, 467; Ice Cube, 309–13; Method Man, 382–83; Tupac Shakur, 400–402

Adidas, Run-DMC and brand loyalty, 79–81

Adler, Bill, Run-DMC management, 69

Adrock (Horovitz, Adam): Beastie Boys' career, 93, 95. *See also* Beastie Boys

"The Adventures of Grandmaster Flash on the Wheels of Steel," recording, 44–45

Aerosmith, "Walk This Way" by Run-DMC, 81–84, 92

African roots and culture, Queen Latifah, 225–28

Afrika Bambaataa: discography, 290–91; Zulu Nation, 265, 269–70

Afrika Bambaataa and the Soul Sonic Force, hip hop timeline, xxiii

Afrocentric fashion, rappers, 220–21

Afrocentric philosophy, Native Tongues, 265

Afro-feminist philosophy, Native Tongues, 278–80

Afrofuturism, Outkast, 470–73

Aftermath Entertainment: Dr. Dre, 324; Eminem, 487, 489

Alcohol and drugs, Dr. Dre and Snoop Dogg, 330–31

Aliveness, Run-DMC, 84–85

All About the Benjamins, Ice Cube, 313

"All Eyes on Kanye West," MTV, 567

All Hail the Queen, Queen Latifah, 224–25, 227, 277–78

AmeriKKKa's Most Wanted, Ice Cube, 301–2

Answer records: female MCs, 124–26; Roxanne Shanté, 53

Anti-Semitism: Ice Cube, 304–5; rap, 179–80, 181

Antiviolence, MC Lyte, 133

Apocalypse '91 . . . The Enemy Strikes Black, Public Enemy, 183–86

Aquemini: Outkast, 462; remaking southern hip hop, 467–69

Are We There Yet?, Ice Cube, 313

Arrests, Ol' Dirty Bastard, 374

Artistic fearlessness, Outkast, 471–72

Artistic influences, Nas, 354–56

Asher D, raggamuffin hip hop, 13

ATLiens, Outkast, 461

A Tribe Called Quest: Beastie Boys and, 112; discography, 291; hip hop timeline, xxvii; legacy of Native Tongues, 287–88; Native Tongues breakup, 285; Native Tongues member, 265, 272–73; reggae and hip hop, 13; rhythm and blues, 266. *See also* Native Tongues

Authenticity: central subject of rap, 357; Eminem, 485; female rappers, 208–9; Kanye West, 563–64; Lil' Kim, 451–52

Bad Boy Records: Jay-Z on Bad Boy Entertainment, 534–35; Sean Combs and, 421–22; Tupac Shakur and Notorious B.I.G., 432–33

Balanced group, Outkast, 478

Barbershop, Ice Cube, 313

Barbershop 2: Back in Business, Queen Latifah, 236–37

Barrier, Louis Eric: growing up, 147–51. *See also* Eric B. & Rakim

Bathtub, soaking records, 12

Beastie Boys: acronym Boys Entering Anarchistic States Through Internal Excellence, 93; adolescent male fantasy world, 102–3; A Tribe Called Quest, 112; California and New York, 99–100; *Check Your Head*, 106–8; Def Jam by Rubin and Simmons, 95–97; discography, 116; gangsta rap, 101–2; *Hello Nasty*, 111–13; hip hop and horror, 369–70; hip hop and rock, 92–93; hip hop outsiders, 98–99; *III Communication*, 108–11; image, 98; innovation, 91–93; interaction with black artists, 99; legacy, 114–16; *Licensed to III*, 100–103; live concerts, 97; members, 93, 95; Mixmaster Mike addition, 99, 112; nasal glide, 97; Nathanial Hornblower, 110–11, 115; *Paul's Boutique*, 103–6; racial chauvinism, 98–99; Run-DMC, 92, 97–98, 101; sampling lawsuits, 104–5; style,

97–98; *To the 5 Boroughs*, 113–14; women in lyrics, 109–10

Beatbox, pioneers of human, 52

Beat Street: hip hop film, 22; Kool Herc in film, 20–21

Beef: Eminem, 491–96; hip hop culture, 54; rappers, 356–57; role in Jay-Z's formula for success, 544–47

Beenie Man, hip hop-generation dance hall DJ, 13

Beneath the Surface: GZA, 372

Benjamin, Andre: 2 Shades Deep, 458; aliases, 457; relationship with Antwon Patton, 457–58. *See also* Outkast

Benzino, Ray, Eminem's rivalry with, 492–93

Beyoncé, duet with Jay-Z, 548–49

Beyond Beef, MTV show, 546

Big Boi: Antwon Patton, 458. *See also* Outkast

Big Daddy Kane, Juice Crew, 55–56

Biggie Smalls: Notorious B.I.G., 417, 419–20; reggae and hip hop, 13. *See also* Notorious B.I.G.

Big-time MCs, oversized MCs, 419–20

Birth of a Prince, RZA, 370

Biz Markie: Juice Crew, 60; storytelling, 122

The Black Album, Jay-Z, 535–36

Black class generational divide, Outkast, 463–64

Black masculinity, Jay-Z, 540

Black pride, Run-DMC, 87

Black Sheep: discography, 291; female-male relationships, 279–80; member of Native Tongues, 273; Native Tongues breakup, 285

Blacks' Magic, Salt-N-Pepa, 203–5

Black Star, reggae and hip hop, 13

Black Thought, MC, 605

Bling-bling, jewelry or something high priced, 468–69

Block parties: 1970s phenomenon, 30; Grandmaster Flash, 30–31; Kool Herc, 7, 19, 23

Blues: hip hop and, 349–50; Missy Elliott, 511

Body tricks, Grandmaster Flash, 28

Bomb Squad: decline, 182–83; Eric "Vietnam" Sadler, 172–73; Public Enemy, 170–71. *See also* Public Enemy

Boxley, James Henry, III: Hank Shocklee, 170. *See also* Public Enemy

Boys Entering Anarchistic States Through Internal Excellence. *See* Beastie Boys

Book of rhymes, hip hop, 359–60

Born Again, Notorious B.I.G.'s posthumous album, 434–35

Branding, Adidas loyalty and Run-DMC, 80–81

Brand New, Salt-N-Pepa, 210–11

Break dancers, hip hop, 519–20

Breakin', hip hop film, 20, 21

Break the Cycle, Missy Elliott, 508

Breakup rumor, Outkast, 479

Bringing Down the House, Queen Latifah, 236

Broadus, Calvin: criminal background, 324–26; nickname "Snoop," 326. *See also* Snoop Dogg

Brother D and Collective Effort, hip hop and reggae, 13

Bubba Spar xxx, white southern rapper, 497–98

Buckshot, MC, 605

Buju Banton, reggae, 13

Bushwick Bill: solo career, 258–59. *See also* Geto Boys

Busta Rhymes, hip hop and horror, 369–70; reggae and hip hop, 13; rhyme style, 284–85

Busy Bee, hip hop timeline, xxii

Campbell, Clive: DJ Kool Herc, 1, 2. *See also* Kool Herc

Canada, hip hop, 120–21

Canibus, MC, 605

Capitol Records, Beastie Boys and contributions, 103

Car culture, hip hop, 571–72

Carnegie Hall, MC Lyte, 137

Carter, Shawn Corey: aliases, 529. *See also* Jay-Z

Categories, hip hop groups, 476–78

Censorship: hip hop and, 398–99; Tupac Shakur, 397–400

Chaka Demus & Pliers, reggae, 13

Chappelle, Dave, block party, 31

Check Your Head, Beastie Boys, 106–8

Chemical Brothers, Kool Herc collaborator, 23

Chi-Ali: member of Native Tongues, 273–74; Native Tongues breakup, 285

Chicago, Queen Latifah, 221, 235–36

Chill Rob G, MC, 603

Chubb Rock, MC, 604

Class experience, Eminem, 485

Clearing samples, lawsuits, 104–5

Clock theory, Grandmaster Flash, 33

Clothing: fashion of Lil' Kim, 448–49; Missy Elliott line, 509; Thug Life ideology, 411

Cold Chillin' Records, Roxanne Shanté, 58–59, 63

Cold Crush Brothers, Run-DMC's idols, 74

Coles, Dennis: Ghostface Killah in Wu-Tang Clan, 365, 378–81. *See also* Ghostface Killah

Collaboration: Dr. Dre, 322–23; Eric B. & Rakim with Jody Watley, 154; hip hop, 92–93, 136–37; Ice Cube, 308–9; Kool Herc, 23; MC Lyte with Sinead O'Connor, 136; Rakim and Dr. Dre, 158–60

Collective. *See* Native Tongues

The College Dropout, Kanye West, 555, 557, 560–62, 563–64

Combs, Sean "Puffy": Jay-Z on Bad Boy Entertainment, 534–35; Notorious B.I.G. and Bad Boy Records, 421–22

Comic books, hip hop and, 379–80

Commitment, MC Lyte, 127

Common: Kanye West and, 565–66; MC, 604

Community health, MC Lyte, 131–34

Competition, beef, 545

Compton, city of Los Angeles area and Dr. Dre, 319–20

Concert violence, Run-DMC, 85–86

Conflict, beef, 54

Conscious hip hop, development, 533–34

The Cookbook, Missy Elliott, 518, 520–21

Cover art, videos and, by Nas, 350–54

Cover Girl spokesperson, Queen Latifah, 219, 237–38

Crack cocaine, rise of hip hop, 395

Crime, Geto Boys' theme, 255

Criminal behavior, Ol' Dirty Bastard, 374

Criminal Minded, reggae and hip hop, 13, 22

Crooked fingers, Eric B. & Rakim, 148

Cross-fader: Eric B., 148; Grandmaster Flash, 35

Crunk, hip hop slang, 470

Culture of death, hip hop, 429–30

Cutty Ranks, reggae, 13

Daddy Freddy, raggamuffin hip hop, 13

The Dana Owens Album, Queen Latifah, 233, 238

Dancers, b-boys and break, 519–20

Da Real World, Missy Elliott, 513–14

Das EFX: MC, 606; reggae and hip hop, 13

Dave Chappelle's Block Party, documentary, 31

Death: hip hop and culture of, 429–30; hip hop's culture of, 429–30; Ol' Dirty Bastard, 374, 375–76; Thug Life ideology, 410

Death Certificate, Ice Cube, 302–4

Death Row, Snoop Dogg, 327–29

Death Row Records, hip hop timeline, xxvii

Debbie D, female MC, 18

Def American, Rubin label, 96

Def Jam: Beastie Boys, 95–97; Def American, 96; hip hop timeline, xxv; logo, 84; *Raising Hell* by Run-DMC, 78–79; Run-DMC management, 70;

Russell Simmons and Rick Rubin, 71; today, 96

Def Jam Recordings, Jay-Z as president and CEO, 536–37

Def Jam South, Beastie Boys, 101

Def Poetry Jam, hip hop and poetry, 495

De La Soul: discography, 291; hip hop timeline, xxvi; legacy of Native Tongues, 287–88; members of Native Tongues, 271–72; Native Tongues breakup, 285; rhythm and blues, 266

Dennis, Willie James: Willie D, 247. *See also* Geto Boys

Denton, Sandra "Pepa": after Salt-N-Pepa, 212; Salt-N-Pepa, 193, 197–98. *See also* Salt-N-Pepa

Detroit, Michigan, hip hop scene, 482

Diamond, Michael: Beastie Boys' career, 93, 95. *See also* Beastie Boys

Diggs, Robert: RZA of Wu-Tang Clan, 368–71. *See also* RZA

Digital Underground (DU), Tupac Shakur, 396

Dirty South, southern hip hop, 458–60

Discography: Afrika Bambaataa, 290–91; A Tribe Called Quest, 291; Beastie Boys, 116; Black Sheep, 291; De La Soul, 291; Dr. Dre, 340; Eminem, 501–2; Eric B. & Rakim, 166–67; Geto Boys, 264; Ghostface Killah, 389; Grandmaster Flash, 49; Grandmaster Flash and Furious Five, 49; GZA, 389; Ice Cube, 315; Inspectah Deck, 388; The Jungle Brothers, 291; Kanye West, 577; Lil' Kim, 456; Masta Killa, 389; MC Lyte, 140; Method Man, 388; Missy Elliott, 527; Nas, 362–63; Native Tongues, 290–91; Notorious B.I.G., 438; N.W.A., 315, 340; Ol' Dirty Bastard, 389; Queen Latifah, 241, 291; Raekwon the Chef, 388; Rakim, 167; Roxanne Shanté, 68; Run-DMC, 90; RZA, 389; Salt-N-Pepa, 215–16; Snoop Dogg, 340; Tupac Shakur, 414–15; U–God, 389; Wu-Tang Clan, 388

DJ Casanova Fly, Grandmaster Caz, 18

DJ culture, women and, 194

DJ Jazzy Jeff, human beatbox, 52

DJ Jazzy Joyce, women and DJ culture, 194

DJ Premier: abandoning tradition, 584–85; career, 581; future goals, 582; hip hop, 580–81; hip hop boundaries, 587; history and context, 587; humility, 584; interview, 579–89; J. Dilla, 588; learning about production, 579–80; love affair with hip hop, 587–88; Missy Elliott, 588–89; passions, 583; paying for respect, 585; people who matter, 581–82; people with icon status, 588; pop-rap, 586; preserving culture, 585–86; producers on upswing, 588; race consciousness, 581; reputation, 582–83; super-producer, 579; watches, 583–84; women rappers, 588–89

DJs, MCs outshining, 17

DJ Scratch: analog vs. digital, 593; behind the scenes, 594; biters, 601–2; Brooklyn, 592; DJing on the radio, 595–96; EPMD, 592, 593; front men, 594; future, 601; handcuffs, 598; history of hip hop, 600–601; inspiration, 592; inspiring producers, 595; inventive DJing, 600; lyrics, 592; mainstream status, 596–97; mentoring, 597; music producer, 595; New York City rap, 591–92; resume, 591; trial and error, 593; turntablism, 598–99

DJ Wanda Dee, women and DJ culture, 194

DMC World Championships, 38–39

D.O.C., reggae and hip hop, 13

The Documentary, The Game, 317

Don Killuminati: The 7 Day Theory: icon status of Tupac Shakur, 404–6; Shakur's alter ego Makaveli, 407–9; social and political commentary, 406–7

Do the Right Thing, Spike Lee and Public Enemy, 180–81

Doug E. Fresh, human beatbox, 52

Doug E. Fresh and the Get Fresh Crew, hip hop timeline, xxiv

Doughboy, Ice Cube, 309–10

Dr. Dre: Aftermath Entertainment, 324; Andre Romel Young, 319–24; collaborations, 158–60, 322–24; Compton, 319–20; discography, 340; Eazy-E (Eric Wright) and, 320–22; Eminem, 487, 488–91; G-funk, 332–33, 335; hip hop and horror, 369–70; hip hop timeline, xxvii; Ice Cube and, 296; N.W.A. reunion, 311; Rakim, 158–60; reggae and hip hop, 13; Ruthless Records, 321–23; signature sound, 332–33, 335–36; studio gangsta, 325–26

Dr. Dre and Snoop Dogg: Andre Young, 319–24; Calvin Broadus, 324–29; discography, 340; drugs and alcohol, 330–31, 332; gangsta hedonism, 318–19; gangsta lifestyle, 330–32; hedonism, 329–32; icons of West Coast gangsta rap, 317–18; status through sexual activity, 331–32; wine, women, and song, 329–32. *See also* Snoop Dogg

Dre, Andre Benjamin. *See* Outkast

Drug addiction, Kool Herc, 22

Drug problems, Ol' Dirty Bastard, 374, 375–76

Drugs and alcohol, Dr. Dre and Snoop Dogg, 330–31

Drug use, rap music, 260–61

Drums: listeners, 37; Roland TR-808 machine, 75, 148, 163

Duets: The Final Chapter, Notorious B.I.G.'s posthumous album, 435

East Coast: Notorious B.I.G. and Tupac Shakur, 432; Tupac Shakur and East-West coast feud, 392–93, 405–6

East Coast vs. West Coast, Beastie Boys, 99–100

Eazy-E: biography, 321; hip hop timeline, xxviii; Ice Cube and, 297; N.W.A. reunion, 311

Education: Ice Cube, 298; Notorious
B.I.G., 418–19; Roxanne Shanté,
63–64
Eightball, Memphis rap scene, 245
Elephant Man, hip hop-generation dance
hall DJ, 13
Elliott, Melissa Arnette. *See* Missy
Elliott
Elzhi from Slum Village, MC, 605
Eminem: acceptance by black hip hop
peers, 487–88; Aftermath Records,
487; authentic class experience, 485;
beef, 491–96; childhood, 481–82;
conflict outside hip hop circles,
494–96; conflict with Royce da 5'9",
494; credibility of white MCs, 93;
Detroit hip hop scene, 482–83;
discography, 501–2; disrespecting
people, 490; Dr. Dre, 487, 488–91;
exploiting bad boy lifestyle, 489;
family life, 486–87; fast rappers,
560–61; hip hop timeline, xxix,
xxviii–xxix; hip hop values, 485–86;
Insane Clown Posse (ICP) vs., 493–94;
making of a rapper, 486–88; musical
inspiration, 485; politics, 496–97;
rapper, not white rapper, 483–84;
rivalry with Ray Benzino, 492–93;
rumors of early retirement, 499–501;
Slim Shady LP, 489–90; style, 488;
white southern rappers, 497–99;
woman troubles, 490–91; worldwide
success, 484
Eric B. & Rakim: crooked fingers, 148;
discography, 166–67; DJ Eric B.,
147–51; *Follow the Leader*, 153–55,
161, 164; hip hop timeline, xxv; J.D.
Salingers of hip hop, 141–42; legacy,
160–65; *Let the Rhythm Hit 'Em*,
155–56, 161; MC Rakim, 146–47;
Paid In Full, 151–53, 161; partnership,
149; Rakim's return, 156–60. *See also*
Rakim
Everlast, Eminem's beef with,
493
Experience Music Project in Seattle, hip
hop exhibit, 117

Fab 5 Freddy: Grandmaster Flash, 45;
hip hop timeline, xxii; *Wild Style*, 20
Fabara, Sandra "Lady Pink," graffiti
artist, 20
Fairy tales, Missy Elliott's videos,
522–23
Farrakhan, Louis, Islam, 149–50
Fashion: hip hop and, 442–43; Lil' Kim,
448–49
Fat Boys, hip hop and reggae, 13
Father figure, hip hop, 351
Fear of a Black Planet, Public Enemy,
182–83
Female MCs: answer records, 53,
124–26; rise, 18; storytelling, 122–23
Female rappers: 1980s, 195–97;
associations with men, 54–55;
authenticity, 208–9; feminism,
200–201; male producers, 205–6;
Queen Latifah nurturing, 229–30.
See also Queen Latifah
Feminism: Afro-feminist philosophy in
Native Tongues, 278–80; Lil' Kim,
446–48; rap music, 200–201
Feud: East Coast vs. West Coast,
392–93, 405–6; Lil' Kim and Foxy
Brown, 452–54
Filmography, Queen Latifah, 241
Financial savvy, Wu-Tang Clan, 366
First Priority record label, MC Lyte,
119–20
Fishscale, Ghostface Killah, 380–81
Five Percent Nation: Infinity Lessons of
Zulu Nation, 269–70; Islam and hip
hop, 149–50; terminology, 143–44;
Wu-Tang Clan, 367
Flash. *See* Grandmaster Flash
Flavor Flav, grills, 186
Flow: Rakim, 163; Snoop Dogg, 337
Fly Ty: Eric B. & Rakim, 153; Roxanne
Shanté, 58–59, 62
Follow the Leader, Eric B & Rakim,
153–55
Foundational groups, rappers, 476–77
Foxy Brown: duet with Jay-Z, 547–48;
feud with Lil' Kim, 452–54
Fresh Fest, hip hop timeline, xxiii

Fresh Prince: human beatbox, 52; sitcoms, 233–34

Friday, Ice Cube, 311–12

Friday After Next, Ice Cube, 313

Fugees, reggae and hip hop, 14

Funk, hip hop, 474

Furious Five: Grandmaster Flash and, 34, 43, 45–46; hip hop timeline, xxiii

Furious Four, Grandmaster Flash and, 43

Fu-Schnickens, reggae and hip hop, 13

Game, *The Documentary*, 317

Gandhi, Mahatma, Nas's reference, 359–60

Gangsta lifestyle, Dr. Dre and Snoop Dogg, 330–32

Gangsta rap: Beastie Boys and contributions, 101–2; Geto Boys, 243–46, 248–51; hip hop's culture of death, 429–30; Ice Cube and emergence of West Coast, 295–97; Lil' Kim, 444, 452; reflective thug, 533; Salt-N-Pepa, 207, 209; Stop the Violence movement, 187; studio gangsta, 325–26; West Coast, 293–94. *See also* Ice Cube

Ganxsta Nip, hip hop and horror, 369

G Dep, MC, 604

Gender ideology, Missy Elliott's videos, 523

Gender role reversal, MC Lyte's videos, 128–29

Geto Boys: Bushwick Bill solo career, 258–59; crime spree, 255; discography, 264; early days, 246–48; future, 264; gangsta lifestyle, 250–55; Ghetto Boys, 246–47; hard-core gangsta rappers, 243–46; hip hop and horror, 369; Houston rap scene, 243, 245, 262; legacy, 260–64; major themes of music, 248–55; nasty and dangerous, 246; psychological breakdown, 253–54; Rap-A-Lot Records, 248, 250, 261, 264; Scarface solo career, 256–58; sexual politics, 254–55; solo careers, 255–60; tales of horror, 251–53; Willie D solo career, 247–48, 259–60; world politics, 254

G-funk sound, Dr. Dre, 332–33, 335

Ghetto Boys: original lineup, 246. *See also* Geto Boys

Ghostface Killah: comic book hero identity, 379; Dennis Coles, 378; discography, 389; *Fishscale*, 380–81; *Ironman*, 380; mask and secret identity, 378–79; *The Pretty Toney Album*, 380; *Supreme Clientele*, 380; Theodore Unit, 380. *See also* Wu-Tang Clan

The Glass Shield, Ice Cube, 310

Glover brothers, Grandmaster Flash with, 43

God's creation, MC Lyte, 134–36

God's Son: album by Nas, 348–49; videos, 353–54

Golden Arms Redemption, U-God, 385

Gooden, Lolita Shanté. *See* Shanté, Roxanne

Goodie Mob, collaboration with Outkast, 460–61

G.O.O.D. Music, Kanye West, 565

Gore, Tipper, music censorship, 398–99

Graffiti artists, *Wild Style*, 20

Grandmaster Caz: DJ Casanova Fly, 18

Wild Style, 20

Grandmaster DST, *Scratch*, 42

Grandmaster Flash: achievements and honors, 46–47; block party, 30–31, 33; body tricks, 28; clock theory, 33; cross-fader, 35; discography, 49; drums, 37; Fab 5 Freddy, 45; Furious Five, 43; Furious Four, 43; growing up, 28–29; hi-fi science, 37–42; hip hop phenomenon, 27–28; hip hop timeline, xxii, xxiii; Keith "Cowboy" Wiggins, 43; L Brothers, 34; legacy, 46–48; peek-a-boo system, 35, 36; performances, 34–35; quick mix theory, 33; recording, 44–45; sociopolitical commentary, 45–46; storytelling, 122; Sugar Hill Records, 43–46; title, 33–34; turntables, 31–33; turntablist, 39–42; violence and hip

Grandmaster Flash (*contd.*)
  hop, 47–48; vocational training, 29;
  Wild Style, 20
Grandmasters, GZA with DJ Muggs,
  372–73
Grand Puba, MC, 604
Grandwizard Theodore: little brother of
  L Brothers, 34; scratching, 17, 28, 32;
  student of Grandmaster Flash, 35;
  Wild Style, 20
Gravediggaz, RZA in, 369–70
Grice, Gary: GZA in Wu-Tang Clan,
  365, 371–73. *See also* GZA
Griff, Professor. *See* Professor Griff;
  Public Enemy
Griffin, William Michael, Jr.: Rakim,
  146–47. *See also* Eric B. & Rakim;
  Rakim
Grills, status symbols, 186
GZA: *Beneath the Surface*, 372;
  discography, 389; Gary Grice, 371;
  Grandmasters, 372–73; *Liquid Swords*,
  372; MC, 604; *Words from the Genius*,
  371. *See also* Wu-Tang Clan

Hard Core, Lil' Kim, 444–45
Hard-core gangsta rap: Geto Boys,
  243–46, 261–63. *See also* Geto Boys
Hawkins, Lamont: U-God of Wu-Tang
  Clan, 365, 385–86. *See also* U-God
Haystak, white southern rapper, 497–98
Hedonism, Dr. Dre and Snoop Dogg,
  318–19, 329–32
Hello Nasty, Beastie Boys, 111–13
Heltah Sheltah, reggae and hip hop, 13
Higher Learning, Ice Cube, 310
Hill, Lauryn: hip hop timeline, xxix; MC,
  604; Ziggy Marley, 42
Hip hop: answer records, 124–26; beef,
  54; blues and, 349–50; book of
  rhymes, 359–60; break dancers,
  519–20; Canada, 120–21; car culture,
  571–72; censorship and, 398–99;
  comic books and, 379–80; conscious,
  533–34, 546–47; crack cocaine and
  rise of, 395; culture of death, 429–30;
  Detroit scene, 482; Dirty South,

458–60; DJ Premier interview,
  579–89; DJ Scratch interview,
  591–602; eras of development, 426;
  exhibits, 117; fashion, 442–43; father
  figure in, 351; funk and, 474; global
  phenomenon, 543–44; grills, 186;
  Hollywood, 21–22; homophobia,
  568–69; horror and, 369–70; Hot 97
  WQHT radio, 453–54; human
  beatbox, 52; Islam and, 149–50; jazz
  and, 165; LA uprising, 306; law and,
  440–41; Mafia and, 377; message,
  274–75; metal and, 189; most
  overlooked MCs, 603–7; poetry, 495;
  post-gangsta political, 190–91; reality
  television, 510; reggae and, 13–14;
  rock and, 92–93; sampler, 334–35;
  sitcoms and, 233–34; skits, 275–76;
  slang, 143–44; slang "crunk," 470;
  Thug Life ideology, 409–12;
  turntables, 32; underground, 15–16;
  wigger as derogatory term, 483–84;
  Wild Style, 20; women in, 218–19;
  year 1977, 19
Hip hop industry, trickiness and Run-
  DMC, 73–76
Hip hop values, Eminem, 485–86
Hip hop video, Run-DMC, 82
Hollywood: Ice Cube, 309–13; Queen
  Latifah, 233–38
Homophobia: hip hop, 568–69; Ice
  Cube, 304–5; Kanye West, 567–69
Hornblower, Nathanial, Beastie Boys,
  110–11, 115
Horovitz, Adam (Adrock): Beastie Boys'
  career, 93, 95. *See also* Beastie Boys
Horror, Geto Boys' music theme,
  251–53; hip hop and, 369–70
Hot, Cool & Vicious, Salt-N-Pepa,
  198–99, 201
Houston rap scene: drug use in rap
  music, 260–61; Geto Boys, 243, 245;
  impact on music industry, 262.
  See also Geto Boys
Human beatbox, term, 52
Hunter, Jason, Inspectah Deck of
  Wu-Tang Clan, 365, 383–84

Hurricane Katrina, Kanye West, 567, 570

Hustle and Flow, rap film, 244

Hype men, rappers, 176

I Am. . ., album by Nas, 347–48

Ice Cube: accusations, 304–5; acting career, 309–13; *All About the Benjamins*, 313; *AmeriKKKa's Most Wanted*, 301–2; Andre Young (Dr. Dre) and, 296; *Are We There Yet?*, 313; *Barbershop*, 313; collaborations, 308–9; collaboration with Sir Jinx, 296; controversy of "No Vaseline," 303–4; *Death Certificate*, 302–4; discography, 315; Doughboy, 309–10; Eazy-E, 297; education, 298; emergence of West Coast gangsta rap, 295–97; *Friday*, 311–12; *Friday After Next*, 313; *The Glass Shield*, 310; going solo, 300–308; *Higher Learning*, 310; hip hop and LA uprising, 306; Hollywood, 309–13; legacy, 313–14; *Lethal Injection*, 307–8; new beginning, 308–9; N.W.A. formation, 297–300; N.W.A. reunion, 311; O'shea Jackson, 294–95; platform by hip hop, 293–94; The Players Club, 312; police abuse, 299–300; *The Predator*, 305–7; Ruthless Records, 297, 301; St. Ides malt liquor, 304–5; social consciousness, 295; Stereo Crew, 296; *Straight Outta Compton* by N.W.A., 299–300; *Three Kings*, 312; *Trespass*, 310

Ice rap, Kanye West, 564

Ideology. *See* Thug Life ideology

Ice-T, hip hop timeline, xxv

Icon's icon in hip hop, Run-DMC, 85

Ill Communication, Beastie Boys, 108–11

Illmatic: album by Nas, 342, 345–46; videos, 351–52

Immobilarity, Raekwon the Chef, 377–78

Infinity Lessons, Zulu Nation, 269–70

Insane Clown Posse (ICP), Eminem's beef with, 493–94

Insane Poetry, hip hop and horror, 369

Inspectah Deck: discography, 388; Jason Hunter, 383; *The Movement*, 384; producer, 384; *Uncontrolled Substance*, 383–84. *See also* Wu-Tang Clan

Intellectualism, Tupac Shakur, 402–4

Interview: DJ Premier, 579–89; DJ Scratch, 591–602

Ironman, Ghostface Killah, 380

Islam: Five-Percenter terminology, 143–44; hip hop and, 149–50

Island Black Music, Salt-N-Pepa, 206

It Takes A Nation of Millions to Hold Us Back, Public Enemy, 176–79

It Was Written: Nas album, 346–47; videos, 352–53

Jackson, Janet, Roxanne Shanté, 65–66

Jackson, O'shea, Ice Cube, 294–95

Jacobs, Marc, fashion of Lil' Kim, 448

Jamaica: Kool Herc, 2, 24; Notorious B.I.G., 423–24

James, Cheryl "Salt" Renee: after Salt-N-Pepa, 212; Salt-N-Pepa, 193, 197–98. *See also* Salt-N-Pepa

James, Rick, Roxanne Shanté, 63

Jay-Z: approach to spirituality, 538–39; Bad Boy Entertainment and Sean Combs, 534–35; beef with Nas, 545–46, 547; *The Black Album*, 535–36; black masculinity, 540; conscious hip hop, 533–34, 546–47; crossover appeal, 544; debut album *Reasonable Doubt*, 532; duet with Beyoncé, 548–49; duet with Foxy Brown, 547–48; family, 530; formula for success, 537–42; future of new recording industry, 549–51; influences, 531; Jaz, 530; legacy, 551–53; lyrics, 537–38; marketability, 544; MTV show *Beyond Beef*, 546; new type of gangsta, 551; Original Flavor, 530; president and CEO of Def Jam Recordings, 536–37; problem

Jay-Z (*contd.*)
  with "99 Problems," 547–49; record
  labels, 530–31; reflective thug, 533;
  Roc-A-Fella Records, 531–32; role of
  beef, 544–47; Shawn Corey Carter,
  529; social issues, 538; symbolic
  representation, 539–40; Tupac-Biggie
  Smalls feud, 534, 544–45;
  underground vs. mainstream, 542–44;
  values and ideas, 544; virtual
  blackness, 540–41; wealth and fame,
  541–42
Jay-Z and Nas, hip hop timeline, xxix
Jaz, Jay-Z, 530
Jazz, hip hop and, 165
Jazz rap, 165
Jazzy Jeff, DJ, human beatbox, 52
Jones, Kimberly. *See* Lil' Kim
Jones, Nasir: biography, 342–43.
  See also Nas
Jones, Russell: Ol' Dirty Bastard of Wu-
  Tang Clan, 373–76. *See also* Ol' Dirty
  Bastard
Jordan, Brad: Scarface, 247. *See also*
  Geto Boys
Juice, MC, 604
Juice movie, Tupac Shakur, 400–402
Juice Crew: Big Daddy Kan, 55–56; Biz
  Markie, 60; influence on Nas, 355;
  Kool G Rap, 57–58; Masta Ace,
  56–57; Roxanne Shanté, 51, 53,
  58–62
Jungle Brothers: discography, 291;
  members of Native Tongues,
  270–71; Native Tongues breakup,
  285
Just My Take, MC Lyte, 133–34

Kanye West. *See* West, Kanye
Kid Rock, white southern rapper,
  498–99
King Tee, MC, 606
K Love, human beatbox, 52
Kool G Rap, Juice Crew, 57–58
Kool Herc: accent, 5–8; block parties and
  Saddler, 30–31; break dancing, 7–8;
  Clive Campbell, 1, 2; collaborator on

recordings, 23; commercialization
  challenges, 15–19; drug addiction, 22;
  exposure to American music, 4–5;
  family, 2; film *Beat Street*, 20–21; first
  party, 6–7; "Herc," 5; hip hop and
  reggae, 13–14; hip hop timeline, xxi;
  "Kool," 5–6; merry-go-round
  technique, 36; mixtape, 11–12; name,
  5–6; parties, 7, 19, 23; record
  selection, 9–10; reggae roots, 2–5;
  sound system, 8–9; stabbing, 19; style
  of playing records, 10–12, 14;
  trailblazer status, 23–24; Trenchtown,
  2; underground hip hop, 15–16;
  VH1's "Hip Hop Honors," 24; year
  1977, 19
Kool Moe Dee, hip hop timeline,
  xxii–xxiii
Kriss Kross, reggae and hip hop, 13
KRS-One, hip hop and reggae, 13
KRS-One and Boogie Down Productions,
  hip hop timeline, xxiv–xxv
Krush Groove, hip hop film, 20, 22
Kurtis Blow, hip hop timeline, xxii
Kutcher, Ashton, prank on Kanye West,
  562

La Bella Mafia, Lil' Kim, 447
"Ladies First," Queen Latifah and Monie
  Love, 225–26, 278
Lady of Rage, MC, 605
LaFace Records: Outkast, 458, 460;
  TLC, 517
Large Professor, Nas and, 344
LaRock, Scott, *Criminal Minded*, 13
Last Holiday, Queen Latifah, 237
Late Registration, Kanye West, 555, 557,
  566–67, 569, 571–74
Lauryn Hill. *See* Hill, Lauryn
Law, hip hop and, 440–41
Lawsuits, sampling, 104–5
L Brothers, Grandmaster Flash, 34
Lee, Spike, *Do the Right Thing*, 180–81
"Lee" George Quinones, graffiti artist,
  20
Legend, John, Kanye West and, 565
Lethal Injection, Ice Cube, 307–8

Let the Rhythm Hit 'Em, Eric B & Rakim, 155–56, 161

Licensed to Ill, Beastie Boys, 100–103

Life After Death, Notorious B.I.G.'s posthumous album, 434

Lil' Kim: authentic rapper, 451–52; discography, 456; fashion, 448–49; feud with Foxy Brown, 452–54; gangsta rap, 444, 452; *Hard Core*, 444–45; hip hop timeline, xxx; inimitable style, 448–49; Kimberly Jones, 439, 441–43; *La Bella Mafia*, 447; legacy, 454–56; *The Naked Truth*, 440, 445–46, 451–52, 455; Notorious B.I.G., 431–32, 443–45; *The Notorious K.I.M.*, 445; notorious life, 441–46; personal feminism, 446–48; plastic surgery, 450–51; prison sentence, 440–41; use of B-word, 454–56

Liquid Swords, GZA, 372

Lisa Lee, female MC, 18

Literacy, Tupac Shakur, 402–4

Live 8 concerts, Kanye West, 567

Living Out Loud, Queen Latifah, 235

Living Single, Queen Latifah, 233–34

Livingston, Theodore. *See* Grandwizard Theodore

Lockers dance group, hip hop timeline, xxi

Lollapalooza, Beastie Boys, 109

London Records, Salt-N-Pepa, 205–6, 209, 210

Lopes, Lisa "Left Eye," TLC, 517–18

Lord Finesse, MC, 605

Los Angeles area, Compton and Dr. Dre, 319–20

Los Angeles uprising, hip hop, 306

Loud Records, Wu-Tang Clan, 365–66

Love, Monie, duet with Queen Latifah, 225–26, 278

Love songs, MC Lyte, 126–27

Loyalty, MC Lyte, 127

Ludacris, MC, 604

Lyrical strategies: signifying, 124–26; storytelling, 121–24

Lyrics: Jay-Z's formula for success, 537–38; treatment of women, 109–10

Lyte. *See* MC Lyte

Mafia, hip hop and, 377

Mainstream, underground vs., for Jay-Z, 542–44

Makaveli, Shakur's alter ego, 407–9

Male producers, female rappers with, 205–6

Mama complex: Notorious B.I.G., 417–19; rappers, 394–95

Marketability, Jay-Z, 544

Marketing, underground vs. mainstream for Jay-Z, 542–44

Marley, Bob, hip hop and reggae, 13

Marley Marl's Juice Crew, hip hop timeline, xxiv–xxv

Martin, Christopher. *See* DJ Premier

Masculinity, Jay-Z, 540

Mask, Ghostface Killah, 378–79

Masta Ace, Juice Crew, 56–57

Masta Killa: collaborations, 384–85; discography, 389; Elgin Turner, 384; *No Said Date*, 384; vegetarian, 385. *See also* Wu-Tang Clan

MCA (Yauch, Adam): Beastie Boys' career, 93, 95; Tibetan Freedom Concert, 109. *See also* Beastie Boys

MC Lyte: answer records, 124–26; antiviolence initiatives, 133; collaboration, 136–7; community health, 131–34; discography, 140; First Priority record label, 119–20; firsts in career, 136–38; gender role reversals, 128–29; Lana Moorer growing up, 118–20; legacy, 138; love songs, 126–27; lyrical strategies, 121, 123–26; music videos, 127–31; name, 135; Rock the Vote, 133; signifying, 124–26; spirituality, 134–36; storytelling, 121, 123–24; subway train, 127–28; womanhood, 126–27; writing books, 133–34

MCs: female, 18; hip hop timeline, xxi–xxii; influence of Grandmaster

MCs (*contd.*)
  Caz, 18; most overlooked, in hip hop, 603–7; outshining DJs, 17
Mean Gene, Grandmaster Flash, 34
Memphis rap scene, 245–46
Merry-go-round technique, Kool Herc, 36
Message, hip hop, 274–75
Metal, hip hop and, 189
Metaphor, technique of rap, 358, 360
Method Man: acting career, 382–83; Clifford Sparks, 381; discography, 388; reggae and hip hop, 14; solo album, 381; *Tical*, 381–82. *See also* Wu-Tang Clan
Michigan, Detroit hip hop scene, 482
Microphone, rhymes, and crowd, Eric B. & Rakim, 145–46
"Mind of a Lunatic," Geto Boys, 253–54
Miss E. . .So Addictive, Missy Elliott, 514–15
Missy Elliott: Adidas-sponsored clothing line, 509; albums, 512–21; awards, 508; break dancers, 519–20; childhood, 504; contributions to hip hop, 510–12; *The Cookbook*, 518, 520–21; *Da Real World*, 513–14; digital identity, 503–4, 521–22; discography, 527; fairy tales, 522–23; hip hop pioneer, 525–26; inspiration of Salt-N-Pepa, 505; *Miss E. . .So Addictive*, 514–15; partnership with Timothy Mosley, 505–7, 509, 511–12; R&B group Sista, 505–6; reality television, 509, 510; spokesperson for Break the Cycle, 508; street credibility, 507; *Supa Dupa Fly*, 508, 512–13; Swing Mob, 506, 511; *This Is Not a Test*, 518; turning point, 504–5; *Under Construction*, 516, 518; videos, 521–25
Mixmaster Mike, Beastie Boys, 99, 112
Mixtapes:, 11–12; promotion, 72–73; Raekwon the Chef, 378; Run-DMC, 79

MJG, Memphis rap scene, 245
Monie Love, duet with Queen Latifah, 225–26, 278
Moorer, Lana: becoming MC Lyte, 118–20. *See also* MC Lyte
Mos Def: breakout star for Rawkus Records, 289–90; MC, 605
Mosley, Timothy, Missy Elliott and, 505–7, 509, 511–12
Motown, Queen Latifah, 229
The Movement, Inspectah Deck, 384
Movies, hip hop culture, 458
Movie soundtracks, RZA, 370
Mr. Xcitement, U-God, 386
MTV, Run-DMC, 82
MTV's "All Eyes on Kanye West," Kanye West, 567
Murder of: Notorious B.I.G., 432–33, 435–36; Tupac Shakur, 392, 397
Murray, Keith, MC, 606
Music videos, MC Lyte, 127–31
  The Naked Truth, Lil' Kim, 440, 445, 451–52, 455

Names, rappers, 135
Nas: artistic influences, 354–56; authenticity, 357; beef with Jay-Z, 545–46, 547; book of rhymes, 359–60; childhood influences, 342–43; discography, 362–63; father figure in hip hop, 351; *God's Son*, 348–49; *God's Son* video, 353–54; hip hop and blues, 349–50; *I Am. . .*, 347–48; *Illmatic*, 342, 345–46; *Illmatic* videos, 351–52; *It Was Written*, 346–47; *It Was Written* videos, 352–53; Juice Crew influence, 355; kings of New York, 356–57; Large Professor, 344; legacy, 361–62; literary techniques, 358–61; Mahatma Gandhi reference, 359–60; major label releases, 343–50; metaphor, 360; Nasir Jones biography, 342–43; *Nastradamus*, 347–48; *Rap Attack* radio show, 354; rap scene, 341–42; rhyme, 360; *Stillmatic*, 348; *Stillmatic* video, 353; *Street's Disciple*, 349;

Street's Disciple videos, 353; videos and cover art, 350–54

Nasal glide, Beastie Boys, 97

Nastradamus, album by Nas, 347–48

National Museum of American History, hip hop exhibit, 117

Nation of Islam: Five-Percenter terminology, 143–44; Islam and, 149–50; Public Enemy, 170

Native Tongues: Afrocentric philosophy, 265; Afro-feminist philosophy, 278–80; A Tribe Called Quest, 272–73, 291; Black Sheep, 273, 291; breakup of collective, 285–87; Chi-Ali, 273–74; context of development, 267–69; defending "pease," 280–82; De La Soul, 271–72; discography, 290–91; disrupting expectations, 275–77; Infinity Lessons of Zulu Nation, 269–70; initial members, 265; legacy, 287–90; members, 270–74; message, 269–70; Mos Def, 289–90; New York City: sixth element, 267–68; philosophy of Zulu Nation, 274–75, 286, 288; Prince Paul, 271–72; princess of posse, 277–78; Queen Latifah, 277–78, 286; Rawkus Records, 288–89; rhyme style, 284–85; rhythm and blues, 266; role of collective, 280–85; selling message, 274–75; skits, 275–76; solidarity and positive thinking, 265–67; speaking in tongues, 282–85; The Jungle Brothers, 270–71, 291; unity of sound, 282–85; women and, 277–80

New York City, Native Tongues, 267–68

Next Friday, Ice Cube, 313

Next Plateau Records, Salt-N-Pepa, 198, 202–3

Nihilism, Thug Life ideology, 410

No Said Date, Masta Killa, 384

Notorious B.I.G.: Bad Boy Records, 421–22; Biggie Smalls, 417, 419–20; big-time MCs, 419–20; Cwest, 419; discography, 438; education, 418–19, 420; formative years, 419–24; hip hop development, 426; hip hop's culture of death, 429–30; hip hop timeline, xxviii; Jamaican heritage, 423–24; legacy, 433–37; *Life After Death*, 434; Lil' Kim, 431–32, 443–45; mother as primary caregiver, 417–18; murder, 433, 435–36; music and short life in limelight, 430–33; platinum era, 424–28, 430; *Ready to Die*, 423, 424–25, 430–31; Sean "Puffy" Combs, 421–22; sex appeal with women, 427–28; suicidal songs, 428, 430; Tupac Shakur and, 432–33, 435–36, 534, 544–45; Uptown/Bad Boy, 422–23; women in his life, 431–32

Notorious K.I.M.. *See* Lil' Kim

N.W.A.: discography, 315, 340; formation, 297–300; hip hop and Mafia, 377; hip hop timeline, xxvi; Ice Cube going solo, 300–301; reunion, 311

Ol' Dirty Bastard: acting out at awards shows, 374–75; arrests, 374; death, 374, 375–76; discography, 389; drug problems, 374, 375–76; *Nigga Please*, 375; *Return to the 36 Chambers: The Dirty Version*, 373–74; Russell Jones, 373; X-rated material, 373–74. *See also* Wu-Tang Clan

Only Built 4 Cuban Linx, Raekwon the Chef, 376–78

Orange Crush, Run-DMC, 72

Order in the Court, Queen Latifah, 230–31

Original Flavor, Jay-Z, 530

Outkast: acting, 467; Afrofuturism, 470–73; Andre Benjamin and Antwon Patton, 457–58; *Aquemini*, 462; *Aquemini* millenium, 467–69; artistic fearlessness, 471–72; *ATLiens*, 461; balanced group, 478; black class generational divide, 463–64; bling-bling phenomenon, 469; collaboration with Goodie Mob, 460–61; fast rappers, 560–61; fighting categorization, 473–76;

Outkast (*contd.*)
funk, 473, 474; Grammy Awards, 465; hip hop timeline, xxviii; influences, 476–78; LaFace Records, 458, 460; legacy, 478–80; litigation by Rosa Parks, 462–64; musical creativity, 475–76; personas, 472; potential breakup, 479; reinventing music, 470–73; relationship, 458; remaking southern hip hop, 467–69; slang "crunk," 470; "So Fresh, So Clean" with Sleepy Brown, 465; *Southernplayalisticadillacmuzik*, 460; *Speakerboxxx/The Love Below*, 466–67; *Stankonia*, 464–65; style, 472–73

Outsiders, Beastie Boys, 98–99

Owens, Dana Elaine: queen of hip hop, 222–24. *See also* Queen Latifah

Paid in Full, Eric B & Rakim, 151–53

Parents' Music Resource Center, hip hop timeline, xxiv

Parks, Rosa, litigation against Outkast, 462–64

Parties, Kool Herc, 7, 19, 23

Patton, Antwon: 2 Shades Deep, 458; aliases, 458; relationship with Andre Benjamin, 457–58. *See also* Outkast

Paul's Boutique, Beastie Boys and contributions, 103–6

"Pease" defense, Native Tongues, 280–82

Peek-a-boo system, Grandmaster Flash, 35–36

Performing art school, Tupac Shakur, 394

PETA (People for the Ethical Treatment of Animals), Masta Killa, 385

Phonte from Little Brother, MC, 604

Pimp persona, Snoop Dogg, 338–39

Plastic surgery, Lil' Kim, 450–51

The Players Club, Ice Cube, 312

Poetry, hip hop, 495

Police, brutality and racist history, 299–300

Political hip hop: post-gangsta, 190–91; Public Enemy, 186–87, 190–92

Political lyrics, MC Lyte, 130–31

Political rap, Public Enemy, 169–70

Politics: 3rd Bass, 344–45; Eminem, 496–97; Kanye West, 566–74

Positivity: Native Tongues, 267, 269–70; Queen Latifah, 217–19, 226

Post-gangsta political hip hop, 190–91

The Predator, Ice Cube, 305–7

Premier, DJ. *See* DJ Premier

The Pretty Toney Album, Ghostface Killah, 380

Prince Paul, member of Native Tongues, 271–72

Prison imagery, Tupac Shakur, 397

Prison sentence, Lil' Kim, 440–41

Professor Griff: controversy, 182–83; "Minister of Information," 180–81; Public Enemy, 170. *See also* Public Enemy

"Proud to Be Black," Run-DMC, 87

Psychological breakdown, Geto Boys' music theme, 253–54

Public Enemy: anti-Semitism, 179–80, 181 *Apocalypse '91 . . . The Enemy Strikes Black*, 183–86; Bomb Squad's sonic boom, 172–73; breakdown of Bomb Squad, 182–83; Carlton Douglas Ridenour (Chuck D), 170; *Do the Right Thing* by Spike Lee, 180–81; early years, 170–72; Eric "Vietnam" Sadler, 172–73; *Fear of a Black Planet*, 182–83; gangsta rap, 184, 186–88; Griff controversy, 180–81, 182–83; Hank and Keith Shocklee, 170–71; hip hop and metal, 189; hip hop timeline, xxv; hype men, 176; *It Takes a Nation of Millions to Hold Us Back*, 176–79; legacy, 188–92; political hip hop, 186–87; political rap, 169–70; post–gangsta political hip hop, 190–92; Professor Griff and Hank Shocklee, 170; *Spectrum Show*, 171–72; Spike Lee, 180, 184–85; Stop the Violence, 187; *Yo! Bum Rush the Show*, 174–76

Public Enemy's Terminator X, Kool Herc collaborator, 23

Q-bert, turntablist, 38–39

Quayle, Dan, censorship of Tupac Shakur, 397–98

Queen Latifah: African roots and culture, 225–28; Afrocentric fashion, 220–21; *All Hail the Queen*, 224–25, 227, 277–78; *Barbershop 2: Back in Business*, 236–37; *Bringing Down the House*, 221, 236; *Chicago*, 221, 235–36; Cover Girl spokesperson, 219, 237–38; creative and financial control, 228–29; death of brother Winki, 231–32; discography, 241, 291; duet with Monie Love, 225–26, 278; early years, 222–24; father, 222–23, 232; filmography, 241; highs and lows, 231–33; hip hop and sitcoms, 233–34; hip hop timeline, xxvi, xxvii–xxviii; Hollywood, 233–38; *Last Holiday*, 237; legacy, 238–40; *Living Out Loud*, 235; Motown, 229; name, 223; Native Tongues, 277–78; nurturing female rappers, 229–30; *Order in the Court*, 230–31; overcoming stereotypes for women in hip hop, 218–19; positivity, 217–19, 226; professional and confident, 221–22; *She's a Queen: A Collection of Hits*, 231; success, 286; *The Dana Owens Album*, 233, 238; Tommy Boy, 224, 227, 229; "U.N.I.T.Y.," 230

"Queen of Rox," Roxanne Shanté, 62–64

Quick mix theory, Grandmaster Flash, 33

Quinones, "Lee" George, graffiti artist, 20

Racial chauvinism, Beastie Boys, 98–99

Racial politics 3rd Bass, 344–45

Racism, Ice Cube, 304–5

Radio show, Nas on *Rap Attack*, 354

Radio station, Hot 97 WQHT and hip hop, 453–54

Raekwon the Chef: Corey Woods, 376; discography, 388; *Immobilarity*,

377–78; Mafia theme, 376–77; mixtapes, 378; *Only Built 4 Cuban Linx*, 376–77. *See also* Wu-Tang Clan

Raggamuffin hip hop, hybrid, 13

"Raising Hell," Run-DMC, 85–86

Rakim: collaboration with Dr. Dre, 158–60; discography, 167; Five Percent Nation and Islam, 143–44; flow, 163; growing up, 146–47; Islam and Five Percent Nation, 149; microphone, rhymes, and crowd, 145–46; retail powerhouse brand, 159; return, 156–60; *Rugrats: The Movie*, 157; style, 142–46, 162; William Michael Griffin, Jr., 146. *See also* Eric B. & Rakim

Rap, anti-Semitism, 179–80

Rap-A-Lot Records, Geto Boys, 248, 250, 261, 264

Rap Attack radio show, Nas, 354

Rap film, *Hustle and Flow*, 244

Rap music: feminism, 200–201; Salt-N-Pepa, 196–97

Rapper-producer dynamic, hip hop groups, 477

Rappers: categories for hip hop groups, 476–78; credibility and law, 440–41; fashion, 442–43; fast, 560–61; hype men, 176; mama complex, 394–95; mixtape promotion, 72–73; names, 135; number exploding, 17–18; vegetarians, 385

Rap recordings, doing away with hip hop DJ, 19

Rawkus Records: hip hop, 288–89; Mos Def, 289–90

Ready Rock C, human beatbox, 52

Ready to Die, Notorious B.I.G., 423, 424–27, 430–31

Reality television: hip hop and, 510; Missy Elliott, 509

Realness, central subject of rap, 357

Reasonable Doubt, Jay-Z's debut, 532, 537

Recording industry, Jay-Z and future of new, 549–51

Red Ant Entertainment, Salt-N-Pepa, 206

Reflective thug, gangsta rap, 533

Reggae: *Criminal Minded*, 13, 22; hip hop and, 13–14; Kool Herc, 2–5

Religious conversion, Run-DMC, 88

Remix phenomenon, *The Black Album*, 535–36

Respect, old-school keyword, 42

Retirement, rumor of Eminem, 499–501

Return to the 36 Chambers: The Dirty Version, Ol' Dirty Bastard, 373–74

Revolutionary vision, Public Enemy, 186–88

Rhyme, technique of rap, 358, 360

Rhyme book, hip hop, 359–60

Rhyme style, Native Tongues, 284–85

Rhythm and blues, range of musical styles, 266

Ridenour, Carlton Douglas: Chuck D, 170. *See also* Public Enemy

Robinson, Darren, human beatbox, 52

Robinson, Sylvia, Grandmaster Flash, 43–46

Roc-A-Fella Records: Jay-Z, 531–32; Kanye West, 556

Rock, hip hop and, 92–93

Rock, Chris, Grandmaster Flash, 44

Rock and Roll Hall of Fame (Cleveland), hip hop exhibit, 117

Rock Steady Crew, hip hop timeline, xxii

Rock the Vote, MC Lyte, 133

Roland Tr-808, drum machine, 75, 148, 163

Roper, Deidre "DJ Spinderella": after Salt-N-Pepa, 212; Salt-N-Pepa, 193, 197–98, 201. *See also* Salt-N-Pepa

Roxanne Wars phenomenon, Roxanne Shanté, 53

Royce da 5'9", Eminem's beef with, 494; MC, 605

Rubin, Rick: Beastie Boys, 95–96; Def American, 96; Def Jam, 71, 78–79; hip hop timeline, xxiv; Run-DMC management, 69

Rumors, early retirement of Eminem, 499–501

Run-DMC: Cold Crush Brothers, 74; concert violence, 85–86; debut, 70, 72–73; defining hip hop, 69–70; Def Jam, 70, 71, 78–79; Def Jam logo, 84; discography, 90; growing up, 76–78; hip hop and reggae, 13; hip hop brand, 70; hip hop branding, 79–81; hip hop timeline, xxiii, xxiv; hip hop video, 82; legacy, 88–89; management team, 69; "My Adidas," 79–81; new look, 84–85; promotion, 74; "Proud to Be Black," 87; "Raising Hell," 85–86; religious conversion, 88; "Son of Byford," 76–78; "Sucker MCs," 72–73; trickiness of industry, 73–76

Ruthless Records: Dr. Dre, 321–23; Eazy-E, 321; Ice Cube, 297, 301

RZA: discography, 389; Gravediggaz, 369–70; influences, 371; movie soundtracks, 370; Robert Diggs, 368; *The Wu-Tang Manual*, 370–71; vegetarian, 385; Wu-Tang Clan, 365, 368–71. *See also* Wu-Tang Clan

RZA as Bobby Digital in Stereo, 370

St. Ides malt liquor, Ice Cube, 304–5

Saddler, Joseph. *See* Grandmaster Flash

Sadler, Eric "Vietnam": Bomb Squad, 170, 172–73, 177. *See also* Public Enemy

Salt-N-Pepa: authenticity of female rappers, 208–9; *Black's Magic*, 203–5; *Brand New*, 210–11; discography, 215–16; early years, 197–98; end of *Black's Magic*, 205–6; female rappers in 1980s, 195–97; female rappers with male producers, 205–6; feminism in rap music, 200–201; hip hop timeline, xxiv; *Hot, Cool & Vicious*, 198–99, 201; inspiration to Missy Elliott, 505; legacy, 212–13; London Records, 205–6, 209, 210; Next Plateau Records, 198, 202–3; officially disbanded, 212; Red Ant Entertainment, 206, 210; rise to stardom, 201–3; strong, independent women, 193–95; Super Nature, 198; *Very Necessary*, 206–7, 209–10; women and DJ culture, 194; women's issues, 196–97

Sampler, term, 334–35

Sampling, lawsuits, 104–5

Sandra "Lady Pink" Fabara, graffiti artist, 20

Saukrates, MC, 606

Scarface: Brad Jordan, 247; solo career, 256–58. *See also* Geto Boys

Scratch: DJ Q-bert, 41; Grandmaster DST, 42

Scratching: DJ Q-bert, 41; Grandwizard Theodore, 17, 28, 32

Sean Paul, hip hop-generation dance hall DJ, 13

Secret identity, Ghostface Killah, 378–79

Selectors, Jamaican term for DJ, 39–40

Sex appeal, Notorious B.I.G., 427–28

Sexual abuse, Tupac Shakur, 397

Sexual politics, Geto Boys' theme, 254–55

Sexual prowess, Dr. Dre and Snoop Dogg, 331–32

Shabba Ranks, reggae, 13

Shakur, Tupac: *2Pacalypse Now*, 396–97; actor, 400–402; alter ego Makaveli, 407–9; C. Delores Tucker, 397–400; censorship, 397–400; clothing, 411–12; controversial *Don Killuminati: The 7 Day Theory*, 404–6; Digital Underground (DU), 396; discography, 414–15; East Coast-West Coast feud, 392–93, 534; embrace of death, 410; formative years, 393–95; hip hop timeline, xxviii; intellectualism, 402–4; *Juice*, 400–402; legacy, 412–13; life after death, 407–9; literacy, 402–4; mama complex, 394–95; meaning of name, 393; murder, 392, 397, 432–33; nihilism, 410; notoriety, 397; Notorious B.I.G. and, 432–33, 435–36, 534, 544–45; performing arts school, 394; prison imagery, 397; sexual abuse, 397; social and political

commentary of *Don Killuminati*, 406–7; Thug Life ideology, 409–12

Shanté, Roxanne: abuse by men, 62–63; answer record, 53, 124–26; Cold Chillin' Records, 58–59, 63; discography, 68; education, 63–64; exploitation, 62–64, 65, 67; Fly Ty, 58–59, 62; innocence lost, 58–59; Janet Jackson, 65–66; Juice Crew, 51, 53, 55–58; legacy, 64–67; Lolita Shanté Gooden, 58; lyric contest with Sparky D, 61–62; Marymount University, 64; "Queen of Rox," 62–64; Rick James, 63; Roxanne Wars phenomenon, 53; teen rap prodigy, 55; U.T.F.O., 53, 61

Sha Rock, female MC, 18

Shaw, Richard: Bushwick Bill, 247. *See also* Geto Boys

Shocklee, Hank, Public Enemy, 170

Shocklee, Keith, Public Enemy, 170–71

Signature sound, Dr. Dre, 332–33, 335–36

Signifying: MC Lyte, 117–18, 124–26; rap names, 135

Simmons, Russell: Beastie Boys, 95–97; Def Jam, 71, 78–79, 96; Def Jam logo, 84; Grandmaster Flash, 44; hip hop timeline, xxiv; Run-DMC management, 69, 74; vegetarian, 385

Sir Jinx, Ice Cube and, 296

Sista, girl group with Missy Elliott, 505–6

Sitcoms, hip hop and, 233–34

Sizzla, hip hop-generation dance hall DJ, 13

Skits, hip hop, 275–76

Slang, hip hop, 143–44

Slick Rick, storytelling, 122

Slim Shady LP, Eminem, 489–90

Smif-N-Wessun, reggae and hip hop, 13

Smith, Will, human beatbox, 52

Snoop Dogg: aliases, 337; criminal background, 324–26; Death Row label, 327–29; discography, 340; flow, 337; gangsta persona, 338–39; hip hop and horror, 370; nickname, 326;

Snoop Dogg (*contd.*)
  persona, 336–39; pimp persona,
  338–39; shooting death and trial,
  327–28; studio gangsta, 325–26.
  See also Dr. Dre and Snoop Dogg
Soaking records, protecting signature
  songs, 12
Social issues, Jay-Z's formula for success,
  538
Sociopolitical commentary, Grandmaster
  Flash, 45–46
"Son of Byford," Run-DMC, 76–78
Soundtracks, RZA, 370
The Source, Eminem's rivalry with
  Benzino, 492–93
Southern hip hop: Outkast remaking,
  467–69; white rappers, 497–99
Southernplayalisticadillacmuzik,
  Outkast, 460
Southern rap, Dirty South, 458–60
Sparks, Clifford: Method Man of
  Wu-Tang Clan, 365, 381–83. *See also*
  Method Man
Sparky D, Roxanne Shanté and, 61–62
Speakerboxxx/The Love Below, Outkast,
  466–67
Spectrum Show, Public Enemy, 171–72
Spirituality: Jay-Z's formula for success,
  538–39; MC Lyte, 134–36
Spivey, George. *See* DJ Scratch
Stankonia, Outkast, 464–65
Status symbols, grills, 186
Steinberg, Leila, influence on Tupac
  Shakur, 402–3
Stereo Crew, Ice Cube, 296
Stereotypes, overcoming, for women in
  hip hop, 218–19
Stillmatic: album by Nas, 348; videos,
  353
Storytelling: art, 122–23; MC Lyte,
  117–18, 121, 123–24
Straight Outta Compton, N.W.A.,
  299–300
Street's Disciple: album by Nas, 349;
  videos, 353
Street style, hip hop DJs and MCs, 16–17
Studio gangsta, rapper term, 325–26

Subway station, MC Lyte in video,
  127–28
Success: definition by Jay-Z, 541–42;
  role of beef in Jay-Z's formula,
  544–47
Sugarhill Gang: hip hop and reggae, 13;
  hip hop timeline, xxii
Sugar Hill Records, Grandmaster Flash,
  43–46
Suicidal theme, Notorious B.I.G., 428,
  430
Supa Dupa Fly, Missy Elliott, 508,
  512–13
Super Cat, reggae, 13
Supernatural elements, Missy Elliott's
  videos, 524
Supreme Clientele, Ghostface Killah, 380
Swing Mob, Missy Elliott, 506, 511
Symbolism, Jay-Z's formula for success,
  539–40

Tables, turntables, 32
Talib Kweli, MC, 605
Teen rap prodigy, Roxanne Shanté, 55
Terminator X, Public Enemy, 173, 175,
  177
Theodore Unit, Ghostface Killah, 380
This Is Not a Test, Missy Elliott, 518
Thomas, Rozanda "Chilli," TLC,
  517–18
Three 6 Mafia: hip hop timeline,
  xxix–xxx; Memphis rap scene,
  245–46
Three Kings, Ice Cube, 312
Thug Life ideology: clothing, 411; death,
  410; hip hop culture, 410–12; nihilism,
  410; Tupac Shakur, 409–12
Tibetan Freedom Concert, Beastie Boys,
  109
Tical, Method Man, 381–82
TLC, R&B trio, 517–18
Tommy Boy, Queen Latifah, 224, 227,
  229
To the 5 Boroughs, Beastie Boys,
  113–14
Treach, MC, 606
Trespass, Ice Cube, 310

Tucker, C. Delores, censorship, 397–400; hip hop timeline, xxvii

Tupac Shakur. *See* Shakur, Tupac

Turner, Elgin: Masta Killa of Wu-Tang Clan, 365, 384–85. *See also* Masta Killa

Turntables, hip hop music, 32

Turntablism: DJ Q-bert, 41; DMC World Championships, 38–39; Eric B., 148

Turntablist, concept, 39–42; DJ, 39

Twista, fast rappers, 560–61

U-God: disagreements with RZA, 386; discography, 389; *Golden Arms Redemption*, 385; Lamont Hawkins, 385; *Mr. Xcitement*, 386. *See also* Wu-Tang Clan

Unbalanced groups, hip hop, 477–78

Uncontrolled Substance, Inspectah Deck, 383–84

Under Construction, Missy Elliott, 516, 518

Underground: hip hop, 15–16; vs. mainstream for Jay-Z, 542–44

"U.N.I.T.Y.," Queen Latifah, 230

Universal Zulu Nation: Afrika Bambaataa, 269; Infinity Lessons, 269–70

Urban Music Association of Canada (UMAC), Canadian hip hop, 120–21

Us Girls, female MCs, 18

U.T.F.O. (Untouchable Force Organization): exchange with Roxanne Shanté, 53, 61; hip hop timeline, xxiii

Vanilla Ice: fake biography, 93, 94; hip hop timeline, xxvi–xxvii

Vegetarians, rappers, 385

Very Necessary, Salt-N-Pepa, 206–7, 209–10

VH1's "Hip Hop Honors," Kool Herc, 24

Videos: Missy Elliott, 521–25; MTV and Run-DMC, 82; Nas, 350–54

Violence: Geto Boys' music theme, 251–53; hip hop and music industry, 47–48; Run-DMC, 85–86

Virtual blackness, Jay-Z, 540–41

Vybz Kartel, hip hop-generation dance hall DJ, 13

"Walk This Way," Run-DMC, 81–84, 92

Wallace, George Latore. *See* Notorious B.I.G.

Watkins, Tionne "T-Boz," TLC, 517–18

Watley, Jody, Eric B. & Rakim with, 154

Wave Twisters, DJ Q-bert, 40

Waxmaster C. *See* DJ Premier

West, Kanye: authentic representation, 563–64; car crash, 559–60; Chicago to New York, 558–59; collaboration with Common, 565–66; *The College Dropout*, 555, 557, 560–62, 563–64; *Dave Chappelle's Block Party*, 557; discography, 577; early years, 557–58; fast rappers, 560–61; G.O.O.D. Music label, 565; hip hop and car culture, 571–72; hip hop timeline, xxix; homophobia, 567–69; hurricane relief concert, 570; ice rap, 564; icon status, 555–57; Kutcher prank, 562; *Late Registration*, 555, 557, 566–67, 569, 571–74; legacy, 574–76; Live 8 concert series, 567; mother's influence, 558, 565, 567; MTV's "All Eyes on Kanye West," 567; politics, 566–74; producer-MC role, 563–64

West Coast: Beastie Boys, 99–100; Compton and Dr. Dre, 319–20; East Coast vs., 99–100, 392–93; gangsta rap icons Snoop Dogg and Dr. Dre, 317–18; Ice Cube and emergence of gangsta rap, 295–97; Notorious B.I.G. and Tupac Shakur, 432; Tupac Shakur and East-West coast feud, 392–93, 405–6

Wheels of steel, turntables, 32

White hip hop artist: Vanilla Ice, 93, 94. *See also* Beastie Boys; Eminem

White southern rappers, Eminem and, 497–99

Wiggers, derogatory term, 483–84

Wiggins, Keith "Cowboy," Grandmaster Flash with, 43

Wild Style, hip hop film, 20, 21

Williams, Tyrone "Fly Ty". *See* Fly Ty

Willie D: solo album before Geto Boys, 247–48; solo career, 259–60; Willie James Dennis, 247. *See also* Geto Boys

Will Smith and DJ Jazzy Jeff, hip hop timeline, xxv–xxvi

Wilson, Simone, Monie Love, 225–26

Wine, women and song, Dr. Dre and Snoop Dogg, 329–32

Womanhood, social commentary by MC Lyte, 126–27

Women: DJ culture, 194; Eminem disrespecting, 490–91; in hip hop, 218–19; Native Tongues, 277–80; Queen Latifah in Native Tongues, 277–78; treatment in lyrics, 109–10

Women rappers, associations with men, 54–55

Women's issues, Salt-N-Pepa, 196–97

Woods, Corey: Raekwon the Chef of Wu-Tang Clan, 365, 376–78. *See also* Raekwon the Chef

World politics, Geto Boys' theme, 254

Wright, Eric (Eazy-E), biography, 320–21

Writing books, MC Lyte, 133–34

Wu-Tang Clan: call-and-response chants, 367; comic book series, 379–80; debut *Enter the Wu-Tang (36 Chambers)*, 367; discography, 388–89; financial savvy, 366; Ghostface Killah, 378–81; GZA, 371–73; hip hop and mafia, 377; hip hop timeline, xxvii; Inspectah Deck, 383–84; legacy, 386–88; Loud Records, 365–66; Masta Killa, 384–85; members, 365; Method Man, 381–83; naming, 366–67; Ol' Dirty Bastard, 373–76; Raekwon the Chef, 376–78; RZA, 368–71; successful solo artists, 367–68; U-God, 385–86; vegetarian rappers, 385

Yauch, Adam (MCA): Beastie Boys' career, 93, 95. *See also* Beastie Boys

Yo! Bum Rush the Show, Public Enemy, 174–76

Yo! MTV Raps, hip hop timeline, xxv

Young, Andre: Compton, 319–20; Dr. Dre, 319–24; Ice Cube and, 296. *See also* Dr. Dre

Zulu Nation: Infinity Lessons, 269–70; philosophy, 274–75, 286, 288